Ladies and Gentlemen on Display

THE *American South* SERIES

Edward L. Ayers, *Editor*

Ladies and Gentlemen on Display

PLANTER SOCIETY AT

THE VIRGINIA SPRINGS

1790 – 1860

Charlene M. Boyer Lewis, 1965-

UNIVERSITY PRESS OF VIRGINIA

Charlottesville and London

The University Press of Virginia
© 2001 by the Rector and Visitors of the University of Virginia
All rights reserved
Printed in the United States of America on acid-free paper
First published 2001

Library of Congress Cataloging-in-Publication Data
Lewis, Charlene M. Boyer, 1965–
    Ladies and gentlemen on display: planter society at the Virginia springs, 1790–1860 /
Charlene M. Boyer Lewis.
        p. cm.—(The American South series)
    Originally presented as author's thesis (doctoral)—University of Virginia.
    Includes bibliographical references (p.) and index.
    ISBN 0-8139-2079-5 (cloth : alk. paper)—ISBN 0-8139-2080-9 (pbk. : alk. paper)
    1. Virginia–Social life and customs—19th century.   2. Virginia—History—
1775–1865.   3. Virginia—Social conditions—19th century.   4. Plantation life—
Virginia—History—19th century.   5. Springs—Virginia—History—19th century.   6. Health resorts—Virginia—History—19th century.   7. Social classes—
Virginia—History—19th century.   I. Title.   II. Series.
    F230 .L67 2001
    306'.09755'09034—dc21   2001026554

For James, my life,
and
in memory of my father,
Ronald James Boyer

Contents

Illustrations

Acknowledgments

A lot of people have been waiting a long time to see this book finished. I, too, have been waiting a long time to thank a lot of people for their advice, assistance, and support.

Sifting through thousands of letters and diaries for this project would not have been so fruitful without the help of efficient and knowledgeable staffs at numerous libraries and archives. I would like to thank particularly the staffs at the Special Collections Library of Duke University, the Southern Historical Collection at the University of North Carolina, the Special Collections Department at the University of Virginia, the Virginia Historical Society, and the University Manuscripts and Rare Books Department of the College of William and Mary, as well as Robert Conte at the Greenbrier. I also gratefully acknowledge all of the institutions who granted me permission to publish quotes and images from their collections.

The researching and writing of this book received financial support at many crucial stages, for which I am deeply indebted. The History Department of the University of Virginia provided me with various fellowships and grants as a doctoral student. An Albert J. Beveridge Grant from the American Historical Association and a Mellon Fellowship from the Virginia Historical Society helped me to finish the final research for the book. At Widener University, a Faculty Development Grant and a Provost Grant enabled me to complete the manuscript.

I cannot think of a better place to have written the dissertation that became this book than the History Department at the University of Virginia. The professors and graduate students fostered a rigorous, yet enjoyable academic environment that allowed me to thrive. The members of my dissertation committee offered encouragement and challenged me not only to revise, but also to reconceive the strange world of the Virginia Springs. Reuben Rainey opened up a whole new way for me to look at the springs with his ideas about landscape architectural history, especially the concept of "healing landscapes." Peter Onuf, as usual, brought out the best in my manuscript and constantly urged me to push for deeper meanings. My fortune in having both Cindy S. Aron and Edward L. Ayers as dissertation advisors is indescribable. They encouraged me to pursue a topic that was largely neglected and helped me to realize just how important the Virginia Springs were. Their kind words, astute comments, and constant support saw me through graduate school. No longer merely professors, I value them as friends as much as I respect them as scholars. Furthermore, Ed has also consummately played the role of series editor for this manuscript.

In addition to my dissertation advisors, numerous friends and colleagues read all or part of the manuscript. Their comments proved invaluable in shaping the final manuscript, even if I did not always follow their suggestions. I am grateful to Joan Cashin, Tom Chambers, Cita Cook, Ruth Doan, Anya Jabour, Cindy Kierner, Dan Kilbride, Jan Lewis, Michael O'Brien, Steven Stowe, and Ron Walters. I would also like to thank the anonymous readers at the University Press of Virginia. My colleagues at Widener University, especially Tom Cragin and Joan Parks, have created a supportive scholarly environment in spite of our demanding workloads. My editor at the University Press of Virginia, Dick Holway, deserves special thanks for his patience, support, and professionalism.

I owe an enormous debt of gratitude to my family. They have never let me down when I needed them. My mother and stepfather, Margareta and Anders Olsson, have continuously provided me their financial and emotional support. Along with my in-laws, Jim and Anita Lewis and Ann and Robert Fear, they have shared my enthusiasm for this project and celebrate its completion. My sisters, Yvonne Boyer and Linda Humphris, have always been my best audience and best friends. For many years, they have listened, without complaint, to just about every historical fact, story, and concept I have learned and have eagerly discussed every part of this project with me. They will never know how much this has meant to me. It is a pleasure to acknowledge them in print.

My husband, James, has traveled every step of the way with me on this exploration of the springs. From its initial form as a seminar paper through its publication as a book, he has read every word and offered brilliant insights. He has made me a better writer and a better historian. He and our dog Cassidy always reminded me that there was much more to life than researching and writing. There are no words to express the debt I owe him for his unfailing love and unflagging support over the years. Indeed, without him, there truly would be no book.

Ladies and Gentlemen on Display

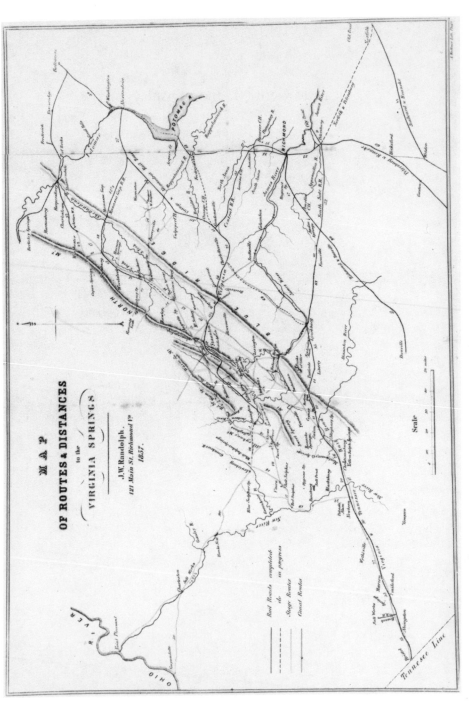

Map from Moorman, *Virginia Springs*, 1857. (Special Collections Department, University of Virginia Library, Charlottesville)

Introduction

"HERE I AM AMONGST THE THRONG, WHO . . . ARE VIS-
iting these mountainous regions, some in search of health, others of pleasure, some travelling because they are tired of home and others because
they are tired of themselves[,] some to make a display and others to see it."
So wrote Samuel Mordecai from the Virginia Springs in 1817.[1] The attractions of the springs resorts amidst the mountains and valleys of Virginia
drew a multitude of visitors from across the country, especially the South.
Each season between 1790 and 1860, hundreds and eventually thousands of
southern men and women left their homes on plantations or in towns and
journeyed to the springs. Most stayed at least three or four weeks, but some
stayed as long as three or four months. Between June and September, more
elite whites congregated at the springs than at any other place in the South.
For the few who had the time and money, the Virginia Springs offered a
healthful, entertaining escape from the diseases and boredom of plantations and towns. While some men and women visited the springs actively
seeking cures, most traveled over the mountains to enjoy the company of
people like themselves, preserve their already-good health, and participate
in an array of leisure and social activities.

The Virginia Springs resorts were scattered through the mountains,
foothills, and valleys of the Blue Ridge and eastern Appalachians on both
sides of the line that now divides Virginia and West Virginia. Most of the
mineral springs that eventually developed into popular resorts were already
known for their curative powers by the mid-eighteenth century. Around

1790 some springs' owners began trying to attract visitors who sought pleasure and fashionable society, not just a cure. Seven decades later, with the
coming of the Civil War, most of the resorts closed or became hospitals.
During the intervening years, the Virginia Springs attracted larger numbers
of elite southern visitors than either northern resorts such as Saratoga or
Newport or other southern springs such as those in Georgia and Arkansas.

Those who frequented the Virginia Springs resorts comprised the top of
antebellum, and especially southern, society. Members of many of the leading families in the South took the waters at the Virginia Springs each season. Most of the visitors came from Virginia, Maryland, and the Carolinas,
but significant numbers arrived from even farther south (including Florida), the Old Southwest (including Texas), and the Caribbean. Presidents,
congressmen, cabinet members, military officers, and wealthy professional
men and their families came from Washington, Richmond, Charleston,
Mobile, and New Orleans. As one travel writer noted in 1839: "The president of the United States is here, and many other distinguished persons.
Ladies of fashion and belles from the principal cities—foreign ministers—members of the cabinet, senators—and representatives, prominent
judges—officers of the army and navy, and polished private gentlemen,
all combining to make the present company, as elegant and select as any
party ever assembled at a watering place." Wealthy families from the West
and North, especially Boston, New York, and Philadelphia, also visited the
springs during the season. Foreign travelers—particularly European dip-
lomats and English and French travel writers—also came to see the famed
waters and society at the Virginia Springs. As early as 1790, "a good deal of
Genteel Company from the Different parts of the Continent & some from
the West Indies" gathered at Warm Springs. That "almost every State in the
Union was here represented" in the "heart of the mountains" impressed
many visitors throughout the first half of the nineteenth century. It was the
southern gentry, however, who filled most of the accommodations, owned
almost all of the private cottages, set the tone, and established the rules at
the Virginia Springs.[2]

Viewing elite southern society from the Virginia Springs offers a new
perspective on the history of the antebellum South.[3] The Virginia Springs
constituted an integral part of a complex, interdependent landscape of distinct sites that created, defined, and reshaped southern society. Too often
southern society has been examined solely from the vantage point of the
plantation or farm. Plantation life was grounded upon interwoven yet

widely varied rituals, rules, conventions, and customs. The myth of the virtuous lady concealed the day-to-day toil and burdens of plantation mistresses. The myth of the chivalric gentleman or doting father disguised the strong patriarchal power of men over their households, plantations, and societies. Professed concerns for "our family white and black" obscured the tensions between master and slave and black and white. Genteel manners marked a person's status and shaped social relations, even as they masked many of the tensions between women and men and rich and poor. Rituals of honor and deference preserved social hierarchies; rituals of romance and courtship celebrated, but also exposed, the sharp gender divisions and hierarchies of the southern elite. Antebellum planters lived in a world of elaborate rituals, conventions, and myths that shrouded, even as they constituted, the hierarchies of class, race, and gender that shaped their distinctive social relations.[4]

Historians generally depict plantation men and women as living in separate yet corresponding worlds.[5] The plantation household possessed its own internal hierarchy and served to reinforce the hierarchies of the Slave South in general. Within its confines, the plantation household included men and women, parents and children, and whites and blacks. An individual's position stemmed from differences in gender, age, and race. According to these historians, clear lines segregated men's and women's work and leisure activities on the plantation. Planter men and women apparently formed their strongest friendships and shared their deepest emotions with persons of the same sex. Accordingly, mixed-gender relationships, except between husband and wife or between siblings, occurred infrequently and met with disapproval from gentry society.[6]

But the plantation neither defined the entire experience of planter men and women nor comprised the only significant place in their world.[7] The southern elite were highly mobile, traveling from place to place according to season and inclination. Masters, mistresses, children, and even slaves spent long periods off their plantations—in towns during the winters, at mountain or seaside resorts during the summers, and visiting relatives throughout the year. The late-winter social season, usually from late January through March, attracted many planter families to southern towns and cities, particularly Charleston, Savannah, New Orleans, and Richmond. From late June through September, they traveled to the shore or mountains, including Cape May and the Virginia Springs. At other times, especially holidays, planters visited friends and relatives at nearby and distant plantations, often staying for days or weeks. Some planters owned a second residence, usually a house in town, and divided their time between their homes, in addition to making other trips.[8] Southern elites created their class and identity in a complex landscape that included plantations, towns, schools, and the Virginia Springs.

Social prescriptions demanded much from southern ladies and gentlemen, offering them few opportunities for even temporary escape. The dull routine of plantation and, to a lesser extent, town life made the limits of their daily environment painfully evident. "Dreary solitude" characterized many of their days at home. This monotony seemed even worse during the long hot summers. It was during the summer months especially that planters and townspeople looked for ways to escape the limits and ennui—and heat—of their regular lives. They eagerly anticipated the change of scene and company and the conviviality promised by their destinations. Fredericksburg, Virginia, as Caroline Richardson complained to a friend one August, was "the dullest place now you ever saw. All the folks are gone to some place for pleasure and cool air and there is a total cessation of business." Plantations and towns around the South became increasingly desolate as the summer progressed. By the middle of the summer of 1838, Lynchburg, Virginia, was bereft of "a great many of our citizens" who had left town for the Virginia Springs for "health" or "pleasure." Leaving home during the summer for cooler and more entertaining places quickly became part of the southern elite's routine—a genteel ritual of pleasure and health.[9]

At resorts and in towns, planter men and women could not count upon the unquestioned status and power they enjoyed at home. As a result, such places forced the southern elite to determine, maintain, and protect the boundaries and foundations of their society with greater care and vigor. At the Virginia Springs, southerners shaped and reshaped their definitions of ladies and gentlemen while pursuing pleasure and health. They defined the limits and characteristics of their class. The experiences of visitors at the Virginia Springs contributed to the idealized view of planters and plantation life held by so many men and women—not just southerners— throughout the nineteenth century (and beyond). At the springs, southerners acquired, and continuously renewed, a richer sense of regional identity. Effectively connected to the rest of the South by its visitors and the media, the Virginia Springs became a central and defining place for the region's mobile, often extralocal, elite. There, every day of their stay, visitors found people, ideas, and attachments that were not limited to just one place, as at home. They traveled to the springs to be a part of a class, to meet those with whom they could identify from far and near. As they shaped resort society by their actions and expectations, they also defined what it meant to be an elite "southerner."

In their quest for gentility, planters borrowed heavily from the English upper classes.[10] More than just architecture, landscape, and furniture designs, elites adopted as well a language of aesthetics and a habit of spa-going that had long been fashionable among the English. They also based their general expectations for master-servant relations upon English models of deference. The very Englishness of these designs and behaviors added to their genteel status. Not wanting to appear outmoded or tasteless, planters eagerly embraced much of what was culturally fashionable in England as well as in the North. Instead of rejecting modern European or northern trends for more traditional notions, elite southerners chose to participate in much of what was up-to-date. Yet they chose carefully. They selected models of fashion from England that they could adapt to their own context and imbue with distinctively southern meanings. Antebellum planter men and women were at once distinctly southern and decidedly cosmopolitan, taking what they wanted from the larger, "modern" world and adapting it to their slave-based plantation world.

Recent work in cultural studies has brought historians' attention to the importance of place, identity, ritual, and contests for power. The insights garnered from this approach should not be underestimated. To make this book more accessible to a wider audience, I have tried to address these important issues with a minimum of the theoretical apparatus and language of cultural studies. Culture, as much as politics or economics, shaped the regional identity of southern planters.[11] Land and slaves made the master class and political power helped protect those holdings, but so, too, did cultural practices and beliefs. Looking at planter society away from the plantation and with a focus upon its culture, moreover, helps us to move beyond the debate over whether planters were aggressive capitalists or paternalistic traditionalists. Recent historiography has emphasized that, to earn their money, planter men and women embraced both modes at different levels and in different ways.[12] As can especially be seen at the Virginia Springs, they similarly spent their money in a complex fashion. They chose to spend the wealth that they were so driven to accumulate to travel to the springs with all of the requisite props to put on a brilliant and conspicuous show for their peers. Yet they also chose to spend their time in an environment that obscured the harshness of their economic and social system and celebrated paternalistic, almost feudal, values.

The importance of power, place, rituals, and cultural practices in the construction of class and regional identities can be easily seen at the Virginia Springs. In their pursuit of health and pleasure, white southerners—visitors and proprietors—created a truly regional community, one that stretched far beyond yet still encompassed their local identities. Spa life revolved around the very rituals and conventions that served to define elite southern society. The social experiences of women and men at these resorts determined and reaffirmed what it meant to be a southern lady or gentleman. In the intensely genteel environment of the springs, elite society made clear the correct rules of refined and fashionable appearance, behavior, and sentiment. In this way the springs served as not only a "stage" but also a "school." Young men and women entering adult society learned much in this public social arena. As an audience, they watched the performances; as performers, they put their lessons into practice. Southern parents regarded the Virginia Springs as a place of learning, especially for young adults who could study the correct behavior of men and women of their class and the correct ways to display their status and power. The social and cultural lessons learned at the Virginia Springs spread throughout the South. Those who could not make the trip received letters from friends and relatives at the springs or read newspaper accounts telling of the exciting activities and elegant people.

The rules and rituals of the springs helped to create elite southern identity. As in England, spa-going was a ritualistic act in and of itself. First-time visitors arrived with preconceived notions of how they would spend their time and how they would need to act in order to succeed on this stage. Returning visitors looked forward to participating in these rituals of health and pleasure. Emulating an upper-class British tradition that had long combined seeking pleasure and health, southerners, as well as professional medical opinion, considered the mineral waters of the Virginia Springs a beneficial therapy for body and mind throughout the decades from 1790 to 1860. A concern about health heightened the visitors' awareness of their own and each other's bodies and helped define the characteristics of a southern lady or gentleman.

The architecture, the landscape, the resorts' staffs, and the visitors themselves all worked together to shape a beautiful and orderly scene—one that could obscure the conflicts in planter society. For its guests the springs environment was intimate, convivial, and, above all, refined. But this affable community existed only in the visitors' imaginations; the visitors narrowed their focus, generally ignoring any object, behavior, or person that did not fit with this wonderful image. Doing so allowed them to regard the Virginia Springs as all that was best of southern slave society.

The reality of the springs world was far different from this imagined world. It was not simply a place to escape the real world and spend a pleasant interlude away from the challenges and competitions of real life. It was not always a smooth and orderly community. The Virginia Springs bolstered and extended the power of the gentry throughout the South, but at the same time the environment of the springs challenged and even undermined some of that power. Having so many elite men and women gathered in the same area made for a tense and intense atmosphere at the resorts. In this competitive environment, planter men and women had to negotiate for their status and even their comfort among peers who watched each other's every move. A visitor's social standing was constantly called into question as he or she competed for admiration and affirmation. At the springs, unlikely people wielded significant power, such as lower-class managers, slave workers, and fashionable women—groups usually considered subject to the patriarchal power of elite white men. Examining these rifts in the community of visitors uncovers the operation of, and resistance to, patriarchal power within planter culture.

At the springs, plantation society's hierarchies became at once more relaxed and more contested; its rituals and rules sometimes changed and reformed; and its gender divisions often softened and blurred. Judging from their days at the springs, men and women did not live in two totally separate and antagonistic spheres. Nor did they blissfully and continuously share each other's lives. It was more complicated than that. They spent much of their time with members of the same sex but still had frequent encounters with the opposite sex. These interactions resulted in predominantly harmonious relations, with important moments of combativeness, such as courtship, between and among men and women. Generally, women and men shared a striking commonality in their springs experience, but their separate gendered experiences remained significant as well. As a place of reunion and relaxation, the Virginia Springs provided the perfect location for women and men to establish, renew, and strengthen bonds with members of their own and the opposite sex.

The Virginia Springs provided a theater of sorts for planter society where contests for power between men and women, fashionables and evangelicals, blacks and whites, old and young, and even northerners and southerners played out. Springs life intensified the power of the rituals, rules, and behavior of planter society. A springs visit was a performance, literally, in which each person played a specific role—with appropriate lines and costumes. The fashionable and beautiful architecture and landscapes of the resorts provided the appropriate scenery or backdrop for the elite visitors' daily performances, while also adding an otherworldly quality to spa life. Southern gentry men and women defined and reaffirmed the traits of their group as they played out fantasies of themselves as romantic cavaliers and ladies. Each performance centered on a plot that highlighted gentility and gender relations—two crucial and tangled elements of planter society. Both harmony and conflict characterized social relations, in general, and gender relations, in particular, at the springs. The demands of gentility created a refined and beautiful place for refined and beautiful people to gather and perform for one another in harmonious affability. But gentility at the springs also fostered a dedication to hierarchy and competition and the exclusion of those who failed to meet genteel standards. The rules and rituals of gentility scripted gender roles, relations, and expectations for visitors. At the same time, women and men had different parts to play in the practice and enforcement of gentility. The class and gender tensions in this society played out on the stage of the Virginia Springs.

In general, visitors remained unaware of the societal or cultural tensions highlighted at the springs. The conflicts spawned by the demands of gentility mattered little to the elite performers at the springs. Their dedication to refinement and sociability made life at the springs alluring, not terrifying. Pleasure-seekers traveled all of those miles to the springs specifically to participate in and watch the drama of display and competition. It is only when we look back at life at the Virginia Springs that many of the complexities in southern society become apparent. Through the social, political, and economic connections made there, southern planter men and women created and solidified the characteristics, boundaries, and power of their class.

Over the years from 1790 to 1860, life at the Virginia Springs changed little for its visitors. The activities, experiences, and identities of springs visitors were remarkably constant. This sameness of life at the springs was exactly what visitors expected when they made the trip. For many southerners, the Virginia Springs was the one stable, unchanging place in the midst of a constantly changing and increasingly unstable world. Of course, the springs underwent some changes over the seven decades before the Civil War—architectural developments, a tremendous increase in visitors, and heightening sectional tensions, for example. But the changes never threatened the exclusivity or gentility of resort life or diminished the importance of the springs for elite southerners.

The Virginia Springs offered new experiences, new identities, and new opportunities beyond those offered by plantation society. By replicating, exaggerating, reshaping, or changing plantation society's social hierarchies, rituals, rules, and gender relations, the Virginia Springs presented visitors with alternative modes of behavior, ways of understanding themselves, and means of ordering their world. Furthermore, the romantic quality of life at the resorts aided both in the sentimentalization and rationalization of all of southern society, including slavery. These alternative modes provided more than a different environment and a temporary experience. Along with plantations, towns, and academies, they also contributed to the formation of southern society as a whole. At this edge of the South, in this rigorously genteel and aggressively leisured atmosphere, elite southern society shaped itself, gaining a greater sense of what it meant to be a southerner and redefining social roles and relations.

PART 1

The Scene

IN THE LATE 1700S CAPT. HANCOCK LEE, WHO SUFFERED from chronic gout, recognized the value—both medicinal and monetary—of a mineral spring that he found in Fauquier County, Virginia. Lee purchased the property and built a wooden lodge for himself and the few invalids already visiting the healing waters. He later sold the property to his son, Hancock Lee Jr., and his son's partner, Thomas Green. Envisioning a full-scale pleasure resort along both banks of the Rappahannock River similar to the ones flourishing in Europe and developing west of the Blue Ridge Mountains, the new owners purchased three thousand more of the surrounding acres.

By 1834 a four-story Greek Revival hotel, "The Pavilion," stood upon a rise as the centerpiece of the resort (see fig. 1). Twelve huge Doric columns supported a wide portico that stretched the nearly two-hundred-foot length of the building, offering strollers "a delightful promenade." Six pairs of small brick cottages formed a crescent on each side of the hotel. Three-story wooden buildings with long porticos on each floor, named "Norfolk Place" and "Williamsburg House," marked the two ends of the cottage crescent. Lee proclaimed that these accommodations were "probably unsurpassed." The springhouse resembled a Greek temple with Doric columns, a domed roof nearly forty feet in diameter, and a statue of the goddess of Health. It stood at the foot of the hill, opposite the hotel, connected to the cottages by serpentine paths. Knowing their importance to his guests,

Figure 1. *Fauquier White Sulphur Springs*, in Moorman, *Virginia Springs*, 1857. (Special Collections Department, University of Virginia Library, Charlottesville)

Lee boasted that "great attention" had been paid "to the proposed amusements of the guests" and that he had procured "the best Wines and Spirits" and "the services of some of the best cooks in the State."[1] After incorporating in 1837 and accumulating more capital, Lee and Green added buildings, creating an elegant resort that catered to their elite visitors' ideas of fashion. "New magnificent chandeliers" adorned the "elegant ballroom." Additional lodging houses, stables, and cottages lined the lawn and nestled in the hills surrounding the hotel. Near the springhouse, a new bathhouse enclosed hot and cold baths and fourteen private bathing rooms. The building had an "Octagon Gothic exterior, whose minerets and spires indicate the determination of the company to please the fancy and gratify the taste" of fashionable visitors.[2] A bowling alley bordered the lawn. To satisfy one of the first loves of Virginians and other southerners, the proprietors put in a one-mile race track across the Rappahannock, the "Victoria Course," with spectators' and judges' stands. By 1850 Fauquier White Sulphur Springs could accommodate eight hundred people; visitors continually filled the rooms during the summer season.[3] Throughout the South, in the nation's capital about fifty miles away, and even in many northern guidebooks, elite men and women touted Fauquier White Sulphur Springs as one of the most fashionable places to spend a summer.

For the South's plantation gentry, the Virginia Springs resorts made up an important part of what historian Richard Bushman has called the "geography of refinement." The springs resorts provide some of the best examples of "places marked by beauty and frequented by mannerly people in proper dress, [who] engaged in elevated activities."[4] For southern planters, a map of such refined places extended from their large, wealthy plantations to elegant town houses and terminated at the Virginia Springs, the spot that epitomized refinement and grace for most of its visitors. The refined areas that marked this map distinguished the men and women who frequented or lived in them from the other, "lesser" members of their society.

In the service of refinement, the architecture and landscape of the Virginia Springs became something like backdrops or stage sets for the genteel visitors who were simultaneously actors and audience, observing, judging, and performing for each other as they moved from resort to resort. The usually graceful and attractive buildings and grounds set the scene for the drama of class-formation and the rituals of planter class power at the springs. In the resorts' hotels, cabins, ballrooms, lawns, gardens, and surrounding countryside, refined visitors played with as well as competed against each other, relaxed as well as defined the limits—and the power—of their exclusive group. The showiness of the resorts' buildings, grounds, and natural scenery matched the showiness of the visitors' display and competition. That the architecture and landscape designs—and the very act of spa-going—were based on English models made them seem even more refined. Though of English origin, the architectural styles and landscape designs symbolized southern society in all its complexity. Without these appropriately genteel surroundings, guests would not have flocked to the resorts. They would not have considered the Virginia Springs the paramount place in their genteel world. At the same time, the layouts and landscapes of the resorts created a fantastic and romantic realm, a retreat from the normal world of the visitors' plantations and towns. This beautiful retreat provided the best stage upon which the all-important creation of class and regional identity took place.

Yet much of the visitors' world was illusory. Just as in the theater, the men and women behind the scenes at the resorts played vital roles in this performance. And the living conditions at the resorts rarely matched the grace and beauty of the surroundings. The lovely and orderly world in the mountains could not have existed without the labor of a resort's staff. Maintaining and managing a well-ordered spa was not easy. Only the hard work of proprietors, managers, slaves, farmhands, and other employees kept these resorts functioning. In spite of their hard work, conditions at the springs contrasted sharply with the refined architecture and landscapes. Genteel visitors rhapsodized about the beautiful buildings, elegant grounds, and sublime scenery even as they complained vociferously about filthy cabins, wretched fare, and lackadaisical or occasionally rude servants. For most of the guests, a stay at the Virginia Springs was so important that they willingly suffered the often poor quality of the accommodations, food, and service. And, even though they usually remained behind the scenes, workers at the resorts sometimes played crucial roles in the gentry's performance. Through their attentions or refusals, the staffs of the resorts, from the proprietors to the lowliest servants, helped to clarify and consolidate status distinctions among the guests as each visitor had to negotiate for his or her comfort. Like the buildings and grounds, resort workers helped to create the genteel atmosphere, but they also occasionally played leading roles in the pageant of competition and display.

∽

"Solidity, Strength, and Grandeur"

The southern elite's search for pleasure, health, and a cooler climate reflected a general trend among the nation's elite. Beginning around 1800, wealthy men and women throughout the United States increasingly traveled for pleasure as well as health. A nascent tourist industry quickly arose to meet the demand. Travel guidebooks began touting scenic sites. Enterprising people constructed new hotels and resorts, often transforming the surrounding areas. Transportation improvements provided easier access to these new leisure spots. The Virginia Springs developed simultaneously with New England tourism and with other seaside and mountain resorts.[1]

Throughout the eastern Appalachians and Blue Ridge, a multitude of mineral springs experienced transformations similar to that of Fauquier

White Sulphur between 1790 and 1860. By the turn of the nineteenth century, most of the resorts destined for later popularity had opened in some
form, creating the area soon known as "the Virginia Springs." By 1860
over seventy resorts—ranging from simple cabins to grand hotels—hosted
thousands of visitors seeking health and pleasure amid the mountains each
summer. While the resorts kept expanding and remodeling over the decades, their architectural styles and landscape designs changed little. The
main buildings and grounds consistently followed British models adapted
to their Virginia context. The Greek Revival style dominated resort architecture. Its stately columns and graceful verandas appealed to the romantic attitudes of the visitors—southerners especially—and were practical as
well in the warm climate. Most of the resorts' grounds followed the fashionable English landscape gardening tradition. To be successful, proprietors knew that their resorts had to look beautiful and grand for their genteel
visitors.

Yet, the buildings and lawns played a more important role at the Virginia Springs than creating beautiful surroundings. They provided the appropriately romantic and refined stages where genteel ladies and gentlemen
could interact and perform. The styles of the buildings and grounds were
more than aesthetically pleasing; they connoted high rank and physically
marked the boundaries between the elite's world and the rest of society.
Though they copied fashionable English designs, the buildings and grounds
received distinctively southern meanings. Visitors delighted in the special
atmosphere created by the architecture and landscape at the Virginia
Springs, for it identified the area as a place of retreat and refinement, a place
that physically embodied their idealized version of the Slave South.

The development of the Virginia Springs district highlights the importance of the architectural and landscape scene and the work behind
this scene in creating this favorite area of antebellum elites. By the mid-
eighteenth century, a handful of springs was already famous for their healing waters. Berkeley Springs, Hot Springs, and Warm Springs drew nearly
two thousand visitors each summer.[2] Berkeley Springs (known in the eighteenth century as Warm Springs and then, in British fashion, Bath) was
perhaps the first famous spa in the colonies. When Lord Fairfax sent a sur-
veying party to his Northern Neck tract in 1748, a sixteen-year-old George
Washington delighted in viewing the "Fam'd Warm Springs." When Washington returned in 1761, he found two hundred men and women there.[3]
The accommodations, however, were primitive at best. In 1762 Dr. Robert

Boyd, a surgeon's mate in the British army, found "nothing but about 40 miserable Hutts and the Baths are done round with Boughs of Trees."[4] After the French and Indian War, improved roads made it possible to tap the springs' economic potential. By 1766 Hot Springs' owner Thomas Bullitt had his slaves construct a small hotel called the Homestead. In 1787 Berkeley Springs' elegant boardinghouse with "piazzas" on both sides contained a large dining room, drawing room, assembly room, and tea room (fig. 2). By that time, Berkeley Springs, following European custom, had become a small town with year-round residents who catered to the seasonal resort crowds. Similarly, Warm Springs grew from a small settlement in Bath County to become the county seat in 1790.[5] These two springs, however, would be the only spas in the region that followed the English pattern by developing into actual towns before 1860.

By the late 1700s Berkeley, Warm, Hot, and Sweet Springs were equally well-known for their efficacious waters and their "polite" society. Visiting in the 1790s, Ferdinand Bayard noted the large numbers of visitors attracted to the springs solely "in search of pleasure and love." In spite of the "very difficult and dangerous" mountain roads that "require[d] a strong well fixt Waggon and a very able Team," many leading citizens of Virginia and the nation visited these resorts. George Washington returned to Berkeley Springs often enough that he had a cottage built there. James Madison also visited Berkeley as well as Warm Springs—the favorite resort of Thomas Jefferson. And Maryland's Charles Carroll owned land in Bath.[6]

It was not until the turn of the nineteenth century, however, that the Virginia Springs district took shape in a flurry of construction. Spurred on by the growing crowd of invalids and pleasure-seekers and the profit they represented, the owners of mineral springs quickly built new hotels and bathhouses. Well-made log cabins and more stylish wooden boarding-houses replaced tents and huts on the lands of both the spring-owners and their neighbors. James Caldwell built the first lodging house at White Sulphur in 1808; rows of fifty to sixty cottages went up by 1810. At the same time, Charles Taylor built a two-story hotel at Taylor's Springs, later Yellow Sulphur Springs. Sometime between 1792 and 1804, the owners of Warm Springs constructed an octagonal bathhouse; by 1810 they raised "The Colonnade," a three-story hotel with large columns supporting a portico.[7]

Beginning around 1810 and over the next five decades, new turnpikes, extended canals, railroads, and steamboats allowed travelers to reach and traverse the mountains in comparative ease and enjoy the scenery along the way. Indeed, in 1828 Louisianna Cocke Faulcon wrote home: "We have

Figure 2. *Berkeley Springs Schottisch,* composed by J. E. Magruder. (Virginia Historical Society, Richmond)

found the roads . . . so vastly improved since Aunt & myself traveled this route together [in 1822], that we scarcely feel as if we were going to The Springs." Easing travelers' woes even more, stage companies planned regular routes from towns in the Piedmont to the burgeoning resorts by the late 1820s. A decade later some of the nation's first railroads drastically cut travel time between major cities, such as Baltimore and Richmond, and Piedmont or Valley towns, such as Charlottesville and Winchester, thus shortening the slow and uncomfortable stagecoach part of a trip to the Virginia Springs.[8]

With these improvements, pleasure-seekers, even more than invalids, flooded the springs. In a circular fashion, those looking for pleasure at the springs propelled the construction of better routes to the resorts, while improved travel encouraged pleasure-seekers to visit the Virginia Springs. As early as 1811, John Cocke grumbled that "more than half" of the visitors at White Sulphur came "from notions of fashion & ostentation."[9] The 1810s and 1820s saw immense crowds of both healthy and ill visitors overflow the resorts. By the early 1830s, most of these resorts stood poised to turn into elegant watering places. A boom in the founding of new resorts and in the expansion of older resorts transformed the Virginia Springs district into one of the premier summering places in the United States. White Sulphur Springs, in particular, became the most fashionable summertime destination in the South. Increasingly, travel guides, newspapers, and correspondence publicized the springs in the way that chemical analyses and medical reports had in the eighteenth century.[10] By the mid-1830s, the beginning of the heyday for the Virginia Springs, nearly six thousand people annually visited the Blue Ridge spas.[11] Throughout the 1830s and especially in the prosperous 1850s, the proprietors of the resorts strove to meet the desires of these visitors. Columns, piazzas, ballrooms, carpets, chandeliers, mirrors, and fashionable furniture became de rigueur at resorts.

By the 1850s, visitors came in droves to the fashionable and famous Virginia Springs to take the waters and enjoy good society. White Sulphur alone held upwards of sixteen hundred, sometimes even seventeen hundred, guests daily. The other large spas, such as Sweet, Rockbridge Alum, Fauquier White Sulphur, and Montgomery White Sulphur could lodge between six and eight hundred. Smaller springs, such as Red Sweet and Salt Sulphur, accommodated around three to four hundred. After 1850, getting to many of the Virginia Springs was no longer a long and difficult trip. Not until after the Civil War would the railroads reach the resorts directly, but during the 1850s the rails stretched far enough into the mountains that most of the resorts were only a short stage ride away from the end of the line. In 1855 the Virginia and Tennessee line promised to carry passengers from Richmond to White Sulphur "without NIGHT TRAVEL, and with but 64 miles of Staging." Montgomery White Sulphur constructed a narrow-gauge railroad, drawn by mules, that linked the resort to a train depot less than two miles away. The trip from Washington, D.C., to White Sulphur now took just over a day—down from about five days by stage. The railroad lines eagerly catered to the spring-going public. One conductor told a passenger in 1858 that even "if only *two* passengers wished to go" to the Virginia Springs the line would readily take them in a passenger car. By the late 1850s, thousands flocked to the grand and luxurious—and still remarkably exclusive—resorts, enjoying elegant public rooms, modernized guest rooms, and comfortable cottages where sixty years earlier there had been only rudimentary cabins or simple boardinghouses for a few dozen people.[12]

The architects of almost all of the Virginia Springs buildings remain unknown. The only identified architects are John H. B. Latrobe, the son of Benjamin H. Latrobe, who designed "six ornamental veranda cottages" named Baltimore Row at White Sulphur Springs (fig. 3), and Henry Exall, a builder from Richmond, who designed the main buildings at Montgomery White Sulphur.[13] Most likely, the resort proprietors were their own designers, telling their builders what they wanted. While the styles drew on fashionable British models, the design process was a regional one, based on what the proprietors had seen around Virginia or in architectural pattern books or carpenter's guides, such as Asher Benjamin's *Practical House Carpenter* (1830) and *Practice of Architecture* (1833).[14] For example, the construction at White Sulphur Springs emerged, according to one visitor, from "no plan, but bit by bit as there was need to enlarge the accommodations." Still, the proprietor made sure the overall layout followed "several lines or parallels."[15]

Designs from Early Classical and Greek Revival traditions became the most popular for Virginia Springs architecture. An interest in classical buildings exploded in the eighteenth century, first in western Europe, especially England, and then in the United States. Reinterpretations of ancient Roman models, such as the works of architect Andrea Palladio and artist Claude Lorrain, renewed interest in Classical Rome. In the early nineteenth century, archeological investigations unearthed ancient Greece's preeminence over Rome and consequently shifted interest to Grecian models. Following the changes in British taste, fashionable Americans turned away from older British styles. The sympathy many Americans felt for the Greeks in their war for independence against the Turks during the 1820s increased the fervor for all things Greek. In the first half of the nineteenth century, the rise of romanticism, with its fascination for ruins and history, further strengthened the American attachment to classical styles.[16]

The South wholeheartedly embraced the Greek Revival or—as southerners described it—"Grecian" style. Spring-owners and their wealthy southern guests loved the gracious look of "a noble colonnaded structure

Figure 3. Baltimore cottages, John H. B. Latrobe, 1832. (Semmes, *John H. B. Latrobe and His Times*)

of brick, which is entered by a broad flight of steps, leading to its lofty portico" (fig. 3).[17] The resort structures reflected the same style as many of the elite visitors' homes on an exaggerated scale. Porticos, pediments, piazzas, columns (usually Doric), wide cornice lines, hierarchical arrangements, and symmetry—all of these classical design elements appeared at the springs between 1820 and 1860.[18] An architecturally appealing resort, according to guests, was one whose buildings were "all of good proportions and in correct taste" and were "planned and commenced upon an extensive scale, uniting elegance, convenience, and durability." [19] The Greek Revival style also served practical purposes in southern climes. Siting the main hotels on eminences, at the top of the hierarchical pattern, allowed them to catch cooling breezes. Symmetrically placed windows and doors on the front and back also aided in air flow. The long columned piazzas and porticos provided much-needed shade for visitors during the summer. Similarly, the high ceilings cooled the crowded public and guest rooms.

The springhouses best exemplified the references to ancient Greece. In every case in which there was a structure over the spring, it took the form of a small temple (fig. 4). White marble slabs usually encased the spring itself. A statue of Hygieia, the Greek goddess of Health, often stood upon the dome or in a niche inside the temple. These statues closely replicated ancient examples, with one hand holding a bowl of remedies and the other extended soothingly or holding a serpent, whose repeatedly shedding skin made it a symbol of renewal. The Hygieia at White Sulphur, for instance, stood "on a beautiful cylindrical pedestal, covered with a snow-white drapery, her left arm gracefully folded in the coils of a serpent, with a bowl in her right hand filled with sulphur water." [20] The guests customarily referred to the springhouses as temples.

Greek Revival remained dominant in the South throughout the antebellum era, even after Gothic Revival became fashionable in the North in the 1840s. While most of the buildings at the Virginia Springs, especially the large ones, were typical Greek Revival, Gothic designs occasionally appeared after 1840. The stone hotel at Salt Sulphur, the castellated bathhouse at Sweet Springs, the Italianate Ladies' Bath at Berkeley Springs, and a handful of other pointed, parapeted, or highly decorated structures probably gave a viewer more of a Gothic than a Classical feel. Resort owners, like southerners in general, easily mixed the two styles. At White Sulphur, a row of Gothic cottages faced a row of Greek Revival ones. The castellated bathhouse at Fauquier White Sulphur stood adjacent to the Grecian springhouse (fig. 1).

Figure 4. *Red Sulphur Springs,* Edward Beyer, *Album of Virginia,* 1858. (Special Collections Department, University of Virginia Library, Charlottesville)

Wealthy visitors relied on springs architecture to delineate the resorts as refined, but they also used the buildings as another form of competition in this very competitive place. At a handful of resorts, some planter families decided that their personal "cottages," which were actually elegant Greek Revival houses, could serve the same purposes within spa society as the resorts did in southern society in general. They would act as badges of status and mark a boundary between the refined and the common. Soon after New Orleans planter Stephen Henderson built his grand cottage at White Sulphur in 1834, southern planters began trying to outdo one another in the elegance of their summer cottages. Planters competed through the cottages' decorative facades, well-furnished parlors and dining rooms, and number of bedrooms. Even though the proprietors reserved the right to lodge other guests in unoccupied private cottages and the owners still paid room and board charges, owning a cottage placed planter visitors higher in spa society and, not unimportantly, guaranteed them a place to stay whenever they visited—a luxury after the mid-1830s.[21]

The landscape design of each resort, like the architecture, was apparently the work of amateurs, probably the proprietors. As with the architectural designs, the proprietors likely drew inspiration from pattern books and examples that reflected aristocratic English fashions. They also occasionally used John C. Loudon's "gardenesque style" and Andrew Jackson Downing's popular and more American designs.[22]

In the pursuit of gentility, the majority of resorts followed the tenets of the English landscape gardening tradition of the eighteenth century: tall shade trees and rounded, flowering bushes dotted sweeping expanses of undulating green lawns. "The valley in front" of Salt Sulphur, for example, was "covered with grass and clover, shade trees & benches or chairs beneath them border the main walk."[23] Also consistent with this English style, tame deer wandered around many of the greens. Numerous graveled, shaded, and secluded paths twisted and curved around the main lawns' perimeters and occasionally crossed their centers. "Many artless paths more agreeable to the foot and eye" curved through the middle of White Sulphur's lawn and along its sides (fig. 5). A sundial marked the central intersection of the paths. Carriage drives, "as fine nearly as in England," wound around the edges of the main lawn and led off into more secluded areas, such as the small cemetery, up the hillsides. At Red Sulphur Springs, "the walks are well planned which intersect the lawns, and abound with large trees, of the sugar maple; a beautiful green hill in the vicinity forms a fine promenade in the evening" (fig. 4). The long porches and piazzas also provided shady places for people to stroll. Tinkling fountains offered sun-warmed strollers cool spots to relax or court. The Greek temple springhouses perfectly fit with the English tradition's love of Greek follies in garden settings.[24]

Perhaps more important than the graceful appearance of Greek Revival buildings and English landscapes was the deeper significance of these styles for planter men and women. There was little that was uniquely American in the resorts' landscape and architecture designs. The Greek Revival style would not have been popular with the southern gentry without its initial popularity among the English elite. Indeed, southern visitors in pursuit of refinement found this Englishness enormously appealing. But, regardless of what they imagined, their society was not an exact imitation of upper-class English society. Those who dominated a slave society necessarily gave different meanings to these British styles—meanings that would more directly harken back to ancient Greece. Southern visitors regarded the Greek Revival architecture at the springs as they did their own plantation society:

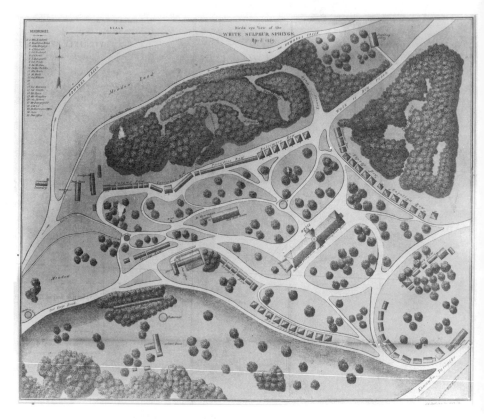

Figure 5. Plan of White Sulphur Springs, 1859. (The Greenbrier, White Sulphur Springs, West Virginia)

as something that was "noble" and worthy of admiration for its "solidity, strength, and grandeur." Their temples of health and columned buildings represented two civilizations—the ancient classic democracy and the contemporary plantation society. While the references to ancient Greece and Rome symbolized their own nation's democratic ideals, the hierarchical arrangement of the buildings at the Virginia Springs mirrored the arrangement of wealthy plantations and of antebellum southern society (fig. 6). Planters designed their home landscapes with an eye for straight lines, symmetry, and hierarchy. The grand house of the master, like the grand hotel at the resort, was the centerpiece of the plantation surrounded by smaller and less-important structures. The romantic style of these magnificent homes—and of the resort buildings—cloaked the social and labor system

Figure 6. *Rockbridge Alum Springs,* Edward Beyer, *Album of Virginia,* 1858. (Special Collections Department, University of Virginia Library, Charlottesville)

that made possible this luxurious mode of existence. Grecian architecture also represented the permanence of a great civilization, a permanence that southerners were increasingly anxious to secure during the 1840s and 1850s. Not insignificantly for wealthy slaveowners, the enlightened and democratic society of ancient Greece had also held people in bondage. The resort buildings of the Virginia Springs carried over the architectural symbols that the planter elite held dear from their plantations.[25]

In 1854 the new owners of White Sulphur, a joint-stock company, began construction of a building that would represent, for many who gazed upon it, the perfect architectural embodiment of all that was best of southern society. The "Grand Central Hotel" (later called the "Old White") opened four years later as the largest hotel in the United States. The four-story, four-hundred-foot-long hotel was in an exaggerated Greek Revival style with a large dome topping the edifice and a central pediment, arcades, columns, and porticos decorating the facade (fig. 7). It contained 228 guest rooms and a dining room that seated 1,200 (also the largest in the country). Although Shannondale, Sweet, Warm, and Yellow Sulphur Springs all sported newly built, enlarged hotels, none matched the gran-

Figure 7. *White Sulphur Springs*, Edward Beyer, *Album of Virginia*, 1858. (Special Collections Department, University of Virginia Library, Charlottesville)

deur—or the overblown architectural symbolism—of White Sulphur's for genteel southerners.

The grounds reflected the same ideal of beauty and order as the Greek Revival architecture. The sweeping greens dotted with trees and bushes in the predominant English gardening tradition were ultimately controlled and orderly landscapes. Ironically, in the opinion of visitors, however, uncontrollable "Nature" often received the credit for beautifying the resorts' setting. "Nature has done much for it," declared Lucy Cocke about Red Sweet Springs, "and I am pleased to see the Proprietor & owner (Mr Sampson) has permitted it to have its way." [26] The popularity of this style with the wealthy in England, moreover, served as a powerful endorsement to southern elites. Gardens laid out in parterres, hedges carefully trimmed and formed into mazes, and graveled, geometrically patterned walks could be found on plantations as well as at the springs resorts. At the Virginia Springs, the landscape designs, like the architectural styles, emphasized beauty, order, and control. Refined and stylish architecture and grounds, whether at the spas or plantations, connoted elite status and fashionable taste. Places with these characteristics formed the southern geography of refinement.

Repeated comments in guests' letters and journals and in travel guide-books and newspapers made clear the importance of the architecture and landscape of the resorts to the guests. Visitors rarely failed to provide descriptions, often long ones, and sometimes even sketches of the buildings and grounds. In the early years, when only rustic log buildings stood at the springs, no one commented that they had traveled to a gracious, almost fanciful, world. Writing from Warm Springs in 1804, William Cox declared the place "a rude uncultivated spot; occupied chiefly by Weeds and Woods, rocks and rubbish, Hogs and Dogs." Visitors began describing places that were better than the ones they had left behind only after the resort owners erected imposing buildings and reshaped the landscape to match the beauty and grandeur of the architecture. Coming from plantations of often-declining fortunes, some must have readily perceived the striking difference between their fading homes and the impressive and stylish resorts, between the harsh reality of their everyday lives and the glowing ideal of southern life at the springs. Once the resorts met elite visitors' expectations for a place in their geography of refinement, then the Virginia Springs could stand out as the premier spot on that imagined map.[27]

Most guests felt that the layout of the resorts—with the small cottages, hotels, and other buildings nestled in valleys and aligned along wide areas of green—gave them the appearance of a lovely rural village or, not surprisingly, an English country park (fig. 8). "The whole place" at Salt Sulphur, according to Jane Caroline North, "has the most quiet rural look & gives one an at home feeling."[28] The whitewashed buildings contrasted pleasantly with the encircling green landscape. For some northern city dwellers, the springs' village-like atmosphere countered "the effects of city living" with "rural solitude."[29] For southern planters, the "villages" at the Virginia Springs countered the intense solitude and boredom of plantation life and relieved its stresses.

The romantic scene of the Virginia Springs appeared almost other-worldly—a place of retreat not just from visitors' daily lives but also from the real world. In many visitors' eyes, no dilapidated shacks marred these fantastic sites. Only the Grecian architecture of the grand hotels, tiny white cottages, columned spring temples, splashing fountains, and green lawns—not the laundry houses or livestock pens—captured their attention, turning these already imagined landscapes into something unreal. Many visitors described the resorts, especially White Sulphur, as a kind of fairyland, as places removed from real time and place. When Mary M. Hagner arrived with her party at White Sulphur at dinnertime, she thought "the whole face

Figure 8. *Roanoke Red Sulphur Spring,* Edward Beyer, *Album of Virginia,* 1858.
(Special Collections Department, University of Virginia Library, Charlottesville)

of things had the look of enchantment. It seemed . . . as if the inhabitants
of some fairy isle were turning out to welcome the coming of expected
strangers." In 1845, after seeing White Sulphur "gleaming in the moonlight," Lucy Walton and her party "fanc[ied them]selves in Fairy Land." "It
seemed like magic," she continued, "& I could scarcely realize that I was
not in Dream Land." That the resort architecture and landscape evoked
words such as "magic" or "dream-like" or "enchanting" from the visitors
reveals their important role in fostering spectacle and in providing the appropriate setting for the creation of an idealized southern identity.[30]

The grounds and buildings of the resorts were more than pretty settings; they formed a central place in the elite South's geography of refinement. The fashionable buildings and well-groomed grounds of the Virginia
Springs worked, as Richard Bushman has noted of other refined spaces,
to separate the "smooth and brilliant" world within from the "plain and
rough" world beyond.[31] This ambience allowed the genteel guests, if they
chose, to participate fully in this beautiful world without being confronted
by objects that did not fit with their picture of refinement. There was a
theatrical quality to the structures' graceful styles, whitewashed exteriors,

and perfect order that befit a stage set for a play. The lawns, walks, benches, ballrooms, porches, and piazzas provided additional settings for social interactions among visitors. "The green during the day," one visitor noted at White Sulphur, was "alive with children & men, the grave & gay, old & young, all seeking their pleasure." The benches around the trees and upon the main greenswards offered space for loungers. The walks and verandas provided "promenade[s] for those who prefer[red] motion" and were "enlivened by gaily dressed belles and beaux." A resort's green was one of the premier spots, along with the ballroom, where the visitors not only played but also performed, presenting and judging fashions, manners, and conversations. Each lady or gentleman provided spectacle and animated the landscape—a necessary part of a "smooth and brilliant" or refined arena. Without the appropriate architectural and landscape settings at the springs resorts, no spectacle could have been achieved; refinement would have found no place.[32]

∾

"A Country More Wildly Picturesque"

The settings of the Virginia Springs juxtaposed controlled landscapes with uncontrolled nature. Wild disorder surrounded tamed order. Rows of rugged mountains, multitudes of cascading streams, and expanses of deep forests formed the resorts' perimeters and contrasted sharply with the refined and well-tended grounds and buildings within their confines. The few valley farms provided pastoral interludes amid the Blue Ridge Mountains. Visitors appreciated and enjoyed the natural landscape of mountains and forests as much as the designed landscape of buildings and greenswards. From his cottage porch at White Sulphur, Samuel Hoffman could gaze upon "a beautiful view of the valley and the Mountains, and all that is going on, on the lawn—a prettier spot I scarcely know." Golden meadows, small wooded groves, and tree-dotted lawns skirted the edges of the resort, mediating between the carefully landscaped grounds of White Sulphur Springs and the wild landscape of mountains and forests beyond (fig. 5). Visitors rarely failed to comment upon the sharp contrast between the manicured greens of the resorts and the wild nature surrounding them. In *Society in America* (1837), Harriet Martineau observed that White Sulphur "present[ed] such beauties to the eye, as perhaps few watering-places in the world can boast." "All is wild, beyond the precincts of the establishment," she noted, hoping it would always remain so. Viewing the scenery around them, moreover, provided elite visitors a chance to utilize their knowledge of fashionable aesthetic theories and language, further displaying their education and refinement.[1]

Experiences with and observations of nature became central topics of the guests' conversation at the spas. Descriptions of the natural scenery and of the feelings it inspired filled visitors' journals and letters throughout the period. In these descriptions, many revealed their familiarity with the fashionable language of viewing nature that derived from eighteenth-century British aesthetic theories of the sublime, the beautiful, and the picturesque. By the mid-eighteenth century in England and on the Continent, learned and artistic men and women reveled in nature's glorious wildness. Unlike their Enlightenment predecessors, who sought signs of reason in nature, these men and women looked to nature to produce an emotional impact. At the end of the eighteenth century, elite Americans adopted this appreciation of nature and borrowed the British aesthetic language for viewing it; they continued to use the language throughout the nineteenth century. Their vocabulary and attitudes derived from such eighteenth-century British and European philosophers and authors as Alexander Pope, Edmund Burke, William Gilpin, and Uvedale Price.[2]

As they did with architectural and landscape styles and other current fashions, elite southerners, hoping to display their gentility, borrowed English intellectual models and then adapted them to their own regional environment. Southerners and other Americans did not accept British eighteenth-century aesthetic theories in their entirety. In particular, Americans did not consider the sublime as terrifying as Burke had; instead, they found the awe-inspiring sublime delightful and developed their own definitions of the concept. After seeing "the purple peaks . . . of a vast mountain chain," Mary J. Windle gasped "in an ecstasy of enjoyment" at "one of the most sublime views." At the same time, they increasingly used "beautiful" for any scene that the viewer considered pleasing or pretty, not merely for "smooth and polished" or "light and delicate" objects. Finally, by the mid-1800s, the picturesque was simplified to apply to any "striking, irregular, spirited forms" or even to any scene that resembled a landscape painting or *tableau vivant*.[3] Influenced by early nineteenth-century romanticists, such as Lord Byron, Samuel Taylor Coleridge, William Wordsworth, and—

the southerners' favorite—Sir Walter Scott, Americans also made "romantic" and "pastoral" key words in their aesthetic vocabulary between the late 1820s and the 1850s. Romanticism placed a premium on strong emotions and sentiment, spirituality and mystery, the strange and the natural. By the late 1810s, visitors to the Virginia Springs described "romantic" scenes and views along with sublime, beautiful, and picturesque ones. Almost all of the visitors' writings show that by the 1820s the fashionable American language of aesthetics included other words, such as "magnificent," "majestic," "grand," "grandeur," and "lofty," in its vocabulary. Nineteenth-century travelers, including springs-goers, always looked for sublime, beautiful, picturesque, or romantic scenes similar to those depicted by Claude Lorrain or Salvator Rosa or described by Burke, Gilpin, or Scott.[4] While American viewers apparently did not use Claude glasses, they nevertheless gazed upon Blue Ridge scenery with the golden images of that artist's and other romantic painters' or authors' works in their minds. For example, the anonymous author of *Six Weeks in Fauquier* gushed: "How rapturous would have been the sensations of Claude, or Poussin, who painted as if their pencils were dipped in the rainbow, at seeing some of these autumnal sunsets!" In 1817 Ellen Mordecai's brother asked her to "tell Gustavus we must take a ride here in search of the picturesque" for "his pencil might have found employment . . . in the Hogarth style." Writing to her family about the route her party took to the Warm Springs around 1820, Martha Terrell described "a country more wildly picturesque than any your favourite Scott ever described."[5]

By the late 1820s, long after an aesthetic appreciation of nature had become a badge of refinement, travel guidebooks, along with paintings and prints, served to popularize the aesthetic language and descriptions found in theoretical or literary works. Travel books set the standards by which the majority of tourists or travelers translated their own experiences of wild nature and designed landscapes at the Virginia Springs, as well as Niagara Falls, New England's White Mountains, and the Hudson River. These books told people not only *what* to see, but also *how* to see, to react, and to describe what they saw. The Virginia Springs region became renowned almost as quickly for its scenery as for its curative waters. Travel accounts and guidebooks of the Virginia Springs chronicled, in the popular aesthetic language of the period and in great detail, the sites, objects, and landscapes that the springs guests would see on their visit. "Here," *A New and Comprehensive Gazetteer of Virginia* (1835) promised, "the painter may find employment in sketching the bold outline of nature's works—the botanist in contemplating the beauties and varieties of the vegetable kingdom—and the philosopher and mineralogist, in speculating upon the unexplored regions of fossil and mineral formations, with which these mountains so richly abound." The guidebooks acquainted visitors with springs life and the surrounding landscapes before their arrival. Visitors knew to expect "romance and adventure in every sedge and cavern and shaded stream, which you pass on your route." Together with romantic and aesthetic literature, guidebooks and published travel accounts constructed guests' expectations and provided them with the language they would use to describe their own views and experiences.[6]

In keeping with the sentimentalism of the era, visitors to the Virginia Springs took pleasure in the variety of emotions that natural scenes evoked within their hearts and minds, from astonishment to pleasure to melancholy. For planter visitors from coastal regions and northern visitors from cities, the first glimpses of the Blue Ridge Mountains were often the most memorable events of the entire trip. Catherine Hall reported that her husband "was struck dumb . . . when we reach'd the Top of the warm Spring Mountain: he said he never could have Imagined anything half so grand." A sleepy Mary Jane Boggs came fully awake upon her first sight of the Blue Ridge. She "enjoyed the view very quietly," but believed "if I had not been ashamed, I should have behaved in a very extravagant manner." Another young woman's "heart literally stood still for a few moments" when "the first mountain [she] ever beheld burst in all its dark blue glory on my sight." Afterward, "indistinct, undefined, sensations of grandeur stole over my senses. I was only alive to the conviction that I really saw a mountain." The settings of the resorts appealed to genteel visitors' romantic leanings. They devoted much of their journals and letters to describing their feelings in language that was both poetic and fashionable as they gazed upon various natural scenes. After beholding, in the light of "the moon and the evening star," "mountain upon mountain towering over above the other in awful grandeur and sublimity and of every variety of hue which the setting sun could possibly impart," C. O. Lyde recorded in her journal that "the whole scene gave *me* feelings I had never before experienced and which I hope *never* to forget."[7]

Some viewers responded spontaneously to nature; others knew from literature and guidebooks that natural scenes should produce certain emotional responses in refined persons. According to these works, rugged mountains, orderly fields, and deep forests should inherently appeal to the gentleman or lady of good breeding because of the beauty or sublimity of the scene. Eighteen-year-old Mary Jane Boggs noted that, while on their springs trip, she and her cousin James "talked about the mountains & the effect produced by looking at beautiful scenery, then we discoursed most *learnedly* upon 'Intellectual Philosophy' &c &c." Viewing awesome wonders and beautiful sights, according to theory, ennobled the individual, cultivated a genteel person's aesthetic sensibilities, and promoted morality and refinement. Most visitors to the Virginia Springs yearned and worked to appear as refined ladies and gentlemen, not only in their letters to friends and relatives, but even in their private journals. Consequently, their descriptions of Blue Ridge and Virginia Springs scenery consistently used the vocabulary and style of the fashionable aesthetic language. For these viewers, the Blue Ridge scenery was always "wild and romantic"; "lofty" mountains and rocky promontories, especially the Natural Bridge, were always "sublime and magnificent"; views from hills and mountaintops were "picturesque and grand"; and valley farms were "pastoral." Describing natural objects and scenery in these terms had become conventional by the 1830s. In fact, doubting their own creativity and vocabulary and revealing the insincerity of fashionable aesthetics, a number of visitors filled their private diaries and letters with descriptions of the spas' landscape designs and the surrounding mountain scenery copied—word for word—from popular published guidebooks. Guidebook writers as well sometimes lifted, without citation, entire sections about the springs verbatim from other published sources.[8]

Judging from the letters, journals, and travel accounts written by visitors of both sexes, gender apparently had little influence on how an individual experienced or related to nature. Planter men, just like planter women, considered the forests, rivers, mountains, and valleys of the Blue Ridge and the natural spectacles, such as the Natural Bridge and Weyer's Cave, objects worthy of admiration. While male pioneers, explorers, and entrepreneurs may have regarded wild nature as something to subdue and master, planter men, like planter women, appreciated nature in much the same manner as the cultured and leisured elite of Great Britain and the North. As ladies and gentlemen, southerners used the same fashionable language of aesthetics to describe what they saw. "Sublime," "romantic," "beautiful," and "picturesque" appeared with equal frequency in women's and men's writings. Both sexes wrote lengthy, effusive, and flowery descriptions. Southern elite men and women apparently differed little in their attitudes toward nature. At the Virginia Springs, gentility—not gender—determined a visitor's reaction to and relationship with nature.[9]

The Virginia Springs resorts juxtaposed the controlled nature of a designed landscape with the uncontrolled nature of mountains, forests, brambles, waterfalls, rock formations, and caves. Planter men and women enjoyed their stays at the Virginia Springs especially because they could be in contact with wild nature, yet remain in comfort and control at landscaped resorts. They found frequent opportunities to use the fashionable (and British) aesthetic language of the period to describe the scenery and the feelings that it inspired. Categorizing the mountains and forests that surrounded the resorts as sublime, beautiful, or picturesque brought these wild and uncontrolled scenes safely into the elite visitors' refined world.

ॐ

"At Great Trouble and Expense"

The Virginia Springs proprietors who envisioned, constructed, and operated the resorts led difficult lives. Their backgrounds, property holdings, and occupation gave them an ambiguous place in southern society. Yet these men and their establishments played an important role not only for planter society, but also in their Shenandoah Valley neighborhoods. Resort proprietors faced tremendous responsibilities. Successfully accommodating, feeding, entertaining, and caring for hundreds or, in later years, thousands of guests each week required business acumen, keen logistical skills, and a polite and eager-to-please attitude. From October to June, a spa owner spent his time making decisions and plans for the next season: how to attract guests, whether and when to remodel, what supplies to order, which musicians and cooks to hire, and whether to buy or hire more slaves. When the spa season arrived, a flurry of activities took place daily that required constant planning and supervision, particularly arranging rooms and preparing meals for hundreds of visitors. The larger resorts, such as White Sulphur and Fauquier White Sulphur, used modern business methods, employing managers and superintendents and dividing the resort into departments in order to handle all of these activities efficiently. How well a proprietor dealt with the challenges and responsibilities of each season determined the success and longevity of his resort.

Resort proprietors came from a variety of backgrounds, though many, like some resorts, left little more than their names in the historical record or remain totally unknown. Men, apparently, owned all of the resorts or were considered the proprietors. Doubtless their wives or other female family members helped to run the resorts, and some women may have owned the springs property in name. Many proprietors had lived in or around the Shenandoah Valley and the Blue Ridge Mountains their whole lives. They inherited their lands from fathers—or fathers-in-law—who had received land grants for military service or were early settlers. If not for John Lewis and his descendants William and John, the Virginia Springs circuit would have lacked two of its most popular resorts—Sweet and Warm Springs. James Caldwell received a springs property from his father-in-law and quickly transformed White Sulphur into a major resort. William Erskine and Isaac Caruthers married two daughters of the Benson family and started Salt Sulphur Springs on Benson land in 1821. Most of the proprietors and their families put everything they had into their resorts; these places represented their only means of livelihood.[1]

A small yet significant number of proprietors came from wealthy families or possessed a medical education. A handful of owners were rich planters living on or owning other lands in the Shenandoah Valley who had recognized the economic potential of their medicinal spring properties. Erasmus Stribling—former mayor and prominent citizen of Staunton—began Stribling Springs in 1817. Dr. John Brockenbrough, president of the Bank of Virginia and member of the state legislature, owned Warm Springs from 1828 through the early 1850s.[2] He visited it often on his rounds as judge for the western district of Virginia, but permanently resided in Richmond, at least until around 1850. Not surprisingly, a number of physicians purchased springs resorts, fully accepting the value of mineral waters for people's health and desiring to promote these therapies. As spa proprietors, they sought both to cure patients and to make a better living than they could as a regular doctor. Dr. Thomas Goode, a Virginian educated in Philadelphia and Edinburgh, purchased the failing Hot Springs in 1832 and transformed it into a full-fledged resort. Goode achieved both goals—curing many guests and receiving some of the highest rates for a physician. Similarly, Dr. William Burke made a good living as the proprietor and resident doctor of Red Sulphur Springs from 1833 until the late 1850s.

Those proprietors for whom a springs resort was their only income and property occupied a strange place in antebellum southern society—neither yeoman nor planter nor professional. Like many of their yeomen neighbors, most held little improved land. These proprietors owned their spring and generally between one and two hundred acres surrounding it. A few proprietors held over five hundred acres, but much of this land was unimproved, consisting of steep, thickly forested mountainsides. Apparently, almost none of the resorts contained large farms or plantations. The proprietors grew enough to feed their own livestock and to provide some, but far from all, of the foodstuffs for the dining room. The early owners struggled just to clear enough land around the springs for guest accommodations and a small farm.[3]

At the smaller resorts, the members of the proprietor's household constituted the entire staff. As in yeoman households, wives, children, and, on occasion, a few slaves contributed their hard work to the running of the resorts either by choice or force. Matilda Stribling's role as hostess was so crucial to Stribling Springs that after her death her husband sold the place. During the 1850s, brothers John and William Frazier ran both Rockbridge Alum and Bath Alum with the labor of their wives, sons, and daughters-in-law. Like most mountain dwellers, the Virginia Springs proprietors apparently owned few, if any, slaves. During 1821 and 1822, the first year of their partnership at Salt Sulphur Springs, Isaac Caruthers and William Erskine purchased only two "Negro Boy[s]" and one female slave.[4] They hired other slaves for short periods of time, usually a month or two. At the larger resorts, of course, the proprietor and his family relied upon more slaves and numerous white employees. Yet, even at the height of its success, the White Sulphur Springs Company must have owned very few slaves, for at the end of its 1860 season the company paid nearly $17,000 for slave "Servant hire." This sum was 10 percent of the total hotel department expenses for the season and was the second largest expense, following "Hotel Supplies." An additional $1,216.77 for slave artisans and repairmen came under "Improvements" expenses.[5]

The springs resorts seem to have been economic engines in their corners of the Blue Ridge region, turning the remote place into a thriving—if only seasonal—commercial area and providing markets and workplaces for farmers and their families. In addition to the resort and its amenities, many proprietors owned stores, taverns, smithies, or tanneries. Salt Sulphur Springs, for example, resembled a small village. Throughout the entire year, Isaac Caruthers, William Erskine, and their employees sold dry goods and enormous quantities of alcohol and "segars," made and repaired farm implements, and crafted shoes and other leather goods. Their neighbors brought produce, livestock, and dairy products to the springs and, in exchange, purchased goods and services from its various enterprises. Both groups profited. The proprietors had ready sources of food for their guests and additional labor when necessary. Area farmers needed to go no farther than the nearest resort to sell their farm products and purchase manufactured goods, shoes, ironwares, or liquor.[6]

The proprietors' occupation and living environment, however, clearly distinguished them from their yeoman neighbors. Like merchants, they engaged in a diversified and commercialized business, depending upon distant clients and responding to economic fluctuations. Like great planters, they lived in elegant and expensive houses surrounded by numerous outbuildings and commanded, at times, dozens of slaves and white workers. The spa owners and their families probably constituted their neighborhood's elite. Yet Virginia Springs proprietors never accumulated enough wealth to match successful urban merchants nor did they generally possess the requisite backgrounds, breeding, or agricultural and slave property to enter the planter ranks.

The awkward position held by springs proprietors in southern society caused their planter visitors to regard them with some ambivalence. As caretakers of the planter elite's favorite places, some garnered respect and even fondness from their guests. A reporter for the *Charleston Daily Courier* regarded the proprietors of Rockbridge Alum Springs as "polished gentlemen" and recommended their spa "to the patronage of our Southern community." Virginia judge Joseph C. Cabell referred to the landlord of Buffalo Springs as "quite a clever, well educated, gentleman." While the majority of Virginia Springs proprietors were simply small landholders and innkeepers, some of them maintained good or even close relationships with their planter visitors over the years. Henry Clay corresponded with James Caldwell, the owner of White Sulphur Springs, from the 1810s until Caldwell's death in 1851. Clay shared political gossip, aspirations, and disappointments with Caldwell over the years. He considered the proprietor, whom he described as "my particular friend," important enough to introduce his son by letter to James Madison in 1828. Planter men also entrusted their most prized possessions—their wives and slaves—to a proprietor's care. As so many planter husbands did, Clay often left his wife Lucretia for weeks at a time at White Sulphur Springs or other spas. Other planters sent sick slaves to the springs under supervision of the spa owner. Proprietors who seemed to care more for money than for the health and pleasure of their guests, however, were considered crass or exploitative. They lost any chance of gaining respect from the gentry and, instead, earned names such as "outrageous extortioner." Richard D. Burroughs believed that the owners of one spa were "the Dirtyest meanest set of people . . . that ever was[;] they think of nothing but getting all the money they can."[7]

Resort owners worked hard throughout the year, enjoying very little leisure themselves as they provided it for others. The hiring of staff and servants took a great deal of a proprietor's time during the off-season. Finding a skilled manager proved no small feat. The positions of musicians, bartenders, washerwomen, cooks, gardeners, and other white employees had to be filled for the hotel and public rooms. Proprietors needed farmhands and dairy workers year round, as well as carpenters, bricklayers, blacksmiths, and other artisans for most of the repair and remodeling jobs. William Erskine and Isaac Caruthers paid dozens of local men for help getting their resort in shape during their first year of business.[8] While many resort workers came from the neighborhood, others arrived from Richmond, Washington, or even farther away. Robert Bailey brought "my bar keeper, my cook and his wife, and some other servants as waiters" from Philadelphia and "house servants" from Georgetown to his Berkeley Springs hotel. His cook was French and his gardener was brought over from Scotland at a wage of two hundred dollars a year. Including these employees, Bailey managed twenty-two "necessary servants" and "every thing seemed to move in perfect harmony."[9]

By the 1850s, White Sulphur Springs employed a small army of people— both black and white, local and cosmopolitan, seasonal and year-round. An echelon of directors, superintendents, and managers guided the large staff, from the hotel dining rooms to the laundry. In 1860, when White Sulphur was the largest resort in the area, and perhaps in the United States, Willis Williams was so impressed that he gave his wife a detailed breakdown of the operation:

> The Hotel springs &c. is owned by a company of about 20 persons. . . . The officers and superintendant are as follows[:] 1 president[,] 5 directors, 1 Superintendant, 1 superintendant of the hotel, 1 for the street, 1 head waiter & 5 assistan[ts]. . . . 136 servants, 4 for the sick. The Kitchen has 4 white bakers with 3 collord assistants, the waiters of the Kitchen 16 males & 6 females[.] Then they have a [*illegible*] Kitchen (for the sick) that has 1 cook and 1 assistant. 1 storekeeper, for the retail, 1 [store-

keeper] & 1 assistant for the whole sale. . . . They have a Laundry . . . that has 50 employees mostly Irish women, 1 to superintend the linen room, 1 for the beds, 1 for the tablecloths, 1 for the crockery room.

The above list failed to include 16 farmhands, the blacksmith, dairy workers, 6 cooks, a couple of bartenders, a fireman, and a lampman. The company had over eighty people listed in its salary account and paid out a total of $16,534.47 in salaries for 1860.[10]

Proprietors contracted with white musicians from Richmond, Baltimore, and, especially, Washington and, from the beginning, used slave or free-black musicians as well for their afternoon and ballroom music during the season. A slave named Sam played the fiddle in the ballroom for an impressive five dollars an evening at Sweet Springs during Robert Bailey's tenure as manager in the 1810s. A black fiddler still played there in 1823.[11] There were a few all-black bands. An especially skilled six-member band composed of black musicians played at White Sulphur in 1838. According to Blair Bolling, they played wind instruments and a bass drum in the afternoons, and added two violins and a bass violin at the nightly balls. Bolling declared their music "excellent."[12] White musicians apparently became the rule for most resorts during the 1840s as more resorts and their guests wanted bands or orchestras that knew the complicated waltzes, polkas, and other "cultured" music of the period. A protracted set of negotiations occurred every year between owners and musicians for the summer season. Bands customarily received their board and a set sum for the season. Some bands reserved the right to play special concerts and charge admission. Proprietors and band leaders exchanged numerous letters wrangling over salaries, musicians, season dates, and benefits. A good band, every proprietor realized, meant successful balls and happy guests; as such, they were worth the expense and aggravation.[13]

The hiring of a large number of slaves as waiters, maids, repairmen, and for other positions was crucial to a successful spa season. In his 1819 advertisement for Berkeley Springs, William Abernathy proclaimed that, "at great trouble and expense," he had procured "first rate cooks [and] honest, attentive and obliging servants." The majority of the hired slaves worked in the ballroom, dining rooms, and guest rooms during the season, but others worked for terms ranging from a few months to a full year. Finding enough servants for the summer required good ties with Piedmont planters who had slaves to spare. In 1842 George Mason Hooe wrote to

Daniel Ward, the superintendent at Fauquier White Sulphur, offering him first refusal of his "very likely & most valuable house servant." Hooe characterized the young man as "particularly brisk & active," perfect for the dining room, and assured Ward that he possessed "no bad habits." The young man even had prior experience at the springs, where he had attended Hooe as a body servant. Once proprietors or managers found the slaves, hiring terms had to be agreed upon with the masters. John Turpin, for example, left little room for haggling with Ward over his pastry cook Lucy. Turpin stated that he had "concluded to let [Ward] have her at the low price of fifteen dollars per month, commencing 1st July, and remain at the Springs, or in your service during the Season." He added that he "expect[ed] to be at no expence for her going and returning." Occasionally, resort owners exchanged a slave's labor for the slave's use of the medicinal waters. Helen Grinnan could not afford to send her son's slave, who was suffering from blindness in one eye, to Fauquier White Sulphur unless he could work as a "horseler" or do "some repairs wanted about the premises." Proprietors also regularly hired free blacks for work around the resorts. Hezekiah Daggs of Botetourt Springs paid Jesse Johnson, "a Free negroe," $14.75 for almost two months of unspecified work. Even in the mountain South, black labor was a necessity for the running of a large enterprise.[14]

Slaves often had their own reasons for wanting to be hired out to one of the springs. Summer hires might have sought to escape temporarily from their own masters. Others hoped for more. Henry Bright spoke with a mulatto waiter who told him that his master said he could earn the eight hundred dollars needed to purchase his freedom by working at the springs. Some slaves desired to join spouses who already worked at the resorts or who lived on nearby farms. Betsy Morton's slave hoped for work as a chambermaid at White Sulphur where her husband also worked. Jeremiah Morton, Betsy's brother-in-law and the manager of the resort, cautioned against it: "My advice is, never to permit a servant to be hired at Springs, especially at the White Sulphur." Hinting that the greater freedom from white supervision and greater power over white comfort made a season working at the resorts "very corrupting" for slaves, he acknowledged that "few are well satisfied afterwards" to resume their plantation duties. "I shall never permit Chapman or any of my young servants to come here again, *if I have my way,*" he explained. There is little doubt that Betsy's slave would have preferred to live with her husband, as her mistress realized, but that was not

the manager's main interest. Preventing a good plantation slave from becoming a corrupted resort slave concerned him most. Morton ended his
letter with a nervous admission: "Of course, what I say in relative to servants, I do not wish to be repeated, as from my position and interest in this
establishment shall have to employ many and do not wish my opinion to
be quoted against me." He would not employ any of his own or his sister-
in-law's servants for fear of corrupting them, but he expected to need the
labor of others' slaves.[15]

Being hired out presented a plantation slave with new opportunities. In
1832 an enterprising slave hired as a blacksmith at Hot Springs, Charles
White, dictated a letter to his master in Caldwell County, North Carolina,
offering him a proposition. White wished to stay at Hot Springs and open
his own blacksmith shop after the end of his contracted term. He pointed
out that his master would earn more money in this way than by hiring him
out again. White probably desired most to stay near his wife who lived in
the vicinity.[16] Resort slaves and slave visitors possessed more freedom of
movement and less white supervision than plantation slaves. Hired and
visiting slaves, both workers and invalids, often traveled back and forth
between their home plantations and the Virginia Springs on public stages
by themselves, carrying money with them for their expenses. Occasionally
one or more slaves drove a carriage alone from home to pick up their master, mistress, or other family members.

The black community at the Virginia Springs looked very different
from its counterpart on plantations, large or small, or even in towns. Some
of its members lived and worked at the resorts throughout the year or, at
least, the season. Others stayed only briefly. Whether the servants of white
guests or invalids themselves, visiting slaves took part in the resort community for a few months, a week or two, or just a few days. In some areas,
local free black families also belonged to a resort's black community. In
1860 at least thirty-seven free black women, men, and children lived and
worked at Fauquier White Sulphur Springs, for example.[17] The large resorts, such as White Sulphur and Fauquier White Sulphur, had communities made up of hundreds of black men, women, and children. Smaller
black communities correspondingly formed at smaller resorts.

Service, not agriculture, dominated the workers' time. At Fauquier
White Sulphur, free black men worked primarily as "Stonefencer[s]" and
farmhands, while women worked mainly as laundresses and chambermaids.[18] Most of the slaves owned or hired by the resort proprietors worked

as maids and waiters. A few held more important positions. George Johnson saw the superintendent of Warm Springs placing an order with a grocer "pretty much according to black Charles's dictation." Visiting slaves served their white masters and mistresses much as they did at home by cleaning cabins, washing and preparing clothes, minding children, and serving food. White guests almost always brought servants when their children accompanied them, and ladies seldom traveled without at least one maid. Yet some white travelers rarely acknowledged the crucial help of their slaves. Lucy Cocke ignored the presence of all six of her slave servants when she recorded in her diary the names of the people that made the trip to the springs in 1850. Others, however, expressed satisfaction with how well their slaves performed on the trip to and in the new environment of the springs. James J. White happily informed his wife that "Bolivar & Sam Christian . . . distribute themselves with an enterprize & energy, worthy of a more profitable investment, upon the parlour & ball room floor" at White Sulphur. George Harrison was more than pleased with Nathan, who "manifested as much vigilance, fidelity & strength as an English mastiff" in the dining room at Sweet Springs. "When any thing was removed which he had provided for me he instantly began to growl & seemed ready to suit the action to the sound." Nathan probably looked out as much for his own interests as his master's—a rule of the dining room gave servants first claim to their masters' leftovers.[19]

Judging from the limited evidence concerning African-Americans at the Virginia Springs, the life of a slave at a resort was assuredly less harsh than that of a slave on a plantation. Even though resort slaves may have led a less restricted and less supervised life at the springs than on the plantation, they still remained subject to all of the indignities and dangers of living at the bottom of southern society. Slave women faced sexual encounters, willing or unwilling, with white men at the resorts. Robert Taylor Scott informed a friend that he could not resist the "charms" of *"the ladies of colour"* at the springs. Nor were slaves at the springs safe from sale. Slave traders came through the area and planters always watched for a good deal. The owner of a hired slave named Israel sought to sell him after his tenure at White Sulphur. A friend of the owner visiting the springs found a "man of worth & wealth" from Alabama willing to buy Israel as a body servant and to convince Israel's free wife to go with him to Alabama.[20]

Visiting slaves and invalids together with resort workers and seasonal hires experienced a different slave culture and, perhaps, more leisure at the spas than at home. At the springs, they met black men and women from across the South, expanding their knowledge of others and their ties outside of their locality. At any given time during the height of the season, hundreds of visiting slaves from various places might live at one resort. Over just three days in August 1852, for example, thirty servants arrived with white families at Bath Alum Springs. These slaves must have come from a variety of backgrounds. There is little evidence of how slaves interacted with each other or with the white servants of northern and foreign guests. Visiting slaves may have had problems fitting in with the resort slaves. Maria Broadus noticed that "the private servants have a hard time too, as those that belong here seem to regard them as intruders." They also received the worst lodgings. In his *Observations on the Mineral Waters*, Dr. Edmondson Horner observed that guests' "servants fare badly at the White Sulphur." Some slept in stable lofts or mangers or their owners' carriages. "The remainder are disposed of in any cranny that may be unoccupied." Nonetheless, visiting slaves seemed to enjoy their stay at the springs.[21]

By the early 1800s, the Virginia Springs resorts competed with each other for guests. The competition intensified throughout the first half of the century as the number of resorts and visitors increased. Guests determined the categories of competition: accommodations and food, service, amusements, fashionable society, and the efficacy of the waters for specific diseases. Resort owners responded by proclaiming that their spring surpassed all others in one or more of these categories. "If you take the word of the *proprietor*," one visitor warned in 1823, "each spring is *best* & none *good* but *his*."[22] Each resort especially made known which diseases its mineral waters could cure. Few, if any, of the spas could excel in all of the categories.

Advertisements for Virginia Springs resorts appeared in newspapers as early as the mid-1700s. From the 1780s and 1790s through 1860, the newspaper advertisements followed a similar style. They stressed the spa's salubrious climate and healthful waters, as well as the quality of its lodgings and service (fig. 9).[23] The notices usually began in May, before the start of the season, and ran through July in newspapers throughout Virginia, around the South, and even in the North. Some resorts ran special advertisements announcing specific events, such as a ball or hunt or Independence Day celebration. Some proprietors sent out broadsides containing descriptions of their resort and testimonials telling of the healing powers of their

MONTGOMERY
WHITE SULPHUR SPRINGS.

Va. 1856

This new and beautiful Watering Place will be open for the reception of visitors on the FIRST DAY OF JUNE, 1856. It is situated on the Eastern Slope of the Alleghanies, near their summit, in Montgomery County, Virginia, within a mile and a quarter of the Virginia and Tennessee Railroad, eight miles from the Alleghany Springs and five miles from the Yellow Sulphur Springs, is one of the MOST ROMANTIC AND PICTURESQUE PORTIONS OF SOUTH-WESTERN VIRGINIA.

These Springs are the Most Accessible in the State, if not the Whole South.

Leaving Richmond, Petersburg, or City Point in the morning, the traveler by the Danville and South-Side Railroads reaches Lynchburg to Dinner; and thence by the Virginia and Tennessee Railroad he arrives at the Springs Station, just after passing the BIG TUNNEL and near the summit of the Alleghanies, at 5 o'clock P. M., the same day; there he takes the SPRINGS COMPANY'S CARS, and passing over their road along an easy descending grade, he is soon transported into the Reception House, without trouble or fatigue. Thus, after a comfortable journey of two hundred miles, part of it through a lovely country, all the way by Railroad, in elegant passenger cars, he finds himself at 5 o'clock, P. M., enjoying all the pleasures and advantages of a watering place, where Nature has done much, and where Art is employed with a liberal hand. The place seems to have been adapted, from the variety of its Mineral Waters, its delicious atmosphere, and magnificent scenery, alike to the wants of the invalid, and the tastes of the seekers of pleasure.

At this watering place there are

TWO WHITE SULPHUR SPRINGS,

Whose waters nearly resemble the Greenbrier White Sulphur, one at a temperature of 54 degrees, and the other 60 degrees and very palatable. There are, besides,

TWO CHALYBEATE SPRINGS,

Near them of good Tonic qualities. The establishment is also supplied with the purest water from the springs rising in the hills overlooking the buildings. These Mineral waters have been resorted to and used to a considerable extent for fifty years by the people of the neighborhood, and have been found efficacious in the following diseases:

Dyspepsia, or Indigestion: Diseases of the Liver and Kidneys; all Diseases of the Stomach, especially of a Chronic Character; and in all Cutaneous Diseases, Tetter, Scald Head, Erysipelas, Salt Rheum, &c., &c.

The Proprietors have, since last season, completed all their buildings then in an unfinished state, and will have completed in addition, a number of other very pleasant rooms, which together, will afford ample accommodation for 1000 GUESTS. They have, also, built a LARGE BATH HOUSE, with Warm, Cold, Plunge and Shower Baths, and have set on the Lawn a number of large Trees, which will afford a fine shade for the approaching season.

They have re-engaged the services of

MR. THOMPSON TYLER,

well known in the Atlantic Cities, whose capacity as a Landlord and Caterer is unsurpassed. Having the advantage of Railroad communication East and West, with a country of extraordinary fertility, the Proprietors are sure the TABLE of the MONTGOMERY WHITE SULPHUR SPRINGS will be supplied in a manner that will give entire satisfaction to the public.

The Dining Saloon is one of the most spacious and elegant to be found at any watering place.

Great care has been exercised in the selection of Servants, and the most vigilant supervision will be observed over the Hotel and Cabin arrangements, so as to promote, in the highest degree, the comfort and pleasure of visitors.

A SUPERIOR BAND OF MUSIC,

(Made up from SMITH'S famous ARMORY BAND) is engaged, and an extensive and beautiful Ball Room, Bowling Alleys and other places of amusement, will add to the sources of healthful and agreeable relaxation at this

New and Beautiful Watering Place.

An arrangement has been made with the LYNCHBURG AND ABINGDON TELEGRAPH COMPANY by which the Proprietors have secured a branch of their line and the establishment of an OFFICE AT THEIR SPRINGS in time for the approaching season; thus affording TELEGRAPHIC COMMUNICATION with all parts of the Union, when the Telegraph is in operation.

Address,

ROBERT H. MOSBY,
President Montgomery White Sulphur Springs Co., Montgomery County, Va.

Figure 9. Montgomery White Sulphur Springs advertisement, 1856. (Rare Book, Manuscripts, and Special Collections Library, Duke University, Durham, N.C.)

spring.[24] Advertising was not cheap. By 1860 the White Sulphur Springs Company spent close to $675 for pamphlets and newspaper advertising in Virginia, New York, and Alabama.[25] A few owners published, in book form, travel accounts of their particular spring or of all of the prominent Virginia Springs. The proprietor-writers usually appended written testimonials after their accounts.[26] Proprietors hoped the heavy investment in advertisements, pamphlets, or books would pay off in the coming season.

A real challenge awaited spa owners every season in the accommodation of hundreds or thousands of guests. Stocking the resort's kitchen and outfitting the guest rooms and public rooms required large amounts and varieties of goods, a huge outlay of money, and keen business skills from the owner and his staff. Ordering supplies and organizing their distribution or preparation occupied the proprietor or his manager the entire year, but reached a frenzy during the peak of the season—from mid-July through early September. On September 1, 1860, Elizabeth Noel reported that at White Sulphur "they bake five hundred pies a day, kill two steers, 22 sheep, 300 chickens[,] cook 40 bushels of corn[,] make from ninety five to 115 gallons of coffee twice a day besides tea & milk." Proprietors wanted the best food and drink they could afford for their elite visitors, especially at the bar. The manager of Fauquier White Sulphur stocked its bar with an impressive array of libations: champagne, "four of the best varities" of claret, sherry, cognac, Irish whiskey, Holland gin, Jamaican rum, and "'Hennessee Brandy' of *great* age." To ensure his guests a good meal and cool drinks, the proprietor of Healing Springs sent to Richmond, via railroad and wagon, for "Tomatoes, potatoes & Ice" at great expense. Supplying a resort required as much time and effort as running it. It was a complicated business.[27]

Providing amusements for the pleasure-seekers who came in droves to the Virginia Springs was a necessity for any resort that desired fashionable visitors and the accompanying profits. An advertisement for Botetourt Springs in 1825 told of plentiful game in the mountains for hunting gentlemen and of "newspapers, books, chessmen, backgammon tables, &c." for those who preferred "more inactive amusements." Amusements for ladies "had not been overlooked" either, with the ad promising "music of the best kind . . . for dancing" and an "elegant" pianoforte. To "promote rational enjoyment and recreation," William Vass of Red Sulphur promised those guests in search of pleasure "a select library of miscellaneous works, together with periodicals, newspapers, &c.," excellent musicians, and "such other amusements." Vass assured a good time for any visitor to his resort.[28]

Constructing or updating resort buildings and grounds also proved popular in attracting visitors. New or remodeled hotels always received special notice, and a heavy advertising campaign usually accompanied their unveiling. The Frazier brothers of Rockbridge Alum cautiously promised potential visitors in 1853 that with their newly added guest rooms, ballroom, reading room, billiard rooms, and "other public accommodations much needed heretofore," "no reasonable effort shall be spared to render our visiters as comfortable as the magnitude of the crowd will admit." Modern improvements, such as gas lighting or indoor plumbing, came at an enormous expense to the proprietor. The White Sulphur Springs Company spent $26,400 on improvements, such as spiral stairs and new guest rooms, and on new furniture, including iron bedsteads, wardrobes, and silverware for the 1860 season. The owners hoped the changes would pay off in the long run.[29]

Not all of the proprietors prospered. Economic downturns, such as the Panics of 1819 or 1837, bankrupted numerous Virginia Springs proprietors. The lingering effects of the Panic of 1837 in the South kept much of the "usual company" away as late as 1842. James C. Bruce reported that "it is thought that most of the proprietors of the watering places will be ruined" for "they have made extensive improvements" and "are in every instance under deeds of trust and must soon be sold." Even worse disasters could wipe out a resort. Berkeley Springs suffered more than its fair share of catastrophes. After its heyday in the mid-eighteenth century, it languished until an epidemic fever struck around 1805, at the height of the season, killing about half of the guests and many of the locals. The resort barely struggled on until a fire in 1844 destroyed almost all of the buildings. Yet the proprietor, Col. John Strother, never gave up. He built a large hotel upon the ashes and Berkeley Springs became a popular spot once again, though it never reclaimed its eighteenth-century glory. Only a handful of resorts, usually those owned by a company or corporation, realized substantial profits. In 1860 the White Sulphur Springs Company made $26,822 in net profits from its Hotel Department alone. The men who could come out a little ahead at the end of every season or borrow until the next one tended to hold onto their resorts for many years. Many others failed entirely after only a season or two.[30]

In 1843 Charles Carter Lee proposed to his brother, Robert E. Lee, that they purchase a springs property. Robert, however, showed little enthusiasm. While he believed that "the prospects" of the property were "very flattering," he wisely reminded Charles that "nothing can be done without money, & it is the very kind of property that requires a large outlay before any profit can be realized." Everyone knew, moreover, that, in the end, profit "will depend upon fashion & prejudice."[31] Neither Charles Carter nor Robert E. Lee became springs proprietors. Running a resort for elite visitors was quite an undertaking. It proved a competitive business that required large sums of money and hard work, but making it profitable still depended upon the caprice of fashion and nature. The resorts constituted considerable enterprises, diversified and staffed with both white employees and black slaves. The larger resorts, especially White Sulphur Springs, were among the biggest employers in the South during the first half of the nineteenth century. Without the labor of proprietors, managers, and slave servants behind the scenes, the resorts simply could not have functioned.

$$\infty$$

"Bribe High and You Live High"

While visitors considered the resorts beautiful or magical, their beauty often failed to offset the poor living. In spite of the glowing descriptions in advertisements, most resorts fell short of their promises of great comfort. As soon as travelers began to expect more than rudimentary accommodations at the Virginia Springs, complaints about the bed, board, and staff began. In 1818 John H. Cocke believed the "present State" of conditions at a few resorts "must be shocking to that refined female delicacy." He vowed "nothing shou'd induce me to bring a female friend to them but direful necessity." The tone of the comments remained the same for the next four decades, even after more resorts opened and the competition for visitors increased. Louisianna Cocke echoed the sentiments of hundreds of other springs guests when she proclaimed: "Oh! this is the dirtiest place I believe in the world, and nothing comfortable about it. The fare is indifferent but we could put up with it better if we knew it was clean." But guests did "put up" with uncaring proprietors, rude managers, crowded or dirty rooms, bad food, and the occasional surly servant. They willingly but grudgingly exchanged an accustomed level of comfort at their homes for health and fashion at the resorts.[1]

A complex relationship took shape between the visitors and the proprietors and their workers in the peculiar labor environment of the springs. Guests relied upon a resort staff made up mostly of people from the lowest ranks of southern society for whatever comfort could be had. Trying to gain entrance into an overcrowded spa and to secure good care while there forced elite whites to negotiate, even beg, favors from those considered beneath them in the social hierarchy. If a planter man or woman could not reach agreement with a proprietor or manager, the only option was to leave the resort. Most visitors acknowledged the presence of servants only in occasional but often vital situations. If visitors ignored or mistreated a slave servant at a crucial moment, they went hungry or slept in filth. Planter men and women always had to negotiate with slaves for their comfort and convenience—and for the comforting illusion of being in control. At the springs, however, elite visitors had to undertake these negotiations with slaves and whites from the lower orders in front of their peers in a competitive environment, not in the safety of their home plantations. Proprietors and their staffs, in a more or less subtle fashion, judged each visitor's claims to high status and enforced the distinctions between them. By evaluating these claims, a resort's staff helped to establish the hierarchy of spa society—a process that had ramifications for the rest of southern society.

Guests ranked resorts, judging which possessed the best or worst accommodations, food, servants, and society. Visitors rarely reached final agreement on these matters, but some resorts consistently stood out in certain categories. Over the first half of the nineteenth century, spring-goers considered Salt Sulphur Springs superior in every way, except in fashionable society and mineral waters, to White Sulphur. In addition to Salt Sulphur, other springs, such as Blue Sulphur, Red Sweet, Warm, and Fauquier White Sulphur, became known as resorts of reliable comfort and a pleasant stay. Red Sulphur and Hot Springs became the favorite spas for those in search of health, while White Sulphur, Fauquier White Sulphur, Rockbridge Alum, and Sweet Springs earned reputations as fashionable and fun-filled resorts. Not surprisingly, the few resorts that did have good food, polite servants, or comfortable accommodations earned loyal guests who returned year after year. Poor food, crude or dirty accommodations, or rude servants could spell doom for a small resort. Guests appreciated "the best ordered and conducted" watering places, but they were incensed at poorly run and ill-equipped ones.[2]

Visitors considered themselves lucky if their lodgings were comfortable. The Frazier brothers were surely correct when they advertised that their new "single and double hair mattresses" at Rockbridge Alum surpassed the "bed and bedding" of any other resort. Many visitors suffered sleepless nights due to wet, dirty, or vermin-infested sheets, mattresses, and pillows. Louisa Maxwell Holmes and her roommate awoke early one morning to hogs "squealing & grunting" under their cabin, shaking the structure like an earthquake. One visitor's wife became "quite sick" from "the shock she received from the horror" of one resort's accommodations. The quality and variety—or lack thereof—of food received frequent comments. While proprietor William Vass advertised that "the most celebrated cook in Virginia has been engaged—and indeed all the servants have been selected with great care," some proprietors apparently had little concern for the expertise of their kitchen and servant help. Terrill D. George, a junior manager at White Sulphur Springs, informed his superior that "there is some grumbling—some think the butter not to good as it ought to be for $14 a week, others say we might, at least, have chickens, but there will be grumblers." Red Sulphur Springs' proprietor informed Samuel Clayton's party that if they did not like the food they could go someplace else. Leaving the dinner table satisfied with the quality of the food and the service was apparently a rare experience for Virginia Springs visitors most seasons. Susanna Harrison reassured her mother only that "as yet I have met with none of the cook's teeth or flies in the apple tarts."[3]

White Sulphur Springs and a few other large resorts, such as Sweet Springs, appeared immune to complaints about accommodations and service because they possessed the greatest drawing card in the competition for visitors: they were centers of fashionable society. White Sulphur Springs received the most frequent and strident complaints about awful food and dirty lodgings but still attracted the largest and most fashionable crowds. James Cathcart Johnston informed a friend that at White Sulphur guests "hang upon one another like bees going to swarm merely for fashion sake," living on "bad food" and "uncomfortably lodged[,] being packed sometimes six in a room intended for two." Other visitors, caught up in the beauty and fashion, loved everything about White Sulphur, despite the reality. Wherever the fashionable held court, visitors went in droves, whatever the resort's conditions.[4]

Except for those who brought their own servants, elite visitors enjoyed almost no control over the quality of their daily life at the Virginia Springs—a situation quite different from that at their homes. No matter how loudly or how often guests complained about their situations, proprietors and their staffs apparently paid little attention. According to James

Johnston Pettigrew, "the immense crowd of the last season" at White Sulphur "might well have convinced [the staff] of their freedom from all de-
pendance upon public opinion."[5] It was entirely up to the proprietor, his
managers, cooks, or servants whether the cabins were cleaned, the food
well-prepared, and the service polite. A visitor's only alternative, and only
source of power, was to leave a resort and never come back. That rarely
happened. Visitors returned year after year to many of the resorts that they
had previously disparaged. Some were desperate for the medicinal waters
at a particular spa; others were willing to give the place another try. Many
others, however, could not resist the lure of a fashionable resort no matter
how many times they had stayed in wretched lodgings or eaten miserable
food. For many, even the South's "aristocrats," comfort seemed a small
sacrifice for seeing and being seen, taking part in the fashionable whirl of a
season at the Virginia Springs. The complaints ultimately meant very little
to the proprietors or the guests.

Visitors had to negotiate constantly with every level of a resort's staff—
from the proprietor to the manager to the servants—not only for their
comfort, but often just for admittance into a resort. No longer possessing
the accustomed authority of their plantations, the men and women of the
master class found themselves in a rare position—forced to accede control
to members of the lower orders. Proprietors and managers served as judges
of their visitors' social status. Out of all his guests, the owner of White
Sulphur distinguished those men and women "that he consider[ed] deserving of his attention, by asking them to take wine sometimes at his house."
South Carolinian James L. Petigru and his family received such an exalted
distinction.[6]

By the 1830s, when the Virginia Springs area became the most fashionable place in the South, the height of the season, July and August, found all
of the large resorts constantly overcrowded. In 1858, two years before the
census listed him as one of the two or three largest slaveholders in the
country, Wade Hampton III wrote that not even he was assured rooms at
White Sulphur Springs at the height of the season.[7] Those who hoped to
gain entrance and a good room were forced to acknowledge, and to seek
favors from, a less moneyed, less educated, and less refined person. Managers and superintendents, who probably owned very little property, came
out of similar, or even worse, social and economic groups as proprietors.
Yet they all held a powerful position. By judging which of the elite travelers
deserved admittance into a fashionable spa, these gatekeepers affirmed, in
a very public way, the high status of a visitor.

Room assignments further distinguished a party's or individual's social worth. Most visitors believed that proprietors or managers determined room availability based on a party's importance, wealth, appearance, or size. After 1830, with the increased popularity of the springs, a shortage of rooms was chronic. Guaranteed entry came to those coming in private carriages with large entourages of servants and horses. The well-known South Carolinian James L. Petigru arrived at the gates of White Sulphur in 1845 and, upon "learning who we were," the "chief superintendent" directed his coach driver to an assigned cottage. Stage passengers, in contrast, often stood waiting in the dust of the departing coach only to learn that they had to go elsewhere for lodging or, if they were lucky, squeeze into a room with strangers. William Vass, the manager at Sweet Springs, "seemed quite at fault in disposing" of William Bolling and his party in August 1841. Vass placed them in "an exceedingly uncomfortable & inconvenient" cabin. Afterwards, Bolling discovered "from Vass himself" that "some 4 or 5 of the best Cabins, & rooms in the Hotel were lock'd up for some favorites expected in a few days."[8]

Like proprietors, those managers who were courteous, efficient, and quiet about the power that they held faded into the background and generally remained unacknowledged, except for passing comments about their capabilities and gentlemanly qualities. But managers who wielded their power unabashedly and unfairly provoked the anger of those clamoring at the gates. While visitors considered White Sulphur's James Caldwell to be a gracious host, his manager, Maj. Baylis Anderson, received few accolades and many complaints. Known as the "Metternich of the Mountains," Anderson ruled entry into White Sulphur with an iron fist. The resident physician, Dr. John J. Moorman, remembered him as a man who "loved better than most other men to exercise authority." He turned away travelers "with as much indifference as he would turn out a flock of sheep" and thereby "flattered his own self importance" and made himself "feel really like an actual proprietor." Visitors had to pass Anderson's scrutiny before being allowed into the fashionable confines. Acknowledging the manager's power, one travel account claimed that before "King" Anderson's "throne," "Senators bow, legislators, judges, professors, are supplicants—flattered beaux, flattering belles sue for his high permission, without which all is lost." But for "'putting on some airs' and telling some truths to Mr. Anderson," Isaac Peck "c[oul]d not have found shelter" for the night in August 1833; even then, he received no better than a pallet on the floor. Once he decided to admit a party, however, Anderson went out of his way to make the honored guests feel comfortable in the overcrowded conditions.[9]

When a proprietor or manager ignored or discounted his visitors' comfort, he received their wrath and condemnation, but apparently only in their writings. Few ever confronted an owner. Most guests politely requested better treatment or simply fumed in silence. The proprietor or manager of a popular resort always held the winning hand. He controlled the place where southern and many northern elites longed to be.

Slave servants knew as well as proprietors and managers the importance or unimportance of particular visitors. Their behavior toward and responsiveness to certain men or women helped to reinforce social distinctions. A rich planter's commands often had little effect amidst the bustle of a resort filled with some of the wealthiest and most influential people in the country. The slaves themselves frequently determined if and when a visitor's wishes would be fulfilled. Unlike plantation slaves, resort slaves found themselves in situations, such as in the huge dining rooms, where they could frustrate an immense number of wealthy men and women with little danger of punishment. Managers and proprietors were apparently unwilling to exercise much control over the behavior of slaves toward guests. Slaves controlled the service in the dining rooms, the preparation of food in the kitchens, and the cleanliness of guest cabins and hotel rooms as waiters, cooks, and cleaners. Another group of servants attended invalids. Because of the crowds, cabin and hotel servants waited on at least a dozen guests; dining room waiters had even more visitors assigned to them. Unless a visitor brought personal servants, getting the best food in the dining room or having one's cabin cleaned early required negotiating with the resort servants.

The large number of guests easily provided an excuse for a slave servant to overlook an uncooperative or inconsequential visitor. One visiting doctor who used an offensive "epithet" toward a resort servant lost all hope of good service.[10] Many resort servants required bribes from visitors to perform their tasks quickly and satisfactorily. Many guests easily went along with the bribing game as just another ritual at the springs and just another facet of the system of rewards and punishments between masters and slaves. Writing from White Sulphur in 1832, Samuel Hoffman informed his wife that he had supped on "delightfully cooked Venison and Beef Steak, Chops and good Tea," "procured by a fee of an odd dollar to the Cook and one to [the] head waiter." Similarly, John H. B. Latrobe secured a pallet, pillow, and blanket "by dint of bribing the waiter and chambermaid."[11] But others, usually foreigners or northerners unaware of the convention or those on tight budgets, bristled at what they viewed as an intolerable state of affairs in the dining rooms and cabins. The unfortunate William Bolling snarled that "the Table is abominable & the dining room disgusting and without *bribing* a servant to attend to you particularly[,] you can get [no] attendance except by accident." Those slaves who had been bribed spent the first fifteen minutes after the dinner bell "cutting & slashing the meats for those they attend." [12] Bolling quickly learned to pay a servant to take care of him. Latrobe neatly summed up the basic rule: "Bribe high and you live high; fail to bribe and you starve." [13] Many of the slaves who worked at the Virginia Springs daily pushed whites farther in a demand for tacit recognition—usually by a few coins—of their role in affirming elite status than the usual plantation relationship between master and slave.

Visitors often believed that resort workers did not care or do enough for their comfort. At the same time, they were reluctant to acknowledge just how much power these laborers, especially slaves, held over their daily lives at the springs. In a place where everyone watched each other's movements, people from the bottom of southern society constantly assessed the social abilities and financial resources of those from the top. The gatekeeping and status-conferring functions of a resort's staff provoked the ire of many visitors. But proprietors, managers, and slaves knew that elites would suffer poor conditions and accept the unaccustomed power of the lower orders in their search for health or pleasure.

Through architectural styles and landscape designs, the resort proprietors carefully created a physical manifestation of the ideal southern place where the elite of southern society could spend the summer in the mountains and put on a show for their peers. The ballrooms, verandas, gardens, and greenswards epitomized the planters' notion of a refined place where genteel people interacted. On an even grander scale than the visitors' often grand homes, the buildings and grounds manifested and supported the refined culture of planter society. Almost anywhere a visitor looked, a gracious and orderly facade or lawn presented itself. Visitors felt comfortable within this setting. But they also experienced enchantment, gazing upon a huge hotel with towering columns and long verandas, immense dining and ballrooms, fairylike cottages, large fountains, Grecian temples, and sweeping acres of landscaped parks and serpentine paths. The mountains and forests surrounding the resorts garnered special attention because of their appearance and because they provided an opportunity for viewers to use fashionable aesthetic language. As at plantation homes, the beauty and order of the landscape and architecture at the springs could be viewed in two ways. On the surface, they presented a picture of a genteel and romantic South that so impressed most visitors. The Greek Revival structures and elaborate landscapes at the springs, however, symbolized not only refinement but also elite southerners' wealth and power and their dedication to hierarchy and slavery—the harsh realities behind the beautiful facades.

The beautiful settings did not always ensure beautiful living. Visitors, especially southern planters, came to the Virginia Springs with certain expectations about the proper deportment of those beneath them, especially slaves, based upon their home and plantation experiences. In the plantation environment, lower-class whites and slaves occasionally failed to conduct themselves according to those expectations. But, at the spas, these two groups frequently failed to meet guests' expectations without some sort of bribe or entreaty. Nevertheless, the happiness, health, and comfort of the guests depended upon the presence and efforts of proprietors, managers, and slaves. Mistreated guests fumed over the perceived indignities of the resort's staff, but they had little recourse, lacking their usual authority to punish the servants. Their desire to see and be seen at a fashionable resort led them to tolerate poor, sometimes abysmal, conditions. Rich and famous planter visitors may have received a nicer room and better treatment from the staff. But, like the other guests, they still had to negotiate for their comfort with slave servants and managers amidst their peers without the accustomed control of their plantation. Though at the top of the South's hierarchy, these men and women clearly wanted to have their claims to high status publicly acknowledged and affirmed by the staff, whether slave or proprietor, of the Virginia Springs resorts.

PART 2

Healing Waters

"IN THE COURSE OF MY LIFE . . . THESE HEALING WATERS have exerted the happiest effects upon my health and constitution," seventy-one-year-old John Hartwell Cocke Sr. recorded in his journal during a trip to the Virginia Springs in 1851. He had come to the springs, as on earlier visits, to improve his "enfeebled health." Cocke made his first trip over the mountains in 1799 when he was just nineteen. At that time, he remembered many years later, the baths had "operated like a charm in restoring me to good health." His future wife, Louisa Maxwell, also visited the springs in the early 1800s as a young woman. Between 1810 and 1860, one or several members of the Cocke family traveled to the Virginia Springs from Fluvanna County, Virginia, on nearly forty different occasions.[1]

Focused solely upon improving his health, the senior Cocke often made the trip with just a servant or one or two male relatives. In contrast, his wife Louisa and their numerous children and grandchildren visited the springs in large groups of family members, relatives, and friends. For example, the brothers Philip St. George and Cary Charles Cocke, their wives and children, a sister, and six servants formed a party of twenty at the resorts in 1850, when Philip praised the "invigorating atmosphere" of the springs. Over the years the Cocke family used the Virginia Springs as a summer home, where they could escape the sickly season and ensure their good health. Lucy Cocke, Cary Charles's wife, noted in her journal in November 1857 that a trip to the springs "was enjoyed by us all" as "the health of each of the party improved" and everyone felt "on all respects gratified by the trip." No one had been seriously ill. All simply desired to drink and bathe in the medicinal waters as a way to preserve their good health. Lucy especially enjoyed the hot "spout" bath at Hot Springs, her "favorite old watering place." On other occasions, the Cockes placed their last hopes in the curative powers of the spring waters for particularly dire illnesses. Louisa Cocke took her epileptic stepgrandson Hartwell to Buckingham Springs in 1840, praying that the mineral waters could cure "his awful malady." The waters failed; the child died soon after.[2]

Upon leaving the springs in 1851, John Cocke considered "the result upon whole favorable" and his "general health bettered."[3] Following the custom of multitudes of visitors and in keeping with his own family's faith in the waters, he returned two years later; other members of his family visited the Virginia Springs every year but one in the ensuing decade to use again their healing waters.

From the late eighteenth century through the eve of the Civil War, Virginia Springs visitors believed that the best course for good health included a trip to the mountain resorts—a trip that revolved around rituals of health as well as of fashion. The springs environment was conducive to a healthy mind as well as a healthy body. Just as the mineral waters assuaged diseases and soothed aching bodies, the change of scene and beautiful surroundings reinvigorated bored minds and cheered spirits. The ennui and physical malaise planter men and women frequently claimed to feel at home disappeared for most of them during a stay at the springs resorts. Beginning soon after the discovery of the springs, medical and popular opinion proclaimed that the mineral waters offered relief or total recovery from all sorts of diseases and illnesses, ranging from the relatively minor, such as rheumatism and facial acne, to the more deadly, such as tuberculosis and malaria. But most visitors traveled over the mountains primarily to maintain their good health, seek amusement, and avoid summer heat and disease. The combined pursuit of health and pleasure had a long history among the spa-going British, and the southern gentry continued the tradition in fine style. The sick and the well both turned to the Virginia Springs for their health, and thus both faced many of the same choices about the best means to achieve their goals. By offering numerous healthful advantages—from their curative waters for specific diseases to the salubrious climate and new scene—the Virginia Springs resorts served in another way: as a retreat for their elite visitors, especially those from the coastal and Piedmont South.

Throughout the eighteenth and nineteenth centuries, medical science as well as popular thinking accepted the efficacy of mineral waters as a cure and, in later years, as a preventative of diseases and other health problems.[4] Even though ideas about health and medicine changed drastically over these decades, visitors and resort doctors always regarded the waters of the springs as beneficial therapy for their acute diseases, chronic illnesses, and general good health. Throughout this period, a tension existed between what orthodox medicine preached and practiced and what the lay public believed and did about their own health and treatment. At the Virginia Springs, this tension was revealed as visitors often decided on their own or with the help of friends what constituted good health and proper treatment. They prescribed for themselves when to make a trip to the springs and which kind of water to use. Visitors' attitudes about health, moreover, became part of their definitions of genteel southern ladies and gentlemen.

Whether sick or not, the spa regimen that they followed cleansed their bodies and steeled them for the coming winter. These rituals of drinking and bathing provided interesting scenes in the daily performance of spa life. Spring-goers experienced a variety of physical sensations not found on their plantations or in their town houses. In a way unknown at home, the body held center stage at the springs. Concern for their health and close observation of the effects of the waters heightened the visitors' awareness of their bodies. This intimate attention to bodies reveals much about the adaptability of southern gentility to different environments in the geography of refinement. Most visitors to the Virginia Springs regarded the springs as natural panaceas or even "miracles." Women especially felt the benefits of these healing waters. "If the accounts of their wonderful virtues are true," Mary Lee wrote to her husband Robert, a person "ought to expect to liye forever."[5] Yet life and death often stood juxtaposed at the Virginia Springs.

ᐔ

"King Cure All"

As some of the first chroniclers of life at the Virginia Springs noted, most people who traveled to the springs resorts were not invalids. From the late eighteenth century through 1860, visitors came not so much to search for a cure, but—in addition to seeking pleasure—to continue the relatively good health that they already enjoyed. In 1829 George Harrison and his wife Isabella traveled to the springs even though their health was "perfectly good." Similarly, writing from Hot Springs in 1847, Robert Hubard declared that he and his family were "enjoying fully as good health as usual." In fact, some visitors even used their health as an excuse to go to the springs in search of pleasure, following British spa custom. In a letter to his mother, Thomas Pollock confessed that there was "nothing" for him to do except "seek my own pleasure & I now see that was the actual though not ostensible object of my trip." [1]

During the summers, the mountainous resort area offered a generally safe retreat within what was the least healthy region in the country throughout the nineteenth century. Epidemic and endemic diseases, such as yellow fever or "summer miasma" (malaria), struck the South's coastal plains and towns every summer. Devastating cholera epidemics occurred in 1832 and 1833; between 1849 and 1854, no twelve-month period passed without the appearance of cholera somewhere in the United States, usually in the South. Typhoid scourged the region, particularly during the 1840s. Yellow fever was classified as essentially a "southern disease" during the mid-nineteenth century; especially lethal epidemics hit Virginia in 1848, 1852, and 1855. The last of these outbreaks killed close to four thousand people in Norfolk and Portsmouth alone. Malaria, the most significant of a number of endemic diseases, and a variety of other "spotted," "bilious," and "intermitting" fevers preyed upon southerners on plantations and in towns every summer.[2] Reaching the mountains before the sickly season began could save many southerners from illness and even death.

For these southerners, avoiding sickness did not depend upon possessing good moral character or leading a sinless life but upon escaping from the sickly summers of the lowlands and maintaining good health with mountain (or sea) air, exercise, and mineral waters. Planter men recognized that their families could catch diseases as easily as any others—black or white. After hearing of cholera's horrible "ravages among the blacks in Norfolk," George Evelyn Harrison feared for his family's safety and put off their return from the springs. Like many other visitors, the author John Pendleton Kennedy spent his months at the Virginia Springs in 1832 preoccupied with the threat of the ongoing cholera epidemic. In every letter to his friend Peter Cruse, Kennedy asked for news about the spread and devastation of the epidemic. With great relief, Peyton H. Skipwith of New Orleans wrote John H. Cocke that his wife and two children had "been spared during the ravages" of a cholera epidemic in 1849. Skipwith had been so worried that they might become infected that he refused to leave any earlier for the springs because of the potentially disease-ridden steamboats. When the threat of disease was especially great, planter fathers preferred to keep their families at the Virginia Springs as long as possible. Dr. Cary Charles Cocke, for example, thought himself "fortunate" that his wife and baby had stayed "in the mountains this summer," rather than at home exposed to the fevers brought about by the oppressive heat.[3]

It was in part the planter family's desire to escape the sickly season that led to the rise and growth of the Virginia Springs resorts in the first place.[4] As early as 1820, the Reverend Jared Sparks proclaimed the area "the Southern planters' paradise."[5] After the first Asiatic cholera epidemic struck the United States in 1832, Dr. William Burke purchased Red Sulphur Springs and Dr. Thomas Goode took over Hot Springs. Even in years without such catastrophes, hundreds and later thousands of springs visitors traveled into the mountains to escape the oppressive heat (and accompanying ennui) of their plantations and in towns. A trip to the springs quickly became a ritual, albeit a healthy one, of the southern gentry and an important part of their year. Those elite families "who can afford to leave their plantations, to fly to the salubrious air of the mountains" often left in late June or, if from the Deep South, even in late May as the summer grew warmer and more disease-ridden.[6] Some did not return to their homes until they felt it was safe, often after the first frost. In 1798, William Gray of Virginia decided not to return home from the springs until the middle of September to "miss the warm weather & return with my health perfectly restored."[7] Like John H. Cocke, Richard Singleton of the always dangerous South Carolina lowcountry first visited Warm Springs in 1818 and thereafter brought his family to their own cottage at White Sulphur almost every summer until his death in 1852. Another South Carolinian, Wade Hampton II, also frequented the springs often enough to warrant owning a family cottage. From 1790 through 1860, families from all over the South, especially the coastal areas of Virginia and the Carolinas, made the journey to cooler and more healthy climes every summer, with the Virginia Springs their favorite destination.

Visitors who drank or bathed in the waters, for curative or simply healthful purposes, thought of them not as medicines but as natural remedies. They considered the thermal and mineral waters "wonderful, and natural phenomena" that could cure many diseases.[8] One only needed to know which particular springs possessed the appropriate waters for his or her specific health problem. Spring-owners quickly made known the specific chemical contents of their waters and listed the specific diseases and health problems for which they were especially beneficial. While a variety of minerals infused each spring, the mineral present in the largest proportion or the color of the water usually influenced the name of the resort.[9] For instance, Salt Sulphur contained sodium; the other sulphur springs, such as White, Blue, Red, and Grey, contained large amounts of sulphur that left colorful deposits. Aluminum, calcium, magnesium, potassium, and even arsenic permeated some of the other springs. Commenting upon a trace of arsenic found in the waters of Healing Springs, J. Taylor of Charleston decided "who cares what the water contains provided it cures diseases," including that of his wife who regularly used the potentially dangerous water.[10] Carbonates and sulfates, especially magnesia sulfate (Epsom salts), made the thermal waters soothing. Many accounts grouped the waters into three categories, allowing visitors to decide which resort to visit based on their health needs. Under "Stimulants" came the waters of White Sulphur, Salt Sulphur, and Blue Sulphur Springs. An example of "Sedatives" was Red Sulphur. "Roborants" (carbonates) included Sweet and Red Sweet Springs.[11]

Newspaper advertisements, guidebooks, physicians, and returning visitors made known the wondrous curative powers of each spring. Dr. John J. Moorman, the longtime resident physician at White Sulphur, declared that its mineral waters "have proved themselves the most indisputably efficacious" for diseases ranging from "Incipent Calculus" (kidney or gallstones) to "Hemmerhoids" and "Cutaneous Eruptions" (facial acne). White Sulphur's waters also became renowned for alleviating stomach ailments. Visitors to Healing Springs considered it "the Balm of 'Gillead' or a 'King Cure all.'" In addition to benefiting syphilis, "dyspepsia, chronic diarrhoea, dysentery, chronic rheumatism and gout, dropsy, gravel, liver affections, uterine diseases, neuralgia, erysipelas, and other cutaneous affections, scrofula, worms, and several other chronic diseases," Red Sulphur Springs was famous as "the resort of the consumptive invalids."[12] The thermal baths at Hot and Warm Springs supposedly cured or at least eased a host of health problems, including general debility, rheumatism, liver complaints, acne, venereal diseases, and especially "uterine diseases" and other female illnesses. Charles Minor informed his brother in 1836 that Warm Springs was "a most wondrous marvellous freak of nature" because it possessed "such an infinite comminglement of all sorts of temperatures, & properties. Hot, warm, cold, very cold, freestone, limestone, sulphur, Iron, magnesia & the d——l knows what all." To add validity to their claims, published works often appended testimonials from cured visitors. In a published pamphlet accompanied by such testimonials, the Reverend Thomas Stringfellow hailed the waters of Fauquier White Sulphur for curing indigestion, diarrhea, other digestive problems, and pulmonary complaints. Visitors to the Virginia Springs in search of a cure for a specific illness needed to know the lengthy list of diseases that each spring claimed to serve. Without this knowledge, recovery was a challenge.[13]

Significantly, neither physicians nor proprietors nor visitors classified the mineral waters of any of the springs as beneficial to only men or only women. Some resorts included specific female illnesses, mainly "uterine disorders," or male health problems, usually venereal diseases, among those diseases benefited by their waters. Still, all of the springs were considered efficacious in some way for both men and women. Husbands, wives, sons, daughters, and traveling companions of either sex could all visit the same resort with hopes that the mineral waters could cure their various problems.

Just as important, masters and slaves believed that the springs would cure blacks as well as whites. Though no published travel account or guidebook specifically mentioned that the mineral waters also benefited black men and women, people seem to have assumed that the springs would help any race. Willingly or not, slaves came to the springs seeking cures for a variety of diseases. Some accompanied their master's families; others went alone or with fellow slaves under orders that entrusted them to the care of the proprietor. Slave invalids suffered from "sore" legs, "affection of the liver," blindness, chest pains, rheumatism, scrofula, "diseased lungs," and generally "delicate" health.[14] Masters counted on the waters to restore their valuable slaves to health. In 1790, Zackary Taliaferro asked Nicholas Cabell to look at his slave's "bad sore Legg" while at the springs to decide whether the mineral waters could cure it. Slave visitors, like white ones, apparently accepted the powers of the mineral waters. Randolph Harrison's slave Anthony claimed that the water at White Sulphur "worked miracles for him." While at Bedford Alum Springs with her baby and two young male slaves in 1855, William Massie's slave Lizzy expressed "strong Hopes that [the waters] will Help us all" in a letter home. Sometimes planters left their slaves at a spa, while they continued on with the visiting circuit. The Duke family, for example, left their son's "mammy" behind at Rockbridge Baths to take the waters for her "delicate" health. A coachman's rheumatic knees led Jerome Napoleon Bonaparte Jr. and his father to leave the man behind at Warm Springs. To their inconvenience, the slave could not rejoin them for two weeks.[15]

Faced with a potentially confusing deluge of published advice, visitors seemed to rely more upon their past experiences or the recommendations of other visitors, especially doctors, than upon the testimonials and guidebooks when selecting the most appropriate springs. Acknowledging that there were a "*multitude* of councellors" at the springs, one doctor advised yielding to "the wonderful discoveries made by the wisdom or the experience of almost every Individual." In 1820, based on his "experience," William Wirt recommended to his close friend Dabney Carr a stay first at White Sulphur for "biliary organs," then at Sweet Springs "to purify the blood and give a tone to the stomach," and finally at Warm Springs "to refresh and invigorate the system." D. C. T. Davis warned his cousin John B. Minor not to "overdo the matter, by beginning too freely" in drinking the waters. He jokingly proclaimed himself "impertinent" for "admonishing a grave & learned Professor," but reminded Minor that he had visited Rockbridge Alum twice, while this was Minor's "first introduction to them." Visiting doctors also diagnosed and advised fellow guests about proper cures for their illnesses. Some charged a fee to cover their traveling expenses, while others dispensed their opinion for free. Dr. Thomas Massie even decided to remain at the springs for the 1849 season "with the view mainly of practising among the visiters." He assured his father that his fees would certainly cover his board. In 1857 Richard Burroughs found "sixteen Doctors . . . from different states in the union all willing to give advice gratis as far as they know" at Red Sulphur. Indeed, at the Virginia Springs, visitors probably encountered more doctors in one place than they ever had before. Medical advice concerning the springs could come in a very roundabout fashion. R. Kean wrote his cousin that he had "received a letter yesterday from Mrs. Randolph" who relayed that "Dr. Buckner in a conversation with Mrs. Carr, told her a few days ago that Jane [Kean's sister] ought to spend about four weeks at the White Sulphur, and go from there to the Red Sweet."[16]

In seeking out advice, spring-goers, male and female, usually turned to male friends or relatives as authorities on the Virginia Springs, even though women used the springs as often as men. Apparently only a few women, such as Louisa Cocke and Charlotte Meade Ruffin, acted as semiofficial advisors on these matters. Cocke took charge of her grandson's health and brought him to several of the Virginia Springs between 1837 and 1840. Ruffin accompanied her husband to the springs, deciding that they should start at White Sulphur since, as she informed her father-in-law, "it would do Mr. Ruffin more good to come here, and drink the water than travelling about from first one place to another." Without her presence, moreover, her husband "would not have remained here two days nor would he have drank the water, except when he was thirsty."[17] Of course, other women may have given advice through these informal channels and left no written record.

The Virginia Springs offered not only a healthful retreat from the sickly season and cures for various diseases but also, from the earliest days, therapy for mental well-being. From Sweet Springs in 1798, William Gray assured his wife that he felt better "both with respect to ease of mind as well as in health."[18] In 1817 another traveler published his belief that a visitor to the Virginia Springs "will feel and think, as he has never done before."[19] During the late eighteenth and nineteenth centuries, both physicians and the lay public recognized a relationship between a healthy mind and a healthy body.[20] Doctors often prescribed a change of scenery to cheer the spirits and to improve physical health. For many people, the Virginia Springs quickly came to mind when searching for the perfect place to rejuvenate body and spirit. Robert E. Lee had great "confidence" in the "continuous journeys" and diverse scenes of the springs for "amusing the mind" and strengthening the body. Accordingly, he planned a trip for his sick and nervous wife to Fauquier White Sulphur and Berkeley Springs in 1836.[21] Visitors and their families alike knew that a sickly person needed good spirits as a part of improving their health. The landscape and atmosphere at the springs eased visitors' tensions, lifted their spirits, and dispelled the ennui and loneliness that so many planters—men and women—felt. The chance to exchange the dull routine of a plantation for the convivial, scenic, and healthful surroundings of the resorts drew hundreds to the springs each season. While northern resorts attracted urban northerners as an escape from crowded cities, most southerners did not need such an escape.[22] What the springs did offer were an atmosphere and a set of experiences vastly different from southerners' normal life. Buffalo Springs, for example, explicitly advertised that it was "very beneficial in the less fatal complaints" of "*ennui*, heart-sickness, hate-of-home, fashionable-hankerings, low-spirits and the like."[23]

The Virginia Springs functioned as a healing landscape. The elegant buildings, cooling pools and fountains of healthful waters, and lush scenery created a landscape that visitors found not only aesthetically sublime or beautiful but also emotionally restorative. Travelers to the springs, "worn down by cares or trouble, welcome[d] the first glimpses of the sparkling fountain, and the verdant lawns encircled by cottage homes" because these features "promise rest, comfort, health." Doctors and visitors both equated the mountain environment with health. In an 1858 guidebook to the springs, Dr. P. B. Tindall credited the "natural curiousities, landscapes, and mountain scenery" for aiding in the cure of invalids. Along with the natural and architectural beauty, the retreat from daily responsibilities and the pleasure of new and strange experiences contributed to the mental well-being of guests. The "change of . . . scene" and the "agreeable society and exemption from care" Jacob Hall experienced at the Virginia Springs were not only "pleasant" but also "very conducive to health of body and mind." For many planter visitors, being in surroundings very different from their homes improved the health of their minds in addition to their bodies.[24]

Many turned to the healing landscape of the Virginia Springs to relieve depression and grief, for a change of scene could cure emotional maladies. In 1801 Joseph C. Cabell prescribed a trip to the springs for his recently widowed brother. Cabell felt such an excursion could "draw him from his gloomy reflections on the subject, carry him into amusing company, make him ride about, and engage his attention with scenes that will dissipate the sorrows of his present situation." "At all events," Cabell concluded, his brother "ought to go to the springs next summer." In 1837 Alexander Stuart took a trip to the springs because he "was quite unwell & almost overwhelmed with the blues." Women, too, found comfort in a trip to the Virginia Springs. In 1803 Rosalie Calvert looked forward to a trip to Bath, where she hoped that "the *waters,* the *exercise,* and especially the *company*" would cure her of her "'*blue devils.*'" Calvert sought out the springs again in 1820 to assuage her heartache over the deaths of two children, as the "losses" had "crushed" her. The trip made her "feel ten years younger."[25]

Since most of the visitors had left homes surrounded by cultivated fields—not lofty mountains, thick forests, and cascading waterfalls—the natural scenery around the resorts apparently proved more of a mental tonic for the visitors than the well-manicured grounds. John McLaughlin delighted in living in "a new world which consists of Rocks and mountains." For those who sought it, mental tranquility came easily in this healing landscape. James Barbour reassuringly informed his mother that at Rawley Springs he had "enjoyed more tranquility & peace of mind than I had hoped for even." Looking out across the mountains and valleys from a hotel piazza, cottage porch, or mountaintop led many viewers to believe that the benefits reached not only their bodies and minds but also their character or souls. "Oh! if I could always behold such scenes," Mary Jane Boggs enthused in her diary in June 1851, "I think I could be better & purer—less selfish & worldly minded." William Burke captured the sentiments of thousands of springs visitors when he maintained that only the environment of the Virginia Springs "can invigorate the enervated constitution, raise the drooping spirits, calm the agitated mind, inspire the finer emotions of the heart, and impart elasticity and strength to the moral and physical powers."[26]

In the healing landscape of the springs, planter men and, especially, women socialized, exercised, gazed upon wild scenery, experienced intense bodily sensations, and breathed cool air far more than was generally the case at home. Such experiences made it easy to shake off the mental and physical malaise of the plantation. The sights and sounds captivated Volumina Barrow of Louisiana, enticing her outside to participate in it all and buoying her spirits in a way unknown at home. "I rise early—take a walk of about a mile before breakfast sometimes on top of the mountain" or amble along one of "the beautiful little brooks [that] wind along the valley falling in mimic cascades over the rocks with a cool splashing gurgling sound that enchants one only accustomed to stagnant bayous." The resort landscapes also contained various forms of recreation, such as racetracks, tenpin alleys, shuffleboards, and bathhouses, which held the promise of fun and relaxation. The social and recreational activities at the springs reinvigorated the mind and emotions of visitors. During his 1808 visit, John Caldwell found a "degree of temperate dissipation, or medicine of the mind" that relieved "the anxiety of worldly pursuits and vexations" and "promote[d] that sunshine and hilarity within, so conducive to the reestablishment of health." James White considered his 1860 stay at White Sulphur Springs successful, for, as he explained to his wife, "I have enjoyed my visit here very much, and feel delightfully relieved from the feeling of lassitude & ennui which had been upon me."[27]

The Virginia Springs atmosphere beckoned visitors to "come, and throw off in this holy place the stuff that gathers on your souls in life's tiresome travels." Plantation masters and mistresses and other elite southerners felt relaxed and unconstrained at the resorts. "This relaxation," James White assured his wife, "is the *only thing* that reconciles me to this painful absence" from home. Many guests immersed themselves in the fun and felt like children again. In 1810 William B. Hare was astonished that John H. Cocke, whose "health & spirits [were] greatly improved," "danced like a Boy of 16 and imparted much pleasures to all about him." At White Sulphur Springs, Samuel Hoffman experienced a return not only of youth but also of romantic ardor. Since his spirits were "as bouyant as those of a boy" of twenty, he wrote to his wife: "I am yet the youthful lover, and when enlivened and animated by this enchanting climate, I yearn for your participation in similar pleasures." During his many years at Red Sulphur, William Burke witnessed the effects of the Virginia Springs upon thousands of visitors' spirits: "The citizen, like a boy let loose from school, rambles over the fields, ascends the hills, culls wild flowers, and is filled with admiration, pleasure, and cheerfulness." [28]

Like their British counterparts, southern and some northern elites easily combined journeys to cure diseases, to alleviate ennui, and to seek pleasure. Thomas Jefferson Peyton, like many, regarded the Virginia Springs as places in which to "[season] good health." Reversing the common wisdom, he insisted that watering places "were intended for healthy people and home for sick ones." [29] A mountain spa's mineral waters and leisured lifestyle rarely failed to promote good physical and mental health in a visitor. The extraordinary benefits offered to body and mind drew people to the Virginia Springs year after year and encouraged extended stays of weeks or even months.

∾

"They All Drink the Waters without the Advice of Any Medical Man"

Examining the attitudes about health and treatment held by visitors to the Virginia Springs and their correspondents provides an intriguing glimpse at popular medical beliefs and practices. In the late eighteenth and early nineteenth centuries, most people held ideas about health and appropriate treatments that differed greatly from those of the orthodox medical establishment published in treatises and pamphlets. Patients had their own traditions of healing methods, or "folk medicine." These decades contained tremendous changes in both orthodox and popular medical theory and practice.[1] Throughout this period of change, the mineral waters of the Virginia Springs always remained a perfect therapy for recovering and preserving health.

Good health meant that the body's system maintained a balance of fluids—that it remained free of "disease," or imbalance. Therapy, therefore, required restoring the natural balance of the body to make the patient well. During this period physicians concentrated on curing, not preventing, disease and generally attended a patient only in serious circumstances. Regarding the body as an interconnected whole, doctors designed treatments aimed to affect the entire body, not just specific parts of it. Furthermore, medical theory argued that the best therapy produced immediate and very visible manifestations of recovery. Through the use of a set of therapeutics labeled "heroics," physicians adopted invasive techniques that restored balance by controlling the flow of fluids throughout the body, usually in an obvious and violent manner.[2]

Heroic medicine relied heavily upon bloodletting, either by opening a vein with a lancet or bleeding a specific area through cupping or leeching. But it also included liberal and regular prescriptions of massive doses of drugs that acted as violent emetics, cathartics, diuretics, or diaphoretics (which produce profuse perspiration). One of the most widely used drugs was calomel (mercury chloride), which caused severe vomiting and produced gray-colored gums, mouth sores, and loose teeth as its poisons dissolved. Physicians considered calomel and bloodletting the two best remedies for almost all ills. Blistering, where a doctor applied a plaster to form one or more blisters and then drew as much fluid as possible from each, was another technique in the medical repertoire of heroics. These treatments severely affected the body, causing extreme debility and dehydration. Yet patients expected drastic responses from their bodies as proof that the cure would really restore balance to their system. It seems likely that these treatments produced more harm than good in many cases. But the ruling medical theory of the day advised an active and aggressive role for physicians in their patients' recovery, leaving little to nature.

With prevailing medical theory before 1830 regarding the body as a system that constantly struggled to maintain a balance of fluids, the Virginia

Springs' waters offered a perfect therapeutic—drinking the waters caused an emission of bodily fluids. Doctors of the time frequently prescribed the springs as a heroic treatment. In 1808 Dr. Charles Everette of Charlottesville suggested that Wilson C. Nicholas try White Sulphur's waters, for they would "act painfully diaphoretical . . . with the additional advantage of clearing out various other impurities." The prominent Philadelphia doctor Benjamin Rush likewise recommended the waters of Berkeley Springs to his patients. Drinking mineral waters produced the expected effects of heroic therapeutics, without being as violent as an emetic or as extreme as bloodletting or as dangerous as calomel. By drinking large quantities, a person quickly responded as the waters acted strongly on the body as cathartics, diuretics, and diaphoretics. An added benefit of mineral waters was that the unpleasant physical effects lasted only a few days. The very visible signs of the impact of the mineral waters easily persuaded drinkers that their body responded well to this treatment and that their system was recovering its balance.[3]

Many visitors combined the use of the waters with the typical heroic therapeutics prescribed by resident spa doctors, including tartar emetics, mercury, and, on rare occasions, bloodletting. They hoped that these therapies would work in tandem with the waters for a quicker and fuller recovery. Even in these cases, most of the visitors apparently tried the waters first before turning to heroic treatments. During his three-and-a-half-month trip to the Virginia Springs, North Carolinian Larkin Newby not only bathed in and drank copious amounts of the mineral waters, but he also had himself bled, blistered, and given pills partially made of Castile soap that encouraged expectoration and another variety that slowed his pulse. Nicholas Cabell bled himself while at Red Sulphur Springs in 1808. In 1813 a doctor at White Sulphur gave Fanny Coalter "a small dose of Calomel," a taste of "Rhuebarb," and later some "opiates."[4]

During this period of invasive and violent treatments by physicians, an attraction of the mineral waters was that a cure did not require the presence of a doctor. Drawing upon advice or experience, visitors often decided for themselves or for other members of their party which spas to visit, how much to drink, and how long to stay. The members of the Cocke family, for example, rarely relied upon the advice of resident or visiting physicians during their visits to the Virginia Springs. With so many family members— including John Sr., Louisa, Philip St. George, and the doctor in the family, Cary Charles—having springs experience, the Cockes monitored their own health needs and determined their own spa regimens. Visitors also often decided for themselves when the waters had done all that they could and what constituted recovery or at least sufficient improvement to return home. Thomas Bolling decided himself that he was well enough to return home, but not until after paying a large sum to one "Doctor who's charges are as exorbitent as he is worthless and good for nothing." During an 1823 trip to the Virginia Springs, Larkin Newby and his fellow guests considered themselves experts on the mineral waters and their effects on varieties of diseases. They conversed "most *learnedly* & *scientifically*" about the different spas they had visited, their numerous diseases, "their origin & the effects of the waters upon them." They did not need a physician to direct them in the proper usage of mineral waters.[5]

The Virginia Springs visitors predated the health reformers of the 1830s in both their skepticism about the expertise of orthodox physicians and their reliance upon nature for assisting in recovering good health. Because they have studied published theories and leading practitioners' writings, many medical historians have placed the recognition and advocacy of these natural benefits only after 1830 and traced them to health reform movements.[6] The voluminous writings left by visitors to the Virginia Springs, however, reveal that from as early as the 1790s both the visitors and the doctors at the springs regarded fresh air, a good diet, and exercise as beneficial to one's health. In July and August of 1792, Ferdinando Fairfax drank mineral waters on a heroic scale, sometimes as much as four pints per dose, and went for vigorous walks or climbs up mountainsides on a daily basis while recuperating at Warm Springs. Two decades later, Virginia Terrell hoped that her kinswoman, Mrs. Carr, would be "completely restore[d]" by the use of Bedford Springs waters "joined to the salutary influence of the mountain air." The widespread acceptance of these natural elements as beneficial remedies shows the divergence of popular practice and thought from orthodox medicine. If most leading physicians failed to recommend regimens of fresh air, exercise, and diet in their published works or medical school lectures before 1830, common doctors and the lay public had long followed a course toward health that relied heavily upon natural therapeutics. Such was the faith in these remedies that in 1822 Nicholas Faulcon considered "abandon[ing] the use of the mineral waters altogether" at Sweet Springs "and rely[ing] wholly, for the improvement of my health, upon the mountain air, and exercise." While the emphasis on diet, fresh air, and exercise as cures increased over the course of the nineteenth century, they had a strong presence in popular therapeutics as early as the late eighteenth century.[7]

Around 1830, medical therapeutics and ideas about health began changing. At that time, many people, such as Catharine Beecher, began commenting upon the poor health of Americans.[8] New attitudes viewed health as something that should be preserved, not merely restored. Good health came to center on the absence of disease and needed to be constantly monitored. Simultaneously, orthodox doctors and practices came under scrutiny and attack after heroic treatments proved ineffectual against the ravages of particularly lethal yellow fever epidemics in the early 1800s and the first Asiatic cholera epidemic in 1832. Echoing the sentiments of multitudes, one Virginian observed in 1823 that there had been little "advancement" in medicine "since the days of Hippocrates."[9] Given that the severe treatments may have killed more than they cured, the antiheroics, antiorthodox stance taken by a large segment of American society was not unreasonable.

This general disaffection with orthodox medical theory and its practitioners led to a more organized and more effective opposition in the second quarter of the nineteenth century in the form of popular health reform movements, particularly the Thomsonians, homeopaths, and hydropaths. Thomsonians advocated the use of botanical preparations as curatives; homeopaths favored the use of minute doses of drugs. Hydropaths based their therapy on the curative value of cold water. Beginning in the early 1840s, these water-cure proponents prescribed cold water bathing and douching of particular body parts, along with a stark diet and regular recreation. Each of these reform groups shared the idea, which was increasingly acceptable to many Americans, that nature had miraculous healing powers. Nature, with perhaps a little help from medicine, could cure any illness. Its powers were also supremely capable of maintaining good health. These health movements and their innovative ideas won over many adherents and eventually forced a reaction from the established medical community.[10]

Orthodox physicians responded by adopting, albeit slowly, the new emphasis upon preventing disease rather than just curing it. Between the 1830s and 1850s, many began to understand that some diseases affected only specific portions of the body. They slowly abandoned the old theories of a balanced bodily system and the heroic therapeutics that targeted the entire body. Medical thought and training turned increasingly to the prevention of disease. The era witnessed a period of rapid and intense identification and differentiation of diseases. Physicians and scientists, for example, distinguished scarlet fever from diptheria, syphilis from gonorrhea, and typhoid from typhus.[11] No longer would a physician actively intervene in the body with copious bleedings or massive purgations. Bloodletting significantly declined during the 1830s, disappearing by 1870. Responding to health reformers, physicians also administered smaller doses of drugs. Calomel and opium remained popular remedies, though now measured in tiny drops. By the 1850s, orthodox medicine had fully accepted nature's role in curing disease, though its exact role was still debated. Now the physician's task required him (and all orthodox doctors at this time were men) to diagnose a specific disease, understand its natural course, and treat the patient by prescribing the appropriate drugs and advising a specific regimen to aid nature in moving the body toward recovery. The essence of medical therapeutics shifted away from an intrusive therapy that relied upon violent bodily responses toward allowing nature, with medicinal aid and medical knowledge, to bring about recovery.

With the changes in medical practices and ideas about health after 1830, the regimen and effects of the Virginia Springs fit perfectly between orthodox practice on one hand and the radical theories of the Thomsonians, homeopaths, and hydropaths on the other. Corresponding with the decline in heroics was an increase in visitors to the Virginia Springs; now thousands, not just hundreds, came to the resorts each summer. Believing that the spring waters excelled "the Drs & medicine" of which he feared his mother had "suffered and from which I wish you to run away," Robert E. Lee suggested that she visit White Sulphur Springs in 1839. Yet the mineral waters also offered a proven alternative to the experimental methods of the health reformers. William Mackay seemed relieved to report from Rockbridge Alum Springs that his brother had "in some measure recovered" the strength that he had "lost by taking so much quack medicine."[12]

There were numerous reasons that the mineral waters of the Virginia Springs remained an appealing therapeutic. Those in search of health could still be attended by a regular doctor if they wished, but their cure did not lie entirely in his control. As they had earlier, visitors often decided what kind of mineral water regimen to pursue; but after 1830 they did so with even less reliance upon a physician's advice. "They all drink the waters . . . without the advice of any medical man," James S. Buckingham noticed in the early 1840s, with the result that resident doctors had "little practice." Many visitors traveled to the springs without any prior discussion with a physician and with only the advice of friends and family to guide their actions. From Alleghany Springs in 1852, Robert Hubard wrote home that his return would be delayed for, after "close observation" of the "effects" of other mineral waters, his own "judgement recommends a longer use of this water." John Speight Jr. had not consulted a physician at Red Sulphur Springs, he informed his mother, because "cosin Lou said she did not think it nesessary." [13]

Familiar methods of treatment remained in place at the springs even while new health reforms influenced much of the theory and practice. Doctors remained available at the larger resorts for emergencies and especially severe cases, as well as for those few visitors who were unsure of the correct regimen. Increasingly, many doctors prescribed specific kinds of waters or, occasionally, a specific series of springs for specific diseases. In April 1839, Dr. Edward H. Carmichael prepared an actual prescription for St. George Tucker Coalter to visit Warm Springs, drink the waters, and bathe daily at one o'clock to cure his particular illness. In 1834 the renowned Dr. Philip S. Physick of Philadelphia questioned whether the waters of Fauquier White Sulphur were appropriate for Lucretia Clay's specific illness. Over twenty years later, a doctor advised Mary Lee to try Warm Springs for her arthritis. Furthermore, guests in ill health still used curatives that produced visible signs toward recovery in the form of severe bowel movements, frequent urination, profuse sweating, and increased appetites. And southern practitioners clung to heroic ideas and therapies longer than northern ones. [14]

While an increased respect for and reliance upon the power of nature to cure could have challenged many physicians', as well as the lay public's, reliance upon the power of God, that apparently did not happen. Southern medical practice as well as popular opinion combined religious and scientific beliefs. [15] In their writings, visitors and their correspondents showed little conflict between their beliefs in the power of nature and in the power of God. With the "minerals of the mountains" and "the blessings of heaven," Benjamin Grigsby, for example, predicted that his friend would recover. Reverend Thornton Stringfellow considered the waters of Fauquier White Sulphur a gift "from the laboratory of God," but believed that the waters healed according to "a law of their own." [16]

As they had since the late eighteenth century, spring-goers continued to regard mineral waters not as a form of medicine but as a natural remedy. Now visitors further believed that the waters effectively aided nature in bringing about improved or recovered health. Since his "dyspeptic symptoms" had been "but little benefitted by medicine," Levin Smith Joynes decided to travel the Virginia Springs circuit in the summer of 1856. [17] After 1830 visitors also placed additional importance upon the natural origins of the waters, sounding something like the Thomsonians, who emphasized botanical alternatives to chemical drugs. Similarly, just as homeopaths administered minute doses of drugs, the visitors at the Virginia Springs could regulate the doses of mineral waters, drinking as little or as much as needed to affect the body.

The water cure of hydropaths and the mineral water regimens at spas have appeared similar to many twentieth-century historians, but they actually differed sharply in the mid-nineteenth century. Those who took the waters at the Virginia Springs believed that the minerals in the water cured their ills, while hydropaths insisted that only pure water could cure the body. Hydropaths disparaged any use of drugs and viewed the minerals in the spring waters in that light. The use of thermal waters, as at Hot and Warm Springs, further clashed with a hydropathic regimen that extolled the virtues of cold water. Hydropathy also encouraged female practitioners, while all of the doctors at the springs were men. In fact, the hydropathic movement had few enthusiasts in the South, particularly among elite spring-goers. Southerners preferred the Virginia Springs atmosphere to the austerity of the hydropathic institutes. Perhaps more importantly, hydropaths often linked their goals with those of other northern reform movements, such as abolition and women's rights. In comparison to the springs, the water-cure movement's popularity was short-lived, reaching the United States around 1840 and essentially disappearing after 1870.[18]

Orthodox physicians and health reformers, such as hydropaths, advocated bathing as an especially valuable remedy for women's health problems; women themselves readily and happily accepted this practice as a therapeutic. In 1853 the proprietors of Bath Alum advertised that their resort's "*peculiar efficacy in female diseases* is becoming generally known and conceded." Nancy Evans, a hired slave at Sweet Springs, urged her "Young Mistress" "to persuade my old mistress to come over here & try this bath," for, as she twice proclaimed, she had "no doubt she would be greatly benefitted." Many women turned to the warm waters of the springs after miscarriages or difficult pregnancies and for menstrual problems. In 1850 Lucy Cocke spent the months of August and September using Hot Springs' spout bath to recuperate from a stillbirth. Tallula Taylor traveled from Charleston, South Carolina, to bathe at Healing Springs, where she improved "very much." No wonder, since these springs, according to her husband, were "said to be peculiarly happy in its effects on the womb where it is affected with any disease." He took heart from a story about a woman who, after using the waters the previous year, "since has presented her hus-

band with a child tho' fifteen years had elapsed since she had one before."
In 1853 James Gray shared information with his brother about their sister
Maria's menstrual difficulties and the relief that they expected to find at
Hot Springs. The resident physician recommended using the waters "untill
her regular time Came round again" in order to "Correct her difficulty
altogether." [19]

An examination of the writings of the southern women who visited
the Virginia Springs, their husbands, and their doctors reveals different
attitudes about women's health from those described in recent scholarly
works.[20] In the mid-nineteenth century, genteel southern ladies do not
seem to have "defined themselves through sickness," nor did their society
"[maximize] their ill health."[21] As in the North, women's health care in the
South increasingly fell under the control of male physicians, but apparently
not with the same ramifications. Carroll Smith-Rosenberg and Charles Rosenberg and other historians have shown that as male physicians gained
control over women's health care by the mid-nineteenth century, orthodox
medical opinion increasingly linked a middle-class woman's health problems directly to her reproductive organs.[22] In the letters and journals of the
southerners who visited the Virginia Springs, however, neither women nor
men, including doctors, described the uterus as the source of all women's
problems. Contrary to northern physicians' attitudes, moreover, a southern white woman's general health was not regarded as in a perpetually delicate state. Southerners, like northerners, paid increasing attention to "female complaints," but they regarded them as problems, not as a woman's
normal state. While childbirth increasingly involved the presence of a physician, only when there were difficulties with pregnancy or menstruation
did southern men and women consider them as health crises.[23]

Many women did visit the springs to bathe in the waters after problematic pregnancies or for menstrual problems, but they came for many other
reasons as well. They suffered from other health problems that neither they,
their husbands, nor their male physicians traced to their reproductive organs. Southern physicians recognized that women experienced not only peculiarly female problems, but also the same health problems as men. In his
1831 work *On Baths and Mineral Waters,* Dr. John Bell recommended the
Sweet Springs baths for "females . . . who have been enfeebled by protracted
confinement, or long nursing their children, deprivation of exercise and of
the enjoyment of fresh air, and who have, in addition to these[,] causes of
dyspepsia." In 1840 White Sulphur's Dr. John Moorman argued that his
resort's waters aided in the cure of "DISEASES of FEMALES, dependant

on *debility* and . . . CHLOROSIS [a form of anemia], &c., &c." He assured his readers that not only had White Sulphur's waters "almost always displayed the most happy and triumphant effects," but they also increased "the life and elasticity of the animal spirits" of women.[24] Unlike mid-nineteenth century northern physicians, southern doctors, at least those at the Virginia Springs, advocated not only restoring but also strengthening a woman's health and the "elasticity" of her "*animal* spirits."

Southern white women and men may have idealized delicate ladies, but they apparently saw no place in an agricultural society for weak or enfeebled ones. Southern women, especially plantation mistresses, had enormous responsibilities to fulfill and labor to perform. They could not afford the sacrifice of productivity required to indulge in ill health, feigned or real. Nor did genteel southern women want to be perceived as fragile. They rarely dwelt upon their illnesses. Many women at the springs barely mentioned their physical sufferings, focusing instead on their hopes for improvement. Instead of dwelling on her declining health, the "magic effects" of Warm Springs' bath made "hope" the "Cherished companion" of the dying Fanny Coalter. Like their husbands, fathers, and sons, gentry women relentlessly worked to attain or maintain good health. Agnes Cabell wished to take her granddaughter to White Sulphur because she feared the girl's "frame [was] too delicate" and "want[ed] to see her more robust." Unlike the northern middle-class women depicted by historians, the elite southern women at the springs wished to be "robust," not pale and weak. They ate heartily and delighted in vigorous exercise. Susanna Harrison hoped to be "as hearty as a mountaineer" by the time she returned from the springs. A sore throat and bad cold did not bother Ellen Wirt, who was "too hardy a mountaineer to mind it much." "Round and rosy as any mountaineers," Lavinia Harrison was "the admiration of the company" at White Sulphur in 1831. While genteel ladies may have been the desired model for southern women, southerners—men and women—saw no need for a weak woman. These attitudes toward women's health may have originated at the Virginia Springs and then spread throughout southern society.[25]

Drawing upon the new health ideas of the mid-nineteenth century, medical theory—lagging well behind popular opinion—increasingly emphasized the benefits of mountain air, diet, exercise, and a change of environment as a way to promote health. Dr. Moorman recommended "regular exercise in good weather," such as "walking,—riding on horseback, or in a carriage," in his 1847 guide to the Virginia Springs. A trip to the Virginia Springs fit the new prescription perfectly. The salubrious climate of the mountains encouraged health; travelers usually felt its effect as soon as they arrived at the first spa. Emphasizing his wife's full restoration of health, George T. Sinclair proclaimed: "There is nothing in medicine to compare with change of air." His wife, moreover, was "a living monument of the value of the waters of the Rockbridge Alum springs." "This climate of itself would restore most people to health," concluded Samuel Hoffman during one of his many trips to the Virginia Springs. By the 1850s, visitors to the Virginia Springs mentioned the invigorating air, variety of food, and kinds of exercise almost as often as they discussed the mineral waters used. According to Jane Caroline Pettigrew, the "bracing air" acted upon her son "like champagne on older people—he laughs out with sheer life & spirits, & shouts . . . from glee & good health." [26]

With further changes in orthodox medicine after 1850, the Virginia Springs waters looked more valuable than ever for curing illnesses or promoting continued good health. "I think the Virginia Mountain Air & Sulphur Waters the best medicine we can take," W. H. Collins declared to his brother-in-law in 1856. Increasingly, orthodox physicians embraced the idea of a healing nature and changed their thinking about therapeutics to focus on helping nature heal the body. In Dr. Jacob Bigelow's *Brief Exposition of Rational Medicine* (1858), mineral waters appeared, along with electricity, under "rational" or "natural" methods of cure. Bigelow declared that particular springs exerted "beneficial effect[s]" on "particular maladies," and proclaimed watering places "arks of refuge to multitudes of chronic valetudinarians." In 1858 Dr. P. B. Tindall, resident physician at Sweet Springs, happily acknowledged the role of nature in medical therapeutics: "We must come back to elementary principles, and substitute natural agents for artificial ones." He heartily endorsed the Virginia Springs as the preeminent therapy: "We must measurably throw away the nauseous drugs of the apothecary, and substitute in their stead the mild and salubrious beverage of mineral waters." [27]

∾

"Every Day Var[ies] a Little"

Whether or not they were ill, all of the springs visitors bathed in or drank the waters. While mid-nineteenth-century orthodox medicine regarded and treated the sexes differently, men and women at the Virginia Springs shared the same routine, drinking the waters at the same times and often in the same quantities.[1] Doctors prescribed, and experienced visitors suggested, that a newcomer start out slowly and gradually increase the amount of water consumed in order to condition the body and soften the harsh effects of the minerals. First, an imbiber had to get accustomed to the taste, temperature, and, if at a sulphur spring, smell of the waters. Levin Joynes found Salt Sulphur's waters *"eggy* in the extreme" and could not believe those who told him that "they have become *fond of it."* Sarah Garland thought that White Sulphur water smelled "just as disagreeable as the atmosphere at home after an explosion on the rail road." After her first dose of Stribling's Springs waters, Susan Stuart wrote home to her mother: "Oh!! aint it awful? And don't it smell?! It made me sick for an hour." After finishing a glass, the drinker might experience warmth around the stomach and a feeling of dizziness. Some visitors enjoyed the sensations; others detested them and never grew accustomed to the smell or the effects. The regimen for bathing echoed that for drinking, with certain kinds of baths prescribed for certain problems. The actual process took various forms, depending on whether a visitor was trying to cure a specific problem or just enjoying him- or herself. These rituals of health were as important to spa life as rituals of sociability.[2]

The daily regimen varied little from spring to spring or over time. Since almost everyone followed the same schedule, drinking or bathing in the waters were social occasions. In 1839 travel writer Mary Hagner outlined a day's schedule at White Sulphur Springs. The first trip to the springhouse occurred before breakfast, when anyone who wished to drink the waters and "exchange the salutations of the day" congregated. "This is an exciting time," Hagner noted, "and for one hour, the whole area around the spring is crowded with the old, the young, the gay, and the invalid." At 8:00 A.M., the guests breakfasted on breads and "all the other necessaries to anticipate the finest appetites." After breakfast, light exercise, conversation, or reading occupied a visitor's time. At noon, guests returned to the springhouse. Physicians prescribed more exercise until 2:00, when the guests sat down for an enormous dinner. Afterwards, the normal regimen called for the visitor to "amuse yourself in social intercourse." By 5:00, everyone reunited at the springhouse. After a small supper, the pleasure-seekers danced, played cards, or engaged in other parlor amusements; those in search of health drank another glass of mineral water around bedtime. "At first view, it would seem that we lead a dull sort of *monotonous* life of it at these Watering places," Larkin Newby wrote after a typical day at Salt Sulphur Springs. "But then though this be true in part," he continued, "it is not, in the whole" for "every day var[ies] a little from the preceeding, in some way or other, so as to give a sort of variety." With only small variations, the visitors followed the same routine every day at every spring, finding comfort in these spa rituals. The days could be filled with activities; those who enjoyed resort life found that they had little time on their hands.[3]

Only those resorts with one or more thermal springs offered bathing. Berkeley, Fauquier White Sulphur, Healing, Red Sweet, Rockbridge Baths, Sweet, Warm, and Hot Springs comprised the major bathing resorts on the Virginia Springs circuit. Sweet, Warm, and Hot received the most celebrity and the most visitors for their baths. Most bathers believed that the thermal waters made them stronger and healthier. Mary Smith informed her niece that "yr ma was a first rate Baptist[;] she took two dips in the bath & came out full of faith."[4] The baths attracted far more people, however, who were not so much searching for a cure as desiring one of the best parts of the spa experience—a warm, bubbling bath. Until around 1800, facilities for bathing remained primitive, often no more than a hole in the ground, surrounded by bushes, and used alternately by men and women. Simple log cabins first housed the baths, but more elaborate structures replaced them as proprietors upgraded and updated the resorts. The octagonal wooden bathhouse constructed at Warm Springs around 1800 was one of the first and set the architectural standard for most of the later bathhouses.[5]

Most of the bathing houses had several dressing rooms—"furnished with a chair, table, looking glass," and fireplace—attached to the main structure.[6] Large circular openings in the roofs above the pools provided air and light. The baths themselves were immense, containing tens of thousands of gallons of water. In these "pleasure," or swimming, baths large groups of men or women bathed together (fig. 10). The Ladies' Bath at Warm Springs measured fifty feet in diameter and held 60,000 gallons of water. The men's swimming pool at Berkeley Springs was sixty feet long and twenty feet wide; at Rockbridge Baths, it measured fifty by thirty. Many bathhouses also had shower baths, individual baths, and smaller baths for invalids and children. In most of the baths, water continuously bubbled up from the bottom, either from the spring directly or through pipes, and ran off, keeping the pool constantly fresh. Most baths averaged between four and five feet in depth; in some cases, such as at Hot Springs, the water could be raised another two or three feet by a hand-operated valve or faucet if

Figure 10. Women's bathhouse at Warm Springs, Virginia, 1832. (Maryland Historical Society, Baltimore)

a bather desired. Steps leading into the pools allowed bathers to immerse themselves gradually. Smooth pebbles covered the bottoms. Unless they had traveled to European spas, visitors had never seen anything like the bathhouses.

All of the popular resorts' bathing facilities contained separate baths and, of course, dressing rooms for men and women. Both Red Sweet and Hot Springs had spout baths for each sex. The bathing room for the "Boiler" was divided in half, with the Gentlemen's Boiler, and presumably the Ladies also, fitting four bathers. At Hot Springs, men and women alternately used the pleasure bath in two-hour blocks. Sweet Springs had separate baths for women and men by 1831. Warm Springs added a Ladies' Bath in 1836; before then, men and women took turns, with a white flag hoisted atop the building signaling a female bather.

The warmth of the waters relieved and pleased the bathers. The temperatures of the waters at Sweet, Red Sweet, and Berkeley Springs averaged in the mid-70s. At Warm and Hot Springs, the waters came, as one visitor

put it, "from some mysterious subterranean furnace" at temperatures between 96 degrees and 98 degrees. Another visitor suggested that everyone,
"once at least in his life," should try "the pleasure of a perfect bath, just
from the laboratory of nature" at Warm Springs. Hot Springs' "Spout
bath" registered 104 degrees at the mouth of the spout and 102 degrees in
the bath; its "Boiler" reached 106 degrees. The Boiler quickly became Mary
Louisa Bolling's favorite. Just ten minutes after their arrival at Hot Springs,
her husband wrote his parents that Mary Louisa was already in the Boiler
where he hoped "she will be *cooked* much to my liking." A cold "plunge"
bath stood next to the thermal bath at both Warm and Hot Springs, en-
abling bathers to go back and forth between the two extremes.[7]

The regimen for bathing was not as fixed as that for drinking. Most
people bathed whenever they felt like it but followed medical advice by not
bathing in cold or rainy weather. Some preferred the early morning hours
before breakfast, others the evenings before bed. But the warm baths saw
use throughout the day as many people bathed two or three times.[8] Visitors
who desired to bathe in the individual baths at popular times might have
to wait a couple of hours. Most people, men and women, apparently wore
loose flannel gowns into the baths, but others may have bathed nude. While
spa doctors advised a gradual descent into the waters, some visitors claimed
"by far the best way" was "to plunge in head foremost, as you are then
instantly transferred to the comfortable element." Others remained cau-
tious. Mary R. Harrison reported that her teenaged daughter "is so much
afraid of being drowned [in the Warm Springs bath] that she will not yet
venture from the steps." Those who took the spout baths at Red Sweet or
Hot Springs stood under the spout and directed the powerful stream upon
aching or diseased parts of their body. Chairs affixed to ropes and pulleys
eased invalids who could not walk or swim into the plunge baths at Healing
Springs and Hot Springs. The amount of time spent in the baths averaged
only about fifteen or twenty minutes. Expert advice cautioned against
long baths, especially for invalids, fearing that they would cause more harm
than good. Still, those who bathed for pleasure often lingered in the baths.
Defying the recommendations of experienced bathers, Dr. Edmondson
Horner remained in the Warm Springs bath "paddling about" for forty-
five minutes.[9]

After the bath, advisors recommended quickly donning one's clothes
and staying warm. Many people considered returning to their beds the perfect end to bathing. Some bathers, especially after taking the Boiler at Hot

Springs, followed hot baths with "blanket sweats." A person would stay in the hot water until "big drops have started on [the] forehead, and begin to chase one another down" the nose, and then retire to the sweat rooms. There, a bather would be wrapped "in flannel from top to toe," led to a cot, and covered with five or six blankets for thirty to ninety minutes, "until the perspiration has freely spent itself from every pore of the body." One avid bather reported staying so long that the sweat soaked through the mattress and "dripped in puddles on the floor." Women as well as men made the sweats part of their bathing regimen. Sarah Rutherfoord took "a blanket Sweat" for a half-hour every day while at Warm Springs.[10]

Servants and bathing assistants played important roles in the visitors' bathing regimen. Some resorts had a bathkeeper, almost always a white man, who oversaw the supply of towels, the fires, and the servants, most of whom were slaves.[11] Female servants attended female bathers and male attendants served male bathers. Assistants monitored the water level and kept track of how long each bather had been in the water. At Red Sweet, Anne Smith "took 7 dips which the woman Kitty the Goddess of the bath room said was quite enough."[12] Slave assistants also performed many intimate tasks for the bathers. Not only did they help them dress for the bath, they also dried their presumably nude bodies with towels upon their emergence from the water and wrapped flannels around naked bodies in the sweat rooms. Apparently, the personal nature of these tasks troubled none of the bathers. Some may have been accustomed to similar intimacies at home. When they commented on them at all, visitors treated the slave assistants and their duties as simply parts of the bathing experience.[13] The social cleavage between white and black, master and slave, made such physical intimacy innocuous.

The regimen at the Virginia Springs had none of the austere character of life at a water-cure establishment. Hydropaths considered spring resorts centers of excess and frivolity. In the *Water-Cure Journal,* James C. Jackson, a hydropathic practitioner at Glen-Haven in New York, proclaimed that well-conducted water-cure establishments definitely did not resemble watering places "where persons in health . . . 'go to debauch.'"[14] Unlike hydropaths, who refrained from consuming alcohol, coffee, tea, tobacco, and even meat, the guests at the Virginia Springs indulged in huge meals, caffeinated beverages, pipes and chewing tobacco, and daily libations. Women as well as men relished the good living at the resorts, especially enjoying the food, even when poorly prepared, and the drinks. According to James L.

Petigru, the sulphur waters encouraged a taste for wine and even for "the attractions of toddy and juleps." Charleston's J. Taylor observed that at White Sulphur all of the guests, including the women, "can eat more than college Boys." "The Ladies too put romance aside & relish Mutton, Beef, & Bacon amazingly—from the appetites of the young people I should say very few of them are in love." The common explanation given by women and men for their indulgences was that the waters stimulated their appetites. Otwayanna Carter confessed to her mother that she was "afraid I shall go home too fat." Larkin Newby called his circle of friends at Salt Sulphur "the greatest *gormandizers* ever known." [15]

As part of the springs regimen, medical guidebooks to the springs included recommendations of the appropriate clothing and activities for health-seekers. Flannels and woolens would protect the sickly against the cool, damp mountain air. The guides cautioned female invalids in particular against gowns that exposed too much of the arms, neck, or chest. Recognizing that their advice would not be heeded by pleasure-seekers, spa physicians warned against excesses in diet, drink, and amusements, especially dancing, for invalids. "Eating too much in the evening, sitting up late, prolonged and immoderate dancing, remaining too long in the cool air of the evening" placed the invalid in danger. But, as one guide warned, "a giddy chase after pleasure and luxurious indulgence" on the part of the perfectly healthy might change the pleasure-seeker into a cure-seeker. [16]

Even though most physicians concluded that the best course for improvement was for a person to use a single spring's waters, many visitors to the springs district spent their time traveling from resort to resort with little regard for the advised regimen. In large measure, the springs circuit arose not out of the visitors' search for health but out of their driving quest for pleasure and fashion. The resident spa doctors condemned this practice for "the invalid *who has something for the waters to do.*" [17] According to the doctors, darting about from spa to spa interfered with the curative powers of the mineral waters and was not conducive to the pursuit of health. Those who were truly ill—always the minority of Virginia Springs visitors— stayed the longest at one resort and usually visited only two or three resorts during their entire trip. All of the visitors remained constantly aware of the effects of the mineral waters' upon their bodies, however, and allowed this knowledge to influence the order in which they visited the resorts. Many recommended that a visitor start the spa circuit at Warm Springs, for example, since its waters eased the aches of traveling and conditioned the stomach, before continuing on to the more vigorous springs.

Visitors in pursuit of fun and leisure bypassed entirely or remained just a day or two at those springs whose waters attracted the largest numbers of invalids, especially Red Sulphur and Hot Springs. In 1804 John Howell Briggs left Hot Springs after only a few hours "with great pleasure" because "the number of invalids, afflicted with various diseases, with limbs distorted by pain, and unable to assist themselves . . . rendered an abode here, very unpleasant." A half-century later, an unsympathetic Jane Caroline North could not wait to leave Hot Springs, or "Crippledom" as she called it, for the fashionable and pleasurable White Sulphur Springs. While waiting for her aunt to bathe in the thermal waters, North wrote her sister that she had never seen "such a collection of miserable looking people" before. Red Sulphur's renown as the gathering place "only of those whose earthly careers were near at hand" led North to refuse even to step foot into its confines. Conversely, true invalids and most doctors regarded the frivolity and fashion at White Sulphur as detrimental to the pursuit of health. Charles William Ashby, who suffered from asthma, informed his wife that White Sulphur was "the great place for the fashionable world," but was "not the place" for him.[18]

The fashionables, however, enjoyed and benefited from the springs regimen as much as the invalids. Whether healthy or ill, all of the visitors to the springs followed to some degree the drinking and bathing regimens. The course of a day usually revolved around visits to the springhouse or bathhouse, even for those mainly in search of pleasure. Those with good health and those in search of it shared in these rituals of health that made up the spa experience.

༺

"The Most Delicious Sensations"

The new sensations of and constant attention paid to the body constituted a major component of the Virginia Springs experience for every visitor — whether in search of health or pleasure. All of the visitors, male and female, closely monitored the function and appearance of their own bodies and often of others' bodies as well. They focused primarily on what went into the body — and what came out of it. Gaining weight and learning, often for the first time, how much they weighed fascinated visitors. Much of the conversation — even genteel public conversation — at the springs and material in letters home concerned these corporeal topics. Bathing, which produced more pleasurable and more novel bodily sensations, may have inspired even more discussions of the body and physical experiences than drinking the waters. Outside the Virginia Springs, there was no place in the plantation South where the body captured so much public interest and produced so much discussion among respectable ladies and gentlemen.

Visitors to the Virginia Springs seemed to delight in the powerful effects of the waters upon their bodies. In 1792 the four pints of Warm Springs water that Ferdinando Fairfax drank "produced a gentle and pleasant Operation" during the night. Even when the effects were less pleasant, the men and women who drank the waters monitored the subsequent functions of their bladders and bowels with rapt interest. "The use of the water & close observation of its effects for 4 days" convinced Robert Hubard to leave Alum Springs for Alleghany Springs in 1852. Daily drinkers kept meticulous records of how often, how quickly, how strongly, and how long the various mineral waters worked on their systems, detailing their frequent urinations, recurrent diarrhea, profuse perspiration, and intermittent vomiting. Larkin Newby's experiences largely confirmed his expectations that White Sulphur's waters "operate freely by the bowels, on the Kidneys & on the pores of the skin." "The two latter I have already realized & the first in a slight degree—In the night I awoke & found myself in a high perspiration," he recorded in his journal.[1] Springs visitors repeatedly filled their letters and journals with such comments about the waters' effect, using phrases such as "acting freely," "most *powerfully*," "agrees wonderfully with me," "had the happiest effect," and "kept my system a little disordered," as well as "entirely inactive."[2] Like many others, Samuel Hoffman felt that his entire "system [was] pretty well impregnated" by White Sulphur's and Sweet Springs' waters.[3] Most visitors believed that the mineral waters totally infused the body and readily welcomed the signs of their effects or "benefits," no matter how uncomfortable.

Many visitors used their journals while at the springs to track on a daily basis their bodily intake and outflow along with recording their activities and encounters. "This day was spent after the fashion of the two last," Hugh Blair Grigsby noted, "water-drinking, good eating, Junius and Morpheus, plenteous evacuations, and so forth." Of the sixty-seven almost daily entries in Larkin Newby's 1823 springs journal, all but fifteen mentioned some kind of bodily condition or function after drinking or bathing in the different waters. As the end of their stay at the springs approached, some visitors contrasted, in minute detail, the strengthened condition of their body with their debilitated state upon arrival. George Carr noted that he had left home with his "bowels disordered, mouth and tongue sore and blistered, evacuations of a watery consistency, and frequently of the color of clay or putty." After a few days using Hot Springs' baths, his "bowels became quiescent[,] evacuations regular and of a healthy color, my mouth and tongue entirely well." The operations of their bodies and the effects of the waters captured the interest of almost everyone at the springs.[4]

The attention paid to the body and its functions went beyond the private confines of journals into the public arena. While at the springs, visitors easily broke the conventional rules of genteel correspondence and conduct by giving detailed accounts of their body's functions, weight, and appearance that echoed those in private journals. Writing home from Yellow Sulphur Springs, John Guerrant, for example, gave his father the details of his discharges of bile and bowel movements in 1806. Such letters home included the same information regardless of the gender of the recipient or writer. Visitors described not only their own condition, moreover, but also that of the people who traveled with them and of the friends and relatives they met. In 1801 Fanny Tucker relayed to her father that her brother had "fattened perceptably" and her sister had "found great inconvenience from tight sleeves and is hungry still 8 times a day." Dr. Cary Charles Cocke informed his father that his wife had "improved very much in strength, as well as in looks" and that the girls gained "strength & *weight* daily."[5]

Visitors happily let friends and family members, especially spouses, know when others at the springs noticed and complimented their improved appearance. John Rutherfoord informed his wife Emily how all of his acquaintances "remark a great change in my complexion, & improvement in my appearance." Frances Stuart probably did not enjoy reading as much as her husband Alexander H. H. Stuart enjoyed writing that he was "getting so fat & handsome" that not only would she "hardly know" him when he returned home, but "the girls [at the springs were] all falling in love with me." Visitors wanted those at home to share in their progress toward good health and included them in the free conversation about the body that was so prevalent at the springs.[6]

Some visitors spared no details, presuming that their correspondents shared the acute interest in their bodily functions and changes. These letters must have made for interesting reading indeed by those at home. During a trip to Warm Springs in 1818, for example, Thomas Jefferson informed his daughter that he was "under great threats" that the water would "work it's effect thro' a system of boils." After a few times in the baths, "a large swelling on my seat, increasing for several days past in size and hardness disables me from sitting but on the corner of a chair." Matters threatened to grow worse as "another swelling begins to manifest itself to-day on the other seat."[7] Writing to his wife, Larkin Newby predicted that his recovery would "require a thorough cleansing of the system—a thorough clearing out of all the vessels, whose operations have been *clog'd* so long, & that this *clearing out* & cleansing must be made thro the great 'Alimentary Canal' & by means of Cathartics."[8] In subsequent letters home, he shared with her the full details of his "cleansing."

In addition to observing their intake of mineral waters, most visitors paid particular attention to what and how much they ate and drank. Lists and descriptions of the variety and amount of food consumed filled letters and journals from the springs. During his stay in 1808, Benjamin Grigsby dined, as he informed his wife, on foods that included "Venison dress'd in a variety of ways—Beef—mutton—Bacon—vegetables—pastry[—] Butter—Bread—milk." Among the "excellent fare" that Sophie Wilson's father enjoyed at Red Sulphur were "Venison & currant Jelly in abundance, fine fat Mutton, Veal & Beef and every thing that can tempt the most fastidious appetite . . . Ice Cream every day and ice in profusion." He found it no wonder that many people came to the springs annually simply "to fatten."[9]

In a period when plumpness meant good health, "fattening" was a goal desired by both men and women. "I am fattening daily," Sarah Harrison wrote home with pleasure, "and have a fine appetite as the fine bread and risen biscuit could testify."[10] Nicholas Faulcon felt that he had not improved much at Sweet Springs for, although "sensible of an increase of strength," "I am still very thin."[11] George T. Sinclair's wife must have indulged in the resorts' heavy meals, for she returned with "her health entirely restored, having gained twenty pounds of weight in two months."[12] Sinclair considered her increased weight and health a testament to the wondrous powers of the Virginia Springs waters. Male and female visitors constantly weighed themselves, fixing meaningful numbers to their bodily growth. Willis Williams felt ecstatic about the results of his frequent trips to the scales at Healing Springs. The five pounds that he put on in five days persuaded him that he was "doing first rate." Two weeks later, he weighed 137 pounds and decided that when he reached 140 he would head home.[13] A young woman happily informed her father that "I gained three pounds last week on the way. I weighed 102 pounds last Friday week, and on last Friday 105. I suppose I weighed about 96 or 8 when I left home." Pleased with her progress, she added that her aunt thought that her face now resembled "the full moon."[14] This young lady stayed at the springs for a number of weeks more and almost certainly returned home heavier and healthier.

The prominence of and attention to bodily functions, appearance, and sensations shattered the normal rules of delicacy in polite society, North and South. In the planters' regular polished circles, ladies and gentlemen considered these topics indelicate and inappropriate subjects for refined conversation and correspondence. Whether they occurred in public or private arenas, these vulgar, albeit necessary, bodily activities were treated as beneath notice.[15] Richly descriptive comments about the body and its workings rarely appeared in the private journals and letters of southern men and women. Yet, as part of the bodily awareness of the spa experience, such accounts were not only commonplace but even expected at the Virginia Springs. Still, whether from greater adherence to genteel codes or from less interest in their bodily functions, women at the springs remained more circumspect than men. None apparently chronicled their bodily functions with the detail or frequency of men such as Larkin Newby, Samuel Hoffman, and George Carr. Instead, women's journals and letters included more general terms, noting that they had been "benefitted" or "operated on" by the waters, though they still emphasized this information. Even though they used more oblique terms, the very fact that southern ladies discussed their bodily functions with other visitors and correspondents remains striking.

Bodily functions and appearance held a central place in public circles at the springs as well as in the guests' private journals and correspondence. The atmosphere of the springs—healthful, natural, leisurely, and intimate—permitted, even encouraged, talk about the body. The physical effects of the various mineral waters, whether successful or not, and the corresponding changes in their bodies reigned as two of the main topics of conversation. "One of the greatest amusements" at the Virginia Springs, as Harriet Martineau noted, "was to listen to the variety of theories afloat about the properties and modes of application of the waters." Edwin Jeffress watched in amusement as a friend "tack[ed]" about White Sulphur conversing with others about his condition and comparing symptoms and effects. Littleton Wickham spent the summer of 1830 immersed in this realm that focused upon the body and health. Near the end of his stay, Wickham, perhaps planning for his return to the normal rules of polite society, hoped that he had improved enough "that after this summer I shall have at least some or only accidental and temporary occasions to speak about" such matters.[16]

As they gathered at the springhouse or socialized in other parts of the resort, guests paid close attention to each other's bodies to see whom the waters had benefited and how. "It is surprising to see the different effect the mineral waters have on different persons," William Latane reported from Sweet Springs in 1826. Visitors regularly monitored the progress of friends and acquaintances for signs of improvement or "fattening." At the springs, they waived those rules of etiquette that normally precluded discussions of their own and other people's bodies. Sally Faulcon's friends told her that she had fattened, although she felt "no change" herself. One man made a special point to tell Richard Burroughs how much he had improved in appearance since they had last seen each other.[17] Guests made sure to compliment each other on their increasingly healthful appearances, encouraging those who needed sympathy and support. "Several persons" that Louisianna Cocke Faulcon had earlier met at White Sulphur were "struck at [her] improved appearance" at Sweet Springs and immediately informed her of it. Writing from Warm Springs, Samuel Hoffman reported that "*Every* one tells me how much better I look." The physical condition of all of the guests, not just of invalids, provided a fit subject for conversation at the springs. Apparently no one shrank from the attention that his or her body received from others.[18]

Being weighed was a public event at the Virginia Springs. Crowds gathered to watch and hear the exact number of pounds called out as each person sat down on the scales. At White Sulphur and Sweet Springs, the scales stood upon the piazza where everyone could witness this spectacle. Many men and women could have observed the proceedings when Mary M. Hagner sat on "the patent scale that stands in the colonnade" of Warm Springs' hotel. According to J. Milton Mackie, every resort had a set of scales prominently placed near the hotel because the "fondness for being weighed is universal." All of the visitors, young and old, male and female, participated in this weighing ritual. "Every man and woman wishes to know how many pounds he, or she, has gained in the last twenty-four hours," Mackie claimed; "nine persons out of ten, here, can tell you their exact weight." Some received quite a shock when they found out what they weighed. Mackie saw one woman—"a matron turned of forty"—leap off the scales "as if she had been shot" upon hearing "the number one hundred and ninety-nine" announced. Even the normally proper Harriet Martineau took her turn upon the scales at White Sulphur. "After tea, we stormed the great scales, and our whole party were individually weighed." Since her weight remained unchanged, she felt that she had added little to the spectacle. "It must be an interesting occupation to the valetudinarians of the place," she rightly concluded, "to watch their own and each others' weight, from day to day, or from week to week." [19]

The physical and mental sensations that male and female visitors experienced while immersing their whole bodies in warm or hot water were a rare, unfamiliar luxury. Most guests did not own bathtubs that could fit their whole body, and bathrooms remained uncommon until the end of the nineteenth century. The majority of Americans washed themselves with a sponge and a bowl of water. Few did even that daily. "It is but seldom in my life," Mildred Halsey explained to her husband, "that I have an opportunity to enjoy these strengthning waters"; as such, she planned to extend her stay at Red Sweet.[20] Nearly everyone who bathed at the springs commented upon the occasion. Over and over again in their writings, they described the sensuous feelings the baths produced as "delicious," "delightful," "enchant[ing]," and "glorious."[21] Many men and women felt that they were "indulging in [a] luxury" when they slipped into one of the warm baths.[22]

Upon entering the bathhouses, the bathers first experienced pleasing visual sensations. The Sweet Springs bath "looked so clear & tempting" that C. O. Lyde "felt inclined to plunge in." The bubbles received everyone's attention. Jane Caroline North became captivated with the way that the Warm Springs bath water bubbled up, "continually breaking in sparkles on the top." The British traveler George Featherstonhaugh described the pool as "playing and sparkling like a vast reservoir of champagne."[23]

Once in the baths, many exercised or simply frolicked in the large pools. Thomas Gordon Pollock enjoyed the "ample room" at Warm Springs "for swimming & playing & every thing of the kind." Another visitor taught Mary and Robert E. Lee's daughters to swim at Berkeley Springs. Other bathers chose just to remain in one place and let the waters bubble around them. The buoyancy of the water made it difficult to keep one's feet, adding amusement to the scene. According to one travel writer, the bathers felt "not much heavier than a feather, and gay enough to dance hornpipes."

Women played in the baths as much as men and children, abandoning, for the moment, ladylike decorum. At Sweet Springs, Sally Faulcon watched as her neighbor "Mrs Woodson plunged in head foremost & so did some others." In 1838 Lucy Baytop encountered two women in the Warm Springs bath. The first, wearing "a life preserver on her neck," appalled Lucy by swimming "about at her full length shewing her whole figure"; the second "was more quiet kept." The women insisted that Lucy and her sister join them. While the sister ventured in "with her wrapper on," Lucy declined.[24]

The baths strongly appealed to female visitors. Southern society expected ladies to be neither openly sexual nor driven by sexual desires. But, at the springs, respectable women could enjoy the sensuous, and almost sexual, experiences of the warm baths, towel rubs, and blanket sweats without restraint or criticism. Female bathers absolutely delighted in the physical sensations and seized every opportunity to "sink into the warm gulph of languor." Louisa Cocke found the pleasures of bathing so exquisite that she worried about taking one on the Sabbath but indulged in the "sin" anyway. A woman at Red Sweet Springs that Jane Caroline North knew bathed "all the time" because it was "exciting." For Mary Pollard, the Warm Springs bath was "the most delightful place I ever was in; it relaxes the sistem[,] every musle." She visited it two or three times a day.[25] For these women and many others, the baths provided an all-female place where women could not only concentrate on their bodies but also indulge in stimulating pleasures from head to toe—a rare occurrence in their lives.

Women who bathed at the springs could deliberately create "exciting" sensations if they desired. In the "spout" baths, they could direct the flow of hot water at any part of their body (fig. 11). Maria Broadus, for example, enjoyed letting the spout at Hot Springs pour down her side. Suggesting the link between sensuous and sexual feelings, some wives thought of their husbands while luxuriating in the warm waters and eagerly wrote to them describing the experience. In 1857 Mary Lee informed Robert that she "often thought of [him] while in that delicious bath" at Warm Springs. Women who published accounts of their bathing experiences at the springs also regularly commented upon the enjoyable feelings. Presumably, they trusted that society would accept these discussions of bodily sensations from a lady because of their context. In her *Life at the White Sulphur Springs,* Mary J. Windle highlighted the "exhilarating effect" as Sweet Springs' "crystal water curved around" her body. Behind the thin veil of her male pseudonym Mark Pencil, Mary M. Hagner explained how the "soft" water

Figure 11. *Spout Bath at the Warm Springs,* Sophie du Pont, ca. 1837. (Hagley Museum and Library, Wilmington, Del.)

of Warm Springs' bath "plays in a most affectionate manner against the body," before adding, "if I may use the expression."[26]

Like women, men found the warm baths, towel rubbings, and blanket sweats enjoyable. Some considered a particular spring's bath the most "charming" or "pleasant" that they had ever taken.[27] William Wirt swore by Warm Springs and recommended it to a close friend because "it makes the blood discourse most eloquent music, and gives spring and animation to the whole system." Men's descriptions of bathing used sexual language similar to that of women. One travel writer noted that he would never forget "the soothing effect of the water as it came over me up to the throat . . . soft, genially warm and gently murmuring," evoking both "dreamy voluptuous and exhilerating influences." Writing to his cousin Mary, Thomas Pollard evocatively described his first experience in the Warm Springs pleasure bath in sexual tones. "While luxuriating in its genial warmth," the "thousands of bright bubbles of gas arising around" his body "soothed" him "into a sort of *dreamy ecstacy of delight* as the transparent water, bright as any gem floated around." The bubbles made the baths seductive. By "creeping up your body," the bubbles slowly "produce[d] a species of titillation the most exquisite, surely, ever felt," according to John Milton Mackie. Being vigorously rubbed down by servants caused a person to feel, in the opinion of one man, "as if he could jump over the moon." John Cocke always enjoyed being "rubbed down & dried with course towels & a strong assistant." The mental sensations produced by the baths were just as pleasing for the visitors as the bodily ones. During John Cocke's 1851 visit to Hot Springs, the spout bath "was not only luxurious for the time being" but also gave him "delightful dreams" that night. The indescribable pleasures of Sweet Springs, according to James L. Petigru, "affect[ed] the imagination so agreeably." Reveling "in the most delicious sensations" while in the baths, according to one travel writer, "transported" the bather into "day-dreams." [28]

Just as visitors discussed the effects of the mineral waters, they also shared the sensations of bathing, whether by speaking about them or bathing together. Featherstonhaugh heard that "sometimes twenty women would be in [the bath] altogether" at Warm Springs. Judging "from the laughter and the noise that proceeded from" the bath, he surmised that the women undoubtedly had "fine fun" together. With the gentlemen's bath capable of holding fifty at a time, "the men, too, are not less gregarious." But Featherstonhaugh detested "mingling" in the waters with "old sick men" and "tobacco-chewing" ones. In such an intimate and sensual setting as the bathhouses, moreover, women threw off not only the social constraints of being decorous ladies but also the physical constraints of their fashionable clothing. "How gay are the bathing scenes!" one female travel writer noted. "In loose robes and slippers," women could "chat and gossip, around the fire" in the adjoining room. In the sex-segregated sweat rooms, individuals lay next to each other, conversing and enjoying the feeling of the sweat "tickling and trickling down" their sides. Women looked forward to sharing these special experiences with each other. Sarah Harrison informed her mother that an old friend told her "to give *her love* to you and tell you she does long to take you by the hand and cut a few capers in the Warm Springs bath, that she thinks nothing would [do] her more good than to see you in the bath." [29]

Bathing at the springs provided more than just therapy for the visitors who entered the pools. The thermal baths did help many with their health problems, particularly women. But it may have been the pleasurable sensations men and women felt while bathing that benefited them, both physically and mentally, more than the minerals and heat. Indulgence in such sensual pleasures was a rare and thoroughly enjoyable experience for the bathers. The baths offered some of the most memorable moments of a trip to the Virginia Springs and provided a major reason for returning.

It seems likely that this private and public sharing of each other's bodies helped to create bonds of intimacy between the visitors. They all experienced similar bodily sensations together at the springhouses, in the privies, at the scales, or in the baths. Even though talk about the body is obviously intimate and obviously gendered, guests easily discussed their bodies with members of both sexes. Larkin Newby's circle of acquaintances at the springs included both men and women who spent much of their time together discussing the "different effects" of the waters "upon our own particular selves" and assessing other visitors' bodies. Peter Saunders recorded a long conversation with his friend Louisa Carrington about her "rapidly gaining health & flesh." Mrs. Clement C. Clay informed Thomas Hill Malone that she could see him "'visibly swelling'" during his stay at White Sulphur.[30]

All of this public emphasis upon and discussion of the body among and between ladies and gentlemen appears surprising, given the stereotypes about prudish nineteenth-century Americans. Nowhere else, except perhaps at other spas, did respectable women and men engage in this level of public or private attention to and conversation about men's and women's bodies. Except for middle-class women at water-cure establishments who felt secure in the overwhelmingly female environment, only guests at the Virginia Springs broke the normally stringent rules of etiquette that prohibited even the acknowledgment of such corporeal activities, particularly in mixed company.[31] The atmosphere of the Virginia Springs—healthful, relaxed, natural, and intimate—must have made possible this openness about the body among men and women. Within this retreat from the "normal" world, men and women permitted, and even enjoyed, a public and private concentration on the body—its appearance, functions, and sensations—that was unknown in the refined society of their plantations and towns. In journals, correspondence, conversation, and social activities, physical experiences and appearance received attention and validation. No longer a subject discussed in whispers or ignored altogether, bodily experiences became something to share publicly among visitors, and they happily indulged in their opportunity to do so at the Virginia Springs.

Not everyone found a hoped-for cure at the Virginia Springs. "Death is everywhere," reported one travel writer. Each resort contained a graveyard, usually tucked away on a mountainside, which became a popular place of romantic fascination and served as a gloomy reminder. A death at a resort attracted the notice of all who knew the person and many who did not. "Promising" young men and "innocent" young women—who always seem to have died in the bloom of their youth, no matter how long they had suffered a debilitating illness—garnered special attention. Conway Whittle sadly beheld the sickly young men and women in whom "the course of nature" had been "arrested" in its "progress." Instead of "advancing in bouyancy and hope to maturity," the poor youths sank "obviously and consciously to the tomb."[32]

In the writings of visitors to the Virginia Springs, contrary to most histories of nineteenth-century medicine and health, sickness and death did not appear as a manifestation of sinful behavior or bad character.[33] Sickness touched everyone: black or white, rich or poor, adult or child, man or woman. At the springs, as well as at home, people of the finest moral character and the deepest religiosity sickened and sometimes died. Even the staunch evangelicals John H. and Louisa Cocke did not regard sickness as a judgment from God for sinful behavior. While at the springs, guests sympathized with and worried over sickly people; they did not make them objects of scorn as sinners. Sickness and death came too easily in the eyes of most southerners to be treated as more than a matter of course, not as a revelation of sin and immorality.

In this atmosphere of beauty, health, and pleasure, a death darkened the scene and saddened the pleasure-seekers. "Of course a gloom has been cast over the whole place by this sad and unexpected event," Sallie Cocke admitted after the death of a young man at Montgomery White Sulphur. Deaths at the springs occurred often enough each summer for all of the visitors to be regularly reminded of the thin line between a happy, healthy life and painful illness or sorrowful death. At the end of August 1851,

John H. Cocke informed his son that an acquaintance had "died here [Hot Springs], a day or two before our arrival." There had been "another death since," and a good friend was so "reduced to a skeleton" that Cocke had sent for the man's sons. The unexpected death of "a gay widow," who had been "perfectly well yesterday," "inexpressibly shocked" Jane Caroline North and her fellow guests at Red Sweet Springs. North believed that after this "sudden death of one in [her] midst" she surely could not "live on the same." But the pleasure-seekers did not stay down-hearted for long. North spent the following day conversing with young men and women and playing music in the parlor. After three days, North never mentioned the deceased woman in her journal again. In 1818 Samuel Clayton observed that "most of those whom I left very low are gone." But "more healthy and more gay company" filled their places rapidly. Many of the frequent visitors to the Virginia Springs witnessed the death of at least one beloved family member or friend, but doing so rarely deterred them from returning for another season.[34]

Like the British upper classes, southern planter families easily combined a search for recreation and fashionable society with a quest for health in their trips to the Virginia Springs. Health and leisure need not, and perhaps could not, be separated from a stay at the resorts. Seriously ill men and women composed just a minority of the Virginia Springs visitors, but all of the guests partook of the mineral waters. Through all of the changes in the theory and practice of health and therapeutics between 1790 and 1860, the waters at the Virginia Springs continued to fulfill the expectations of orthodox physicians and the lay public about therapy and recovery. Both orthodox and popular opinion agreed upon the effectiveness of these waters as therapy for body and mind. The mineral waters offered a natural cure and the mountain air and spa regimen provided their own healthful benefits. The springs also offered a degree of emotional and mental well-being that not only improved the health of visitors, but also provided a much-needed balm for many weary, bored, or depressed planter men and women. These rituals of health placed a tremendous emphasis upon the body—its appearance, functions, and sensations—at the springs that was almost unknown in the parlors and dining rooms of plantations and town houses. Genteel men and women never shied away from these topics while visiting the springs. Instead, they indulged in the experience, observation, and discussion of their bodies, often in mixed-sex groups, adapting their rules of proper etiquette to this new environment. After experiencing all of the physical sensations and mental stimulation available at the springs, even visitors who were not sick often felt like "new beings." [35] In this healing landscape, their mental and physical health was rejuvenated, allowing them to return to their homes ready to face the long, quiet months until the next summer and, possibly, the next trip to the Virginia Springs.

PART 3

Community and Competition

WHEN JANE CAROLINE NORTH AND HER RELATIVES ALIGHTED from the stage at Warm Springs, their first stop on the Virginia Springs circuit, she "felt a little *scared*" at the fashionably dressed visitors staring at her and the other "dusty[,] weary & travel worn" newcomers. The South Carolinian feared, as well, the sight her unkempt group would make in the dining room. Luckily, everyone else had already eaten. During the rest of her long stay at the springs, North always appeared among the company fashionably dressed and achieved the desired results, noting on one occasion that "the effect seemed to meet with the approval of the company." Twenty-three and single, North found herself in the midst of the most exclusive circle of society congregated anywhere in the South. And she had a marvelous time.[1]

North traveled through the springs area with her aunt, uncle, two young cousins, and a slave servant during the summer of 1851, seeking the "more lively" resorts in order to have fun and associate with fashionable people. Her winning ways made her quite popular among both young and old. "Uncle H. tells me I display great capacity for gaining popularity," she recorded in her journal while at Warm Springs. She endeared herself to older women, formed fast friendships with other young visitors, and collected male admirers. During her season at the springs, North met such visitors as the Calhouns, Rutledges, and Singletons of South Carolina, the Porters of Georgia, the Dulaneys of Maryland, and a host of distinguished Virginia families, as well as the South Carolina sportsman William Elliott, the novelist John Pendleton Kennedy, and Sarah Gales Seaton, the wife of the *National Intelligencer*'s editor—all members of some of the most prominent, wealthiest, and oldest families in the South. North even saw President Millard Fillmore on several occasions. A fortunate friendship with Isaetta Coles, of another prestigious Virginia family, quickened North's entré into the "best" circles at the springs. North fully understood the value of this friendship: "Knowing the Coles was a great advantage to us, they knew everybody, & we consequently were introduced to many pleasant people." Coming from the well-known Petigru family, North possessed all of the qualifications necessary for a welcoming admittance.[2]

Everyone seemed to get along famously. North and her friends and acquaintances gathered daily in parlors or cabins or on the lawn for conversation and assorted amusements. As a fashionable young lady, she performed the latest steps at balls and dances nearly every evening. At other times, she attended occasional sermons, bathed in the waters, and engaged in pleasurable outdoor activities with various friends, relatives, and acquaintances. On a single day at Salt Sulphur Springs, North rolled tenpins on the lawn with friends, rode into the mountains and climbed to an old observatory to enjoy the views with an escorting "cavalier," and attended the evening ball with her family.[3] She had so much fun at White Sulphur Springs that she neglected her journal for ten days.

During her stay, in her journal and letters home, North described, often in minute detail, many of the men and women she met—noting what they wore and how they acted and criticizing or complimenting them. She found a Mrs. Vanderhorst "perfectly rich!" and her son "a stiff youth full of himself, but gentlemanly and polite." One woman was "a marvel of ugliness" to North and another "a foolish, talkative girl, without discretion, or one interesting quality." She characterized dear male friends as "such insignificant looking little men." She preferred to avoid visitors who failed to meet her standards of behavior and appearance, laughing at them privately. After dancing one evening with a Miss Jackson who "capered & cavaulted!" North resolved "never again" to "form one of such an exhibition, too dreadful!" And she became considerably offended at the condescension of Susan Rutledge, a member of one of Charleston's leading families; "Miss Susan Rutledge is as up & down as a pine tree & has about as much polish," she recorded. Likewise, the "twanging tone" of Virginians surprised North. "'I reckon so' meets one in every phrase and this from people whom . . . are 'of the right stripe.'" Nor was she fully satisfied by her fellow South Carolinians and "their narrow absurd conduct" toward President Fillmore. North always remained outwardly polite and sociable, even when she disdained the person with whom she conversed. Constantly aware of her own appearance and behavior throughout her stay, she always monitored and assessed the appearance and behavior of others. It is no wonder that she was an undeniable success at the Virginia Springs.[4]

In an 1842 travel guide, resort proprietor William Burke succinctly explained the problems of Saratoga Springs while extolling the virtues of the Virginia Springs. First, because of the easy railroad access, "persons in every condition of life, and at a trifling expense," could travel to the various northern watering places. Thus, "the mass of visiters" there was "composed of all sorts of people." "The knowledge of this fact," according to Burke, made visitors "distrustful of each other's standing, and shy and reserved." At the Virginia Springs, on the other hand, "an entire feeling of equality, a relinquishment of formality, a republican simplicity of manners, a reciprocity of kind, courteous, but unpretending civility, and an easy, unaffected social intercourse" characterized the atmosphere. For Burke and many other southern travelers, these attributes rendered the Virginia Springs resorts "peculiarly agreeable." According to Burke and other southern visitors, Saratoga lacked important qualities of gentility: exclusivity, order, intimacy, affability, and chivalry. In essence, it lacked the hallmarks of southern plantation society. The absence of these cherished southern traits led southerners to consider Saratoga's women "as chilling as isicles" and its men "nothing but a set of statues." If a cold reserve characterized northerners, hospitality and "easy, unaffected social intercourse" made southern women and men a different, and superior, breed, at least in their own eyes. While some southerners enjoyed Saratoga, most believed that it could not compare with the Virginia resorts. They clearly preferred a place where southerners and southern ways held sway.[5]

The Virginia Springs experience intensified the power of southern society's rules, rituals, expectations, and boundaries. Life at the springs made the contours of two crucial and intertwined elements of elite society— gentility and gender relations—readily apparent. Gentility's rules and rituals helped to set gender roles and expectations. On the other hand, women and men had important, though often different, parts to play in the practice and enforcement of gentility. Regional identity and class-creation, moreover, relied heavily on the cultural connections between gentility and gender. Examining southern society at the springs starkly reveals the rich complexity of southern gentility and gender roles and relations, as well as the various ways in which class and regional identities were created.

From the late eighteenth century until the Civil War, the Virginia Springs remained the enclave of the southern elite. At this central place in the southern gentry's "geography of refinement," society revolved around the ideas and behaviors of gentility. On the surface, gentility created refined and beautiful places where refined and beautiful people gathered to amuse each other and to perform for everyone in a spirit of harmonious camaraderie. At the same time, however, southern gentility emphasized social differences and class boundaries and encouraged fierce competition, harsh judgments, catty behavior, and petty disputes among men and women who viewed themselves as genteel.

Genteel men and women would not have labeled themselves snobbish, petty, or censorious, nor were they hypocritical. They did not feign sociability. Visitors regarded the Virginia Springs, and themselves, as embodying only gentility's best qualities without ever recognizing that the springs, or they themselves, also cultivated its worst aspects. They saw the Virginia Springs only as a beautiful place where fashionable and hospitable people shared a marvelous experience.[6] Yet genteel spa society encouraged not only easy intimacy and sociability among the visitors but also stern rules, stiff competition, and firm exclusions. Southern visitors boasted of equality at the springs yet remained devoted to hierarchy. The renowned informality of the place coexisted with a strict attention to etiquette. The visitors were remarkably intimate with each other, but they desperately sought position above one another. Within this relaxed and informal atmosphere, they remained obsessed with personal display. Their refinement was unquestionable, but so was their competitiveness. Their desire for an orderly and pleasant society required excluding those who lacked the requisite attributes. The resulting tensions could have made life at the springs complicated and unpleasant for visitors. The true ladies and gentlemen, however, skillfully maneuvered on both the surface and the underlying levels of gentility with little recognition of doing so.

The demands of gentility strongly affected gender roles and relations but, at the springs, did not prohibit men and women from interacting freely and easily with each other. The world of the springs was not a simple one. In this retreat from the normal world, harmony and, to a lesser extent, conflict characterized the interactions and performances of men and women. The leisurely and playful springs environment encouraged harmonious gender relations but exaggerated gender roles in ways that could cause conflict. While some of the plantation world's usual rules of conduct for ladies and gentlemen intensified at the springs, its usual gender divisions eased or changed. At least at the springs, elite southern men and women interacted more easily and more regularly than most accounts of southern gender relations suggest. They participated in more mutual and less divided relations than supposedly on the plantation. Except for courtship, competition and status-seeking did not center on exchanges between men and women. Interactions with the opposite sex at the springs were neither problematic nor anxiety-ridden but anticipated and enjoyed. In spite of the remarkable mutuality at the Virginia Springs, however, male and female visitors experienced resort life somewhat differently; the significance of the trip also varied for men and women. The Virginia Springs provided a place where men and, especially, women could create, strengthen, and renew bonds with members of their own sex. Along with the ties created *between* men and women at the Virginia Springs, the bonds formed *among* men and *among* women strengthened the planter elite's collective power and collective identity.

The Virginia Springs environment exaggerated the roles that men and women normally played in elite southern society in a variety of ways. In this public arena women wielded significant social power. As judges of appropriate genteel behavior and appearance, they set the social standards and helped enforce the boundaries of their class. Furthermore, the competitive demands of gentility often caused tensions between members of the same sex, as men and women vied with each other for status and acclaim. And, although everyday gender relations were harmonious, courtship at the springs (as at home) often produced sexual conflict. The heightened importance and prominence of gender roles at the springs defined and reaffirmed what it meant to be an elite southern lady or gentleman at home.

The Virginia Springs simultaneously acted as both a "stage" and a "school" for elite southern society. The springs provided a stage surpassed by no other upon which men and women could perform for, compete with, and even challenge their peers. At the same time, there was perhaps nowhere else that elite young adults could so easily learn how to behave and how to display the power of their dominant class. As a stage and a school, the springs served to bolster the elite's sense of rightful dominance. The springs experience heightened the showiness and self-consciousness of elite power and provided many opportunities for the South's leading men and women to exercise that power. Yet, as a place of conflict as well as harmony, the intense but amiable springs environment constantly sparked contests for a right to power. The competition for status, attention to display, and judgment of performance seemingly belied the intimate and sociable atmosphere of the springs, but the dedication to affability and refinement transformed what could have been a vicious experience into part of the allure of a season at the springs. Through display, contest, and scrutiny, southern ladies and gentlemen defined themselves and consolidated their claims to status. While these processes occurred within the unique environment of the Virginia Springs, they reflected and influenced southern society in general. As the elite gathered from throughout the South every summer in this truly regional community, they reformed and renewed their regional identity to a degree unknown in their plantation and town communities.

☙

"A Never Ceasing Scene of Stir, Animation, Display, & Enjoyment"

The Virginia Springs environment highlighted and intensified the characteristics prized by the southern gentry. The exclusivity of the resorts and the orderliness of life there strongly appealed to the visitors. Guests relished the amusement and leisure that pervaded the spot. The exclusivity and dedication to order, refinement, and gentility also created an easy and amiable, almost familial, atmosphere. Beginning soon after 1790, the Virginia Springs emerged as a place of regional unity for the large numbers of southerners who came from plantations and towns all across the South during the summer.

Before the springs became places of resort in the late eighteenth century, they had primarily attracted people from the surrounding countryside. Once the proprietors decided to cater to an elite clientele, construct hotels, and charge high prices, the Virginia Springs resorts became enclaves for the privileged and prominent. As Judith Rives remembered, "A visit to the Virginia Springs was rather an aristocratic distinction, since it was an indulgence only to be attained by persons who could command their own carriages, horses and servants." Throughout the South, gentry men and women knew about the springs and traveled great distances to spend a summer in this fashionable and popular place. The duration and expense of the trip necessarily made the resorts exclusive. Poorer small farmers did not have many, if any, slaves to work their fields or a small fortune to pay the enormous expenses of even a short visit (fig. 12). But wealthy planters and others with the time and money to travel to one or more spas over the summer could afford the trip across the Blue Ridge. A two-week stay in 1816 at White Sulphur, for example, cost Richmond's John Wickham $167 for board and lodging for himself, his wife, oldest daughter, two children, four servants, and six horses, though this included a hefty bar tab. By the late 1850s, an entire season, mid-July to mid-October, at Fauquier White Sulphur totaled close to seven hundred dollars for Chief Justice Roger B. Taney and his family.[1]

To put these resort charges in perspective, a day laborer in Virginia in 1850 received only 65 cents per day and a skilled carpenter just $1.22. In South Carolina, the same kinds of workers received 66 cents and $1.40, respectively. Female domestics earned 96 cents a week, including board, in Virginia and $1.42 in South Carolina. In 1850 a farmhand worked for a monthly wage of $8.43, including board, in Virginia and $7.72 in South Carolina.[2] Such wages prohibited a trip of any duration to the springs for laborers and small farmers from outside the immediate area. It was only by accompanying her wealthy employers that a free domestic could visit the springs.

The well-known exclusivity of the Virginia Springs pleased most of its visitors. These men and women wanted to appear select and sought to frequent select places, as genteel persons should. Exclusivity guaranteed them a level of society that met their expectations. The southern gentry could feel comfortable at such places, for, as John H. B. Latrobe noted of White Sulphur, "there is something eminently aristocratic about the place, and you feel that you are with your fellows here, more than at any other place of its kind in Virginia." Foreign visitors likewise readily discerned the refined, even aristocratic, feel of White Sulphur. There, the English novelist Frederick Marryat proclaimed, "You feel how excessively aristocratical and exclusive the Americans would be." "Spa [Belgium], in its palmiest days, when princes had to sleep in their carriages at the doors of the hotels, was not more in vogue than are these white sulphur springs with the *elite* of the United States." Despite the large crowds at the springs by the mid-nineteenth century, the guests still believed that only the best of society

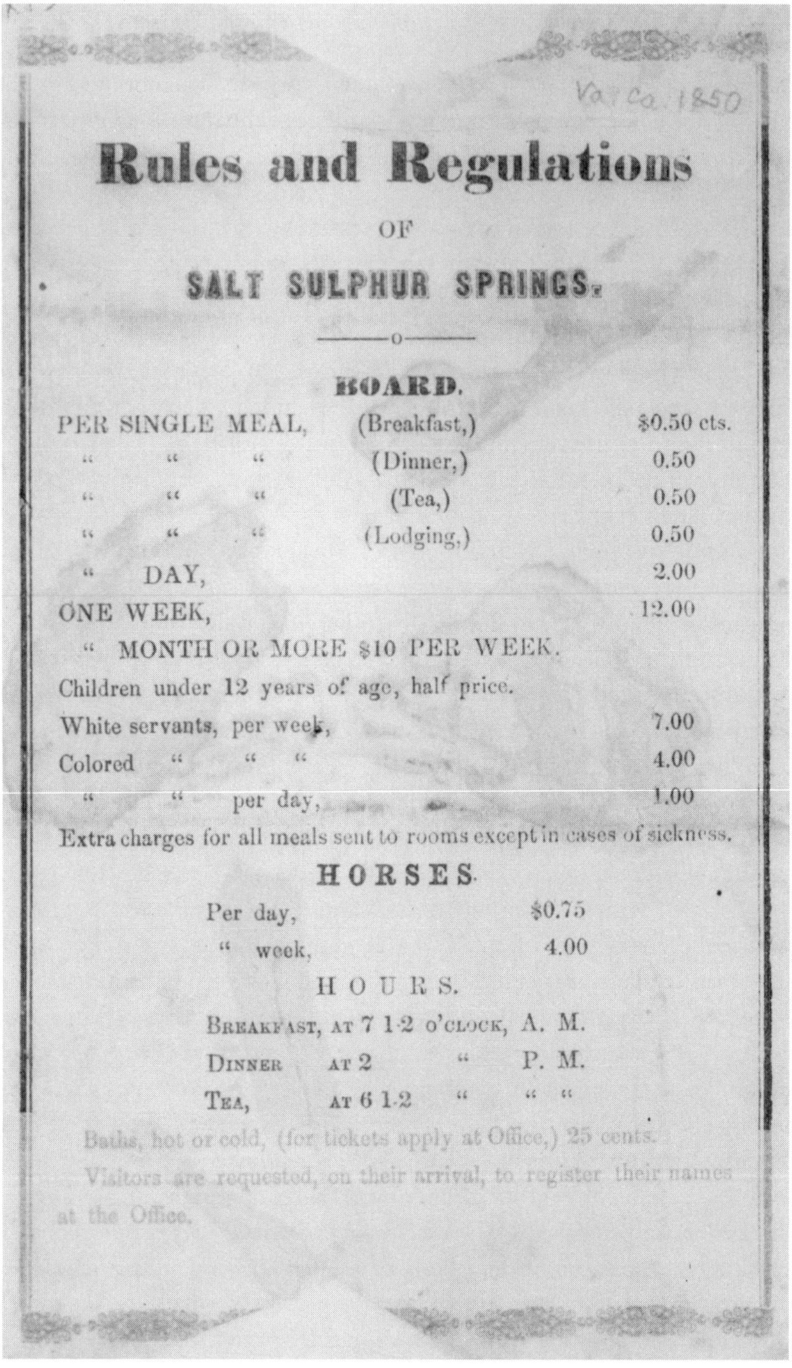

Rules and Regulations

OF

SALT SULPHUR SPRINGS.

———o———

BOARD.

PER SINGLE MEAL,	(Breakfast,)		$0.50 cts.
" " "	(Dinner,)		0.50
" " "	(Tea,)		0.50
" " "	(Lodging,)		0.50
" DAY,			2.00
ONE WEEK,			12.00

" MONTH OR MORE $10 PER WEEK.

Children under 12 years of age, half price.

White servants, per week,	7.00
Colored " " "	4.00
" " per day,	1.00

Extra charges for all meals sent to rooms except in cases of sickness.

HORSES.

Per day,	$0.75
" week,	4.00

HOURS.

BREAKFAST, AT 7 1-2 o'clock, A. M.

DINNER AT 2   "   P. M.

TEA, AT 6 1-2   "   "   "

Baths, hot or cold, (for tickets apply at Office,) 25 cents.

Visitors are requested, on their arrival, to register their names at the Office.

Figure 12. "Rules and Regulations of Salt Sulphur Springs," ca. 1850. (Rare Book, Manuscripts, and Special Collections Library, Duke University, Durham, N.C.)

surrounded them. In 1860 Thomas Pollock reported to his mother that "the crowd here is immense—some fourteen hundred people—the most elegant & refined of the Southern country."[3]

By itself, the assured exclusivity of the Virginia Springs drew planter and wealthy professional visitors to the resorts. People always assumed that travelers to the Virginia Springs were of the "better class." Guests who sought to create or strengthen ties at the resorts knew that they would socialize only with those from their own social level. This fact alone placed the Virginia Springs ahead of Saratoga in the opinion of most southerners. At Saratoga and other northern resorts, according to southern accounts around 1840, an inexpensive day trip allowed the places to be "resorted to by every would-be fashionable, by every class, colour, and condition," including "the sickening fop and conceited nincompoop." Such a situation could not develop at the antebellum Virginia Springs. With the company at the southern resorts more homogeneous, "more exclusively confined to the well-bred classes . . . [and to] those who are in opulent or at least in easy circumstances," a visitor could expect to "sit at table beside the highest and best in the land." This expectation led many southerners, as well as those from other parts of the country and abroad, to choose the Virginia Springs as their summer destination.[4]

With only the "highest and best" at the springs, visitors, especially young women and their male protectors, showed little concern about meeting rakes or pretenders. A planter father need not fear that his daughter would dance or stroll with "one with no prouder title than papa's tailor, or boot-maker," as at northern spas. Because of the exclusivity and homogeneity of the guests, the tightly woven yet extensive kinship and friendship networks of the southern gentry enveloped every social occasion at the springs. Some gentleman or lady could generally provide assurances that an unfamiliar visitor came from a respectable family and had a good reputation (and, of course, sufficient wealth). During her stay in 1851, Jane Caroline North received "the history" of various visitors from Sarah Gales Seaton. The standing rule in the ballroom at White Sulphur established that "no gentleman [would be] suffered to be introduced" to a young lady "unless known to some [other] gentleman." This rule apparently never caused any problems.[5]

According to their devotees, the exclusivity of the Virginia Springs ensured the true gentility of the guests, while the democratic atmosphere of the northern spas allowed for masqueraders with false claims to gentility.

Thus, real ladies and gentlemen could never feel as secure at northern resorts as they did at the Virginia Springs. While staying at the Virginia Springs in 1817, southerner Samuel Mordecai contemplated the problems for genteel persons at northern spas, such as Ballston: "I know that every fellow, whatever his degree may be at home, thinks he must assume importance at such a place as Ballston, to be thought a gentleman—and that the swaggering airs of a fashionably dressed chap who perhaps made the Coat or boots he wears, must . . . only disgust those whose gentility is inherent." For Mordecai and many others, true gentry could only feel comfortable at the Virginia Springs. Over and over again throughout these decades, visitors and travel writers remarked upon how much the gentility, respectability, and sociability of everyone at the Virginia Springs impressed them. In his well-known *The Mineral Springs of Virginia,* William Burke acknowledged that it "would not be true" that "all the *elite* of the nation are annually seen" at the Virginia Springs, but asserted that he could claim without "exaggeration" that "a large portion of them, and of the learning, wit, beauty, elegance and fashion of the States is here assembled."[6]

Since it ensured their preeminence, the leading class of southerners had come to regard order as one of the most valued attributes of their society. Elite southern men and women expected orderliness from society in general and from individuals in particular at the Virginia Springs. On the whole, this expectation was gratified. Dandridge Spotswood Sr. considered the gathering at White Sulphur in 1848 to be "the most genteel & orderly set of people it has ever been my lot to associate with[;] we have not one disagreeable person among them." A Charlestonian voiced similar sentiments fifteen years later: "I have never before seen a more orderly, sober & decorous crowd collected any where." For those at the top, life at the springs ran smoothly as long as people acted within the accepted range of behavior, which depended upon their status, and the social hierarchy remained preserved.[7]

In the eyes of elite visitors, the relations between master and slave at the Virginia Springs generally took on an orderly and pleasant guise. Even though the servants often required a bribe or two to perform their tasks quickly and properly, they did not seem to pose a threat to the stability of the social hierarchy. Southerners often described the servants at northern watering places as unruly and disrespectful and, thus, sources of disorder and disruption. One incident in a Saratoga Springs dining room during the summer of 1845 dramatically highlighted this difference. "The folks of

Saratoga were thrown into great excitement by the occurrence of an affray at the 'table d'Hotel' by a gentleman from Georgia's slitting the nose of one of 'Africa's Sons' who was an impertinent waiter," as Patrick Henry Aylett related to his mother. The gentleman ultimately gave the waiter a hundred dollars. Aylett sided with the Georgian, telling his mother: "I most devoutly wish that the South Carolinians had the insolent negroes of the North in their cotton fields for a term of months each year." Most visitors at the Virginia Springs viewed the slave servants there as delighted to serve the guests. According to one travel writer, the resort servant, "tak[ing] his summer life easily," "constantly [gave] back the picture of his grinning face," so much so that the Virginia Springs "might better be called the Laughing Waters."[8]

Ill-favor fell upon those guests whose undeserved mistreatment of obedient slaves disrupted the order at the springs. While at Red Sulphur in 1838, William Stabler related a story about an invalid man who received sympathy from the ladies and gentlemen. But, when the man replied to a slave's offer of assistance by using an "epithet" and "saying that when he wanted him he would send for him," he lost this sympathy. "Conduct like this," Stabler reported, "has turned the feelings of the community away from him."[9] Guests could not remain a part of the springs community if they became unruly, even toward slaves. Elite visitors could tolerate an occasional surly or lazy servant, but they insisted upon constantly controlled behavior from their peers.

The neighboring "country people" who came to the Virginia Springs either to deliver goods or to use the waters seemingly never disrupted the orderly life of the elite visitors. The fashionables found them interesting, admiring their appearance and way of life more than deriding them. To James Kirke Paulding, the country people who stopped at White Sulphur in 1817 possessed "a striking air of conscious independence," "the finest characteristic of our countrymen." Some genteel visitors viewed these men and women in an even more sentimental light. In 1844 Mary B. Blackford wrote to her son about a group of poor people "encamped here now on the banks of the Stream, a little above the Springs in the woods." She liked "to walk by and look at them," for they reminded her of a "Gipsey camp when they are sitting round their fire eating as they were yesterday, and one of their number playing the fiddle most merrily." They must "lead a merry life in the Green Wood," she romanticized. By appearing infrequently and remaining distant from resort life, such people never challenged elite southerners' ordered expectations. At northern resorts, in contrast, the presence of "a rabble from the country, to which we may add a few cooks, and chambermaids, from the cities . . . fairly eclipse[d] the fashionables," creating an unsettling disorder in the eyes of southerner Anne Royall. Without an urban lower class and with a rural lower class that acted only in an acceptable and frequently invisible manner, the Virginia Springs remained a decorous environment for Royall and other southerners.[10]

A feeling of being at leisure and a commitment to amusement were as crucial to the genteel environment of the Virginia Springs as its exclusivity and order. The wealth of activities and number of people produced a constantly changing and enjoyable scene. "The scenes presented at a watering place" reminded J. Taylor of Charleston of "the pictures of a Kaleidescope, which as *you know* vary with every turn of the instrument." The social and recreational activities offered the visitors a respite from the labor and routines of their plantation and town lives. Furthermore, gentility rested upon the idea that, within refined places, refined people would come together to amuse each other and promote happiness. Visitors to the springs vigorously put this idea into action. "What adds very much to the pleasure," Thomas Smith noted in 1826, "is the apparent disposition of all to make the time of each other pleasant and agreeable." The determination of genteel visitors "to contribute to the general happiness" heightened the already merry and leisurely atmosphere.[11]

Visitors traveled to the Virginia Springs as much for genteel amusement as for health. Those in search of pleasure knew that they could find it there. "The gay, young, agreeable and handsome of both sexes," one travel writer remarked, gladly came to the resorts "to see and be seen, to chat, laugh and dance, and each to throw his pebble on the great heap of the general enjoyment." Though surrounded by invalids suffering and dying from diseases, most visitors quickly and easily embraced the convivial life at the resorts. Relaxation and recreation pervaded the Virginia Springs, and most visitors found it difficult to resist their allure. The guests devised a variety of amusements and entered into them with relish. Many threw themselves into the whirl so deeply that they had little time for anything else, including writing home. Elizabeth Taylor complained to a friend that her daughters were "so taken up with the company" that they had no time to write their friends or tend to any other responsibilities. Taylor indulged her daughters at the springs, hoping that, when they returned home, the girls would "return to their duty, and a rational mode of spending time."[12]

Given the inherent sociability of genteel places, visiting appropriately constituted the guests' preeminent leisure activity. "Visiting founded in idleness and sharpened by curiosity is a very brisk business," Mary Thompson informed a friend in 1848. Visitors to the springs brought their home rules for social intercourse but willingly and easily adapted them to the peculiarities of the springs environment. Most resort guests believed that, as at home, meeting someone required the social ritual of introduction. Yet at the springs, where so many people knew each other, visitors found it very easy to get an introduction or to circumvent a formal one. Even the ever-cautious Jane Caroline North felt safely within the bounds of propriety, if a little daring, in introducing herself to Sarah Gales Seaton, even though her only connection was having met Seaton's daughter in Charleston the year before.[13]

The elaborate rules of paying and receiving visits took on a life of their own among the guests at the springs, with some home rules remaining in place, or slightly altered, and others abandoned completely. Guests established "a regular system of visiting from Cabin to Cabin" to which new arrivals quickly adapted. Sarah Harrison assured her mother that she strictly followed the etiquette of visiting, returning visits of those who called upon her and calling upon others with whom she wished to establish ties. This "great deal of formality among the ladies" at the springs surprised Harrison, especially since "all" of the ladies told her "it is without their consent"; the self-perpetuating cycle of visiting demanded their acquiescence. As she probably soon discovered, however, women more than men kept the continual rounds of visits going at the springs, just as they generally did at home. Springs visitors not only roamed from cabin to cabin at one resort, they also constantly moved among the resorts seeking out friends and acquaintances. When Judith Walker Rives visited the Virginia Springs in the early nineteenth century, she and her party "amused" themselves "in fluttering daily from one to the other" resort, "remaining longest where society was most attractive." Even though these ladies and gentlemen entertained in simple cottages rather than in grand houses, they maintained much of the usual ritual of visiting by leaving calling cards, serving tea, and having servants announce visitors.[14]

The living arrangements at the springs dictated some changes in visiting etiquette. Guests staying in the hotels exchanged civilities in the hotel reception rooms. For those in the cottages, "a totally different etiquette" prevailed. Cottage-dwellers visited from cabin to cabin. If a friend was away,

Figure 13. John H. B. Latrobe with the Claiborne family at Botetourt Springs, John H. B. Latrobe, 1832. (Semmes, *John H. B. Latrobe and His Times*)

callers might simply write their name and the hour on a post of the porch. The size of the cabins also forced the inhabitants to receive visitors in their bedrooms rather than in parlors as they normally would. Because of the scarcity of chairs, moreover, beds substituted for sofas; this practice became so commonplace and accepted that beds were nicknamed "Spring Sofas." Inviting someone into a bedroom and having them sit on a bed, especially in mixed company, clearly violated traditional rules of etiquette. Yet no one seems to have complained about this forced intimacy. John H. B. Latrobe simply recorded that within these usually female-only confines he had made "some very pleasant visits" (fig. 13). In the relaxed atmosphere of the springs, genteel society accepted transgressions required by the peculiar accommodations. The visitors' dedication to appearing as ladies and gentlemen permitted an intimate bedroom to be viewed as a parlor and an even more intimate bed as a sofa.[15]

On porches, in parlors, at the springhouses, or under the trees on the lawns, groups of men and women gathered for pleasant conversation, often over tea or stronger drink or cards. The rules governing such conversation at the springs generally carried over from the elite's home environments. Men and women encouraged discussion but not heated debate. In conversation, gentlemen and ladies carefully chose their words and studied their answers. As at home, genteel conversation at the springs included literature, religion, nature, and gossip. But, importantly, conversation at the springs included both men and women and rarely avoided subject matter usually considered "male." In 1796 Ferdinand Bayard at his boardinghouse in Bath spent one evening "talk[ing] politics" with two couples. "The ladies took part in the debates; both defended vigorously the President of the United States, when Mr. Am. or anyone else, refused to share the enthusiasm which he inspired during the war." Fifty years later, British traveler Robert Playfair whiled away his evenings in the ladies' drawing rooms conversing about Sir Walter Scott, slavery, politicians, and the Mexican War. A conversation between a Dr. Davis and Edmund Ruffin "on the best method of teaching agriculture to 'young Virginia'" intrigued John B. Minor's female cousin so much that she could not finish writing him a letter. At the springs, traditionally male subjects such as politics and agriculture became perfectly acceptable topics for drawing-room conversation among men and women. Even more striking, what would have been considered a serious breach of etiquette at home—the public discussion of a person's body—became an appropriate and favorite pastime among refined men and women at the springs. Polite conversation in mixed company at the springs included many subjects that genteel society forbade in the presence of ladies at the visitors' homes. Apparently no one objected.[16]

The springs' leisure spaces served an important purpose in the guests' enactment of gentility. Porches, ballrooms, parlors, and lawns provided common gathering places where visitors counted upon finding friends, lively discussion, and entertainment—and upon showing off their genteel manners. James Seddon believed that the parlor, dining hall, and ballroom at White Sulphur composed the "main *life*" of the resort as the rooms contained "a never ceasing scene of Stir, animation, display & enjoyment."[17] Within these leisure spaces, groups of men and women came together not only to converse but also to play instruments, sing, or play backgammon and chess. On their cabin porches, they watched the sun set and gathered for ice cream or watermelon parties. They sipped mint juleps, "sangaree," and other strong drinks on porches, at the tavern, or under the trees. And they frequently played cards. Next to conversing with friends

Figure 14. Men gambling at White Sulphur Springs, John H. B. Latrobe, 1832.
(Semmes, *John H. B. Latrobe and His Times*)

and acquaintances, card playing seems to have been "the rage" at the springs from the late eighteenth century through the mid-nineteenth century. While both men and women played whist, women do not seem to have participated in the betting games of faro and poker. Gentlemen gambled in their rooms or in the drawing rooms or on the lawns with little condemnation from genteel southern visitors, including women. "Gambling went on openly, and near our cottage men assembled to play," Joseph Packard reported from White Sulphur (fig. 14).[18] Some of the guests spent quiet afternoons in the parlors or their cabins during the heat of the day reading and napping. Joseph C. Cabell used his trips to the spas to catch up on his reading because he was "more at leisure" there than at home.[19] Many of the guests would have agreed with him.

Amusement also came from outside the springs for the visitors' enjoyment, and their money. Itinerant entertainers, merchants, and showmen appeared at the springs throughout the summer season. As early as 1791, an acting troupe performed at Bath, putting on "tragedy, comedy, comic opera and the farce." In 1846 Jerome Napoleon Bonaparte Jr. reported that an acting company from Richmond played at White Sulphur Springs three or four nights a week for fifty cents a show. Two large red wagons containing a traveling museum showed up at the springs in 1838. According to one account, "it was Peale's museum in miniature, for they appeared to have a little of every thing curious, wolves, bears, wax figures, Indian dresses and arrows, a large crocodile, shells, minerals, and many strings of rattles." Phrenologists always garnered attention, often negative, once they began traveling to the springs during the 1830s. In 1844 John Wickham warned his brother about "an odd one sided faced, red cockeyed red haired man who calls himself doctor Baylis, Phrenologist[.] A most amusing ass who will talk most ridiculously on the science." Valley residents also came selling and showing objects around the resorts, from maple sugar cakes to trained squirrels to rattlesnakes. By the 1850s, photographers appeared at the springs and attracted many customers interested in the novelty. Even more novel, Peter Saunders witnessed "a balloon ascension" in 1860 at White Sulphur. "It went up very prettily," and "the Aeronaut . . . came down very safely." The Virginia Springs offered a large variety of recreational activities, along with many of the social entertainments found in cities. These enjoyable activities further enabled the visitors to "contribute to the general happiness" and provide an amusing place in which genteel ladies and gentlemen could come together.[20]

The exclusivity and order of the springs, the gentility of the visitors, and the spirit of leisure and amusement combined to produce communal feelings of warmth and intimacy among the guests. No female "icicles" or male "statues" walked the grounds of the Virginia Springs. Visitors and travel writers believed that elite society amidst the mountains relinquished its formality, though not its gentility, seeking instead an affable, open, familial atmosphere. "Indeed Mama," Jane Caroline North Pettigrew wrote on her second trip to the springs in 1855, "old acquaintances, & new ones are all so warmly friendly that I think we must be a very winning party!"[21] The assured homogeneity of a genteel crowd, the comfort of an orderly hierarchical environment, and the ease that came from being at leisure allowed the men and women to create and share in a warm, intimate community of visitors. With their emphasis upon familial sentiments and sociability, the Virginia Springs once again appeared to southern elite visitors as the embodiment of what was best in their society.

The pervasive familial feelings among unrelated visitors no doubt found inspiration in all of the reunions that took place among actual families at the resorts each season. The certainty of reuniting with family, friends, and acquaintances became a leading reason for traveling the long distances to the Virginia Springs as they grew in popularity. John Brodnax and his party "met with a great many acquaintances here. Cal & Mrs Baily[,] Mr Garret

& his Daughter[,] Mrs John Coleman[,] John Cunningham & his wife . . . & Jannie. Old Man Edmond Ruffin[,] young Edward & his daughter and a host of others." And it is no wonder—"1500 to 1900 people" crowded into White Sulphur during the 1860 season. Some planned trips to the springs expressly to gather with kin, especially those whose children or siblings had left the old states of Virginia and the Carolinas for the new frontier states of Mississippi, Alabama, and Louisiana. These families could always look to the Virginia Springs as a place of reunion. In 1849 Virginian Emily Rutherfoord and her family "found Uncle Tucker & Aunt Helen" at Hot Springs, where her "Aunt Selina with Cousin Peyton" had also arrived the previous night. Emily and her party had just left "Uncle Stevenson & his wife with Uncle [Richard] Singleton [of South Carolina] at the White Sulphur." She then moved on alone to Warm Springs to stay with her "Uncle Edward & his family." Most visitors knew that at the springs they would see friends and acquaintances that they might never see anywhere else. St. George Tucker Coalter had a wonderful time at White Sulphur Springs in 1833 with "some fifty acquaintances." A spirit of cheerful reunion with dear friends and loved ones consequently pervaded the resorts and contributed to the affable and communal atmosphere.[22]

In the unique environment of the Virginia Springs, wealthy southern visitors seem to have felt less reserved and more informal than at public gatherings in their home communities. One Charlestonian urged a friend to join him at White Sulphur for "most people are very social, having left their stiffness at home." Walter E. Preston's sisters expressed their delight and relief at finding Sweet Springs not "so frightfully ceremonious and stylish as they had expected." In 1837 Philippa Barbour "became better acquainted" with neighbors from her own county at Rawley Springs than she ever had at home. This relinquishment of formality and reserve convinced northern and southern observers alike that the company at the Virginia Springs remained "free from aristocratic pretensions and ridiculous attempts at exclusiveness." In an ironic twist, the exclusivity of the springs allowed the visitors to appear communal and friendly, rather than exclusive and formal. New acquaintances regularly became close friends before leaving. During an 1831 visit, the Wilson family of Charleston met "two families from Mississippi[,] Mr Mercers & Mr Elliotts, with whom we got acquainted, [and] on their leaving the Springs, we mutually exchanged cards, and good feelings." Good feelings created at the Virginia Springs often continued elsewhere.[23]

While socializing almost entirely with people of one's own status eased any stiffness at the springs, being at leisure in nature and away from the plantation contributed to the familial feelings and informal atmosphere as well. "Nature smiles" at the springs, Anna Cora Ritchie proclaimed, "and draws us out of ourselves." At these retreats, visitors did not throw out all social rules—genteel standards still guided their conduct; but they did relinquish the more formal modes of behavior of their home communities. Louisa Emmerson remembered that a friend credited nature's "reflection on surrounding objects" with causing the visitors to be "more natural, less affected, and [to] enjoy life here." Such informality came easily to visitors who gave free rein to "the buoyancy and frolicksomeness of childhood" experienced at the resorts and roamed amid "the fields and forests" and "beneath the lofty trees." The temporary escape from normal restraints on public behavior and social intercourse certainly caused Virginia Springs visitors to feel less constrained or formal in their behavior. James Alexander Seddon confessed to his brother-in-law that "I have been so metamorphosed that I hardly know myself," changing from a "saturnine and unsocial" being into one who threw himself into "the giddy whirl" of society and amusements at the springs. Visitors who relaxed in this leisurely environment probably interacted with a more carefree quality than they would have in their home communities—places that required and expected restrained behavior from its leading members. The well-known jurist James L. Petigru noticed that at the springs fellow South Carolinian Richard Singleton was "a different man entirely from what he is at home. There is an indefatigable planter and the inveterate turfman. Here is the politest man of the age, scrupulously attentive to his dress and marked in his civility to the ladies." The signs of Singleton's refinement actually intensified in the leisurely yet always genteel atmosphere of the springs. He became more intensely genteel in his manners, sociability, and devotion to harmony among the guests.[24]

In these conditions, making new friends and acquaintances came easily—so easily that one recently arrived visitor remarked that he had "more acquaintances now than I know what to do with." Genteel men and women always strove for harmony and affability, instead of the ceremony or coldness that would have destroyed the purpose of gentility as they viewed it. After criticizing a party from Baltimore for being "very little inclined to mix," Lucy W. Cocke recorded in her travel journal what could have served as the Virginia Springs motto: "At a place of this kind sociability is very desirable, every one should try and make themselves useful and contribute to the amusement of the company." [25]

The "harmonious and equitable enjoyment afforded to the visitors" no doubt added to the appeal of the springs for many guests and, more importantly, helped to strengthen the southern elite. The perceptions of intimacy and family, when added to the emphasis upon sociability, made the southern elite more cohesive by easing relations and promoting strong ties among these wealthy and influential men and women. With each visitor "having nothing more depending on them than the other, and all placed on the same footing, having the same conveniences & inconveniences to bear," one perceptive woman realized, "you become interested, and attached." Attachments made at the springs could have lasting importance. [26]

For many, the very "southernness" of the springs guaranteed a pleasant stay. These visitors believed that gentility, exclusivity, order, sociability, informality, and hospitality—the traits that the southern gentry saw in themselves—made the Virginia Springs into the premier place in the South. One Fauquier White Sulphur guidebook assured readers that a visit to the springs would be most agreeable because the gracious southern welcome, "'right hardy' and sincere," would instantly cause the visitor "to feel that he is not a stranger in a strange land," but in the "quiet and comfort of their own homes." Northern travelers also believed that they benefited from the southern ways of the springs. For one northern travel writer, "the infusion of the Virginian or southern element—a frank, cordial address and good humor—adds not a little to the pleasures of the northern visitors, who, with excellent intentions, are not remarkable for that ease of manner and confiding speech which invite intimacy." Thirty years earlier, Virginian Anne Royall ranked the Virginia Springs ahead of northern resorts because of their southernness and southern clientele. The "frank, open and sociable" Virginians, their "very agreeable" ladies, and the South Carolinians who were "still more so" drew out the "reserved and distant" northerners creating a harmonious community. The perceived "southernness" of intimacy, openness, and harmony served to ensure that southern hospitality and manners prevailed, easing the process of forming friendships and courtships and promoting a genial company. [27]

Precisely because of this harmonious atmosphere, some people viewed the Virginia Springs as a place to unite not only the South but also the entire Union. In 1844, Englishman George Featherstonhaugh remarked upon the usefulness of a place where visitors could, "by communicating to each other the information they bring from their respective countries, reciprocally enlarge their minds, carry home useful information, and become, in every sense of the word, more united as citizens of the same nation." In cabins, ballrooms, and other social spaces at the resorts, guests "from the different states" mingled; through these individual encounters, according to a visitor in 1838, "another link is added no doubt to the chains that bind together this mighty union." Since the "family" at the springs happily embraced northerners of the appropriate background, some northern visitors also acknowledged the potential benefits of the cross-sectional congregation at the springs. New Yorker Charles Hoffman believed that, "if the tour were more common with people of leisure from the north, it would tend much to root out the prejudices which three generations of pedlers have sown everywhere south of the Potomac and west of the Alleghanies." In 1851, as relations between North and South grew increasingly strained, Virginian William Burke pointed to the Virginia Springs resorts as the perfect place to overcome sectional animosities. An environment conducive to frank and easy conversation could "make the two great sections appreciate each other" and no longer alienate the South, "a generous, chivalric and warm-hearted portion of this great family of republics." Since southern generosity, chivalry, and warm-heartedness formed the basis of society at the Virginia Springs, surely, Burke and others believed, these attributes could provide the basis for national unity.[28]

For many visitors, England's Bath, Europe's Aix-la-Chappelle, or New York's Saratoga lacked "that calm repose, that freedom from restraint, that omission of conventional usages, which render the society of our Virginia Springs so delightful."[29] When exclusivity, order, a sense of leisure, and a commitment to gentility combined in their intense form at the Virginia Springs, they produced amity, informality, sociability, equality, and community. These characteristics assigned to the Virginia Springs by its devotees were the same traits the southern gentry tried to cultivate among themselves. It is no wonder that elite southern men and women felt so comfortable, so familial in such an environment.

☙

"Forming Violent Friendships in Three Days Time"

Most studies of plantation life suggest that, outside of their immediate families and households, elite southerners possessed few opportunities and little desire to interact with the opposite sex, much less to form close friendships. These historians conclude that a vast emotional gulf between men and women and a sharp segregation of daily lives prohibited mutual understanding and inhibited real intimacy.[1] At the Virginia Springs, however, the strict gender divisions of the plantation lessened and visitors encouraged interaction between men and women. Harmony generally characterized gender relations at the resorts. Men and women, married and unmarried, came together willingly, easily, and frequently. Seemingly in contrast to their lives the rest of the year, men and women easily became acquainted, thoroughly enjoyed each other's company, and frequently formed friendships with the opposite sex during summers at the springs. The clear divisions between men's and women's daily lives on the plantation almost disappeared at the springs, where a typical day included far more interactions with far more people of the opposite sex. Some of the plantation's rules of mixed-gender relations remained in force, but most of the forms were relaxed or changed. Since the competition for status rested upon genteel behavior and communal acclaim, rather than gender relations, interactions between men and women could be more relaxed and informal. Furthermore, an emphasis on leisure, nature, and pleasure promoted conviviality between the sexes and offered numerous opportunities for them to be together. Male and female visitors spent a good deal of time in each other's company, delighting in the daily social activities that promoted such mixing. They not only had fun together but also comfortably shared serious moments, thoughts, and feelings. While their closest bonds remained with members of their own sex, male and female visitors to the Virginia Springs happily participated in mixed-gender activities and easily socialized with members of the opposite sex.

If planter women and men usually worked and socialized separately at home, they experienced a rare mutuality in their daily regimens, activities, and attitudes at the Virginia Springs. Both male and female visitors took the waters in the same ways and felt similar effects. They shared similar experiences in nature and similar sentiments about the scenery that they viewed. They conversed together, talking comfortably about what were usually viewed as gender-specific topics. With only a few important exceptions, most of the social and recreational activities at the Virginia Springs, unlike at their homes, were not sex-segregated. The constant round of balls, card parties, picnics, and other social gatherings brought men and women together for amusement and conversation. Quieter pastimes also appealed to both men and women, including fishing in nearby streams and ponds.

Such games as tenpins, shuffleboard, and quoits brought the sexes together in physical competition. In 1854 Blanding DeSaussure proclaimed his delight at rolling tenpins with women during the day and waltzing "with the dear creatures" at night.[2]

Departing from customary nineteenth-century notions of appropriate female behavior, women at the springs fully and joyously participated with men in most of the sporting events at the resorts. In 1823 Larkin Newby competed with a Miss Dorsey in a shuffleboard tournament at Sweet Springs, noting that, outside the springs, women "do not usually play." Newby admitted that she "beat me a 'rubber' with the greatest ease!" Women also enjoyed playing tenpins. Rolling tenpins was "like indulging in an agreeable extravagance," providing Charlotte Ruffin and her female friends "much amusement." Each morning after breakfast, a "crowd of ladies" rolled tenpins during Anna Ritchie's stay at Fauquier White Sulphur. Ritchie found it amusing to watch some of the "expert players" "flinging the balls boldly, then standing erect to see what execution is done, while the blood mounts to the cheek, and exultation dances in the eyes." Women seemed to relish both participating with men in the games and sports that the resorts offered and receiving male and female attention during these activities. None of the visitors, male or female, regarded women's participation in these amusements and physical competitions as extraordinary or unfeminine enough to mention.[3]

A few activities remained exclusive to men. Male guests alone could take fencing and boxing lessons. Beginning in the late 1700s, gentlemen at the springs considered billiards a beneficial form of indoor recreation and a pleasant diversion. Small groups of men hunted on foot or horseback for deer, fox, or birds, often accompanied by servants and occasionally using hounds placed at their disposal by the proprietors. During his 1831 visit, Archie Harrison tramped about all day so "entirely devoted to field amusements" that his family only saw him "when he [came] in to prepare for meals." At Fauquier White Sulphur, Warm, and White Sulphur Springs, however, the grand, season-ending fox and deer hunts involved all of the guests—men and women. The men pursued the game on horseback, while the women rode along in carriages or on horses. These organized hunts were so popular, according to one travel guide, that every man "who likes, can join in this spirit-stirring sport, provided he owns, or can beg, borrow or steal a horse."[4]

Day and night, men and women—usually in mixed groups—took

walks or rode in carriages around the lawns, in the resort groves, and in nearby woods. Some rambled daily through the woods, enjoying and studying the flora and fauna that they found. And both men and women climbed nearby hilltops, mountain peaks, and rock outcroppings for the exercise and the views (fig. 15). Picnicking on such occasions was quite popular. "You never thoroughly understand the philosophy of the word pic nic, until you come here," one travel guide noted. "Ask a lady who has spent a summer at the White Sulphur to tell you." In the woods, groups of men and women dined sumptuously and sometimes drank champagne, danced, read poetry, or sang. Though thoroughly genteel, these ladies and gentlemen heartily enjoyed "sporting gayly in the midst of the wild mountains." Longer excursions to admire and explore various Indian mounds, Falling Spring, the Peaks of Otter, Weyer's Cave, and especially the Natural Bridge for an entire day or overnight became accustomed parts of a trip to the Virginia Springs for men and women (fig. 16). "Scarcely have we got through the rides and excursions of one day, ere new ones are proposed for the next," complained one guest in the 1830s: "'Miss —— has never been to Lewisburg, or Miss —— has never seen the cascade, or would like to see it again.'" The men and women who went on these excursions often an-

Figure 15. *View from the Hawks Nest,* Edward Beyer, *Album of Virginia,* 1858. (Special Collections Department, University of Virginia Library, Charlottesville)

Figure 16. *The Drums . . . Weyer Cave,* Edward Beyer, *Album of Virginia,* 1858.
(Special Collections Department, University of Virginia Library, Charlottesville)

ticipated and enjoyed the intimate socializing on the trip to these sights as
much as the sights themselves.[5]

The experiences that visitors shared at the Virginia Springs blurred the
lines that often separated men and women and fostered easy and enjoyable interactions between the sexes. Participating in the same regimen and
spending so much time together in the same social and recreational activities brought women and men physically and emotionally closer together,
making gender relations less divided and less problematic than at home. At
the Virginia Springs, men and women did not just spend time together,
however; they often formed close relationships. These relationships became
a significant part of a visitor's daily life at the springs. With friends and
acquaintances, men and women chatted, gossiped, exchanged accounts of
their bodily experiences, joked, flirted, tended one another, and shared personal feelings and thoughts. Such closeness and ease has been found by
historians studying other parts of the South only between husbands and
wives and friends of the same sex.[6]

The visitors' recorded exchanges and activities repeatedly reveal little sign of being uneasy with or alienated from the opposite sex. Few women showed any apprehension about interacting with so many men, and most men expressed their pleasure about the company of numerous women. Apparently neither men nor women sought acquaintances and friends only among members of their own sex. Writing to her future husband, Eliza Harwood, for example, reported that she had "made a number of very pleasant and agreeable female friends, and a few among the gentlemen." And both men and women wrote poems and other endearments in Eliza Cave's friendship book from Rockbridge Springs. Far from preferring their own sex, men and women worked to spend time with each other and arranged activities that allowed them to do so. J. K. Lee boasted to his sister that he had met "a great many" ladies at the resorts and was "constantly going from morning to night, first with one & then with another."[7]

At the springs, the unique environment, the common experiences, and the easy interactions allowed friendships to form quickly between male and female visitors who had not even known each other a few days earlier. William Elliott's "Girls" enjoyed themselves "in earnest" at the springs, "forming violent friendships in three days time" with both men and women. Many women spent almost as much time with their male as with their female friends. As a young widow in the summer of 1816, Louisa Maxwell Holmes came to the Virginia Springs from Norfolk with her sister and brother-in-law but spent much of her time alone with male friends. "In the afternoon," she wrote in her diary, "I was surprised by a visit while I was sitting alone in my Cabin, from Dr. Lewis, & Mr. Goodwin," two men whom she had met just the day before. Dr. Lewis quickly became a close friend. One day when she was "in too bad spirits" to enjoy a conversation with a group of women, Holmes went to the spring where she "had the pleasure of finding Dr. L[ewis] with whom I took a long walk through the woods." Upon their return, she found that two more male friends had arrived, helping to boost her spirits even further. While these relationships may not have been as intimate as those between same-sex friends, they were close enough and comfortable enough to permit discussions of a wide range of personal matters. Jane Caroline North quickly became close friends with the brother of Isaetta Coles, a new female friend. He hoped over the next two weeks to "understand" her "character." Holmes discussed religion and the afterlife with Dr. Lewis and felt free enough with him, though a relative stranger and a man, to express "my sentiments very freely on the subject." Again and again, female and male visitors recorded conversations with members of the opposite sex that included self-revelations as well as social chitchat. These exchanges were warm and pleasant, not strained and aloof. Unless they felt that a friendship had progressed further toward a romance than they desired, women delighted in becoming friends with male visitors and spending time with them. Such friendships were often rekindled whenever they saw each other again, whether at the springs, in towns, or at home.[8]

While participating in these activities, women and men often stepped beyond the prescribed limits of genteel gender relations. Yet their reputations remained intact since spa society permitted temporary transgressions as a part of the springs experience. Supposedly reserved husbands and wives mixed with single persons as easily and frequently as they did with other married men and women. A Mrs. Stanard was "a very good companion *for the Springs*," according to H. B. Tomlin, but she was "too fond of admiration for a married Lady and too *easy* manners" by the standards of the real world. Married men entertained and complimented single women. While unmarried, both Louisa Maxwell Holmes and Jane Caroline North took walks, played cards, talked, and danced with married men. With his wife at home, Edwin Jeffress spent an entire evening chatting and playing music with a male friend and a group of five sisters. Married men also squired married women whose husbands were absent. Taking "the ladies—sometimes married ones, at others single"—for carriage rides composed part of the typical day that Samuel Hoffman described to his wife. And, in accordance with the courtly cavalier tradition, married women had their trains of unmarried male attendants. Charles Bruce "found some amusement" in watching a Mr. Quitman, his wife, and her attending "cavalier." Bruce noted that the husband, whom he described as "amply large," watched the children, while "the knave guards the wife."[9]

Occasionally married visitors' interactions with unmarried ones went beyond the normal limits of "polite" conversation, but not beyond the relaxed standards of the springs. After returning home from a summer at the springs, South Carolinian Blanding DeSaussure knowingly informed a friend, "At one time there were fifteen married women at the springs whose husbands were in Washington so judge what a time we had, flirting &c." "In the absence of his beloved spouse," Hill Carter "appear[ed] to have taken quite a fancy" to Louisa M. Collins. She confessed to a friend of "the *prodigious flirtation* that is going on between us. . . . 'Tis most shocking; and *worthy of France*." Normally decorous matrons even engaged in flirtations with married men at the springs. Mildred Halsey playfully informed her husband that she had been *"regularly courted* to day, by Gov: Foot, and as I could not accept during your lifetime, reserved an interest, in the *event of becoming a widow.*" Similarly, Alexander H. H. Stuart warned his wife that, unless he received a letter from her, he would "fall in love with Mrs Riggs. Her husband will not be any obstacle for he is never with her." [10]

The relaxed gender relations and rules for visiting at the springs allowed socializing in unusual places. When married or single women entertained men in their bedrooms, especially if unchaperoned, they violated one of the most stringent rules of southern society. At home, these women would have found it very difficult to redeem their reputations after such a misstep. But most springs visitors evinced no concern about spending time alone with members of the opposite sex and apparently suffered no social stigma following such occasions. Often Louisa Maxwell Holmes and her attractive single roommate Miss Peacham were the only women in a group of six or seven and felt at ease. On many occasions, they strolled to nearby resorts or rode out on horseback accompanied by several gentlemen. When Miss Peacham or other women were not around, Holmes often chatted in her cabin or went on walks with one or two men. She even "rode on horseback with Mr. R.[,] Mr. W. & two other gentlemen to visit a cave not far distant" without any other women present.[11] Though gender relations were relaxed at the springs, these women and men always remained ladies and gentlemen. They may have had more freedom in their behavior toward the opposite sex than at home, but they almost never abandoned polite conduct and refined manners.

The easing of gender relations at the springs did have its limits. Spa society relaxed some rules concerning male-female interactions, but left others intact. On rare occasions, men and women took advantage of the lowered barriers between the genders and the easy mingling between married men and women at the springs. These rare transgressions demonstrate that spa society still saw a clear demarcation between the relaxed rules of the springs and socially unacceptable behavior. During the height of the 1832 season, South Carolina congressman Joel R. Poinsett and a Mrs. Woolsey Rogers of New York caused, according to Samuel Hoffman, "every body in this quarter" to be "open mouthed." Since Mr. Rogers had returned to New York, Poinsett had escorted Mrs. Rogers and two young ladies from Charleston to the springs. At Warm Springs, Poinsett and Mrs. Rogers shared the same cabin, ostensibly sleeping in separate but adjoining bedrooms. The two young ladies were placed, "on this and subsequent occasions," in rooms "distant from the Amours." At Salt Sulphur and Red Sulphur, the party had similar lodgings. The couple's "deportment" at these two resorts, according to Hoffman, "was that of Man and Wife—the *chambermaids* believing them to be such." Hoffman left unstated whether the servants had been questioned on this matter or had volunteered the information. He also noted that the two young ladies "expressed their abhorrence of the lovers deportment" but not whether they had made their feelings public (which is unlikely) or offered them to someone in confidence. Unwilling to "propogate scandal," he cautioned his wife not to reveal this piece of rich gossip to anyone in Baltimore. Still, he remained confident that the news would spread throughout the South by other means. The affair, Hoffman and the other springs visitors who discussed it predicted, would "effectually down Poinsett." [12] They proved wrong. In 1837 President Martin Van Buren appointed Poinsett secretary of war. Whether or not it "downed" Mrs. Rogers remains unknown.

At the Virginia Springs, women and men interacted with little stiffness or formality and within established, if relaxed, rules for genteel ladies and gentlemen. Gender relations at the resorts showed that women and men, whether married or not, took pleasure in being with one another and felt comfortable sharing their private thoughts. These casual, and often close, mixed-gender relationships lacked the inequality and hierarchy common in many women's relationships with their male family members, but still conformed to the expectations for relations between ladies and gentlemen. At the springs, visitors made acquaintances and friends of the opposite sex for purely pleasurable reasons. When she eventually parted from friends—old and new, male and female—who had "become very dear to me indeed," Louisa Maxwell Holmes's "tears flowed abundantly." [13]

∾

"You Might Have Supposed Them All Quite Intimate"

Even though men and women who visited the Virginia Springs shared a remarkable mutuality, their experiences differed in some ways; women enjoyed more leisure than men and experienced a sharper contrast with their lives at home. At the springs, planter women enjoyed a release from their duties and a freedom of movement and behavior unknown at home.

Planter men rarely forgot about their affairs at home, though they easily combined business and pleasure on their trips. This continued attention to business and their duties afforded male visitors less leisure and relaxation at the springs than women—a striking reversal from home. Perhaps more importantly, the springs environment allowed both men and women, in various ways, to build their own distinct communities. For southern women, a trip to the springs offered a rare opportunity to meet or reunite with female relatives, friends, and acquaintances from across the South. In the same way, visits to the springs permitted men to meet with other men, allowing them to form or renew vital economic and political connections and close friendships. By reuniting at the springs and renewing their bonds, the men and women of the southern elite strengthened not only their same-sex communities, but also their collective power and collective identity.

Whether in search of health or pleasure, most female visitors delighted in the change of scene and the leisurely pace of resort life. A trip to the Virginia Springs offered an escape for plantation mistresses and other elite women from the routine, boredom, and duties of their daily lives. Despite their often-romanticized image, planter women led a life of little leisure. While slaves undoubtedly worked harder physically than the white women on a plantation, mistresses spent much of their day supervising and assisting their slaves with domestic chores. Such duties prevented Louisa Cocke from accompanying her husband John to the springs in 1822. She had "Children to teach, and cloth to weave, & poultry to raise, and the Kitchen and Dairy, and Store Room & Dining room to attend to," John explained to a friend. The chance to exchange the work and tedium of life on a plantation, or even life in a southern town, for the excitement and novelty of the Virginia Springs led many southern women to long for the start of the resort season and a trip over the mountains. In order "to accomodate the professors wives & daughters" who wished to "frolic over at the springs" at the height of the season, the University of Virginia's Board of Visitors revised the summer vacation schedule in 1826.[1]

The southern women who traveled to the springs sought relief from daily domestic responsibilities, not from their families and marriages, unlike some of the female patients at northern water-cure establishments.[2] Female visitors regarded the springs as a place to reunite with family rather than to escape from it. While a few women went without male family members, propriety prohibited an elite white woman from traveling without a male escort, so most were accompanied by a husband, brother, or son at least. The pleasures of the springs easily persuaded a husband or other male relative to act as an escort. Most women traveled with multiple family members, and mothers regularly brought at least one child if not the whole brood. In 1850 Courtney Cocke worried about "carrying her 7 children to the Springs," but she and her husband could not leave their loved ones behind. Unless seriously ill, children usually caused little trouble as most families brought along a slave to look after them. Judging from the early disappearance of children from their letters and diaries, most mothers apparently felt quite free of parental and, more generally, domestic duties. But mothers and daughters did not entirely forget their responsibilities. Even as they enjoyed the company at the springs, they still wrote home frequently, informing those at home of the health and activities of the travelers and inquiring after those left behind, especially the children. Mistresses also occasionally sent instructions to husbands or servants concerning specific domestic matters under their responsibility that might need attention. Still, after giving her daughter directions to sell fowl and purchase cider, Elizabeth Noel added, "I try not to think any more about home than I can help."[3]

Even when children, husbands, or other family members accompanied them, women at the springs cherished the reprieve from their daily responsibilities and the opportunity to relax. Running a household sharply constrained women's leisure time while at home. At the springs, women probably enjoyed more free time than during the rest of the year. After returning home from a wonderful trip, Mary Thompson fondly recalled the "happiness" that she "enjoyed in the mountains, where I never saw a key except the one belonging to my chamber door, and where I never thought of dinner or breakfast until I heard the bell which summoned me to partake. Where I could read several hours every day, and take two long walks, and in the interim have a few pleasant friends to talk with." Thompson realized "the value of [her] present blessings" both at the time and, even more forcefully, upon her return home. "Not for twenty years" had she "enjoyed such repose, such *rest,* such bodily health and such happiness."[4]

Similarly, many women experienced a new sense of freedom from traditional restraints on their behavior while at the springs. Genteel gender conventions prescribed decorous behavior for ladies, especially married women. While at the resorts, however, married and unmarried women engaged in behavior that would have normally seemed improper. Female visitors took pleasure in the bodily freedom and sensations of the baths. And they interacted freely and easily with men. Judging from visitors' accounts, moreover, some women apparently drank more alcohol at parties and picnics at the springs than at home. The British traveler James S. Buckingham noted that the women at the springs showed "more than a feminine share of taste for juleps, cordials, and champaigne." At a ladies' luncheon, the hostess, to a northern woman's "amazement," presented a large tray of mint juleps and "*hoped* her company were as fond of them as she was." Needless to say, the luncheon "passed off agreeably." Finding the "incentives to liberty and enjoyment" at the springs "irresistible," women happily spent entire days outside—strolling, hiking, climbing, riding, fishing, picnicking, and playing lawn games. Plantation or town mistresses' domestic responsibilities rarely allowed for a whole day spent at such enjoyable outside activities. Some may have found time for short morning rides or evening walks, and young unmarried women certainly had more opportunities than their mothers for outdoor recreation at home. But, at the springs, single and married, old and young women all took advantage of the myriad opportunities for outdoor amusements and exercise.[5]

A few women displayed their sense of freedom from traditional expectations about a lady's behavior in truly exceptional ways. In 1791 a group of women at Bath challenged each other to a race on horseback. Sometime before 1840, Mary Randolph became legendary when she rode her horse to the craggy summit of a mountain and tied her handerkerchief to a tree. Over eighteen years later, one visitor reported that "in honor of her heroic horsemanship they have kept continually moving 'pon the tree the little white flag." In 1839 James Buckingham heard a story of a young lady who, while standing on one foot upon a tree trunk at the edge of a precipice, "turned herself round three times, waving her handkerchief in the air, giving three huzzas for Georgia, her native State, and challenging, as she might safely do, the other States of the Union to produce a lady who would beat this." Impressed with her courage, Buckingham called her "the Amazon of the West."[6]

The freedom to move about the individual resorts and the springs district unescorted struck female visitors as one of the greatest changes from life at home. While most women relied upon husbands, sons, brothers, uncles, or male family friends to get from home to the springs, once they made it over the mountains they often went around the resorts alone or in groups of only women. Once at White Sulphur, a Mrs. Starke became "too busy" to attend to her husband, for she knew "everybody and [was] going all the time." One older unmarried woman returned calls by herself; as there were plenty of other single women doing the same thing, she did not feel "conspicuous in [her] maidenhood." This unaccustomed freedom of movement thrilled many women. Eliza Harwood declared that Fauquier White Sulphur was "a famous place to display an independent spirit. The ladies go about from one place to another without seeming to mind it at all; it makes no difference whether to the ballrooms or the dinner table." Indeed, it was "a common occurrence to see half a dozen ladies marching about entirely unattended." Some women went off on excursions by themselves or with a party solely of women. In 1807 Sarah Brunet provided herself "some little amusement" by climbing Warm Springs mountain alone. Over fifty years later, Mildred Halsey, a "Mrs. G.," and two young ladies walked in the moonlight without a male attendant from Red Sweet to Sweet Springs. Men could always travel by themselves; but the opportunity to move about on their own was one of the special charms of resort life for women.[7]

Surprisingly, given the prescriptive restrictions on elite southern women's mobility, a few women had little choice but to move about the springs unescorted when no man had accompanied them. These women seemingly felt unashamed about traveling with their mothers, aunts, or other female companions. In 1837 John C. Rutherfoord's sister visited the springs with her aunt. Every summer, a Mrs. Taylor of Norfolk spent over two months with her three young children at the springs, apparently without her husband. Some husbands brought their wives to the resorts before leaving on business in the area. Joseph Cabell and other circuit court judges often left their families at White Sulphur while they held court in the area. Other wives stayed at the springs while their husbands traveled to Washington, D.C. In 1854, Blanding DeSaussure reported flirting with fifteen married women whose husbands were in the nation's capital.[8] In 1834 Henry Clay sent his ailing wife Lucretia to White Sulphur, accompanied by their young grandson and a servant. He hoped that the owner of the springs and his good friend James Caldwell would "take good care" of her and noted that he had provided her "with a sum which, accidents excepted, will be sufficient for her whole journey." Years later, Clay's friend William Mercer left his daughter and two other young ladies at White Sulphur while he went on to Cape May, New Jersey.[9] The presence of a substantial number of unaccompanied women at the springs attests to a more generous sphere of women's movement than historians have found elsewhere in the South.

Even though women at the springs experienced a freedom from responsibility and of movement unknown at home, many still succumbed to traditional prescriptions of male control over their movements. When the male head of a party had to leave early or unexpectedly, it often necessitated finding a suitable male relative, friend, or acquaintance who could take charge of the women and children in his party. In 1817, for example, Randolph Ross assured John Preston that he would come to Richmond as soon as he could "in propriety" leave his wife at the springs. Many women submitted to the convention while finding it a bother. From White Sulphur, Mildred Halsey complained to her husband: "It is trouble to have our movements governed by others—If I were only a man I should be off tomorrow." [10]

While women escaped from most of their home responsibilities at the springs, men did not. At home, planter men had more control over their time and thus more free time than their wives. In their social and agricultural activities, they combined work with leisure. At the Virginia Springs, planters and professional men often continued to combine business and pleasure. Circuit judge Alexander H. H. Stuart visited White Sulphur in the course of his duties in the area. Philip St. George Ambler incorporated an excursion to Warm and White Sulphur Springs into a business trip to western Virginia in 1829. Though it was disagreeable to him, James Bruce had to keep up with his business correspondence while relaxing at the springs. Taking advantage of the presence of a large number of wealthy planters, horse traders often brought herds of quality carriage or riding horses to sell in the springs area. And George Hancock struck a profitable cattle deal while at Sweet Springs in 1805. Some men even made arrangements for buying or selling slaves while at the springs. Thomas Walker Gilmer negotiated the sale of a friend's slave, who had been hired by Warm Springs, with an Alabaman in search of a body servant. In 1860 Horace Hunley arranged to purchase "three or four negroes" while at Montgomery White Sulphur for his brother-in-law, Robert Ruffin Barrow of Louisiana. [11]

Except for the young men who caroused and courted women, male visitors usually worried about their crops and other affairs throughout their stay. For the principal southern crops, the fall harvest began during the height of the springs season in late August and early September. Most planters kept in regular contact with overseers, friends, or family members about the weather, crop prices, and farm operations. During his stay in September 1858, for example, Georgian William Mackay sent his overseer "an order to get a Two Horse power Threshing machine should the Harvest be so successful as to warrant it." While at the springs, many husbands relied on wives who remained at home, believing them perfectly capable of handling plantation matters in their absence. They sent instructions to their wives for their overseers and slaves, fully expecting the workers to obey the mistress as their surrogate. In 1808, in a letter from the springs, Nicholas Cabell gave his wife Peggy detailed farm instructions, including how wide to plow the fields. Almost fifty years later, while at Red Sulphur, Richard Burroughs directed his wife Caroline to watch the prices for wheat, to sell it at a certain price, to set aside a fixed amount for seed, and to store it in a specific place. He also told her how to wean cows and repair outbuildings.[12] Planters also frequently inquired about how well their slaves worked in their absence. Sometimes those at home gave them reason to worry. Two of William Pettigrew's slave overseers, Moses and Henry, kept him abreast of plantation matters during his long stay at the springs in 1856. Henry must have caused Pettigrew great concern when he wrote: "I have some secrets to tell master but I will keep them untill master comes home[,] you will excuse this master."[13]

Like wives and mothers, husbands and fathers missed and worried about family members. When away from home, men wanted regular news about their family's welfare. Their letters home reveal a sincere concern and love for their wives, children, and other family members. Indeed, men cherished their families as much as women did. Larkin Newby declared to his wife of seventeen years that he had never realized how much he loved her until their separation. He felt like "some love-sick swain," thinking about her "all the day" and dreaming of her "every night." While at the springs, Benjamin Temple missed "those feelings of fond security" with his wife's arms around him "in our own bed & under our own comfortable roof." These men felt keenly their role as protector and head of the family and sought constant reassurances that their loved ones remained well. "Its the hardest effort to turn myself from home, from thinking of you[,] my babies[,] my business &c.," Willis Williams confessed to his wife. Many of these husbands vowed to return to the springs with their wives, if not their entire families, in tow.[14]

Male visitors to the springs did not feel the same release from traditional gender conventions as female visitors. Many men could not relin-

quish the responsibilities of being a gentleman who protected, and sometimes controlled, their wives, children, and other female relatives. But for
his mother and sisters, James C. Bruce would have left White Sulphur early:
"[I] should be ashamed to leave them in the mountains without a protector
as they have kindly proposed." "In delaying my departure so long," he
explained to his wife, "I feel that I am in the line of my duty"—a sacred
duty for an elite southern male.[15] The protection of women by men at the
springs sometimes extended to a woman's health regimen. Husbands, fathers, or male friends often directed a woman's use of the waters. John
Faulcon, for example, assured his in-laws that he saw "daily, nay hourly . . .
sure evidences of the rapid amendment in [the] Health" of his wife Louisianna midway through the regimen he had settled upon for her. Three
weeks later, however, George Harrison found Louisianna Faulcon to be "in
wretched health, aggravated it is said by the imprudent use she made of the
water here, in consequence of the advice of her sapient husband."[16] Even
though they relaxed at the springs, many men could not relax their expectations of themselves as protectors.

At the Virginia Springs, women and men created, renewed, and
strengthened social networks and personal ties with members of their own
sex. Elite southern women used the springs to reunite and renew bonds
with distant female friends and relatives. They also met and formed bonds
with new female acquaintances from all across the South and even the
North. Female visitors enjoyed being in the company of a large group of
women who shared similar concerns and provided support for those who
were unwell. The Virginia Springs functioned as one of the sites where elite
southern women could build such bonds with one another. Resorts, academies, towns, visits, and letters provided the vehicles by which these women
created and sustained communal networks that extended beyond their
households and neighborhoods. A community of elite women existed in
the antebellum South that centered around not only female kin and neighbors but also close friends and acquaintances scattered throughout the
South. Many elite southern women considered themselves a part of this
community—a member of an intimate, if large, circle of female friends
and relatives with whom they shared the joys and sorrows of life and gained
a sense of themselves as privileged white women.[17] While planter women
had no interest in extending their networks across class or race lines, they
did form relationships with women like themselves across geographic lines
and outside their households and families. They did not have to share
bonds of communality with yeoman or slave women to believe that they

belonged to a female community. While a planter woman's primary identity came from her family, that identity did not prevent the formation of close ties or a feeling of connectedness with other women. Because of meeting places such as the Virginia Springs, southern women's networks included not only neighbors and kin but also old schoolmates, new acquaintances, resort friends, and other women from across the region.

Planter women cherished this communality with other women and considered it a crucial part of their lives. Yet elite southern women almost never regarded these bonds as the basis upon which to organize formally in order to challenge their society through feminism or abolitionism.[18] Though they recognized and perhaps resented many of the constraints upon their lives, these women enjoyed the privileges of their wealth and status. Instead of organizing for change, southern women created a community based upon common interests, sentiments, and rituals and a common place in southern society. They formed relationships with other women to broaden their emotional and practical support networks, not to broaden their sphere relative to men's. While these women held many of the same values and attitudes as their husbands, fathers, and brothers, they considered their female networks very important. At the same time, their involvement in this women's community and in close, supportive same-sex relationships did not preclude strong friendships with men or easy participation in the heterosocial atmosphere of the Virginia Springs.

Traveling to the Virginia Springs comprised just one part of an array of visits, trips, and correspondence that created and sustained the extensive women's community throughout the year. In combination, these links to other women kept the plantation from being a place of isolation, at least in the more settled areas of the South.[19] Women paid each other long visits during the spring and summer and at holidays as well as for weddings, illnesses, and childbirths. And they spent time with each other during trips to the Virginia Springs in the summer and to large towns and cities in the late winter social season. The steady flow of letters between women kept these bonds strong until the next visit.[20] Connection and contact, not isolation and solitude, characterized the lives of planter women. While they occasionally expressed a sense of loneliness in letters to friends and family, such professions usually came in between visits and trips, when they were no longer surrounded by women. But these very letters, like their other correspondence with women, helped to alleviate these feelings of solitude even as they maintained the bonds of community between elite southern women.

Many factors combined to create these bonds among female visitors at the Virginia Springs. A simple desire for each other's company, especially that of old friends and relatives, brought many women to the springs. Emily Rutherfoord and her cousin Isaetta Coles "were scarcely ever separated" while at the springs; "indeed we could scarcely have been happier." Mary Randolph Harrison and her female friends "were constantly together" during their stay and hoped "to meet again at the Sweet Springs."[21] Female visitors' common concern about health, open discussion of their bodies, and shared sensual experiences contributed to a greater feeling of intimacy in a shorter time than would have been possible at home.[22] At the springs, they found others who shared and understood their ills. Their sensuality was not only permitted but also encouraged. This physical openness unquestionably fostered an emotional closeness between women. At the baths, Catherine Hall, dressed only in her nightgown, became closely acquainted with a woman who wore only blankets. Hall's daughter entered the pool with "at least one dozen Ladies and children," and after five minutes "she had something to say to every one of them." When they met again in the drawing room, "you might have supposed them all quite Intimate."[23] The presence of so many women also provided a supportive environment for female invalids. In 1845 James Petigru brought his sickly daughter Caroline Carson to White Sulphur Springs. Before Caroline went to bed, Mrs. Bull Pringle and Mrs. Matt Singleton and her daughter came to offer assistance. Mrs. Singleton engaged a maid for Caroline and sent over a pheasant for dinner. Soon after, five more women, including the wife of Virginia's governor, called on the invalid.[24]

The extended leisure time and relaxed setting that women found at the springs, moreover, gave them valuable hours, rarely found at home, for getting to know each other and enjoying each other's company. In the mornings and afternoons, groups of women gathered in parlors or on porches to converse, offer advice, sew, sing, and sometimes dance together. They often took carriage rides around the resort or walked in the woods on sunny afternoons. Women quickly became close friends at the springs. When Ferdinand Bayard returned to the resort where he had left his wife, he found her "surrounded by tender hearted women." During her 1851 visit to Warm Springs, Jane Caroline North was introduced to a young lady in the morning. And "before night," North recorded in her journal, she "was so intimate as to relate me all her tender experiences."[25] In general, younger, usually unmarried, women spent less time in homosocial circles than older, usually married, women. While her daughter spent much of her time with a young mixed crowd in the ballrooms, Volumina Barrow exercised and visited "among the ladies." She usually bathed, strolled the grounds, and walked to nearby sights with the same two married women. In 1812 Hannah Cabell informed her son that she had "met with some agreeable old acquaintances and made some new ones"—almost all of them married women. Mary Bolling's primary circle of friends at Hot Springs consisted of the wife of one of her husband's old schoolmates, "Mrs. Judge Cabble," and a Mrs. Abbot. The foursome used the "boiler" together daily.[26]

The heterosociality of the springs in no way hampered the efforts of women to create and strengthen ties with one another. Although women conversed, shared activities, and formed friendships with men as often as they did with women, their relationships with women were generally more intimate and intense than those with men. As often happened at academies, some young ladies became infatuated with each other at the springs, acting toward one another as they did with men during courtship. Virginia Heth thought that F. Caldwell was "the prettiest little creature I ever beheld." Caldwell looked "so artless, and innocent" that she "won" Heth's heart "completely."[27] Writing from Alum Springs, Helen Fitzhugh assured the recently departed Fanny Coalter that "none of the new comers have taken your place in my affections" and hoped that Fanny would "not let any one cut me out" at White Sulphur. "An eternal friendship" formed between Chloe Whittle and another young lady at Sweet Springs resulted in "a correspondence."[28]

The ties that female visitors established or strengthened at the resorts with women from outside their families and neighborhoods often extended beyond the springs in the form of letters and visits. "It was not without much real regret" that Louisa Cocke took "an affectionate leave of our good Mrs. Canty (who had been every thing to us)" when the 1837 season ended. The two maintained a correspondence after returning to their homes in Virginia and South Carolina. Like Louisa Cocke and Mrs. Canty, women often pledged to write or visit their new friends. Writing from home in October 1846, Bettie Fontaine remembered Martha Minor's charge not to forget her and their promise to visit each other. She assured Minor that it would afford her "the greatest pleasure to avail myself of some early opportunity to accept your kind invitation." In 1851 Sarah Gales Seaton affectionately parted from Jane Caroline North, declaring that she must visit the

Seatons in Washington. North also received "repeated & pressing invitations" to visit the Howell women in Columbia and to spend Christmas with a Mrs. Vanderhorst in Charleston. Four years later, her younger sister Lou was "quite inclined . . . to accept all the invitations made her."[29]

The informal gathering of elite women at the springs resulted in an expanded and strengthened women's network across the South. The Virginia Springs provided a leisurely place in which these women created and strengthened communal bonds with each other. These relationships proved important in the lives of planter women, connecting them to women far beyond their own neighborhoods and giving them a sense of belonging. Whether frolicking in the baths, gossiping in the parlors, or drinking mint juleps on their porches, female visitors enjoyed their leisurely time spent with other women.

As with women, the Virginia Springs fostered bonds of community among men. Southern men—planters and professionals—developed networks on a local level at many places, such as courthouses, on a state level at fewer places, such as assemblies, and on a regional level at only a handful of sites. With its large number of visitors from throughout the South, the Virginia Springs served as the premier gathering place for southern men. Men's social networks were wide and varied compared to women's, but they too benefited from coming together at the springs. Men often traveled to the resorts with other men and frequently made new friends and acquaintances. An already well-connected man could renew and extend his connections with men from his own state or across the South by visiting the resorts. In 1852 Virginian Robert Hubard became acquainted with at least ten men from seven different counties in Virginia, including "a fellow collegian of mine, whom I had not seen since we parted as good friends in 1826." Joining old friends and relatives, many of whom lived far away, made for a special occasion. William Rives hoped that his good friend John C. Rutherfoord would "make [his] indisposition an excuse for a visit to the Springs" in order to join him there. Rives proclaimed that, if Rutherfoord could be persuaded and if another friend "can be induced by your eloquence to join us, what a glorious 'time of it' we should have!" Pleading "come, come for God's sake, for my sake," Robert Taylor Scott entreated Charles Cooke and William Aylett to meet him at Fauquier White Sulphur in 1852. Reuniting with old college friends especially appealed to male visitors. Thomas Pollock spent much of his time at the springs "pleasantly employed in talking over old college friendships" with men from Yale and the

University of Virginia. Like women at the springs, men quickly became intimate with each other and treasured their new relationships. Samuel Hoffman and a new friend spoke "freely and confidentially at all times" and, along with several other male friends, moved "about together with mutual satisfaction." [30]

For many male visitors, the Virginia Springs served an economic function as an informal marketplace for goods and services. At the resorts, male visitors met with the leaders of southern society—politicians, doctors, lawyers, judges, large planters, and military officers—and sought their advice. Friends readily lent money to each other. Conversations kept them abreast of the latest news, especially in politics and agriculture. When his son John visited White Sulphur in 1836, Thomas Rutherfoord wanted him to learn "the state of the wheat Crop in most parts of our State, as you will see many intelligent Gentlemen there, from all parts of the country: I wish you therefore to obtain what information you can & to transmit it to me." [31] Rutherfoord knew the male community at the springs could serve as a valuable source of useful information.

Politics provided men with another source of contacts and connections at the Virginia Springs. Many men engaged in political discussions throughout their stay. Although Sarah Ashby gave her husband "orders" that he was not "to talk politics," he found it "hard to do" in the potentially volatile summer of 1860.[32] Male visitors discussed a wide range of state and national political matters, including both individual elections and candidates and larger issues, such as nullification, the tariff, and secession. On his annual trips to the springs in the late 1850s, for example, fire-eater Edmund Ruffin engaged influential southern men in conversations about disunion and slavery whenever possible, believing that he could persuade anyone. These conversations among men from across the South surely influenced voters' decisions.

At the resorts, politicians openly sought support among their male friends and acquaintances, who often invited them to give speeches. Visitors honored former and current presidents, congressmen, and judges with public dinners. In his published account of the springs, William Burke wondered, "Is there a Presidential nomination in agitation, where else can the aspirant play his card with equal success, or gather with more certainty, the probabilities for or against him?" During his many bids for the presidency, Henry Clay frequently used the Virginia Springs to garner support informally and congenially and to survey voter opinion, all the while appearing as a relaxed planter at leisure rather than a worried candidate at work. On his way to White Sulphur in 1832, Clay stopped to see Judge Francis T. Brooke, Governor James Barbour, and James Madison. While at the springs, he narrowly avoided his arch-enemy President Andrew Jackson. Society at the springs permitted electioneering, but frowned upon heated debates that could lead to incivilities. When a political convention met at White Sulphur to decide the Whig candidate for governor of Virginia in 1852, William Rives and James Lyons reportedly "indulged in some quite animated & personal remarks." But this ungenteel behavior created a sensation throughout the male community at the springs.[33]

The resorts often served as the setting for political events. The Whig Party held well-attended conferences at White Sulphur Springs in 1837 and 1841. At the latter meeting, men from "a large number [of] different States of the Union" adopted "several resolutions" condemning President John Tyler for vetoing the Bank Bill. In 1849 the Virginia legislature convened at Fauquier White Sulphur to revise Virginia's civil and criminal codes after fleeing Richmond in fear of an Asiatic cholera epidemic. The House of Delegates occupied the ballroom and the Senate took over Rowdy Hall, the bachelors' hotel. Keeping the congressmen at their important task proved difficult, as tenpins and billiards, the leisured atmosphere, the beautiful scenery, and the female company lured many away. Other political conventions and party meetings took place over the years at various resorts. The impact on southern or even national politics of large numbers of elite men coming together at the Virginia Springs, whether for formal political purposes or merely to exchange political opinions, can only be imagined.[34]

The 1860 season made clear the importance of the springs as a central meeting place for elite southern men. As tensions between North and South grew, southern visitors seized the opportunity to discuss their options for the future. Writing from White Sulphur in 1860, James L. Petigru informed a South Carolina friend that "the chief discourse, here, is about Lincoln, for the election is only another name for the topic that involves the many shades of opinion concerning the probable results of having such a President." One man offered to wager five thousand dollars that the Constitutional Unionist candidate John Bell would carry Kentucky—a winning bet if he found any takers. The Virginian Edmund Ruffin considered the springs the perfect place for fomenting discontent and building support for secession. In packing for his annual visit in 1860, Ruffin brought his "usual travelling supply of pamphlets" supporting southern rights and slavery.

When he arrived at White Sulphur, its sixteen hundred guests included South Carolina Senator James Chesnut, Richmond *Examiner* editor Patrick Henry Aylett, and Mississippi Governor William McWillie. According to Ruffin, "the prospects & reasons for a dissolution of the union" furnished "most of the subjects of conversation here among the men." Still, he found himself alone "as an avowed disunionist *per se*," though he declared his "disunion doctrines to all proper persons." As men had for decades, Edmund Ruffin and his influential friends believed that the Virginia Springs comprised one of the best places for elite southern men to come together physically, politically, and ideologically.[35]

The community of men at the springs did not revolve solely around business and politics, however. Like the members of the female community at the springs, male visitors also acted as caregivers, showing great concern for the health not only of wives and children but also of male friends. Many fathers interrupted busy schedules to take sick children to the springs or to meet them there. When Abram Cabell's father heard of his adult son's wretched state at the springs, he "sat off as soon as he could possibly make his arrangements for the journey." In turn, many sons accompanied sickly fathers to the springs. At Red Sulphur in 1808, John Edwards Caldwell noticed with pleasure Congressman John Wayles Eppes nursing his father. The son performed "the *double duty* of the most dutiful son, and the most affectionate friend" by "smoothing the bed of death, and gently tending the expiring lamp of the author of his being."[36]

A close and supportive relationship often developed between an ailing man and the male relative or friend who accompanied him to the springs. Edwin Jeffress and his "agreeable" roommate, Thomas Adams, enjoyed a mutually supportive relationship at the springs. "When I complain & begin to lament my condition," Jeffress noted in his diary, "he is my consoler & when he complains, which is more frequent than I do, I endeavor to console him." William Pettigrew spent the summer of 1856 attending James Cathcart Johnston, a longtime family friend, at various resorts. As Pettigrew explained to his sister, "my time [is] entirely at the disposal of my excellent friend whose happiness & welfare I desire to promote." Attending each other in sickness was as much a part of the men's community as the women's at the Virginia Springs.[37]

The friendships and other connections that men formed at the Virginia Springs often served them well after the end of the season. As with the women's community, visits and letters sustained and strengthened the men's community throughout the rest of the year. After one trip, John Cocke promised to send "Gooseberry Cuttings[,] Sea Kale seed & Hudson bay strawberry plants" to male friends he had met at the springs.[38] Political, economic, and social ties established during a summer at the springs bound men together later at their homes. The men who traveled over the mountains valued the community of men at the Virginia Springs—a community that discovered its common interests and strengthened its common bonds each season.

Many visitors—male or female—would have agreed with one travel writer's assertion that the friendships formed at the Virginia Springs "by persons who are strangers on their first meeting, are generally of the most agreeable and endearing kind, and often the most lasting."[39] The enjoyment of one another's company, the friendships renewed or formed, and the connections established at the Virginia Springs broadened and solidified both women's and men's networks in the South.

℘

"You Are Now Just Entering upon That School of Life"

The atmosphere at the springs provided the perfect place where young men and women could, perhaps for the first time, socialize with a large group of their peers from across the South. These "beaux" and "belles" became the pulse of the resorts, the driving force behind most of the social life and competition. A season at the springs served for many planter children as a part of their entrance into adulthood. Like most people their age, the young ladies and gentlemen excitedly watched and carefully assessed each other. Young adult visitors formed their own social circle at the resorts. They modified some of the normal rules of genteel society and indulged in their own modes of behavior. At the springs, young women and men learned and practiced interacting with the opposite sex as adults in a social setting unlike any that they would encounter at home.

Many southern adults considered the Virginia Springs an excellent arena for their young people to embark upon a new stage of life. The springs could serve as a "school" in which to instruct young men and women in the lessons of southern gentility and gender relations. The gathering of people from all over the South, parts of the North and West, the

Caribbean, and Europe made the Virginia Springs the ideal place to observe adult society, manners, and fashion. In the view of many parents, moreover, the socially homogeneous world of the springs made it an especially safe one in which to introduce gentry youth, particularly young ladies, fully into southern society. In 1840 Alexander H. H. Stuart promised his three little daughters that "when you get large enough, I mean to bring you out to spend some time" at the springs, for they were "a very pleasant place for young ladies & gentlemen."[1] Standing at the threshold of their entrance into adult society, young visitors could learn much in such an environment. At the springs, as their parents knew, young men and women would witness southern genteel society at its most intense. Parents expected their children to watch and learn from the fashionable society that surrounded them. They hoped to see their children put into practice the lessons of gentility that they had learned at home and at academies. For many planter youths, a trip to the Virginia Springs was a critical step in their ritualized entrance into adult society.

Some parents explicitly informed their children that they expected the Virginia Springs to be a place of socialization. Even though he disliked the frivolity of spa life, the evangelical John H. Cocke encouraged his older children, especially his daughters, to visit the springs. When his youngest daughter, Sally, made her first trip in 1833 at the age of seventeen, Cocke advised her: "You are now just entering upon that school of life, where all you have been acquiring at your former schools is to be turned to account." He knew that she would find at the resorts "the most instructive subjects of observation." While urging her "to [be] shrude" "without being cynical," Cocke warned that "while you mark the follies of the Vanity-Fair in which you are participating, take care that you do not make yourself the just subject of con[sideration] to some shruder observer than yourself."[2] Almost twenty years later, his daughter-in-law, Lucy Cocke, offered similar advice to her daughters: "This is one of the best places I know for one to study human nature, one meets with persons of all characters and dispositions."[3]

Virginia's Rutherfoord family also considered a trip to the springs important in the coming of age of planter youth. When John C. Rutherfoord admitted to his parents that he had become "'a Ladies man'" at the springs, his father assured him that both he and his mother "think that nothing is better calculated to refine and polish a youth then the company of the Ladies, whether the conversation be learned and profound, or playful and gay." Indeed, it was probably to receive exactly this kind of social refinement that they had encouraged their son to make the trip. The father hoped that his son would continue "to cultivate" the society of ladies, for "nothing is better calculated to impart proper self-possession."[4] He trusted that what his son learned at the springs would serve him well in his future as a southern gentleman.

It was not only Virginians who viewed the Virginia Springs experience as beneficial to youths. Henry D. Mandeville Sr. of Natchez, Mississippi, accompanied his son on an extended tour of the springs, introducing him to friends from throughout the South, encouraging his acquaintance with numerous young ladies, and taking pride in watching him make use of all of the social graces he had learned.[5] Throughout the South, elite parents believed that the Virginia Springs provided the best place for young unmarried men and women of the plantation and town gentry to socialize with a large number of their peers and be socialized into elite southern society.

While their parents expected them to take away valuable lessons from their springs trips, young visitors apparently put little conscious effort into drawing these lessons. They mainly sought pleasure—both in amusements and in the company of the opposite sex—amidst the largest gathering of their peers in the South. Deeply concerned about their appearance, they brought fashionable clothing and paid particular attention to their comportment, knowing that they would be competing with one another for attention and acclaim. Whether male or female, young single visitors to the springs expressed an interest in meeting people of their own age, getting to know one another, flirting, and possibly finding romance. They especially sought freedom from close supervision by adults. Many of the young men and women had spent time at same-sex academies and arrived at the springs ready for the new social realm of mixed-gender friendships, flirtations, and courtship. They had an enjoyable time laughing, talking, joking, strolling, and dancing. At White Sulphur, Henry Mandeville Jr. declared one week to be "one of the gayest in my personal annals for years." Between the "Fancy Ball, and the constant association with pleasant women, morning walks, and evening flirtations," he had been "swept into a whirl of excitement." The belles' and beaux's constant search for pleasure provided the driving force behind much of the conviviality, romanticism, and social "whirl" at the Virginia Springs.[6]

Within the larger community of visitors at the springs, belles and beaux formed their own community of young people, with their own modified set of rules for personal behavior. For many young adult visitors, their days at the springs signaled their first social experience out from under their parents' or relatives' watchful eyes. While they learned and followed most of the rules of proper society, they did not allow these strictures to prevent them from having fun with each other. Perhaps most importantly, in this mixed-gender environment, the young adults were also socialized by *each other.* They not only learned the rules, rituals, and behavior befitting ladies and gentlemen from their parents but also educated each other in gender-role expectations. Their own youth culture, not just the culture of their parents, provided them with models of social success and failure.

Away from their parents' scrutiny, young visitors conducted themselves according to rules that blended those of traditional genteel society with those established by their own peer group. Like most of the visitors, they strove to appear as refined ladies and gentlemen, but they placed an even greater emphasis upon romantic and carefree behavior and sentiments. Young visitors sanctioned more private, unchaperoned interaction between couples than their parents would have allowed at home. Henry Mandeville Jr., for example, happily pursued a series of "little romance[s]" with various young women while on secluded morning walks or after the evening dances. In a letter after they parted at the springs, John Rutherfoord reminisced with Ann Roy about "the moonlit portico, the deserted parlour—those morning and evening walks—that rustic seat beneath the leaning sycamore." Young visitors also assumed, and accepted, that courting couples would engage in more intimate behavior than permitted by polite society. When one young woman ended up in the carriage of an engaged couple on a trip to view mountain scenery, some of her friends considered her "an object of pity" as they assumed that the couple's intimacy might make her uncomfortable. Much to the woman's relief and surprise, the couple "behaved themselves *properly.*" While these young visitors stretched the rules of their parents, they rarely violated them directly. For example, even though one young man possessed "every facility for falling in love" with a woman at his dining table, it proved an obstacle that he had "*not been introduced to her yet.*" [7]

Elite young men spent much of their time at the springs indulging in the pleasures typical of their age, status, and gender. They flirted with pretty girls, drank heavily, gambled late into the night, and bragged about sexual encounters. On a tour through the United States in the early 1830s, two

English ministers met with some youths at the springs who "were pursuing pleasure in the gratification of their passions, and were mortified to find themselves still displeased and miserable." Just as in towns and on plantations, gentlemen-in-training at the springs were permitted to participate in these more dissipated pursuits, causing little conflict within spa society as long as they refrained from doing so in the presence of ladies, especially young ones. Those who went beyond the bounds of acceptable public behavior received severe condemnation. When a "Mr. S" "carried his merriment so far as to fire pistols whilst in bed" or when an "intoxicated" Joe Alston "behaved badly in the ball room," especially by "insulting a gentleman in the presence of a lady," spa society quickly censured them.[8]

Many of the resorts had a row of cottages designated for bachelors in order to isolate less-acceptable behavior. At White Sulphur, the row received the nickname "Wolf Row." One man warned that only those "young and foolish—fond of noise and nonsense, frolic and fun, wine and wassail, sleepless nights, and days of headache" should stay in this row's cabins, for "Mercury and Nimrod have taken up their abode there, and Macbeth-like, nightly murder sleep." Particular bachelor activities, such as sexual experimentation, certainly happened with more frequency than recorded in letters and diaries. It is rare to find a comment such as Robert Taylor Scott's boast to a friend: "I resisted the charms of all the young ladies at the Springs, (*the ladies of colour, of course* excepted)." In 1827 F. R. Bolling and four college companions "frolicked so much at the White Sulphur and lost so much sleep" due to "surrounding pleasures, and sensual amusements" that, he confessed to his parents, "it was rather disadvantageous than otherwise" to his health. Still, his parents did not call him home. South Carolinian Blanding DeSaussure engaged in similar "sensual amusements," presumably with female servants, that quickly undermined his health. "As to those big tales about [John M.] & Jack Parr putting thro' nine women &c. . . . it is all a lie," he confided to a friend after a trip to the springs, "for the very first thing he put me to over there clapped both of us. It wd. have amused you to have heard the cursing I gave him." "Fortunately," DeSaussure reported, "the sulphur water cured me, in a few days and I believe he was convalescent when I left." Bolling's and DeSaussure's health, but not their reputations as gentlemen, seemed to be endangered at the springs. Young men took full advantage of all the opportunities offered to them as members of the male community at the springs.[9]

Male behavior at the springs includes some surprises. Even though young gentlemen from across the South passed weeks or months together in the competitive environment, few real affronts to honor apparently occurred. Occasionally, men swapped insults. But the disputes always ended quietly with each man's honor and reputation preserved. Shooting competitions occasionally took place, but duels apparently did not. In 1792 "a very disagreeable altercation in the Course of a Political Discussion" between two men resembled an affair of honor as their friends formed a "Counsel" to decide "the properest means of bringing it to a peaceable Termination." By the next morning, one man acknowledged that he had "used improper expressions" and the other accepted this gentlemanly apology. Even more interesting, young men occasionally donned women's clothing for the masquerade balls, seemingly without anxiety about their honor (though probably not without discomfort). With the help of another visitor's French maid, William and George Brice "went as young girls" to a Sweet Springs ball in 1840. At a "fancy Ball" at Red Sulphur, "some of the men dressed in full uniform . . . some like [Indian] squaws[,] some with skirts & Breeches and fancy stockings." Richard Burroughs considered them "really worth looking at." One comic masqueraded as the suffragist Lucy Stone in bloomers and a long skirt. He proved quite amusing to the company, capering through a quadrille and abusing "the sterner sex in the sharpest language." Apparently, a young man could mask himself temporarily as a woman without risking his honor as long as he and his peers considered him a true gentleman.[10]

Young women, on the other hand, evidently did not indulge in similar dissipated behavior at the springs and thus remained within the behavioral bounds set by their parents. Ladies-in-training drank alcohol on occasion, but none gambled in public. They rarely violated the rules for ladylike appearance. After asking Isabella Ritchie "to look carefully at her," Rose Freelaw mortified the matron by wearing no "drawers" while dancing in the ballroom. Freelaw responded that "she had not a pair in the world and had never worn them." The next morning, Ritchie sent her a pair. Some may have flirted heavily with numerous young men and reached the limits of propriety. At White Sulphur in 1837, Louisa Collins witnessed "a regular *race* here the other evening by moonlight, between, a Miss Frazier of Charleston [and] Miss Erskine of the Salt Sulphur," that tested these limits. During the evening ball, some of the young men had placed bets on which belle would win. After the ball had ended and "the company had retired to their cabins," the two young ladies, "who have been seeking notoriety the

whole summer at this place, came out upon the Lawn to decide the bets."
Even though a flirtatious belle herself, Collins considered the whole affair
disgraceful and, "together with a number of other Ladies, determined not
to witness the exhibition." Disgraceful or not, Collins must have watched
the event, for she gave her cousin a full account of the race: "One gentleman called out for them not to start until he had walked his *filly*, and after
the race was over, the winner of the bet, proclaimed his to be the *best
bottomed nag*. Did you ever hear the like! For my part, I think the appelative
'lady' is inappropriate." The loser of the bet "gave a great supper the night
after, and kept it up till day-break." Young women out with young men at
night engaging in mild sexual pranks pushed the boundaries of appropriate
behavior for young ladies as far as they could go. But young women apparently, and not surprisingly, did not engage in sexual experimentation at the
resorts. As compared with young men, their sexual behavior was more limited and less dangerous to their health—and, thus, their reputations.[11]

Generally, young women and men happily went about their activities
with little interference from older visitors. Unless sick, young visitors pursued their own pleasure, eschewing anything resembling family duties.
"Young people have no time for writing," Emily Rutherfoord explained to
her brother in apology for the tardiness of her letter.[12] Whenever possible,
young visitors escaped from the supervision and potential criticism of the
older generation in carriages, on horseback, in the woods, or at remote
scenic sites (fig. 17). A typical afternoon at White Sulphur saw young men
and women in "parties and couples" "straying in the beautiful paths of the
mastin wood, in the rear of the hotel," and "extending their steps as far as
Lover's Retreat, a romantic spot, in the same direction."[13]

Having escaped family duties and accepted more relaxed gender relations, the circle of youths at the springs enjoyed a degree of unsupervised
contact between young men and women rarely seen at home. Unmarried
youths at the springs mixed not just for a few hours at parties, dances, and
picnics, but for entire days or even longer. The party of "young folks" that
Eliza Harwood belonged to was "constantly together" and "sometimes
[spent] the night with each other." Philippa Barbour and her friends at
Rawley Springs enjoyed "romantick rides and walks" as well as fishing trips.
Some young visitors went on unchaperoned excursions with other youths
that their parents had never met. In 1801 Fanny Tucker traveled from Sweet
Springs to a nearby plantation with a party of nineteen people "all of
whom," she informed her parents, "you are unacquainted with." They re-

Figure 17. *The Christiansburg Party,* Lewis Miller, 1853. (Abby Aldrich Rockefeller Folk Art Museum, Williamsburg, Va.)

turned very late at night. Young visitors participated in these unsupervised outings for the sheer enjoyment of sharing each other's company and having a good time. When Louisa M. Collins and her friends proposed "a riding excursion" in 1837, the men in the party chartered a stage since they "wished to be all together on the principle of 'the more the merrier.'" The group set off "at a furious rate over the mountains, and returned about dark, singing songs, duetts, relating anecdotes." "In fact," she informed her cousin, "we were as excited a set of persons as you would wish to see." Another young woman and a party of friends traveled from White Sulphur to Sweet Springs to spend "a delightful day" and attend the evening ball.

They did not return until the next morning; adding to her "enjoyment, Mr Peyton Coles drove me over and back again in his buggy."[14]

Most parents and relatives, however, expressed little concern over these excursions or other mixed-gender mingling at the springs. Except for evangelicals, most southern parents and chaperones approved of the amusements offered for young adults at the Virginia Springs, as long as they did not lead to dissipation—particularly on the part of their daughters. Levin Joynes "warmly [envied] the gay young people who seemed to enjoy [White Sulphur's charms] with all their souls."[15] Older visitors could take comfort in the fact that young ladies encountered only wealthy and respectable young gentlemen at the exclusive resorts. And they counted upon them to follow the rules appropriate to genteel society. In 1840 Samuel Hoffman simply reported to his wife that her single sister was "enjoying herself prodigiously, visits, walks with beaux and sees a great deal of company at her cabin." Whenever his "girls had beaux," James White stayed out of the ballroom. While young visitors believed that they had escaped from supervision, their parents and chaperones actually encouraged them to get acquainted, form friendships, and possibly find spouses from among the large gathering of socially acceptable youths.[16]

Young people took advantage of the special opportunities for mixed-gender interaction at the springs. Eighteen-year-old Mary Jane Boggs found a new female acquaintance happily "engaged in a romp" with "at least a dozen gentlemen," and on "the *public* porch too." Young visitors came to the springs anticipating a rare opportunity to spend unsupervised time with their peers, especially those of the opposite sex. Occasions for a young man to touch a young lady's body, while rare on the plantation, were frequent at the springs. Nightly dances, mountain climbs, carriage rides, sporting games, and other activities routinely allowed for physical contact between men and women. The excitement evoked by these occasions was memorable. Robert Taylor Scott boasted to one friend about dancing at the springs with a cousin, "the prettiest woman, I almost ever saw." And he revealed a sense of awe when he described the effect of putting his arm around her waist. "I'll swear," he confessed, "I felt like I was in the seventh heaven . . . it made a fellow breathe awful fast, I'll be darned if it didn't."[17]

In their writings, young men and women made clear their comfort with new and old acquaintances and friends of the opposite sex. Evidence from the springs suggests that planter youths enjoyed close relationships with the opposite sex even before they engaged in serious courtships. Jane Caroline North, for example, had many male acquaintances and friends at the springs with, at least in her opinion, no marital intentions involved. Old male friends from South Carolina and new ones from across the South called on North throughout the day and almost every evening during her 1851 trip to the springs. In her journal and letters, she made clear distinctions between those whom she considered friends and those who courted her. One of her "great friends," Willie Calhoun, for example, was "so perfectly delighted" to meet with her at the springs that he "almost embraced me outright." [18] The informality of their relationship and the closeness of their friendship—a closeness reestablished at the springs—appeared not only in his warm welcome, but also in North's reference to him by his first name, which she did only with close friends, male or female. With her more formal relationships, including such beaux as a Mr. Harvey, she used "Mister" or "Miss" and their last names.

Marriage moved a young man or woman out of the culture created by gentry youths at the springs. Their culture revolved around being both single and young. Four years after her successful visit as a belle, North returned to the springs as a married woman. She still spent time with other men, though in more restrained activities and not as part of the unmarried throng. Along with her young charges, she attended the parlor and danced at the balls but, as she informed her mother, "with the becoming degree of motherly dignity which marks my exalted place as Ladyhead of the party." [19] She watched the younger women in her party participate in the social whirl that she had enjoyed so much as a belle and took pride in their success. North had now moved fully into elite adult culture, leaving the springs' youth culture behind. Most of the young visitors at the springs would eventually follow in her footsteps.

Over the first half of the nineteenth century, a trip to the Virginia Springs increasingly became a part of the coming-of-age ritual for planter youths. While they pursued pleasure and each other, these young men and women learned the lessons of their society. Their participation in and observation of elite southern society at its most intense marked for many their entrance into adulthood, their transformation into ladies and gentlemen. The community of young people that they created every season allowed them to test and improvise their own forms of behavior and gender relations in a relatively safe environment.

ॐ

"A Great Deal Is Affected, but Nothing on the Heart in It"

Most wealthy visitors regarded the Virginia Springs as a place of pleasure and leisure, yet their very presence made the resorts places of intense ritual and competition. While visitors eased some rules of gender relations, they did not relax their general expectations for proper southern ladies and gentlemen. If anything, the demands of such roles became clearer. At the springs, elite society clarified the rules of genteel and fashionable appearance, behavior, and sentiment. These rules defined individual actions and simultaneously provided guidelines for group competition. Success or failure at knowing and following the rules often determined a guest's status in springs society. The concentration of so many elite men and women in such a close setting intensified the competition for status—to be the prettiest or handsomest, the most fashionable or graceful, the most respected or popular. The exclusivity and homogeneity of the guests fueled this need for differentiation and acknowledgment. Lacking the inherent status of plantation or town environments that readily distinguished them from their neighbors and slaves, elite men and women found themselves forced to compete with members of their own group for a top place in the springs hierarchy. And the competition was fierce. One mistake in word, deed, or dress by a visitor could create a sudden loss of status, perhaps even a scandal. The demands of gentility and competition at the Virginia Springs required visitors to serve in various capacities at once. The guests participated in spa society as serious competitors, shrewd spectators, or stern judges. They relaxed and played while they competed and performed. They acted while they watched. They observed while being observed and judged those who judged them. Yet most of the women and men willingly played the game by displaying their mastery of the art of being a lady or gentleman. Their willingness to play this game—to follow the rules of polite society while jockeying for status—fostered an atmosphere at the springs that was both gregarious and competitive.

While visitors rarely commented upon the tensions created by intense competition and status obsession within a leisurely, familial atmosphere, they clearly considered the Virginia Springs a perfect arena for social competition. A member of a prominent Virginia family, Philippa Barbour determined early that at the fashionable resorts "a great deal is affected, but nothing on the heart in it," as "each family of wealth endeavours to excel the other in regard to their personal appearance and splendour of their equipages." This aspect of resort life followed a long tradition in gentry society. Throughout the eighteenth and nineteenth centuries, particularly in the South, when ladies and gentlemen gathered, they used contest, performance, and display to define and evaluate members within their own circle. Through their public display of manners, talents, and dress, women and men revealed the communally sanctioned hallmarks of membership in the southern gentry. The contest gave rank and reputation to the participants. This concern with public display reflected an emphasis on the physical form and outward signs of gentility in a society that rested upon the community for the bestowal of status, honor, and personal worth. This tradition reached its zenith at the Virginia Springs.[1]

Many visitors went to the springs primarily to participate in and witness the display and competition. Young men and women, the beaux and belles, especially enjoyed the "little follies" and "various artifices" of life at the Virginia Springs. They usually threw themselves into the whirl with verve, competing with each other for popularity and admiration while having a marvelous time. Martha Terrell envied her sister's "natural gayety" and delight in "the confusion of the crowd." Correspondingly, young singles received the most attention—and thus the most criticism or acclaim—as major players in the status contest. They also had the most at stake since their reputations might decide marriage partners and, for men, future business and political prospects. Walter Preston expressed his pleasure that his two sisters found "no difficulty in getting along as well as any." More importantly, he predicted that "they will have sufficent confidence in themselves after a while to aim at and succeed in surpassing all who may undertake to compete with them." He wanted them to leave the springs as winners.[2]

Simply by going to the Virginia Springs, men and women laid claim to a high level of status. A long trip to the Virginia Springs became a badge of distinction within the southern elite. Almost every planter man or woman wanted to spend at least one season at the springs during a lifetime and the real fashionables went almost every year. Even families in hard times, such as after the panics in 1819 and 1837, often scraped together enough money to send at least a daughter or sister, with her chaperone, for a visit during the height of the season. Robert Hubard borrowed one hundred dollars in order to take a pleasure trip to the springs in 1825.[3] The cachet of a season at the springs—the seat of fashion in the South—imparted a sense not only of wealth but also of gentility.

Upon arriving at a resort, the display and competition began. Guests flaunted their status by arriving in large entourages with men on horses and family and servants in carriages and coaches. Otwayanna Carter took distinct pleasure in the picture her party's arrival presented with "three carriages[,] two gigs[,] a barouche and the two young Boyds on horseback with two servants." The group "made quite a *dash*." Even before the visitors descended from their conveyances, the style of a party's carriages and the quality of the horses had already produced a sensation. Duly impressed, Philippa Barbour informed her sister that a "Mrs Hampton has a splendid coach and four; she has three carriages here, and twelve horses; her coach of course the most splendid." Crowds assembled at the receiving rooms of the resorts to stare at newcomers and make an early judgment. While waiting for their room or cabin assignments in dusty and unkempt travel clothes, the new arrivals suffered under the intense scrutiny of freshly and nicely dressed onlookers. Like Jane Caroline North, Harriet Martineau keenly felt the stares as she stepped out of her carriage and into the crowd, at once recognizing the importance of her first appearance at the springs. "We were heated, wearied, shabby, and all of one dust colour, from head to foot . . . looking very sheepish under the general stare. Every body else was gay and spruce, and at full leisure to criticise us. Gentlemen in the piazza in glossy coats and polished pumps; ladies in pink, blue, and white, standing on green grass, shading their delicate faces and gay head-dresses under parasols." Those who owned their own cottages often drove directly to their residence in order to avoid this embarrassment. By making such an easy entrance, they immediately proclaimed themselves "the high aristocracy" and therefore one of the most influential groups at the springs.[4]

The southerners who came as pleasure- and status-seekers usually traveled to the springs with other family members and several slave attendants. "Mrs. Clay, a little grandson and myself compose the white members of our party," Henry Clay informed the proprietor of White Sulphur. "Then, we have four servants, two carriages, six horses, a Jack ass, and a Shepherds dog—a strange medley, is it not?" As Clay clearly knew, a large number of horses and servants added to a visitor's status. Isaac Peck discovered that "horses & servants are the best recommendations a man can bring & a person with these are preferred & recd. [by the managers] where stage passengers are not." One South Carolina family brought eleven horses and seven servants to ease their stay and show their wealth. Elite families displayed their horses, carriages, and servants like their clothes and manners. "Near sun down," according to one visitor in 1856, "handsome equipages turn out . . . beautifull carriages[,] splendid horses, driver and footman on the box, two grooms behind. all in handsome livery[.] ladies on horses that cost 500 each, with grooms riding after them." Such a show generally produced the desired effect.[5]

Those who wanted to stay in the popular crowd, and thus in the competition, had to keep up with its movements from spa to spa. Each resort that catered to pleasure-seekers had a peak period for a few weeks of the season. At the start of the season in June and at the end in late September, Warm Springs was the place to be. Sweet and Salt Sulphur Springs received the fashionable crowds just before Warm's finale. White Sulphur experienced the longest fashionable season, extending from mid-July to early September in some years. "It will be too late for the White Sulphur after the 5 or 6th of September," George Randolph warned his sister, "for nothing is worse than the dregs of a season at a watering place." Some smaller resorts, such as Botetourt, Capon, and Red Sweet Springs, could be all the rage one season and unpopular the next. Pleasure-seekers, not the invalids who needed the curative waters, created the famous Virginia Springs "circuit." It included those resorts that aimed as much at amusing their guests as healing them. Status-conscious visitors traveled from one resort to the next, trying to stay with the fashionable crowd and to add to the amusement that could be had. "People in the mountains are like the wild pigeon," a South Carolinian observed, "never satisfied in one locality—they flit about from place to place." It is unclear who decided when the in-crowd would move on to the next resort. Presumably, those persons whom spa society considered the social leaders in other respects—the wealthy Baltimoreans, aristocratic South Carolinians, and prominent Virginians—led the crowd around the circuit. In 1828 Henry Clay's departure from White Sulphur in mid-September provided "the signal for breaking up the camp," according to Benjamin Temple. Many visitors shaped their itinerary accordingly, desiring to arrive in the thick of the fashionable crowd. In the opinion of one travel writer, "like the worshippers of Juggernaut, the votaries of pleasure are willing to be crushed to death, to obtain a chance of laying their offerings on the shrine that fashion has set up in this happy valley."[6]

The most glorious spectacle of competition occurred every season at

Figure 18. The lawn at White Sulphur Springs, John H. B. Latrobe, 1832. (Semmes, *John H. B. Latrobe and His Times*)

White Sulphur Springs, the "Queen of Watering Places." From early on, White Sulphur earned a reputation as *the* most fashionable resort on the Virginia Springs circuit. Throughout the nineteenth century, elite society crowned the place "the grand Emporium of Fashion—the gay metropolis of the Springs." By the 1830s hordes of people sought entrance to White Sulphur, since, as a later visitor noted, "there is more fun[,] frolick[,] life & annimation at this place than all the rest of the springs put together" (fig. 18). In spite of its notoriously wretched accommodations, almost every southern visitor concurred that White Sulphur ranked higher in fashion, display, and society than any other spa in Virginia, or New York, or even Europe. By the mid-1850s, White Sulphur could accommodate over 1500 — too many to include only the top echelon of southern society as in earlier years. Increasingly, Sweet Springs became better known for its exclusivity. In 1856 Levin Joynes judged the company at White Sulphur "inferior" to that at Sweet, for White Sulphur's crowd, though bigger, contained "a smaller proportion of the *upper ten,* and a larger one of the *million.*" "All agree that the company at the Sweet has been unequalled for selectness, for elegance, and for beauty," he concluded. Yet these changes never stopped a multitude of elites from crowding into White Sulphur during the height of its season, when everyone who was anyone still appeared. One perennial visitor caustically commented that many of the travelers "no doubt would have died right out had they not been crowded & pack[ed] into the White Sul at the height of the Fashionable season." By missing out on the competition at White Sulphur, they would have lost the chance to succeed there and to achieve some of the highest accolades of elite southern society.[7]

Those who were considered the leaders of southern society provided the models for appropriate and fashionable appearance and behavior at the Virginia Springs. Visitors often regarded famous men or women—such as Henry Clay, Dolley Madison, and Elizabeth Patterson Bonaparte (the ex-wife of Napoleon's brother Jerome)—as the paragons of fashion and gentility. Clay, who was known as the "lion" of White Sulphur, "was for many years, a central object of attention among the visitors" and "was always the most noted, honored, and observed by all observers," according to Dr. John J. Moorman.[8] In her *Life in Washington, and Life Here and There,* Mary J. Windle coyly referred to a "Mrs. ——, of Washington" from whom "every one seems anxious to receive the law from her lips on all points of fashionable etiquette. Her influence in [springs] society is remarkable." Considered the prime "aristocrats" in the South, almost all Charlestonians, especially the Singletons, Rutledges, and Hamptons, served as leading examples. According to James L. Petigru, Richard and Rebecca Singleton appeared at White Sulphur in 1845 "in the character of persons giving tone to society." Wealthy Baltimoreans and New Orleans French also had their admirers. Early in the 1838 season at White Sulphur, "the Baltimoreans carr[ied] the day." Louisa Carrington described them as "people of great wealth," who made "'a great dash.'" As in southern society generally, family name helped to confer prestige and influence in spa society. Thomas Pollock noticed in 1860 that "all the great names flourish largely—the Pinckneys & Rutledges &c &c." Since Pollock was traveling with a distinguished family, he also had "the entire 'swing' of the place." [9]

In their pursuit of fashion, obsession with public display, and desire for public attention, refined southern men and women differed drastically from those who sought refinement in the North. By the beginning of the nineteenth century, a growing middle class had begun to transform the meaning of refinement from gentility to respectability in the North. Respectability, unlike gentility, prized individual worth over communal acclaim. It emphasized taste, not fashion, for fashion privileged appearance over character and could corrupt morals. Refined northerners avoided spectacle and rarely engaged in public display. For them, respectability meant never calling attention to one's self, especially in public.[10] But southerners remained devoted to the more eighteenth-century aristocratic form of refinement that emphasized gentility with its hierarchy and public display. For fashionable southern society, one's outer signs of refinement still mattered more than one's inner goodness.[11] Competition for status remained dependent upon external, easily measurable indicators of gentility. Status and acclaim, according to elite southerners at the springs, could not be granted upon one's invisible and unjudgeable inner moral worth. Few hesitated to draw attention to themselves and their mastery of the rules of southern fashion and gentility.

Observing and being observed occupied a major portion of a visitor's day. From early in the morning at the springhouse to late at night in the ballroom, a visitor was on display and judging others' displays. Daily, Louisiana's Volumina Barrow and her party spent the evenings "on our galleries conversing & watching the promenaders or else promenade ourselves." Everyone watched everybody else—from cottage porches and hotel verandas, at the springhouse, along the graveled pathways and lawns, and in the parlors, ballrooms, and dining rooms. Mary Thompson likened her cottage porch to "a sort of Lense" through which she could observe spa society passing back and forth all day. Some contented themselves simply with being spectators, not wanting to participate in the whirl of fashion and competition. Mildred Halsey informed her husband that her group of friends met three times a day in the parlor, with its "constant promenading round and round." She had been "in the stream several times, but [found] it pleasanter to sit in a quiet corner, and comment on the beauty and fancy-dresses constantly passing."[12]

Surrounded by their peers, elite southerners were more on display at the springs than on their plantations or in towns, where they worked and lived surrounded by slaves, poorer whites, and only a few elites. The outward appearance and behavior of both women and men received more scrutiny on the "stages" of the Virginia Springs than at any other place in the South. To determine the winners and losers, the competition at the springs required observers and judges, many of whom were simultaneously participants. Yet none of the guests seemed even remotely aware of the potential tensions arising from their dichotomous roles. Their observations and judgments often involved censorious and petty behavior. Visitors of lower social rank or lacking the requisite knowledge of the rules of high society—if they even dared to venture onto the sophisticated scene— became objects of criticism, scorn, and, often, humor. So, too, did those elites who indulged excessively in fashionable clothing, haughty manners, or rowdy behavior. The genteel men and women at the Virginia Springs intensely scrutinized the behavior and appearance of those deemed worthy of ruling their society.

Everyone—male or female, rich or poor, black or white—recognized the clear signs of appearance and conduct that marked a visitor as a member of the gentry. Ladies and gentlemen appeared beautiful and fashionably dressed in public and conducted themselves gracefully and politely. Such signs reflected elite southerners' emphasis upon breeding and refinement, and not just wealth, as requisites for high social status. Family name might carry a visitor far in spa society. When "Gen. [Zachary] Taylor's son" arrived at White Sulphur in 1847, Elizabeth M. Maben shrewdly calculated that "he will be quite a high lion, on his father's merits & bravery." But mere wealth without family background or good breeding had little impact. From Rockbridge Alum in 1859, Charles Bruce, an eminent Virginia planter, wrote his wife that "there are several families from the South, with retinues of Servants, and rich displays of dresses." But, despite their trappings, their lack of genteel manners and imperfect knowledge of genteel etiquette had quickly revealed themselves. "The rough exterior, the uncouth manners, and unpolished Conversation of the men prove that their affluence is of recent origin," Bruce concluded. Presumably, the men in the family, not the well-dressed women, gave away the entire group. Try as they might, any nouveau riche without the proper background or signs of good breeding had little chance of winning a prominent place in the springs hierarchy. Spa society could quickly identify a visitor as fashionable and genteel, and thus worthy of respect and intimacy, or as a respectable middling sort, worthy of politeness and toleration, or as an inferior interloper, worthy of only ridicule and contempt. Even though he was not of the planter class, North Carolinian Larkin Newby knew the secret for acceptance into privileged society: "With these men, the appearance & manners of the gentleman (which I flatter myself I am not entirely destitute of) is enough." Adherence to the rules of gentility, even without the associated wealth, could sometimes gain a person acceptance into the circle.[13]

Members of Virginia Springs society brought rules for social behavior, fashion, and the ballroom from plantations and towns to the springs resorts. By concentrating so many elite men and women in one place, however, the springs environment intensified some of these traditional codes of conduct. That a person's societal worth as a lady or gentleman could be quickly revealed and discerned through the outward signs of etiquette and fashion made the rules that much more important at the springs. Furthermore, the rules served as the basis in the contests for status. Although familiar to most visitors, the manners and customs at the springs still appeared quite elaborate. Travel accounts often included a specific section devoted to the customs of springs society. When his granddaughter made her first visit to the Virginia Springs in 1856, John H. Cocke considered it a perfect occasion to give her a book entitled *How to be a Lady,* certain that she needed guidelines for her debut into spa society and its complicated and critical etiquette. The young girl liked the book and believed that "a great many ideas might be taken from it" for her venture into society. Even as many visitors believed that the springs atmosphere fostered a "free and easy manner at which you are at liberty to deport yourself," they did not abandon all of the rules of decorum. Singing and laughing on carriage rides, romping through fields, scrambling up rocks, dancing in the woods, and rolling tenpins found acceptance at the springs in a way unknown at home, but guests still had to comport themselves according to the appropriate spa rules for gentlemen and ladies. Visitors engaged in more playful behavior than at home, but they remained aware of the limits of propriety.[14]

The glaring exception to this intensification of normal rules at the springs appeared in the dining rooms—one of the preeminent places to display refinement at home. The conditions in the resorts' dining rooms forced a suspension of the rules of genteel dining (fig. 19). "The prevailing manners . . . were good, except at meals," proclaimed one travel account. "There decorum is forgotten in an overwhelming sense of self-preservation." Dozens of similar comments from different times and resorts echoed this observation. Never sure when a servant would swoop in and pick up a dish to pass it on to another table, diners grabbed as much food as possible as quickly as possible. Some plantation mistresses pleaded for specific foods and some plantation masters demanded that their meals be brought or not taken away. William Stabler observed "two ladies, ladies of some character too I suppose for they were part of Chapman Johnson's company, beg hard for a glass of milk a piece but while I remained at the table they got none." A gentleman who sat near Mary Steger at the dining

Figure 19. *The Party at Supper & Breakfast, Chapmans Springs,* Lewis Miller, 1853. (Abby Aldrich Rockefeller Folk Art Museum, Williamsburg, Va.)

table at White Sulphur "gets into a regular passion at meals, but as the servants are too busy to find it out, he generally fumes in silence." The widespread acceptance of grabbing, begging, demanding, and fuming at the resorts' tables revealed a side of the southern gentry not normally seen in their elegant dining rooms.[15]

Even as spa society relaxed or suspended many of the rules guiding social intercourse and behavior, some rules intensified in importance with the concentration of so many ladies and gentlemen. One set of rules, particularly those concerning bodily carriage and deportment, gained added importance at the springs by providing the starting point for status competition.[16] A visitor had to present a clean body and clothes. Good posture remained imperative, as did graceful and dignified movement. Careless bodily actions seemed even more glaring amid the extremely genteel company of the springs. In order to enter the competition for admiration and acclaim, men and women first had to understand and then follow these basic rules of bodily deportment, along with the more modified rules of visiting and conversing. Another set of rules, specifically those concerning fashion and the ballroom, gained in intensity and importance at the springs as they established the standards for status competition among the visitors.

At the Virginia Springs fashionable dress constituted one of the clearest signs of gentility and social rank and sparked some of the fiercest competition, especially among women. Private letters and journals and published travel accounts, guides, and fictional works reveal that visitors paid a tremendous amount of attention to their own and each other's clothes. Fashion provided an easy and obvious yardstick with which to measure a visitor's refinement. Observers carefully scrutinized clothing for stylishness, richness of fabric, quality of work, and expense of decoration. Men and women brought their finest clothes to the springs, well aware of the crucial role of fashionable dress in the competition for admiration and status. To Mary Jane Boggs, the bonnets and dresses that she packed for an 1851 springs trip were her "artillery." [17]

The men and women who sought status and attention in spa society knew that they had to dress finely and in only the latest fashions. Henry D. Mandeville Jr. always went to the ballroom dressed "in his best, hair and moustach perfumed and arranged with elaborate attention." Those vying for status never appeared in public dishabille, taking so long to ready their elaborate costumes and coiffures that they sometimes visited the springhouses hours past the scheduled time for drinking or arrived late to dinner and other entertainments. Stylish visitors promenaded before the start of evening activities to display their finery and grace. Recognizing the theatrical quality of the promenades, Susanna Harrison likened the parade of fashionably dressed women and men to a puppet show. Only those visitors who followed the rules of fashion could succeed in springs society. [18]

In the ballroom, the rules for social intercourse, behavior, and appearance intensified to their highest levels. Almost every night women and men crowded the ballrooms, anticipating the pleasures of dancing and socializing—and of performance and competition—beneath the brilliantly lit chandeliers. The guests cherished the balls for their "more than usual" "life and animation." Men and women demonstrated their mastery of genteel etiquette, conversation, fashion, and dance styles and competed through this display in front of a large audience. They donned their most fashionable clothes and their most polished manners for the ballroom. Like fashion, dancing provided an excellent way of displaying status and an easy measure of a visitor's refinement. Everyone entering the ballroom needed to know the proper attire and the difficult steps for any fashionable dance. The popular men and women danced minuets, cotillions, reels (especially the Virginia reel), waltzes, polkas, and schottisches as each came into vogue. Men needed to know how to ask a woman for a dance and women needed to know how to accept or reject a proposal politely. A female acquaintance of Thomas Malone's created a small sensation when *she* came up to him "holding out her hand, and coquettishly" proposed that he waltz with her. Dancers also needed to know the appropriate topics of conversation for the ballroom.[19]

The popularity of balls led resort proprietors, or even the visitors themselves, to schedule one almost every night. At White Sulphur during the 1840s, for example: "On Mondays, Wednesdays, & fridays they have balls, & appear in full dress. On Tuesdays, Thursdays, & Saturdays, they also attend the Ball Room dressed plainly, & have what they call '*a Hop*' & break up early." Of course, this schedule forced truly fashionable women to own numerous ballgowns. The balls at the Virginia Springs became celebrated affairs as newspapers reported, with detailed descriptions, the appearance of the southern gentry. A correspondent for the *Charleston Daily Courier* admitted that he could not "attempt to do justice to the raven tresses, fair hair, blue, black, hazel, and all manner of colored eyes, dimples, blushes, ruby lips, white teeth, pretty feet, and gentle accents." He did single out a few dancers, including "a lady from Baltimore, with a fine Spanish face, in a superb crimson brocade," and a "Lieut. ——, of Washington, *en grand toilette*, gold band and buttons."[20]

A familiarity with fashionable dance steps and a graceful performance of them ensured the attention of the crowd and a visitor's status. In 1833 a Miss Chapman drew crowds to White Sulphur's ballroom solely to watch her dance, as she was "universally allowed to be a most graceful & beautiful waltzer." If a dancer performed the steps incorrectly or awkwardly, however, he or she became a comic spectacle for the onlookers. C. O. Lyde recorded in her travel journal that she had met a man whose personality was agreeable, "but his manner of dancing was so droll it was with difficulty I could keep from laughing." A visiting Englishman struck Eliza Harwood as "a well educated man, exceedingly interesting in conversation, and intelligent, but the most awkward figure, and the most ungraceful creature in all his movements that I ever beheld." She and her group took pleasure, "while he was here, to go in [the] ballroom, to see him dance; he has no more idea of time or [*illegible*] than a cat." Such failures in the ballroom colored one's reputation among society at the springs. In the ballroom, even more than at the resort in general, grace and style proved critical.[21]

Upon entering the ballroom, both men and women felt the pressure to perform, expecting to receive close attention and careful assessments of their skills. But most dancers, especially the young adults, enjoyed being in the spotlight. At every ball, John Rutherfoord's "girls" were "on the floor from the time they enter the Ball Room until they break up." William Elliott took pride in his granddaughter because she "attract[ed] much attention" and "danced the Virginia reel so as to vindicate her descent from a dancing stock." Those participating in the performance had to watch themselves carefully, making sure that they did not cross the line from competitive display to public spectacle. When a Miss Erskine at Salt Sulphur "whirled untill her head was quite giddy" in a waltz, Mary Cameron considered it "a disgusting sight." Like Cameron, many attended the balls merely as spectators. At a ball in 1838, Blair Bolling observed "a good display of Beauty," fine dressing, and "some arogance." Spectators crowded into the ballrooms to witness the splendor and exhibition and to judge the competition. "Such a scene never was seen," James C. Johnston reported after "a large masquerade ball." "The Ladies stood on the seats to see the masqueraders & the crowd was so dense" that the weight broke the floor supports "& one end of the room gave way with a great *crash.*" Players and observers alike looked forward to balls, for there the real competition and display took place. In a single night, a high rank in the springs hierarchy could be won or lost.[22]

In the resorts' ballrooms and other public spaces, women received more attention to their clothes, behavior, and bodies than men. At the springs, they competed for status especially through fashionable dress, spending more time worrying about the suitability of their clothing and changing their clothes more often than men. Elite southerners expected their women not only to ornament society but also to reflect their men's status. Wives and daughters did both by dressing richly and fashionably. Many of the women who visited the springs brought trunks of clothes—enough to allow them to change outfits four or five times a day. Morning hours, visits, promenades, exercise, dinner, and evening entertainments all required different types of dresses, at least according to fashionable etiquette. A Miss

Dent of Alabama reputedly brought "19 trunks, and 75 dresses" for her trip to the springs in 1856. Many women enjoyed the constant dressing; others found it a chore or approached it with trepidation, fearing the consequences of a mistake. One woman acknowledged that, with the company "so select as that now here," "improprieties in dress . . . strikes one the more glaring." Travel writer Mary J. Windle recorded the dramatic tale of "one lovely girl" who had been "condemned, executed, and given over by a jury of her fashionable friends, for being guilty of wearing a Berthe of *Guipure* lace, with sleeves of *'Point d'Alençon.'* " To remain safe, some dressed plainly, though still fashionably. Hoping to persuade a friend to join her at the springs, Roberta Burwell assured her that "you may wear any thing and not appear singular in such a crowd." Burwell's definition of "any thing," however, ranged between a plain silk dress and "as much finery as you choose to pack on." Her own luggage included "quite an elegant & abundant wardrobe." [23]

Because of this close scrutiny, women—not men—were the fiercest competitors at the Virginia Springs. At the springs, women competed in their display of ballgowns and jewelry, and even in the size of their hoop skirts. During an 1860 trip, Maria Louisa Fontaine related a particularly revealing episode of the importance of dress and the seriousness of competition among women at the springs. Attired for a fancy ball at White Sulphur, two ladies faced off in the parlor in a rich, public display of fashion while an audience that was at once admiring and judgmental watched: "Mrs Senator Gwinn and Mrs Battaile vied with each other in splendour of apparal[.] the former eclipsed Mrs B in dress, but cant compare with her in person, Mrs G was blazing in Diamonds[,] white velvet and Black point lace with scarlet trimmings[.] they promenaded the Parlour long enough for every one to see and admire, and it was amusing to see with what eagerness every one looked on, many rising from their seats to get a good look and some contending the point, as to which was most elegant." [24]

Social relations were usually harmonious and easy at the springs, but the demands of genteel competition could sometimes break through the layer of sociability and politeness that elite men and women so staunchly preserved. Even though female visitors looked forward to reuniting with one another, supported each other, and shared unusual experiences, the community that they formed at the Virginia Springs was hardly idyllic. The fierce competition and harsh judgments could promote catty behavior and petty disputes among the competitors as they vied for status and acclaim, dividing the usually affable female community. In 1829 Jane Harrison Randolph wrote home about a Miss Wilcox and a Mrs. Tabb who "do not *speak.*" "It was really painful to see the satirical *contempt* with wh. the former treated [the latter]," Randolph noted. "Miss W. acknowledges that Mrs. T. waited on & apologized for not knowing her on a former occasion, but *she* does not *chuse* to *come down.*" As early as the 1830s, author James Kirke Paulding found "a certain odd sort of rivalship prevailing among the ladies of the different sections or states of the Union." Women who arrived at the springs with a hint of scandal about them felt the sting of the community's scorn. Mrs. St. Romain Robb's daughter from Louisiana, "who had sold herself soul & body for fame and that Spaniard" and was in the process of getting a divorce, created quite a sensation among the women at Montgomery White Sulphur in 1859. Mrs. Robb's daughter probably found cold shoulders instead of welcoming embraces from the community of women at the springs.[25]

Similarly, the men's community at the springs had its own special, but less public, forms of masculine competition. Status competition among male visitors often occurred while drinking or smoking or playing cards or billiards. It seems that every resort had a bar and most had a gaming room or house. These spaces constituted the only exclusively male preserves at the springs, and served as arenas of gentlemanly contest. While certain excesses brought expulsion from refined society and from the competition, using tobacco, drinking alcohol without becoming too drunk too often, shooting billiards, and gambling without falling too deeply into debt remained the privileges of the southern gentleman and his community.[26]

At the Virginia Springs, gentlemen indulged in these privileges, using them as genteel forms of masculine competition. Evidence from the springs suggests the pervasiveness and extensiveness of drinking. Guests' account books list heavy charges for libations and resort owners' ledgers reveal staggering purchases of alcohol.[27] Male visitors apparently imbibed freely and frequently. In his 1851 travel journal, temperance advocate and tobacco opponent John H. Cocke noted: "I discovered several shy drunkards who thought they had the art to conceal their besotting sin." A few days earlier, Cocke had observed a youth "drinking Brandy" and using tobacco who was, in an odd form of competition, "distinguished for smoking the longest Cigar of any person at the Springs." Gambling on cards and billiards was equally common. Gambling had long reigned as a form of competition among southern gentlemen. As early as 1791, "gambling coteries" gathered

"at the billard-table and in taverns where they would often spend the entire night." From Sweet Springs in 1798, William Gray informed his wife,
"Nothing uncommon going on here[.] a young man lost last night in the
next room to mine $800 at Cards." In 1847 Lucy Tucker complained that
she never saw her husband after tea time since "he is in [the] billiard room
untill 2 oclock at night." The tavern, the gaming house, and the activities
within each played crucial roles in bringing men together for camaraderie—and competition.[28]

At the Virginia Springs, elite women not only embodied their class
through personal display but also determined and enforced the boundaries
of their class—they were the main judges. If we look at the social aspect
of class-formation, instead of just the economic or political aspects, we
can see the importance of women in the creation of the southern elite. In
southern planter society, married women performed the critical functions
of both representing and determining gentility. White southerners' emphasis on outward signs of status—of gentility—ultimately gave women a crucial role in shaping class and regional identity. By setting the rules of appropriate behavior and appearance, they drew the social lines that excluded
not only other white women but also white men from their exclusive circle.[29] They determined the social limits of their class and the social characteristics of genteel southerners. Southern women may have possessed little
political or economic power, but they did hold social power, which could
prove just as effective.

In the very public arena of the Virginia Springs, older women wielded
this power in especially obvious ways. As paragons of refinement, they constantly and carefully guarded entrance into their social group at the resorts.
More than anyone else, these women decided which visitors, male and female, would succeed or fail in fashionable spa society. In her *Life at the
White Sulphur Springs,* Mary J. Windle told of one "Mrs ——, of Richmond," who was "omnipotent in the fashionable world" and only needed
to "shake her head with an air of mistrust to secure the ostracism of any
one." The community of women at the springs possessed a keen sense of
"us"—those who belonged at the springs and in their social group—and
"them"—those who intruded upon this place of fashion and society. As
early as 1791 visitors commented that women held the power to define the
social circles at the springs. In his *Travels in the Interior of the United States,*
Ferdinand Bayard witnessed this power in action at ladies' tea parties. "A
deep silence follows the entrance of each invited guest; and all those ladies

are as grave as judges on the bench," taking stock of the newcomer and deciding where he or she would rank in the circle. This power was obvious as the closed circle of older matrons were "ever on the watch to repress any innocent ebullition of vivacity, and to poison every little moment of youthful gayety, by sour looks of reprehension, sideblow innuendoes, and appalling shakes of the head." Whether a guest could be considered a member of fashionable spa society—and, therefore, at the top of southern society in general—apparently rested with these elite women who carefully and staunchly guarded its boundaries.[30]

The social power of these women affected both men and women. An aspiring man needed the approval of elite women. Without acceptance into the social circles that women controlled, men stood little chance of advancing into the upper echelons of southern society, regardless of their political or economic accomplishments. Women were especially unyielding in their exclusion of gamblers and drunkards from their company. These women usually decided which gentlemen actually merited the title and should be introduced as such. Acknowledging this fact, Thomas Pollock made "it a point to cultivate the married ladies" at White Sulphur in 1860. They also determined who really deserved the title of lady. "When a female arrives," James Kirke Paulding noticed during his stay, the group of fashionable ladies "sit in judgment upon her directly; and if she does not possess the mysterious, inexplicable attributes of bon ton—whew! marry come up!— and all that sort of thing." Young ladies could not become belles without the approval of these older women, no matter how many men fell in love with them. And female visitors could not gain entry into their circle without passing their judgment, no matter how many dresses and jewels they brought.[31]

In their roles as judges and protectors of their class's boundaries, female visitors occasionally differed with one another about just which women should hold the top places in the ever-changing spa hierarchy. As they routinely and closely scrutinized one another, some judges found themselves holding a minority opinion concerning the virtues of a competitor. After careful study, Volumina Barrow intensely disliked the woman that Montgomery White Sulphur Springs society had "generally conceded to be the prettiest and most elegant woman at these springs." Although she found Mrs. Frank Williams "to be graceful and to dress with taste," Barrow could not "admire her at all—or think her pretty"—because of her "low forehead and an eye whose expression *can* charm, but in whose depths lurks a hidden something I distrust and cannot confide in." Barrow believed that she alone had discerned Mrs. Williams's true character, calling into question the decision of the other judges. She preferred a Mrs. Quitman who was, to her "taste," "the most elegant and distinguished woman here during her stay." She admitted, however, that "since her departure there have been a perfect galaxy of reputed beauties."[32]

The female judges at the springs apparently ranked women according to attributes of beauty, fashion, manners, and character. Only true ladies could enter into the competition or serve as judges.[33] "Being neither amiable nor pretty," a "Mrs. C———y," who accompanied Ferdinand Bayard and his wife to Bath in 1791, "was sought after very little by women who could appreciate and choose their companions." Instead, she "launched out into the society of devout women," who ignored the dictates of fashion and frivolity.[34] Evidence such as this suggests that there might have been a hierarchy of women—with the most attractive or most fashionable on top, the merely convivial or genteel next, the evangelical or unfashionable below that, and the invalids last—created and controlled by women at the springs. They determined just how popular and influential a female visitor would become. Successful belles, of course, made up a large percentage of the women at the highest level. But fashionable married women, such as Mrs. Frank Williams and Mrs. John Quitman, or especially famous women, such as Dolley Madison and Elizabeth Patterson Bonaparte, held the same top rank. Women who possessed only one or two of the requisite characteristics of the upper echelon rose only to second place. A friendly and graceful but unattractive woman rarely led in the community of women, remaining instead a genial follower. The leading women often simply ignored those who chose not to dress fashionably and compete socially, such as "Mrs. C———y." Women whose infirmities kept them from participating in the social whirl fell to the bottom of the hierarchy, of course, having little influence because of their poor health. Unlike religious or unfashionable women, however, they received sympathy from the leading women and might return to claim a higher rank in the female hierarchy another season. This hierarchy of women at the springs, based on competition and judgment, bolstered southern women's power in determining membership in their class. Through their attention to the fashions, manners, and background of the other visitors, older, and generally married, women controlled who became a member of fashionable spa society. And their judgments spread beyond the mountains.

Elite southern men seem never to have conceived of women's control over the social boundaries of their class at home or at the springs as a challenge to their overall authority. They, like women, regarded this exercise of social power as falling within the women's sphere and, therefore, naturally under female control. Planter men were well aware that to be a man of "influence" meant more than possessing large numbers of slaves and cultivated acres. He had to possess the requisite social characteristics, dictated by planter women, to shine within elite circles. Some men openly credited women with setting the genteel tone of springs society.[35] Planter men could grant women the power of determining the cultural characteristics of their class, since men ultimately held the lion's share of power by controlling its political and economic aspects. At the same time, women apparently never used this power to challenge the assumptions underlying their society. Indeed, they enjoyed both their elite status, especially at the springs, and their role as the definers and enforcers of that status. They protected their class as fiercely as their men did.

Rating and ranking the players in the contest for status relied upon gossip and even scandal. Everyone agreed upon the worth of some guests. Others found favor with only a few. The "intellectual game of scandal" at the Virginia Springs, one travel writer alerted visitors, required an "acute observation" that "will enable you to detect any little manouevering amongst mothers, any imprudence on the part of young ladies, or violation[s] of propriety." She then added, "It is your imperative duty not only to tell all you know, but all you have heard, not failing to suggest probable circumstances." The reliance upon gossip and scandal fueled half-truths, scathing criticisms, and petty comments. Despite their sociability and intimacy, visitors whispered about one another, snubbed each other for perceived indignities, and watched and waited for a breach of etiquette or something even more scandalous. When Littleton Wickham arrived at White Sulphur, the company asked: "When did you get here? When do you leave? What is the news? give a famishing sinner a morsel[,] I am dying for a bit of scandal no matter how stale or tough." The virtues and flaws of visitors provided much of the fodder for lively gossip. One northern visitor heard a number of "*stories*" about other guests, the "*married ladies*" near her "*being the ringleaders.*" Visitors frequently discussed inheritances and incomes, especially those of marriageable women. Levin Joynes told of a problematic case for the gossiping judges. A young woman from a genteel Alabama family had brought trunks and trunks of clothing to the springs, but "it is whispered that her father is not worth a dime, being bankrupt." Those who conferred status had to decide where to place this young lady in the spa hierarchy. Even as they gossiped themselves, in conversations at the resorts or in letters home, visitors understood that they too provided material for gossip. After criticizing many and complimenting few in a letter to her mother, Otwayanna Carter added: "As to what is said of *me* I refer you to your next meeting with George Willis," a friend of the family who had been at the springs.[36]

Personal journals and letters home became the repositories of much gossip and many caustic comments and served as ways for guests to pass on their tantalizing information. Hannah Cabell assured her relatives that she could "fill a volume, and I would say two," with news from the springs, even though she had "lost some" while she tended to her sick son. Most related with great relish and in less than genteel terms the events at the springs. In August 1827 Mary Thompson informed Frances Lewis: "We have a whole family of Smiths from Charleston, all mighty ugly. Some Ringgolds from Fredericktown, but tho' they dress like fiddles, they look stiff and stupid, so I have contented myself with a general inspection of their laces and flounces without aspiring to a more intimate knowledge." Even friends and family could become subjects for gossip. George Randolph hoped that his sister could join him at the springs so that the two could enjoy "a quiet dish of scandal at the expense of some of our common friends and relatives." The civility and intimacy of the guests often did not run very deep.[37]

Visitors who failed to keep up with the standards of fashionable appearance and genteel etiquette became prime targets. In the confines of her journal, Mary Jane Boggs ridiculed a number of guests with whom she had socialized: a married couple that she derided "as ugly as Toby's own self," a woman she described as "a real slab of a woman with a purple dress," "another slab" wearing "an imitation crepe shawl," and "a whole parcel of other queer people." Peter Daniel and his group considered Mrs. Riggs, "the wife of a parvenue of Washington," odd, "very weak," and "not a little ridiculous." But, the Riggses' new home, "an immense Gothic Castle," earned much envy among gossipers. Visitors at the springs constantly looked out for those men and women who could not fulfill genteel standards. Judged to be "failures," they became the subjects of gossip and condescension, isolating them from the competition and, perhaps, even from genteel society altogether.[38]

Like those visitors who failed to understand the rules or meet the requirements of fashionable society, those elites who exceeded the normal bounds of genteel conduct or appearance received the censure of their peers. Though Samuel Hoffman considered his party, known as "the Balt[imore] Caravan" or "the Big Drove," "decidedly the most distingué" at White Sulphur in 1840, Robert E. Lee believed they only displayed "ridiculous pride, superciliousness & shallowness." Lee considered the Hoffmans the height not of gentility but of elite excess and bad taste. Just as it criticized poor performance or dress, spa society would not tolerate haughty attitudes or extravagant clothes. A Mrs. Thomas "sadly disappointed" Otwayanna Carter, who found her "very haughty" though rather "common *looking.*" Thomas's haughtiness toward "others would have prevented my ever being acquainted with her," Carter noted, if she had not "*condescended* to ask an introduction." Jane Caroline North wrote to her sister of the rude Susan Rutledge who, after being urged to dance with their uncle, turned "with a grand air" and insisted: "'When Miss Rutledge says *no* she never retracts!'" Not surprisingly, North spread the word about Rutledge's behavior around the springs and in letters to friends and family. Extravagance in dress or cosmetics especially drew censure. One young lady's "fantastic dress and appearance causes merriment wherever she goes," reported Samuel Hoffman. Not even a former First Lady was safe from derision. James C. Johnston informed a good friend that Julia Gardiner Tyler, the "Expresidentiss," was "in full swing of skirts & rowling of her eye balls, shewing an immense mouthful of artificial teeth & cheeks painted up to the eyes." Whether at home or at the springs, those who fell short of or who went beyond the rules for conduct and appearance found themselves ridiculed by genteel society.[39]

Through the medium of gossip, the impact of social life at the Virginia Springs extended beyond the resorts' confines and influenced much of southern society. Those who did not make the trip to the springs received letters from friends and relatives or read newspaper and travel accounts telling of the exciting activities and elegant people. Even as visitors lamented that their friends and family members could not join them, they relished their position as privileged informants. Their letters suggested that if the readers had made the trip over the mountains as well, they too could have participated in this wonderful, exclusive world. Roberta Burwell wished that her friend Lucy Tidball "could see the variety of faces & characters here," for then she "would see the world, in one sense, in miniature." Burwell had seen the world at the springs, garnering the status and enjoying the experiences inherent in such a trip. Visitors to the springs reveled in the prestige of their position, even if they tried to hide it. After receiving numerous letters from her brother that suggested that she knew "how things stood" at White Sulphur, Mary Pettigrew finally wrote him that "I have never been there. A visit there is a pleasure I have in anticipation at some future day to be consummated"—a pleasure that her brother indulged in at that moment and flaunted in front of her. Similarly, Henry D. Mandeville Jr. regaled his sisters with his tales of the "fascinations of society" and his "exciting pursuit of pleasure." Nevertheless, he assured them that he looked forward to returning, at some as-yet undetermined date, "to the quiet nest of home"—a quiet that the two young women probably would have swapped in an instant for the excitement of the Virginia Springs.[40]

Through letters, newspapers, and travel accounts, people who had never traveled to the springs learned the behavior and appearance expected of a southern lady or gentleman. The springs again served as a "school" of gentility's rules and rituals, but now for those outside its confines. Visitors passed on fashion tips so that those at home, away from this center of refinement, could at least dress like the stylish spring-goers. With an air of authority, Thomas Pollock wrote his mother: "Tell the Girls there is a new dance 'the Imperial' which is in vogue[,] some little like the Can can but prettier. Hoops are not worn by the ultra fashionable & bonnets never—a new hat the shape of a china bowl inverted takes it place."[41] Alexander H. H. Stuart and George Johnson each sent their wives the minute details of what women at the springs wore, including the types of shoes and the latest hairstyles, providing Frances Stuart and Marguerite Johnson with the correct tips for fashionable dressing from one of the South's centers of fashion.[42] No less importantly, those at home heard about the successful competitors at the springs—the most graceful or attractive or popular or honorable men and women. Travel accounts and newspapers played an especially important role in the dissemination of southern elite society's successes, as thousands of people read of Virginia Springs society in their printed pages. Both of Mary J. Windle's works, *Life at the White Sulphur Springs* (1857) and *Life in Washington, and Life Here and There* (1859), included extended sections filled with detailed descriptions of the apparel and conduct of male and female visitors, even providing their names and hometowns.[43] Newspapers from Charleston, Richmond, Washington, and elsewhere throughout the South kept track of the celebrities and activities each summer at the Virginia Springs. Their articles extolled the "exquisitely

lovely" faces that looked like moonlight, gushed over the "tranquil gentle-
ness" of young ladies' "movements," and praised gentlemen's "modest
good sense" and "total absence of pretension."[44] These accounts not only
presented a clear picture of how ladies and gentlemen of the finest circles
looked and acted but also bestowed high status on anyone who visited the
springs and took part in the exclusive society there.

The winners in the competition for admiration and status successfully
put together the whole package of gentility. With great skill, they mar-
shaled all of their assets for the best display and performance at the springs.
North Carolinian William Eaton's "distinguished daughter," for example,
made quite a striking impression "in her Parisian dresses[,] talking Italian."
Ranked as "one of the most observed here," she even knew how to compose herself as a lady of leisure, "looking most languishing[,] lolling lan-
guidly in a splendid carriage covered with plate drawn by four elegant bay
horses." Mary Bell became a "great figure" in the 1838 season because of
her "dressing[,] flirting[,] talking & giving water melon frolics." In 1848 a
party of New Orleans Creoles captured the crowd's interest by leading spa
society in "all the fancy and ornamental part of Spring-life." During the
day, they led the parlors, and "at Night, they were always in full dress in the
ball-room, at the head of the Polka's and Mazurka's and quadrilles." In
August 1854, Henry D. Mandeville Sr. of Natchez wrote home to his daughters that, at a ball the previous night, their brother, "equipped in his best,"
had had "many a bright eye looked on him admiringly after having given
full scope to critical observation, and none of either sex, so far as I could
judge, disparagingly." The exclusive company, "by universal consent," declared him "the most unexceptionably and splendidly attired Gentleman in
the room and the most distinguished in style and courtly bearing." Their
brother had passed through the scrutiny of spa society and come out on
top. Of course, the father implied, the sisters—and the rest of southern
society as well—should deem him a success, just as the select society at
the springs had. But winners often reigned only for brief moments. Only
rarely did a man or woman hold a commanding position throughout the
season. Too many newcomers and too many competitors vied for the top
spots, creating a constantly changing hierarchy of popularity. Everyone
who achieved a modicum of success, no matter how fleeting, at the Virginia
Springs took great pride in the fact. John C. Rutherfoord noted that his
family had "heard that Sally was very much admired at the Springs, and
Mama is afraid it will turn her head."[45]

The men and women who came out on top in spa society won more than just the admiration of other resort guests. When details of the display and competition at the Virginia Springs spread throughout the South, all of the winners' peers, not just those at the springs, could then know of their success at the font of fashion. Success at the springs had lasting ramifications. For men, success in spa society could translate into greater influence in business and politics and, if unmarried, better marriage prospects. Successful women also improved their position in husband-hunting; more importantly, since a southern lady's reputation determined her public persona, a stellar performance at the Virginia Springs ensured a high standing throughout fashionable circles in the South. Furthermore, winners at the springs became the models held up for emulation by the rest of southern society. They were actually, however, models of both the best and the worst of genteel southern society—representing the most sociable and beautiful as well as the most competitive and status-obsessed aspects of southern gentility.

∾

"Love-Making May Fairly Be Set Down as One of the Amusements of the Virginia Springs"

As the springs environment intensified the good and the bad characteristics of southern gentility, it also exaggerated the gender expectations and roles of young adults in ways that could produce conflicts. Belles and beaux knew the importance of a good performance at the springs, and they played their parts of ladies and cavaliers to the fullest extent. In the romantic atmosphere, courtship varied from the rituals of the plantation, becoming even more of a scripted masquerade between men and women. In the unique environment of the springs, the game of gentry courtship intensified gender differences even more than at home.

The young male and female communities at the springs often met in the realm of courtship. Because of its crucial importance to the perpetuation of the gentry class and its inherent competitiveness, courting was not only a central activity for the circle of young adults at the springs but also one of the main entertainments of spa society. Much of the courtship at the springs rested on deception and display. Gender roles became performances as young adult visitors all played, with various levels of skill, at the game of courtship. The romantic, almost fantastic, atmosphere of the resorts inspired highly ritualized courtship behavior and exaggerated the differences between "cavaliers" and "ladies." Conflict characterized courting rituals that combined the fun and risk of competitions for status and reputation with potential marriage partners. Men and women often regarded each other as adversaries in courtship. The language of love was often that of warfare. While they mingled easily with each other, beaux and belles donned masks of perfect cavaliers or ladies and strove to best perform that role. They hid their true selves as they followed the script that genteel society had written for them. But these young adults still sought companionate marriages, based upon an intimate knowledge and deep love of each other.

Though the circle of young adults at the springs sought to remain separate from their parents, ultimately the desires of parents and children converged. The parents' concern for gentry socialization and the children's desire for heterosocial pleasure led to the same final goal—finding a suitable spouse. Courting proved to be an activity that both parents and children encouraged while at the resorts. Children thought that they were escaping parental supervision, but parents actually encouraged them to engage in activities that could attract a spouse. A successful season at the springs, according to both parent and child, often ended with a young couple returning home to plan a wedding. Finding a suitable husband or wife from the exclusive circle at the resorts marked the end of a young adult's socialization and, at the same time, perpetuated the southern elite's status and power.

After the late eighteenth century, as the best of southern society came to the springs for more than merely health reasons, the resorts increasingly achieved renown as the premier place in the South for seeking a spouse. "Love-making," according to travel writer J. Milton Mackie, "may fairly be set down as one of the amusements of the Virginia Springs." Southerners had long regarded marriage as the perfect mode for strengthening and reproducing their class, even after they began placing more and more emphasis on individual choice, companionate marriage, and romantic love. The Virginia Springs facilitated the process of elite spouse selection and provided the appropriate environment for the new ideas of courtship and marriage. Since the springs brought together elite families "from every part of the country," as Judith Page Rives recognized, "alliances were often negotiated among these romantic scenes, which brought hearts together widely separated before." The chances for success looked good. Parents with children of marriageable age traveled to the springs knowing that they would meet with some of the best families in the country and find a large field of potential spouses. Older widows and widowers as well went to the springs in search of a new husband or wife. By acting as a central gathering place, the Virginia Springs served yet another important function for elite southern society by providing a marketplace for marriages.[1]

Some visitors literally regarded the springs as a "market" for spouses. The "want of a good parlor" at White Sulphur struck Levin Joynes as "a great misfortune [for] the belles, who are fairly entitled to a good *exhibition-room*, or (if you choose,) a *market-house*." James Kirke Paulding similarly labeled the resorts "great marts" of eligible young ladies and "rich bachelors." Many visitors single-mindedly pursued potential spouses at the springs. Plenty of men came with the primary intention of finding a wife. Kitty Harrison expected that her friend, Fred, would "court about a dozen Girls" while at the springs. Women, too, searched diligently for appropriate men. At Red Sulphur, Richard Burroughs found "some few Ladies here looking for Husbands," but they stood "a poor chance" as "no men [were] looking for wives" at the resort that season.[2]

By the 1830s, the presence of so many of the most eligible and cele-brated belles added to the Virginia Springs' fame. The safe and homogene-ous environment increasingly led many parents to bring their daughters to the springs for their debut, confidant that they would meet only acceptable young men. Belles from across the South, as well as from many northern cities, came every season; the beaux followed. In addition to "Virginia's most choice and beautiful flowers," "beautiful, fascinating, blooming girls" from the cities and "the fair and lovely, the gay and interesting daughters" of the rest of the South gathered in one area. White Sulphur especially achieved renown as a marriage mart. At the height of the season, "when nobody can get accommodations," J. Milton Mackie noticed that every-body insisted on being there, for "the most beautiful ladies of Virginia and the South hold their court of love at this fountain; and, their fame going abroad through the mountains, the guests of the other Springs hasten to this centre of attraction." Levin Joynes concurred: "To any young gentle-man on the look-out for a fashionable beauty, whether to flirt with or to make love to, I cannot imagine a more charming field for selection" than at White Sulphur. Every season, the rise and fall of various courting couples entertained both the visitors and their correspondents at home. News of possible engagements and predictions about whether some suitor would win his belle's hand filled visitors' letters. "News! News!" Alexander Stuart excitedly wrote to his wife in 1837: "McClelland told me last night that Miss E. Cabell is engaged to be married, very shortly, to Wyth M[unford,] Elvira's old beau! What think you of that[?] Elvira Daniel is also *certainly* to be married to Mr Ellett, & Miss Parke Carter is to marry some fellow from Lynchburg."[3]

The Virginia Springs presented a "splendid theatre for a young lady who might wish to be a belle." The culture of the springs demanded a belle's full range of talents. Staying atop the demands of spa fashion required even more trunkloads of clothes and changes of attire for the constantly watched belles than for other women. The fashionable whirl of the resorts meant a constant round of amusements and socializing. Many of the activities centered around belles and beaux. Louisa Cocke flatly described one evening in the White Sulphur's crowded ballroom during her 1837 visit as "an exhibition of the belles & beaux." The more intimate and relaxed gender relations of the springs allowed belles regular interactions and frequent flirtations with men. The refined yet competitive atmosphere played to a belle's strengths. She knew her role well and thrived on the attention and contest for male admirers. Even in the midst of the most intense scrutiny and competition, few single young women found the springs atmosphere unpleasant. According to her father, Virginia Hall felt "quite in her element, surrounded by beaux and belles" at the resorts. Success as a Virginia Springs belle gained a young lady a prime distinction in the South. One male visitor recognized the importance of his female friends becoming "something of belles" when he called that title "the greatest disideratum to young ladies visiting the Springs."[4]

Onlookers, as well as the other belles and beaux, determined which young women were the prettiest, wittiest, gayest, most popular, or most graceful. A young lady could become a belle in many ways. During the 1840 season at White Sulphur, a Miss Swan gained admiration "for her ladylike appearance and deportment, Miss Johnson for her fresh looking complexion and uniformly cheerful manners, [and] Louisa Ann for her ladylike manners and amiable deportment." Receiving the appellation of "belle" required the agreement of both women and men. During Jane Caroline North's stay at White Sulphur in 1851, the popular Betty Mason was "an universal favorite with man, woman, & child," as was North herself. To be considered a belle subjected a young woman to constant scrutiny, but most of them apparently relished the attention. According to Virginia Heth, a Miss Tapscott "looks as if she knew she was a Beauty, and expects admiration from every eye which she invariably gets."[5]

Belles recognized that the contest for beaux at the springs was a highly competitive one; one woman's success made another's less likely. The competition evoked a variety of responses in belles, from jealousy to admiration. At the springs, belles competed against young women from across the South and parts of the North, not just from their plantation district or town. Male admirers and communal acclaim served at once as the goals and the measures of their competition. In 1822 Virginia Heth playfully complained about the sensation that her correspondent Mary Carter had created at the springs. Having heard that Carter had "taken such a host of Beaux from the Sweet Springs," Heth feared that "there will be no such thing as my ever *seeing* one." She "*had* hoped to have made my fortune this year, but shall be compelled to put it off until another Billious fever makes me retreat to the mountains again, or you are out of the way." After describing her most recent conquest, Amilie Rives's friend coyly asked, "*Don't you envy me?*" During the 1833 season at White Sulphur, a Miss Chapman from Philadelphia became such the "centre of attraction" that Courtney Bowdoin worried that she would probably "eclipse" all of the other belles. Although the competition sometimes led to cattiness, the participants generally remained friendly. Young women usually admired and praised the successes of other belles.[6]

While belles competed with each other to collect admirers, beaux competed with each other for a belle's affection. At Bath in 1791, Ferdinand Bayard encountered a young widow, a "Mrs. B.," and her "brilliant circle of young men." They constantly surrounded her, "happy to see her, to hear her and to lavish their compliments on her." "All the places which she embellished with her presence became the rendezvous of all the amiable young men that the town could offer," Bayard noted. The men enjoyed the competition for her affection, as Mrs. B. "seemed to be . . . a prize desirable enough to make them tolerate the rivalry with resignation." Within the genteel confines of the resorts, the rivalries rarely broke into physical conflicts between men. When two young men fought "fisty-cuff cur like" over a wealthy belle from Cuba in 1835, it was a rare occurrence. Even then "they inflicted very little injury on each other," and the affair was quickly settled. Most often beaux competed amicably against one another in the courtship game.[7]

The power of belles over their suitors seemed especially obvious at the springs. While young male and female visitors generally interacted easily and flirted lightly, the true belles held sway when it came to serious courting. In her travel account, Mary J. Windle reported that the arrival of "several new beauties" at White Sulphur caused such a stir as to resemble "a popular panic." "All the gentlemen join in the general pæan, and vie with each other in attentions." In 1811 the happily married John Coalter wrote of a Miss Mayo who, "dressed out in all the splendor, & elegance," had "descended upon us in all her power," captivating the men. Men found belles alluring, but also dangerous. James Kirke Paulding warned young men of Virginia Springs belles, whom he considered "the most numerous class of ladies to be found at these resorts." "Regular built, systematic, determined, and invincible," they went "about as roaring lions, seeking whom they may devour." Some men undoubtedly agreed with Paulding. Even as Littleton Wickham enthused about Eliza Nicholson's "great kindness and . . . sweet face and animated conversation," he predicted that it could be "a charming romance, but . . . a very dangerous one." Though Bella Stuart held only a few "dangerous darts in her quiver," a number of gentlemen still wished to be "trophies of her archery."[8] The matrimonial "danger" presented by young women at the springs often came out in the language used to describe them. Young men regularly used the language of warfare to describe courtship. Belles, such as Bella Stuart and Eliza Nicholson, engaged in "battle," made "conquests," and took "captives."[9] This martial language hints at the potential conflict caused by women having power over men, no matter how temporary and limited.

As at home, belles at the springs thoroughly enjoyed the fleeting moments of power that courtship gave them.[10] Single young women coming to the springs fully expected and excitedly anticipated the numerous flirtations and possible courtships. The letters from young women at the springs usually centered on men and romance. Writing from Alum Springs to her friend Fanny Coalter at White Sulphur, Helen Fitzhugh joked that she hoped that "scores of beaux are being well flirted with by Maria & your *mischievous, good* for nothing self," warning Fanny not to "flirt *too hard*." Demanding that she give her "all the news," a friend of Louisiana Hubard's asked: "When do you expect to return home & how many squires will you have in your net?" The number of her beaux vied for importance with the feelings in her heart throughout each young woman's brief period of flirtation and courtship. Yet even belles could occasionally become impatient with the beaux surrounding them. The popular Lucia Harrison complained in 1827 that "the gentlemen swarm[ed] like bees" around her at the springs.[11]

Jane Caroline North exemplified and relished the role of the belle perhaps better than any other woman at the springs. North excelled in the art of being a belle, receiving the admiration of other belles and the adoration of a host of beaux. In her journal and her letters home, she wrote with a connoisseur's eye about the beaux she met. "Mr Harvey," she reported to her sister, "is the best specimen of the Virginia beaux I have yet seen." While on her first trip to the Virginia Springs in 1851, North collected at least three professions of love and left a string of broken hearts. Two weeks after meeting Stricker Coles, whom she thought "wonderfully romantic & Byronic," he proclaimed "'you know I love you . . . you know your power.'" Unmoved by the profession, North "thought it time to stop." She parted from Coles "with real regret," even though he accused her of having "a great deal of experience" and amusing herself with him. At Salt Sulphur, John Vanderhorst "attach[ed] himself" to her party, though North coyly asserted: "I dont know what brought him." Though warned by her aunt not to be "so encouraging" toward him, North could not resist "torment[ing] him a little" by dancing and talking with him. When Vanderhorst left, she only regretted that she had lost an "attendant." North's conquests continued with a Lieutenant Riall whom North already knew from Charleston and considered "a poor man, somewhat crackbrained" from a fever, and very bothersome. A few days after their reacquaintance, Riall, according to North, "put the china to his annoying behaviour by proposing to me after supper. I have done every thing to avoid it, but found by so doing I was only prolonging my own discomfort." Like any true belle, North's own discomfort or happiness, not those of her admirers, remained her primary concern throughout her stay at the springs.[12]

Parents and chaperones, no less than the belles themselves, closely watched their young ladies' success at collecting admirers. James White took great pleasure in informing his wife that "my 'girls' are considered the best looking on the premises & are having various & Sundry beaux." But the solicitude of parents for the success of their daughters could easily become excessive, earning condemnation rather than admiration for both. Mothers who shrewdly "exhibited" their daughters much like wares at a market opened themselves to ridicule. One travel writer noted the presence in a drawing room of "long rows of anxious, manoeuvring mothers 'that cannot take their tea without a stratagem.'" In 1829 George Harrison's cousin "subjected herself . . . to unpleasant remarks by her too palpable eagerness to show off her daughter Carter." Visitors expected parental interest and pride in a daughter's achievements but rejected such obvious calculation as inconsistent with their ideas of gentility and romantic courtship.[13]

Courtship at the springs differed significantly, though by no means completely, from courtship at home. In addition to offering more choices of potential spouses and taking place amidst more relaxed gender relations, courtship at the resorts often moved at a faster pace. At visitors' homes, courtships ending in engagements took anywhere from a few weeks to a few years. At the resorts, the same process could occur in a matter of a few weeks or even a few days. After all, the eligible young men and women believed that they only had the season to find and fall in love with someone in order to give or receive a marriage proposal. Emily Rutherfoord wrote home about a divorcee who became engaged to a man that she had met at the springs after only a "fortnight's acquaintance." Furthermore, the youth culture of the springs created more opportunities for unsupervised courtship than existed in plantation neighborhoods. Much of the courting at the springs took place within groups of young people or even between two people alone. Flirting couples could be seen not only dancing in the ballroom or chatting in the parlors but also conversing in secluded areas or walking alone in the woods. While walking before breakfast, one travel writer came upon a young man and woman exchanging intimacies in a hidden spot on a hillside. The very landscape of the springs fostered seclusion. Vine-covered porches, as Mary J. Windle recognized, afforded "an American Juliet" enough privacy to "murmur melodious nothings in the ear of her Romeo." At White Sulphur, a group of shady paths meandered through the woods with names that reflected their intended romantic uses: Lovers' Walk led to Courtship Maze which branched off into Hesitancy, Lover's Rest, Acceptance (which led directly to Paradise Row), and, at the end, Rejection and Lover's Leap (fig. 5).[14]

The lack of parental supervision reached its greatest extent when courting couples made secret arrangements to see each other at the springs, as occasionally happened. In the summer of 1827, Elizabeth Powell planned to meet Robert Conrad at the springs unbeknownst to her parents. When she asked her father for permission to make the trip, she told him that it would be with two female friends without mentioning Conrad. Though concerned that it would not be proper for her to go with just women, her father reluctantly agreed. Powell and Conrad probably enjoyed their time together, for they married soon after. Ironically, twenty-five years later, Robert and Elizabeth's daughter wanted to go to the springs with a group of female friends. Robert replied that she had to have a male chaperone and should have the protection of her mother as well. Perhaps he remembered his and his wife's youthful escapade. For two summers in a row, Emily Rutherfoord's parents worried that a beau that they particularly disliked would try to meet her at the springs. W. S. Harding of Louisiana recorded that one of his daughter's beaux "was quite shocked when I told him that Harriet was not coming on." He surmised that Harriet "must have promised to meet him here or he would not have made such a fuss about his disappointment." For Harriet Harding, Elizabeth Powell, Robert Conrad, and assuredly many others, the Virginia Springs presented a rare opportunity to spend some time alone with a would-be "lover." [15]

Courting women and men knew well the "script" that genteel ladies and gentlemen were supposed to follow in the drama of courtship. The springs environment instilled a heightened sense of the romantic in courtship rituals and exaggerated the roles that women and men played. From 1790 to 1860, the courtship rituals at the springs changed very little. They followed the same pattern of grand romantic gestures and overblown performances by "maidens fair" and "cavaliers." Admirers presented roses or other flowers as signs of their feelings to their favorite belles. Some years it was the fashion for courting couples to exchange rings. Both men and women found inspiration in the sublime scenery to write poems or romantic tales. One of these poems, "The Maid of the Cascade," told of a rock at the bottom of a waterfall where

> 'Twas said if on that rock, engraven there
> By maiden hand, a lover read his name,
> That then by all most beautiful and fair,
> Her hand! her snow-white hand, he then could claim. [16]

While at Fauquier White Sulphur, H. B. Tomlin received "a very poetical quotation" from a young lady and replied in kind.[17] Serenades at young ladies' cabins after dark occurred regularly, reflecting both the rituals of springs courtship and of the youth culture that permitted late-night activity. Sometimes an admirer arranged for the resort's band to perform; more often, a small group of men with a guitar or flute serenaded their favorite belles. This ritual dated to the earliest days of the springs. When Philip Vickers Fithian visited Warm Springs in 1775, he recorded hearing "soft & continual Serenades at Different Houses where the Ladies lodge" "from twelve to four this Morning" as well as "An Accusation against one [serenader]—for breaking, in the Warmth of his Heart, through the Loge & entering the Lodging Room of buxom Kate."[18] The serenades continued over the decades. In the late 1830s, one travel writer awoke at midnight to "a strain of sweet music" and a voice singing "We're all a'noddin'" beneath a woman's window.[19]

With various levels of success, courting men and women acted out the romantic idea of themselves as cavaliers and maidens fair. These men and women played their parts as well as they could, knowing that the best performers would receive the most admirers and the resulting communal acclaim, status, and wider range of marriage choices. Having walked to "Lover's Retreat"—a "very lonely part of the wood, which had been the scene of so many courtships, and romantic adventures"—two miles from White Sulphur Springs, a woman, her friend, and two male escorts "*tried to feel very sentimental*" as one of the men told a romantic tale of a dashing count and a virtuous lady. The appropriately named *A Trip to the Virginia Springs, or the Belles and Beaux of 1835* acknowledged the superficial aspect of elite southern courtship as it provided guidelines for courtship to future visitors. The author commended those men and women who knew how to put on the correct masks and give superb performances. With detailed accounts, the author set the scene for flirting and courting couples at the springs and suggested the appropriate lines and actions. Under the "embowering shades" of oak trees, "lovers may sit by moonlight to talk soft delicious nonsense, and flirts wile away a weary hour sheltered from the mid-day glare." A startled horse "only gave the gentlemen an opportunity of displaying their gallantry, and the ladies their bravery, or timidity, whichever they deemed most becoming." Whichever part a courtier chose to play, whether gallant, brave, or timid, it had to be played according to the standards of gentility in order to achieve the desired results. Courting visitors happily followed gentility's dictates, studied their parts well, and responded to the heightened romantic atmosphere of the springs.[20]

In their efforts to appear properly romantic, courting gentlemen performed chivalric deeds for deserving ladies. When a young woman at White Sulphur dropped a bracelet while walking one evening, an anonymous gentleman returned it with an attached poem that read:

> Fair lady! there ne'er was a pleasure like mine—
> That this bracelet which dropped from an arm so divine,
> Should by chance, so unlook'd for, have fallen to me,
> To restore the bright treasure uninjured to thee.

The man had learned well his lessons in chivalric courtship. Another young man and woman acted their parts perfectly when their party came to a wide stream during a walk in the forest. Seeing that the young woman was "somewhat timid," the young man "gallantly caught her up in his arms, and bore her across, amid the bravos of the gentlemen, and the approving smiles of the ladies." After secretly meeting Elizabeth Powell at White Sulphur, Robert Conrad sent her a note asking if "the peerless ladies upon the hill choose to repair to the fountain of health . . . this afternoon, upon horseback?" If so, he would make sure that "three ambling palfrey's—fleet as the cloud . . . will be in waiting at the gate at 4 oclock precisely." He then added that "the young knight McCormick is burning with zeal to protect them, with his life, through the dangers of the journey." Each of these young men and women readily accepted a role as "knight" or "lady" in the romantic courting games of the Virginia Springs.[21]

Underneath the masks and scripts, courting men and women at the springs hoped to find that special individual to know and love intimately. In their letters and diaries from the springs, young men and women revealed not only their familiarity with the rituals of courtship but also their expectations for companionate love. William S. Pettigrew surmounted a number of obstacles in his effort to get time alone with a "Miss F. B." who "captivated" him because of her "ingenousness" and the "frankness & sincerity" of her "countenance." After one private conversation in which he felt comfortable enough to express his "real sentiments," he "had fallen quite in love" with the woman and dreamt of marrying her. A friend of Louisiana Hubard's inquired not whether she had made many conquests at the springs but whether she had "lost [her] heart." John H. B. Latrobe quickly fell in love with Charlotte Claiborne's "pretty face and figure and pleasing manners" after meeting her at one resort in August 1832. When Charlotte and her family moved on to Botetourt Springs, he accompanied them. Only eighteen days after their initial meeting, he proposed on a stroll to the resort's "romantically situated" graveyard and she accepted.[22]

Much to their own and their parents' satisfaction, a number of young men and women emerged victorious from the courting competition each year, returning from a trip to the springs ready to plan a wedding. Richard Bruce, for example, met a Miss Lowry at the springs, "followed her to her home and married her" in 1857. Some families relied heavily on the Virginia Springs for finding their children spouses. The prominent Coles family of Virginia had great success at White Sulphur. Rebecca Coles met her future husband, South Carolinian Richard Singleton, there; her family considered it an "excellent match" since he was "a man of wealth and great Style," which suited Rebecca "exactly." Isaac Coles married one of the Singleton women. Rebecca's sister Emily capped off a springs romance by marrying John Rutherfoord, a prominent Richmond lawyer. Sally Coles married Andrew Stevenson, speaker of the Virginia Assembly and later minister to Great Britain, whom she met at the resort. Finally, Angelica—the daughter of Rebecca Coles and Richard Singleton—fell in love with President Martin Van Buren's son, who had accompanied his father on a visit to the springs. The springs remained a romantic place even after a successful courtship, becoming popular with southerners as a honeymoon spot from an early date. In 1810 Virginia Terrell's friend and her new husband "sett off for the Springs" soon after their wedding. Almost fifty years later, Henry Jones's cousin Alfred took his new bride to Rockbridge Alum.[23]

Whether viewed as a marriage market or as a singularly romantic place, the Virginia Springs provided an immensely valuable service to the southern elite by bringing the "best" young men and women of their society together and encouraging courtship between them. Some of the belles, beaux, and other unmarried men and women came simply for the fun and flirtations. Many young women hoped to shine as belles, wielding a momentary sway over men. Others searched long and hard but had to return to the springs another season. They suffered the fate of Sally Taylor who, having "caught nothing" on a fishing trip, decided that it was "*emblamatic of my trip this summer*" to the springs. But some were "more fortunate in their feelings, and attachments[,] and in the attentions they had received," they "left, pleased, and anticipating future happiness." Yet a too romantic courtship at the Virginia Springs may have brought disappointment to many couples when they started new lives together. Most of the time, married life little resembled their courting days at the Virginia Springs.[24]

❧

"They Seemed to Sink into the Deepest Insignificance"

Part of southern gentility involved constructing rigid boundaries that de-marcated fashionable white society. At the resorts, the elite defined itself by whom it accepted into the inner circle and whom it shunned. Despite the feelings of community, intimacy, and harmony at the Virginia Springs, the lines that elite men and women drew between themselves and others pre-vented excluded groups from exercising any real social influence at the re-sorts and often from joining fashionable society entirely. Some of these boundaries were physical and obvious; others were invisible and subtle. But all of them had power and fostered conflict. Place of residence, religious beliefs, attitudes toward fashion, economic standing, and race all served as grounds for exclusion. The excluded could be elites themselves or, as in the case of slaves, essential components of the springs experience. Yet they re-mained outside the competitive realm of status-seeking, whether by choice or by force. They lacked the power to set rules or enforce them. Some of the excluded groups, especially evangelicals and slaves, formed their own communities and experienced the springs in an entirely distinct manner. Relegated to the periphery, they watched but rarely participated—remain-ing marginal, or even invisible, to those who dominated spa society.

Elite southerners' exclusiveness could even turn inward and create di-visions among themselves. Individual planters separated themselves from the group when they built the large, elaborate cottages that served as an architectural embodiment of their crowning, and therefore ultra-exclusive, place in spa society. William Elliott, the owner of nine plantations in South Carolina and Georgia and a well-known writer, considered those "who own the handsome ranges of private cottages" at White Sulphur "the high aristocracy."[1] Southerners' united front sometimes fell apart as loyalty to state surpassed loyalty to region. An awareness of subregional differences among southerners seems to have increased after 1830, perhaps because of the growing numbers of visitors from the entire South, not just Virginia and the surrounding states, or perhaps because of the growing tensions among members of the southern planter class. Even before 1830, cottage rows at various resorts had taken their names from the state of the majority of the cottage owners. At White Sulphur, for example, southerners physi-cally divided themselves and declared their state loyalties when they stayed in cottages on Alabama, Baltimore, Carolina, Georgia, Louisiana, or Virginia rows.

Virginians especially regarded themselves as separate from, and better than, other southerners. From Rockbridge Alum Springs, Charles Bruce wrote to his wife in 1859: "I turn with [*illegible*] from the ostentatious display, and vulgar manners of the Southern people, to the poor, honest, quiet unpretending Virginians with their polite and considerate bearing." Some Virginians apparently did not even classify themselves as southerners. Because Montgomery White Sulphur "was filled with Southerners almost entirely," Virginian Louisa Venable "did not fancy it at all." The character of women provided L. H. Bolling with the material for a comparison of his beloved Virginia and the rest of the country, including the South: "We have had the elite of the North & South, and the 'Old Dominion' has lost nothing by the comparison. There is something in the graceful ease & dignity of the Virginia ladies far more captivating and loveable than is to be found in the boistrous gaiety & bespangled finery of the far south or the cold and formal propriety of the gaudy 'down Easters.'"[2]

South Carolinians at the springs also claimed a distinctive place in the South, particularly during and after the Nullification Crisis of the early 1830s and the sectional tensions resolved by the Compromise of 1850. By the 1820s, Salt Sulphur Springs had become known as the gathering place for South Carolinians. Around 1833 the resort named a row of cabins "Nullification" or "States' Rights" for its leading guests. All of the "Carolinians" that Edward Tayloe of Virginia met in 1832 were "nullifiers" and, according to him, "beset with a strange delusion which no reason can vanquish."[3] Similarly, from White Sulphur in 1852, South Carolinian James L. Petigru worriedly informed his friend Alfred Huger that "there has been more than one fuss out here, and our countrymen each time, had a hand in it."[4] An intense sense of state or even local identity among southerners at times divided them, overwhelming the feeling of shared community that they usually enjoyed with other southerners at the Virginia Springs.

Though they occasionally divided among themselves along geographical lines, southerners at the springs generally united in excluding from positions of social power and influence those not from the South. Southerners often admired the finery and wealth of northern and foreign visitors and readily accepted them into their circles; but they never permitted them to set or enforce the rules at the springs. "Among the Rich is a family from Phila named Bard," Virginian Agnes Cabell wrote to her daughter around

1836. "They hold their heads very high—and are classed among the exclusives in their own City. Nobody seems to take to them here." With the exception of Philadelphia Row at Red Sulphur, no cottage rows carried a northern name. Southerners noticed the appearance of northerners and foreigners at the springs. But, as Agnes Cabell observed, they often were not fond of the northern urban elite visitors. In 1838 Alexander Stuart informed his wife of the arrival at White Sulphur of "a daughter & several grand-daughters of John J. Astor of N. York & Genl Talmadge & his daughter, who is said to be the belle of N. York"; she may have been "the belle of N. York," but she was not likely to be one at the Virginia Springs where southern women usually held that distinction. Another northern family was "said to be very rich," but was "evidently pretty up-startish" and made few friends among the southerners. Southern planters also admired foreign visitors, especially those with titles or high offices. But they believed that these foreigners sometimes put on "airs." Caribbean planters formed an exception to this rule; southerners apparently accepted them as part of their own group.[5]

As sectionalism intensified, many southerners and northerners found it difficult or uncomfortable to travel to resorts outside of their own region. When Philadelphian William Short contemplated summering at the springs in 1833, he had to inquire about Virginia laws governing his free black servants. Writing to John H. Cocke, he asked whether Virginia law prohibited the entrance of "free people of color" into the state. "Nothing could induce me to take a free man with me where he would be exposed to be sold as a slave," he explained, refusing to visit the springs if such a law existed (and it did).[6] Conversely, personal liberty laws restrained many southerners from traveling north with their slaves. In combination, such laws increasingly led planters to view the Virginia Springs as *their* resorts. After spending the summer of 1850 traveling with the Van Buren family through the North, South Carolinian Mary Singleton concluded that "she would not give the old Virginia Springs for *all* the Northern watering places."[7] With increasing sectional tensions, southern planters turned more and more to their exclusive world in the mountains, where they happily encountered their own kind.

In the end, not even the increasingly homogeneous company of the Virginia Springs could protect the planters' genteel and convivial atmosphere from the growing sectional conflict. When President Millard Fillmore and his party arrived at White Sulphur in August 1851, the New Yorker received little attention or respect from many guests, probably because of his part in finalizing the still-controversial Compromise of 1850. The South Carolina gentlemen refused introductions to the president and, according to Jane Caroline North, "the Carolina Ladies declared not one of them would attend" the ball held in his honor. By the late 1850s, the southern gentry believed that elites who did not uphold their values deserved rude treatment. And the sectional feelings, as well as the exclusion, at the springs deepened. In 1857 Maryland's Richard Burroughs "met with many kind friends from the south and the old Virginia, but let the North pass."[8]

Unfashionables, those without the money or the interest to participate in the competition and display, were even more excluded than elite northerners from fashionable spa society. Not only did they lack the power to set rules or influence society, they also became almost invisible. Elite southerners at the springs used their standing and influence to force these unwanted members from their community. Poorer whites never stood a chance of acceptance as they could not afford to stay more than a few days or to own the costly accoutrements of fashionable society. Unfashionables stayed at the bottom of the spa hierarchy; but, as long as they remained respectful and unobtrusive, the fashionables tolerated their presence. These excluded men and women never entered the competition, for they had no hope of receiving admiration and status. If they ever danced in the ballrooms or promenaded on the piazzas or gossiped in the parlors, their presence went unnoticed in the letters, journals, and travel accounts of elite visitors. Fashionables noticed them only as objects of derision or pity. Recognizing their low position in the spa hierarchy, these men and women generally accepted their place without demanding recognition.

While prohibitive travel costs and hotel prices kept out most of the "lower" elements that elite visitors disdained, a number of unsavory characters slipped into the scene every season. In 1840 Edmund Randolph ran into some "black-guards, with hairy faces and adventurers of every trick [who] throng upon one another" at White Sulphur. To amuse his sister, he described them in detail: "There is a man who sells air-guns, an auctioneer who sells cheap books, a phrenologist who tells fortunes, a couple of dentists who draw teeth with their fingers, all like so many spiders setting their nets in different corners to catch the silly flies who buz about on bank-note wings."[9] Most of these unwanted guests, like the ones that Randolph described, were itinerant merchants and entertainers who passed through the springs area during the summer. They never attempted to stay long at the resorts or enter fashionable society, so the well-to-do visitors worried little about their presence.

Judging from the numerous complaints about their unwelcome appearance and pernicious influence, professional gamblers received most of the visitors' ire and little of their renowned hospitality. Many respectable guests regarded professional gamblers as a separate class of people, as "*Vultures*" who "entrap[ped] the young & thoughtless." Visitors clearly differentiated professional gamblers from those gentlemen who gambled as an avocation, simply enjoying the competition of a good game of cards. Gamblers ran faro games, initiated wagering on billiards, and arranged poker parties, and made a living by doing so. Elite guests especially despised gamblers who had once been members of their class or had the wealth and accoutrements necessary for a gentleman. According to Nelly Custis Lewis, the entire company at White Sulphur in 1834 refused to notice or speak to a man that she called only "C. S." "He is not received in any genteel home in N[ew] Orleans," she explained to a friend, for "he kept a gambling house last winter." Because so many of the visitors were familiar with one another to some degree, everyone quickly knew who the "real '*blacklegs*'" were, even if they at first looked to be of "genteel appearance." Most of the time the ladies and gentlemen ignored or even shunned them. Harriet Martineau traveled to the springs in a stage with two self-declared gamblers whom she found insufferable. After their arrival, "it was a comfort" for Martineau "to see how poor a figure they cut at the Springs." All of the guests ignored them and "they seemed to sink into the deepest insignificance that could be desired." The gamblers must have attracted enough gentlemen to do a good business or they would not have returned every year. But the genteel company, especially the women, would never permit them to participate in regular spa society.[10]

Some guests chose not to enter fashionable society and its competition, foregoing admiration and high standing. They chose to remain outside the circle of influence for a number of reasons. Some traveled to the springs strictly to seek a cure for a serious illness and mainly visited the resorts that catered to invalids. Other guests considered fashionable society inane or wasteful and quickly became bored with the scene. Finally, evangelical visitors regarded fashion and display as sinful and stayed within a distinct religious circle at the resorts.

Invalids remained aloof from and were not sought out by the pleasure-seekers. They often willingly excluded themselves from fashionable spa society by staying at resorts primarily for invalids. When Henry Watson traveled to Red Sulphur in 1856, he found that all of the visitors were "pale[,] feeble, Emaciated, coughing all about & spitting." There was "not the same *crowd* as at the other places," he informed his wife. Because the fashionable crowd stayed elsewhere, Watson believed that a less rigid form of conduct prevailed at Red Sulphur than at the more popular resorts. His neighbors spoke to each other without formal introductions and "can continue to be sociable without Even Knowing Each others names."[11] At the popular resorts, invalids separated themselves from fashionable society by their choice of activities. When not at the springhouse or in the baths, most of those suffering from illness spent their time in their own rooms, reading, sleeping, or writing. Few ventured into the parlors or ballrooms. They received visits from kind friends but only returned calls if they felt up to it. Their outdoor excursions usually consisted of a carriage ride or perhaps a short walk around the resort. The fortunate ones regained their health and returned to the Virginia Springs solely for pleasure.

Not everyone enjoyed the glittering society and social competition at the Virginia Springs. Some elite southerners regarded spa life as frivolous and dissipated. These visitors grew bored during their stay, but usually could not leave either because they sought to maintain their health or because the rest of their party loved the place. The springs and its society "disgusted" Volumina Barrow's brother, Horace Hunley, for example. Only the scenery could "recompense me for the waste of time and money—but a 40 horse power engine and a cable chain could not drag me to the waste of two weeks more at the 'Montgomery White.' The insipidity of the place is as a dose of Castor oil to my taste—I endure it how ever for the pleasure of Volumina & the children."[12] Some considered the emphasis on display and competition merely a useless pursuit of fashion, devoid of any real value. Mary Brison regretted "the folly and fashion of these poor souls, who vainly strive with earthly toys to fill an *empty* mind, for to judge from appearance, they have nothing very solid to build upon." Others could neither enjoy nor endure the forced life of leisure, the usual activities of the resorts, or the accompanying feeling of idleness. In addition to finding society at White Sulphur as "unsociable and selfish as any I have ever seen any where," Robert Hubard became bored with "no amusements except dancing, gambling and riding" and took no pleasure in the routine of drinking the waters, "eating and lounging and dressing."[13]

Some visitors believed that spa life centered around and encouraged dissipation and led pleasure-seekers to squander valuable time. Elizabeth Bryan pitied the invalids that she saw at the springs; but she pitied even more "the healthy & vain throng who had gone in search of pleasure & dissipation, & were mirrours of fashion & extravagance." When an 1840 newspaper article promised that "'nothing which money and labour can procure will be wanting to make the Warrenton Springs attractive to all,'" Robert Eden Peyton protested vehemently. In an angry letter, he inquired of the editor: "I suppose this last sentence means to include cock fighting, farrow tables, roulette & such like things." "What if some of them should be against [the] law? It is easy to dodge that. Am I right in this conjecture?" He warned that he would consider the editor's silence "an assent." Peyton obviously understood that he represented a minority opinion yet wanted the public to know just what sort of dissipation took place at the springs and who encouraged it. Still, the opportunities for gambling, dancing, hunting, dressing, visiting, lounging, competing, and various other pleasurable and fashionable activities lured more visitors—perhaps even because of the element of dissipation—than they repelled. Even those who complained, moreover, generally enjoyed some aspects of the trip, especially the medicinal and scenic, and often returned to the springs.[14]

Many devout visitors, especially evangelical southerners, found people at the Virginia Springs not only dissipated but irreligious. Eighteenth- and nineteenth-century evangelicals, primarily Baptists, Methodists, and Presbyterians, regarded dancing, fancy dressing, drinking, and sabbath-breaking as sins. One could not love both frivolity and God, in their view. Little wonder, then, that they regarded spa life and the fashionable pleasure-seekers as sacrilegious. In 1789 the prominent Methodist minister Francis Asbury described the wealthy pleasure-seekers at Bath as "sinners" and, later, called Bath "that seat of sin." Since White Sulphur received praise as the pinnacle of fashion, it also received condemnation as the pinnacle of sin. The "fashion and extravagance & show" at White Sulphur convinced Lucy Baytop that "surely Satan has his seat here." Paulina Storrs thought it "was like Sodom and Gomorrah was when it was destroyed with fire and brimstone. The people seem to be entirely given up to the gratification of every sin." Because the corporation "derived a large revenue from the renting & licensing [of] a gambling House, Faro Bank & also the sale of Liquors," the devout Joseph Ficklen turned down the opportunity to purchase five thousand shares of stock and a "cottage Priviledge" at White Sulphur. To have done otherwise would have caused a "stain & infringement on my moral & religious scruples." The group of visitors that included Baytop, Storrs, and Ficklen among its numbers turned away from the frivolity and the empty pursuit of fashion on account of their religious beliefs. As they chose to remain outside the fashionable circle, they formed their own small but distinct communities at the resorts.[15]

Religion never played a major role at the springs. In the decades from 1790 to 1860, resort owners built hundreds of buildings of various kinds— none of them apparently a church. Those visitors who wanted to hear a sermon every Sunday had to travel to nearby towns, such as Union, Lewisburg, or Lexington. The conduct of both visitors and proprietors who willingly violated the Sabbath appalled and angered evangelicals. In 1856 Lucy Cocke was aghast when Dr. Thomas Goode of Hot Springs disallowed sermons on Sunday mornings because they interfered with bathing. In an 1820 tavern bond, the proprietor of Buffalo Springs was only willing to promise "no unlawful gaming, and no more drinking than was necessary on Sunday." Springs society also showed little interest in the evangelicals' temperance movement. "The Temperance cause seems at a low ebb at these Springs [Red Sweet]," Mary Blackford noted; "some of the people seem to think they must take a julep on coming out of the bath." Finding "negroes more ready to receive moral instruction then the Whites," John H. Cocke "accordingly persuaded several of the Servants at the Hot Springs of the value of the temperance reform."[16]

Evangelicals did attempt to bring some salvation to the sinners. Ministers visited the springs every season, representing every denomination from Methodist to Unitarian and including such leading lights as Lorenzo Dow and Jared Sparks. When a visiting minister stayed at a resort over a Sunday, he generally preached unless sickly. In 1837 Louisa Cocke took pleasure in the rare "plentiful supply of the clergy" at White Sulphur, which consisted of two from Norfolk, one from Richmond, and one from Culpeper.[17] To her relief, their presence promised plenty of Sunday sermons. Ministers gave the occasional sermon in the resort's ballroom and they were usually well-attended. On the whole, however, most guests did not seem to mind the absence of a Sunday sermon; in fact, some appreciated not having to endure one. Those who really felt the lack of a sermon observed the Sabbath with prayer and Bible readings in their cabins or rooms. They also found kindred spirits among the other pious visitors.

Despite their concerns, plenty of evangelical visitors, even ministers, came to the springs to improve their health, see friends and family, and

enjoy some of the amusements. They gathered into their own small community, which included some elements of the larger society. They followed
many of the rules and rituals of genteel society and generally considered
themselves refined. But they avoided fashionable society, refused to participate in the display and competition, and struggled against the temptations
of spa life. In 1854 James Pleasants warned his recovering daughter Ann
that "the 'flesh-pots' will tempt you from a rigid self-denial and permanent
triumph over disease. Forsake, therefore, the pleasures of sin," at least "for
a season." Fearing that she was "too easily led into temptation and it would
not be for my soul's good to be much in company of the sort to be found
at the Springs," Caroline Richardson decided against meeting a dear friend
there. But every season a few could not resist. Two years later, she heard
about a young man who, "though he is religious[,] danced away at the
Springs." The young man's father, however, "was truly glad to see it. He
knew full well there was no sin in it." But Richardson thought otherwise.
Alexander Stuart similarly expressed surprise at seeing "among the spectators who seemed to take the liveliest interest in the scene" at a ball, a
Mr. Williamson, "Mr Jone's deputy in his revival operations . . . the fellow
who sung the psalms & made such a fuss in Staunton."[18]

The deeply religious Cocke family of Virginia remained staunchly opposed to the follies and frivolities of fashionable society; yet its members
frequently visited the Virginia Springs throughout the nineteenth century
and occasionally struggled against the temptations of resort life. When she
ventured into the Amelia Springs ballroom to watch an assembly in 1840,
Louisa Cocke received "a timely reproof from husband [John H. Cocke]
for being tempted to go to such a scene." Returning to her cabin to find
the Miss Robertsons, "two dear young converts," conversing quietly with
the other evangelical matrons, she felt even more the sinner. John H. Cocke
in particular believed that evangelical visitors needed to set themselves off
from the sinners at the resorts. In 1818 he despaired of acquaintances who
participated in the "odious & destructive vice of Gaming." Over thirty
years later, he watched as a longtime friend drunkenly "sunk down into the
first Chair he could reach in the piazza [and] fell to sleep." There he left
him, "a spectacle of beastly drunkenness to every passerby." To reduce the
sinfulness of the springs, Cocke conferred with Dr. John Brockenbrough,
the proprietor of Warm Springs, and his wife about building a church at
the resort in 1844, since an increasing number of visitors appeared "more
seriously inclined" and some had even inquired "'What they must do to be

saved.'" In Cocke's opinion, a church would help to instigate "a secession" of the pious from "the hair-brained dancers & airy aspirants for fashionable distinction." With his financial help and leadership, Cocke believed that Brockenbrough could create at least one resort "where sober minded & sedate people could congregate without having their toes trodden upon & themselves elbowed into corners by the impudent & presumptuous fashionables of the day." Despite Cocke's efforts, vice won out, corrupting, in his view, "one of the most distinguished gentlemen of Va." Instead of building a church, Brockenbrough "contracted for a large & expensive Building for gambling purposes." The sinners had triumphed.[19]

John Cocke's proposed church may not have accomplished all that he hoped. Even when it made its presence known at the springs, evangelical religion often had a limited impact on the activities of the fashionables. At Sweet Springs during the revivalist upsurge of the 1790s, many visitors "attended a methodist sermon yesterday and heard card playing and dancing condemned as damnable sins." But shortly after the sermon ended, "some of the gentlemen returned to the card table, and others joined the ladies to receive their approbation for an assembly. Whether the ladies were convinced by the arguments of the preacher or the beaux a little time will determine." Within ten days, however, all of the preachers had "withdrawn," "yield[ing] to the ascendency of loo and whist"—to the rule of the pleasure-seekers. Hearing of an upcoming camp meeting near Sweet Springs in 1825, the fashionable Robert Hubard thought that he would "delight to see the Capers of the Methodists." The fashionables attended the same sermons as the evangelicals, but continued pursuing pleasure, competing for status, and enjoying the display and spectacle. The pious watched from the sides and prayed for their souls.[20]

While fashionable society paid little attention to the evangelicals, who willingly isolated themselves into their own communities, it actively excluded free and slave black workers, who ultimately formed their own community as well. White guests rarely recognized the important role that slaves played in fashionable society. Without the work of black men and women, there would have been no leisure for white visitors. Without the presence of slaves, white visitors could not have felt like feudal lords and ladies. As in southern society in general, black workers always remained the most excluded group at the springs. Ironically, they received more attention from the powerful and fashionable than poorer whites, evangelicals, and other unfashionables. Around their duties, free and slave blacks, whether visitors or workers, created their own community at the resorts. They had their own leisure experiences and sometimes claimed the same spaces as whites. They even shaped their own version of fashionable society, with its own rules and competition for status.

Slaves proved essential not only to the operation of the resorts but also to the workings of fashionable society. For example, they played important roles in the spread of spa gossip. Through their connections with other servants, some slaves knew a great deal about the private lives of ladies and gentlemen. Black workers—and not just those traveling with white families—visited back and forth between the resorts just like white guests, picking up and passing on news. Their information often proved valuable to white guests as prized gossip in the competition for status. Slave maids had passed on the crucial information concerning the private behavior and sleeping arrangements of Joel R. Poinsett and Mrs. Rogers during their scandal at the springs in 1832.[21] Even more importantly, resort slaves functioned as a necessary audience for the white visitors' displays. The black men and women who crowded around the ballrooms' windows or alongside the tournament fields reaffirmed both the southern hierarchy and the image that planter men and women held of themselves as cavaliers and ladies.

At the same time, resort slaves and slave visitors had leisure experiences that were separate from, but often similar to, those of fashionable white society. The small theater at White Sulphur had a gallery for blacks. Some resorts had separate springs "where the negro servants assemble and drink in imitation of their masters." With no church services, one visitor noted that "the only indication" that it was Sunday was "the appearance of the blacks in their best attire and in their highest spirits."[22] Elizabeth Gray's slave Margaret attended "quite an elegant *dinner party*" and drank enough champagne to make her sick. About the whole affair, Gray sighed, "What we have not seen [from the slaves] since we have been here."[23]

Clearly, resort slaves believed that they possessed certain rights even in the presence of rich white men and women. Their insistence upon these rights, such as bribes for good service or drinking champagne to excess, often caused conflict between whites and blacks at the springs, as they did on the plantation. On some occasions, white people felt that black people had gone too far. In a letter published in the *Charleston Daily Courier* in July 1858, "A CAROLINIAN" protested "negro waiters being allowed to ride *within* and upon the stage occupied by ladies and gentlemen" and urged the proprietors of White Sulphur to use their influence with stage companies to prevent such a breach in race relations. "You may imagine my horror," he explained, "when, on starting the stage, the driver was stopped by the agent, and two black waiters were put *inside,* in close proximity with the ladies." After stepping out of the stage for a moment and losing his seat to a white man, one of the slave waiters demanded it back and, to the Carolinian's mortification, received it.[24]

How, when, and where resort and visiting slaves spent their leisure time often brought them into conflict with white visitors. The Carolinian's continued complaints provide a fascinating glimpse into slave life at the springs, revealing other important ways by which enslaved men and women challenged the system of bondage and the denial of their humanity. In addition to the horror of "negro waiters" on the stages, the anonymous author called the proprietors' attention to another "evil"—"the privileges and conduct of the black waiters and maids" at the resort itself. He demanded that the proprietors "suppress . . . the promenading of waiters and maids in the only walks attached to the Spring." He considered the walk "a most lovely spot." But the scene became "marred when high-dressed maids are permitted to frequent those spots, which to such, should be inviolate! and negro men are allowed to fill the air, which should be pregnant only with the odor of flowers, with the fumes of bad segars!" He suggested "that there be at once made an entire revolution in the arrangement of other 'walks' which have been promiscuously used, so outraging decency and propriety as to be most truly revolting to all well bred Southerners."[25] He was clearly upset not only that black men and women used the walks and the stage coaches, but also that they dressed like whites, promenaded like whites, and enjoyed the scenery like whites in places that should have been reserved for white ladies and gentlemen. Most alarming to the author was the fact that the slaves believed, as their behavior and attitude showed, that they possessed an equal right to these spaces.

As evident in this diatribe, the black community at the springs had their own signs of status and fashion. Like the elite white community, slaves at the springs competed with one another for status and acclaim in a variety of ways, ranging from courting to dressing to dancing. The champagne-drinking Margaret, for example, became a "great belle" among the black community at Rockbridge Alum Springs. In a remark strikingly similar to comments about white women, her owner Elizabeth Gray noted that she "never saw a *greater belle,* you scarcely ever see her *without* an escort." The black men vied with each other over "which shall pay her the most attention." Margaret, like any white belle, delighted in the attention. Her conquest of the "'head dining room servant'" was considered "the *greatest*

Figure 20. *Kitchen Ball at White Sulphur Springs,* Virginia, Christian Mayr, 1838. (North Carolina Museum of Art, Raleigh, Purchased with funds from the State of North Carolina)

catch of the Springs for the colored gentry."[26] As on the plantation, there was a hierarchy of black men and women at the springs and Margaret received standing for "catching" one of the highest men in the hierarchy, just as a white belle would have.

Another powerful portrayal of the black community's fashionable society, leisure activities, and mutual competition at the springs appeared in a painting by Christian Mayr. In 1838 Mayr, a German artist, painted *Kitchen Ball at White Sulphur Springs, Virginia,* his best known painting (fig. 20). The simple details of the kitchen and the fact that Mayr portrayed "all the well-known coloured people in the place," including "the band of musicians," suggests that he witnessed an actual event.[27] Even more than the newspaper complaints, the painting provides rare insight into the often-hidden community of black people at the springs. The central presence of a man and woman finely dressed in white suggests that the ball celebrated a wedding, an important social and communal occasion for the black community. The kitchen ball provided much-needed entertainment and leisure for the slaves. Slaves who worked all day could dress up and dance all night. The slave musicians who played for whites in the after-noons and evenings could play for their own community at night, though they may have played different music and danced different dances. Mayr's painting reveals more than merely slaves at leisure. Like the white com-munity, black men and women apparently competed for status through dance and dress. With his attention to clothes and other details of finery, Mayr showed the variations in status of the black guests. Interestingly, the lightest-skinned persons wear the finest clothes. Some desired the spotlight, while others remained on the sides as spectators and possibly judges. At this ball, however, black men and women did not simply mimic white vis-itors. Instead, they participated and shared in their own temporary leisure experience in their own temporary community.

The process of defining and establishing boundaries at the Virginia Springs proved an integral part of southern planter class-formation and reproduction. Excluding those men and women who did not meet genteel southern standards from influence and prominence protected the power and position of the reigning elites. Like the rules for behavior and appear-ance, the status competition, and the personal display, social boundaries helped to define what it meant to be an elite southerner. At the Virginia Springs, those lines probably appeared more obvious and more fixed than at any place else in the South. Within the springs' unique environment, the South's leading men and women found opportunities to create and test the boundaries they would implement and enforce at home.

❧

"Honor to Those Days of Chivalry"

The "southernness" of the Virginia Springs appeared in its most explicit form in a series of special events that brought together and revolved around all of the characteristics of the southern gentry. After about 1830, elite southerners, influenced by romanticism, increasingly linked themselves and their way of life with the feudal aristocracy of the Middle Ages. Draw-ing upon romantic themes, southern visitors organized hunts, costume balls, and *tableaux vivants* at the springs that gave form and substance to this imagined link. The tournaments held at the end of the season at some resorts represented the ultimate manifestation not only of the southern elite's attachment to medievalism but also of the characteristics of Virginia Springs society. These events, especially the tournaments, embodied southerners' devotion to hierarchy, commitment to gentility, and love of games. They combined refinement and beauty with competition and display, satisfying the dual demands of gentility. Tournaments and other romantic events also highlighted and heightened the different experiences of men and women. Furthermore, these events that took place on the "stage" of the Virginia Springs made clear to all who observed them and read about them in newspapers and letters the power of these men and women and the dominance of their class. Because the springs most closely approximated their idealized view of themselves and their society, the visitors knew that life there offered a wonderful alternative to the real world of home. Medieval tournaments perfectly captured the fantastical or theatrical quality of life at the springs. Visitors, whether participants or spectators, considered these events the crowning experience of a season.

The romantic movement, in Europe and elsewhere, emphasized sensibility, imagination, sentimentalism, a love of nature, and the exotic. Southerners created their own form of romanticism centered mainly on the cult of chivalry and a concomitant fascination with the Middle Ages. Southern women and men formulated their image and understanding of the Middle Ages primarily from Sir Walter Scott's stories of heraldry and chivalry. Scott's novels achieved more popularity in the South than the North. As a place that seemed both out-of-time and out-of-space, the Virginia Springs provided a perfect setting for such southern romanticism. Describing one resort to his daughters in 1840, Alexander Stuart perpetuated this fantastic view of the springs. "This is a very beautiful place, & there are a great many people here. It is like a town, but there are no shops, & ugly houses, & all the people are dressed nicely, & amuse themselves walking about, & visiting each other." In such a setting, visitors could easily envision themselves in medieval forests and castles. "We went forth in gallant style," wrote one woman who accompanied a hunting party that set out from the "castle" at White Sulphur, "and only wanted the hawkers, to have imagined ourselves in the reign of Queen Elizabeth on a Holy-rood day." That the members of her party were well aware of their invocation of medieval images and fictional personas is clear: they quoted passages from Scott on their ride.[1]

Inspired by their romanticism and their emphasis upon display, visitors organized and participated in masquerade balls and dramatic tableaux. They excitedly awaited every costume ball that took place during their stay at the springs, trying to attend as many as possible. The combination of fanciful costumed display and competition drew immense crowds to the resort ballrooms. Details of the balls filled letters home and newspapers. Henry D. Mandeville Sr. described a costume, or "fancy," ball held at Salt Sulphur in 1854 using the same language that viewers used when describing mountain scenery. "The contemplated fancy Ball came off last night, and proved to be quite a splendid picturesque and Charming spectacle. I do not possess the requisite descriptive powers to pourtray it—but will only observe that many of the costumes—female & male—were well conceived and imposing—most of them gay and brillant." Men and women took great care in their choice of costumes, drawing from their own American locale, exotic places, literature, the Middle Ages, and even the ancient world. In her travel account, Mary J. Windle included a twelve-page description of the "Grand Fancy Ball" at Red Sweet Springs in September 1856. "The whole scene seemed enchantment. Noble lords, Indian princesses, Italian peasants, Turkish sultans, Di Vernons, and stately dames of the olden times, passed before us in rapid succession." Angels, Spanish privateers, Titania the Queen of the Fairies, Sappho, Joan of Arc, and, remarkably, Greek slave girls also made their appearance. Not every guest indulged in the fantasy. The curmudgeon Edmund Ruffin regarded the fancy ball that he witnessed as an absurdity since many of the dancing partners dressed as characters "who never possibly could have come together." [2]

The *tableaux vivants* that visitors staged for admiring audiences similarly allowed the participants a chance to imagine themselves as romantic figures for a moment. The always-popular tableaux consisted of a group of suitably costumed men and women posing on a stage, like a still life, offering a static representation of a specific scene from literature, mythology, or history. One young man who participated in a "grand Exhibition of Tableaux Vivantes" at Red Sweet listed the "principal scenes" and the names of the actors and actresses in a letter home. The first, amazingly, depicted a "Turkish slave market, wherein the Grand Turk, as they called him, was surrounded by any number of Circassian beauties." After a "Corsair Prison Scene" came, not surprisingly, a "Scene from [Scott's] Lady of the Lake." The tableau "generally considered the best" featured a "Miss La Doux[,] a French lady from Louisiana, representing a Nun, about to have her hair shorn off preparatory to taking the black veil." The closing tableau included the " 'To be or not to be' " soliloquy and an exchange between Hamlet and Ophelia.[3] Women, as well as men, apparently felt perfectly comfortable performing on this actual stage in front of other visitors.

Tournaments provided the supreme example of the southern qualities of refinement, exclusivity, hierarchy, chivalry, display, and competition. In the two decades after 1840 or so, Capon, Jordan White Sulphur, Red Sweet, Shannondale, White Sulphur, and perhaps other springs held medieval tournaments at various times. But the grandest and best-known tournaments occurred annually at Fauquier White Sulphur. Held at the end of August or beginning of September, the tournaments often served as the grand finale to the fashionable season. Newspapers and periodicals throughout Virginia, in Washington, in large towns across the South, and even in some northern cities announced upcoming tournaments and published details of the events. In 1848 an advertisement in the *National Intelligencer* proclaimed that at the Fauquier White Sulphur Springs tournament the "sons of Maryland (twice victorious) are to appear on the occasion of their own studs; and, if again successful, will be acknowledged as entitled to the palm of superiority." Often the tournament events lasted for a few days, beginning with a deer or fox hunt. At White Sulphur, the hunt started in lordly style at a grand structure, named the "Wolf," built upon a hill and decorated inside with antlers, bearskins, firearms, and bugles.[4]

The jousting events and masquerade balls attracted not only resort guests but also their slaves and sometimes hundreds of spectators who lived in the surrounding countryside. The elite participants thus displayed their position and dominance in front of a crowd. In 1852 Robert Taylor Scott's grandmother, who lived at Oakwood plantation near Fauquier White Sulphur, ordered him to escort several of his cousins and sisters to the resort for the grand tournament and fancy ball. "Carriages well filled with men & women & children, horsemen without number, and gangs of country folks on foot" came "from all quarters" for a jousting tournament at Red Sweet Springs in 1840. The male participants at a White Sulphur tournament a week earlier considered the event a success because "nearly all the ladies & gentlemen & servants" watched their feats of bravery and horsemanship. The "rush of vehicles and horses was so great" at a Shannondale tournament in 1848 that "gentlemen and ladies were borne over in the large ferry boat as thick as they could stand." In the early 1850s, "country-people gathered from miles around" to view the masqueraders at a Sweet Springs ball. The presence of the "lower orders" and their admiration of those at the top of the social hierarchy reinforced the feudal element of the tournaments and reaffirmed the elite status of the participants.[5]

Figure 21. *Tournament-Grounds on the Rappahannoc River, Knickerbocker Magazine,* Sept. 1858. (Van Pelt Library, University of Pennsylvania, Philadelphia)

The tournament ground at Fauquier White Sulphur was a smooth meadow three hundred yards long on the banks of the Rappahannock (fig. 21). Along its shady slopes, the judges and spectators gathered. Trumpeters announced the arrival of the participants. The knights, with such names out of Scott as Wilfred of Ivanhoe and Brian de Bois-Guilbert, wore colors, plumed hats, and coats of arms. At an 1848 tournament, the knights "presented an imposing and brilliant spectacle" with their "peculiar and picturesque costumes" and "their tall lances glittering in the sunbeams." The fair maidens in the stands held the colored ribbons of their favorite knight. A "Herald" gave a brief speech and then announced the knights. The tournament itself consisted of men on horseback running lances through rings or at wooden dummies for five or six trials over the course of about two hours. Samuel Hoffman considered it "a manly and active sport, no child's play." The victorious knight chose a maiden from the audience to crown the "Queen of Love and Beauty." Caught up in the

feudal atmosphere at Fauquier White Sulphur, one spectator wistfully reported that the scene "would inspire to something like the ancient feats of
arms, and we might expect to see the lances shivered, and the helmets
dashed away, were not the age of chivalry really past." A costume ball with
a medieval theme followed the games in the evening, with the winning
knight and his queen presiding. Princesses, huntsmen, and knights in "Ar-
mor"—including an irreverent Don Quixote—danced at the ball following an 1840 tournament at Red Sweet Springs.[6]

As the ultimate competitive activity, medieval tournaments brought the
images that the plantation gentry held of itself as feudal lords and ladies to
their ultimate expression. The visitors were not simply imitating characters
found in Scott's novels. They were playing out their own fantasies—fantasies that they had constructed based upon their ideas of honor and gentility
and the realities of land and slave ownership. One herald addressed a crowd
at Shannondale in such "eloquent tones and elevated and inspired sentiments, that the dullest bosom was roused to the highest daring and the true
spirit of ancient chivalry was revived." These wildly popular events carried
the southern elite's self-definition as chivalric cavaliers and virtuous maidens to the extreme. Men accepted the exaggerated, and active, role of
knight—brave and skillful participants; women accepted the exaggerated,
and passive, role of maidens—lovely and appreciative spectators. Even
without considering them in relation to tournaments, most travel writers
and many visitors already idealized the members of springs society as perfect ladies and gentlemen and the Virginia Springs as the perfect place for
them. In 1851 William Burke declared that "beauty, wit, elegance and grace
characterized the fair visiters, and honor, refinement, urbanity and disin-
terestedness distinguished the male portion of the assemblage." For a day
or two, the tournaments permitted women and men to live their romanticized ideal of themselves in full by playing the roles of maidens and
cavaliers.[7]

At the springs tournaments, southern visitors deliberately exaggerated
or intensified the gendered images of lady and cavalier. When young women
played the virtuous maiden, then young men could play the chivalric cavalier. Men could perform as jousting knights in mock tournaments as long
as women watched in admiration along the hillsides and accepted the
honor of Queen of Love and Beauty bestowed upon them by a victorious
knight. Like the men, women relished playing at courtly ladies and gentlemen. As at home southerners of both sexes at the springs expected elite
white women to embody the ideals of their society. Expectations dictated

that these women should be the most beautiful, fashionable, charming, witty, nurturing, pious, and virtuous.[8] According to the standards of the time, young women possessed these attributes most fully. Most young women knew these expectations and willingly participated in bringing this conventional mythical image of southern womanhood to life at the springs. They took their symbolic status seriously and apparently found pleasure in their public roles as beautiful and virtuous symbols of southern society.

While the hunts, tournaments, and costume balls provided amusement and recreation for the guests, they represented much more. Publicly announced and widely attended, these events allowed the gentry to perform not only for each other, as in many of the recreational and social pastimes at the springs, but also for the other elements in southern society. The presence of such witnesses affirmed the participants' elite status, even as their competitions established a hierarchy within the elite. The tournaments also reaffirmed the roles that southern society assigned to each gender through the exaggerated performances of cavaliers and maidens. Through this role-playing, the southern elite sought to link their lives to a chivalric medieval past, establishing themselves as courtly lords and ladies worthy of controlling a society. This significance was not lost on the participants. In 1845 one newspaper assured its readers that an upcoming tournament promised to "do honor to those days of Chivalry." Increasingly under attack in the late 1850s, southern planters clung to these romantic images. Summing up a tournament one visitor noted: "The really attractive part of the scene is the display of youth and beauty beneath the green boughs, and the happy faces that look on, fondly thinking that they gaze upon the sports of those chivalrous ancestors, whose deeds of gallantry and daring civilized dark ages." These events reassured planters that they still lived the romantic and honorable lives of supposed medieval ancestors who had civilized the dark ages, just as southern elites believed that they had civilized their own society. With such an ancestry, these men and women could regard themselves as the rightful leaders of their society. While everyone recognized the pretense in these romantic scenes, the role-playing strengthened and reaffirmed the image that elite southern men and women held of themselves and their society even after they left the springs.[9]

In the eyes of their devotees, the Virginia Springs were genteel, exclusive, affable, and orderly—embodying what was best in southern society. Yet the resort environment was also competitive, censorious, hierarchical, and dependent upon the labor of slaves. Within the more liberating atmosphere of the Virginia Springs, elite southerners could improvise, adapt, and test the rules and relations of their society. They bent some traditional gender lines while they strengthened others, just as they bent some traditional rules of gentility and strengthened others.

The Virginia Springs served many purposes for the men and women who visited them. Since life there changed so little over the decades, southern visitors could rely on the springs to perform essential functions for their society each season. The resorts provided a place for women and men to create and strengthen ties of community with others of their sex. Men combined business with pleasure, frequently discussing crops and politics and conducting business. For planter women, the springs offered a cherished escape from plantation responsibilities and boredom and a welcome source of feelings and freedoms rarely known on the plantation. For these women, the Virginia Springs also provided a public place where they could play key roles in their society, whether by physically symbolizing its ideals or actively determining the social boundaries of their class. Women, at least at the springs, determined whether a man or woman gained acceptance into the "best circles" and just what the requisite social attributes of southern gentry society would be. These public roles provided them with a sense of influence and direction in a society that usually placed them under some man's control. The Virginia Springs offered elite women not only relief from the tedium of their lives but also alternate experiences that undoubtedly formed an important part of their self-identities as southern ladies.

The high level of gender integration and the apparent ease with which the southern elite created and participated in a relatively untroubled mixed-gender world at the Virginia Springs challenges what historians have told us about the patriarchal, sex-segregated, and gender-divided plantation world. If, as many historians have argued, patriarchal values and practices controlled plantation life, then they were broken down at the springs as male and female visitors became quickly acquainted, thoroughly enjoyed each other's company, and frequently formed friendships. And patriarchal authority was further diminished as young men and women formed their own circle, modified traditional rules to suit their own purposes, and learned gender-role expectations from each other instead of simply from their parents. The atmosphere of the Virginia Springs apparently eased the strict gender divisions of the plantation world and encouraged interaction between the sexes. Judging from their letters and diaries, neither male nor female visitors regarded this high degree of sexual integration as a problem.

Instead, ease, comfort, and enjoyment characterized their relations—a drastic change from the usual view of planter gender relations.

The Virginia Springs also highlighted the tensions that arose from the dual demands of southern gentility. While gentility fostered sociability and refinement, it also encouraged divisions and exclusions. A layer of sociability, intimacy, and refinement obscured social boundaries that remained rigid and strict even, and perhaps especially, at the springs. At the springs, elite southerners interacted with their own kind, secure in the knowledge of their crowning place in society even as they competed amongst themselves for status. As on the plantation, a person's reputation largely determined his or her acceptance into or rejection from elite society. Yet the stakes were higher at the springs. Attention to the rules of conduct and appearance never mattered more. The scrutiny of other ladies and gentlemen never occurred as often or carried as much value. Failure in the fashionable contest based upon social rules and personal display at the springs, moreover, meant failure before a crowd of one's peers. But the rules of gentility also softened the competition, giving it a veneer of politeness, affability, and refinement.

The benefits of success repaid the risk of competing. After a successful evening in the ballroom at Salt Sulphur Springs in July 1841, for example, a young woman from New York received the ultimate accolade—acceptance into southern elite society. Because of her "spirit" while dancing the reel, a southern gentleman mistook her for a southerner; a southern lady, she recorded in her diary, "considered me *quite good enough* to be a southerner," telling her that "this was the highest compliment she ever paid a lady." [10] Few northerners ever achieved such a distinction. Through their competition and display at the springs, especially in the ballrooms and at the tournaments, southern ladies and gentlemen intensified and exalted the codes of genteel conduct and appearance and provided the models for successful social behavior for the rest of their society. The rules followed by the best of southern society at the Virginia Springs ultimately influenced those who rarely or never traveled over the mountains, helping to create a regional identity for this dominant group of southerners.

Conclusion

IN EARLY JULY 1861 MARY BOYKIN CHESNUT ARRIVED AT Fauquier White Sulphur Springs with a large group of women and men, including her husband James, Robert Barnwell, Mrs. John Preston, and other members of Confederate President Jefferson and Varina Davis's inner circle. Across the lawn they saw former Supreme Court Justice John A. Campbell and his family, "disconsolate" since resigning his seat "for a cause that he is hardly more than half in sympathy with." Even as Chesnut and her party enjoyed the effects of the water, they suffered—with great "self-control under such trying circumstances"—the company of various Union sympathizers and an "antique female" rumored to be "a Yankee spy." Chesnut characterized most of the young ladies at the springs, however, as "enthusiastic" in their support of the Confederacy and its soldiers. A day or two after their arrival, the men of the party headed for nearby Manassas, while the women stayed at the resort. Chesnut and her friends tried to keep their spirits up by reading, chatting, and joking, but eventually news from the front caused them to fear for the safety of their husbands and friends. Even the otherworldly springs could not keep out real disaster. On July 11 Chesnut noted: "We did hear cannon today," "saw lights glancing about among the trees, and we all heard guns." [1] After staying up all night, the terrified women left the threatened place the next day for Richmond. Fauquier White Sulphur escaped that early action but later became a casualty of the Civil War. On August 25, 1862, Union artillery fired upon the Confederate-occupied resort, leveling many of the beautiful buildings. [2]

The Civil War dashed the hopes of proprietors and visitors for the Virginia Springs. As late as the summer of 1860, many had held great expectations for the resorts' future. George Tucker, for example, predicted that, once the railroad was completed "the year after this," White Sulphur Springs "will be the most frequented watering place in the United States."[3] With sectional tensions on the rise, some visitors regarded the springs as the last refuge for elite southerners and the last enclave of their idealized version of gentility. Yet, as Mary Boykin Chesnut and her party discovered, the Virginia Springs could not remain isolated from the disruptions and destruction of the Civil War. The Virginia Springs finally faced dramatic change. Many of the resorts became military hospitals or, like Fauquier White Sulphur, suffered fires or other damage as a result of their proximity to battlefields. Others succumbed to the four-year absence of visitors and fell into disrepair.

After the Civil War, only a few of the prewar resorts reopened for visitors. Not surprisingly, White Sulphur Springs took the lead, becoming renowned once again as the summer home of a newly popular and beloved southern gentleman—Robert E. Lee. The railroads slowly made their way to some of the resorts. By 1870 the Chesapeake and Ohio had reached the vicinity of many of the Virginia Springs. The cars, however, carried a new mix of visitors. The isolation and expense that had ensured the exclusivity and homogeneity of the springs disappeared in the face of progress. The romantic world of planters amidst the Blue Ridge Mountains changed fundamentally. While elite southerners still made up the majority of visitors at the resorts, many guests came from other parts of the country and from lower classes of society, diluting the influence of previously dominant families. In her memoirs, Letitia M. Burwell recalled hearing from members of the old leading families of Virginia and South Carolina that society at the Virginia Springs "was never so good after the railroads and stages brought 'all sorts of people, from all sorts of places.'"[4] For many of the old visitors, the exclusive and genteel life at the springs became part of their nostalgia for the antebellum years.

The Virginia Springs also lost visitors to new amusements and new resorts that arose during the postwar decades. Railroads made travel to other sites across the country, such as Atlantic City, Niagara Falls, and Yellowstone Park, relatively easy and inexpensive. The trains also began to erase the regional distinctions that had previously characterized most resorts. As leisure became a regular part of more and more Americans' lives in the form of the vacation, new kinds of entertainment emerged to meet the insatiable appetite for pleasure. Resorts no longer constituted one of the few places of leisure. Parks, railroad excursions, beaches, dance halls, sporting events, and amusement parks all offered pleasure-seekers entertainment and respite from ordinary life. The Virginia Springs now competed for visitors when they had once turned them away.[5]

Every June through September from about 1790 through 1860, more elite whites congregated at the Virginia Springs than at any other place in the South, creating a community based upon their values, ideas, and manners. Here, only the cultivated and pedigreed could enter and become part of the leisurely romantic surroundings. The assurance of an exclusive and well-ordered environment placed the Virginia Springs above Saratoga Springs and other northern resorts in the opinion of many elite guests, especially southerners. Most of the visitors thoroughly enjoyed their stay at the springs and reluctantly left the convivial atmosphere, pleasant diversions, leisurely life, and new friends to return to the more routine and lonelier lives of their plantation homes. Saying farewell to the temporary community of family, friends, and acquaintances gathered at the springs proved difficult. Louisa Maxwell Holmes's "tears flowed abundantly" when she said goodbye to male and female friends "who have become very dear to me indeed," for she feared, with the uncertainty of life, that she might never see them again.[6]

The world of the springs was deceptively simple. The gloss of refinement, sociability, and romance prevailing at the springs and elsewhere usually concealed the complexities and contradictions of southern society. It enabled the women and men who abided by the modes and ideals of gentility to live their lives with little concern for the tensions and paradoxes of the Slave South that historians have found so problematic. The environment of the Virginia Springs enveloped guests in continual contrasts, between romance and reality, life and death, sociability and competition, modern and traditional, the unusual and the ordinary.

It was the image of the Virginia Springs as an orderly, sociable, and genteel place—an especially southern place—that captivated thousands of elite southern men and women from the late eighteenth through the mid-nineteenth centuries. In spite of an increase in guests and transformations in architecture, medicine, the economy, and sectional politics, genteel visitors regarded the springs for over seventy years as a refuge—as perhaps the one stable and almost unchanging place in their increasingly disordered world. The architecture at the spas, based on aristocratic British styles, served as an appropriately beautiful and grand setting for the performances of the visitors; its exaggerations matched those of their society. Natural and man-made landscapes presented viewers with sublime and beautiful scenes very different from their home landscapes and offered a balm for their minds. The waters cured many of their ills and encouraged a concentration on the body in genteel society. The exquisite sensations found in the baths provided a rare indulgence in sensuality. Recreational and leisure opportunities beckoned guests to throw off their reserve and participate in amusement with relish. The intimate and friendly feelings of the visitors made almost everyone feel like a part of a big family. Rules of etiquette and fashion enabled genteel ladies and gentlemen to compete for attention and acclaim but to do so with civility and affability. The relaxed atmosphere fostered easy relations between men and women. The romance of the springs heightened the romance of courtship. The informality of the resorts provided normally separated people with the perfect place for creating bonds of community. All of these elements combined to make the Virginia Springs critically important to the lives and the world of the southern elite.

At the Virginia Springs, visitors believed that all of the best qualities of southern women and men could be found in one place. It was the place where elite southerners could be the most southern. The perceived attributes of society at the Virginia Springs highlighted the characteristics of the ruling elite and strengthened the communal ties of that group. The springs environment, moreover, often stood in opposition to the plantation environment that, because of its slave labor system, could often appear unrefined and disorderly. Planter men and women's experiences at the springs defined and reaffirmed what it meant to be an elite southerner. Spa life revolved around the rituals and characteristics of aristocratic southern society. Elite southern visitors valued the Virginia Springs as a place where the hallmarks of their class gained added importance. Masquerade balls, hunts, and tournaments brought their intensification to its peak by allowing male and female visitors to live out chivalric fantasies of being cavaliers and ladies. Even as they reinforced the standard characteristics and roles of planter society, the Virginia Springs could offer men and women alternative experiences and identities.

The springs experience was not always a pleasant and comfortable one. Nowhere was the dedication to, and the conflict inherent within, gentility

more evident than at the springs. The dual demands of gentility—its posi-
tive and negative characteristics—shaped springs life. Even as the springs
strengthened their collective power, elite visitors continuously faced challenges to their accustomed power, often in the name of gentility. At the
springs, planter men and women had to define themselves relative almost
exclusively to their own class. Their plantation roles provided the status
that gained them entrance into spa society but could not guarantee them
status once inside. Elite men and women had to compete among their
peers without the shield of the plantation, its household hierarchy, and its
inherent status. Furthermore, slaves, servants, and lower-class managers
often played important roles in this competition for status, wielding an
unusual amount of power and publicly undermining the gentry's illusion
of control.

The Virginia Springs acted as a theater in which elite white southern
society could perform in a contest for social status before a judging audience of their peers. On the "stages" of parlors, ballrooms, greenswards, and
cabin porches, visitors displayed their fashions, manners, and talents, even
as they watched and evaluated the displays of others. Acknowledging the
demands of the springs, some grew "tired & weary & long[ed] for the moment where the play shall be over, the curtain shall drop, & they shall be
once more homeward bound."[7] Few questioned the need for performance, competition, and assessment, for most visitors desired renown and
admiration. Etiquette, decorum, and fashion provided the outward signs
by which elite guests, especially women, could easily distinguish their peers
from those who stood outside their circle. They also provided the rules by
which these status-obsessed visitors could compete for preeminence in the
spa hierarchy. Everyone had to play by the same rules so that they could be
judged by the same standards. Only those who had mastered the intricate
and complex rules for social intercourse, behavior, fashion, and the ballroom could be considered successes, reaffirming the boundaries of their
class. Ultimately, the intensely competitive and judgmental environment at
the Virginia Springs defined the characteristics of southern ladies and gentlemen for all of southern society. Through this process of self-definition
at the springs, elite southerners helped to fashion a culture for their entire
class.

The springs experience was neither limited nor fleeting. In this truly
regional place, more so than in their plantation or town communities,
southerners constructed and strengthened the social aspects of their re-

gional identity. The Virginia Springs, contrary to what we might expect of a leisure environment, did not merely allow visitors to escape temporarily from some of the restraints of traditional society, only to return refreshed to their regular roles. The springs also magnified the rituals, expectations, and images of elite southern society, along with the tensions central to that society. This romantic place that stood apart from "normal" life did not allow visitors to forget about society's demands; instead, it accentuated their ultimate importance. The effects of a season at the springs lasted throughout the year—maybe even throughout one's life—with the personal, political, and economic ties created or strengthened there continuing in the form of letters, visits, partnerships, and marriages. The memories of a springs trip could transcend the boredom of plantation or town life as well. While at White Sulphur around 1815, William Maxwell stored "charming things . . . in the corner of my imagination, to refresh myself with thinking upon in the winter evenings that are coming." In the fields of his plantation under the hot sun, A. Braxton could recall "the Lawn & fine oaks of the White Sulphur." And in the evenings at home, his thoughts "would again wander" to "the ball room at the White Sulphur . . . the swell of music, the thrill of the dance—& the radiance of beauty." The temporary role-playing of feudal lords and ladies strengthened the image that elite southerners held of themselves throughout the rest of the year. The lessons that they learned in personal display and gender relations served them well at home. Indeed, the southern elite was as much a product of the Virginia Springs as of the plantation.[8]

Notes

INTRODUCTION

1. Samuel Mordecai to Solomon Mordecai, 8 Aug. 1817, Mordecai Family Papers, NcU. I have capitalized Virginia Springs throughout because I treat them analytically as a single area, and nineteenth-century visitors generally referred to them as one place. Also, for a more comprehensive bibliography, see my dissertation, "Ladies and Gentlemen on Display: Planter Society at the Virginia Springs, 1790–1860," Ph.D. diss., University of Virginia, 1997.

2. Pencil, *White Sulphur Papers*, 40; Lawrence Butler to Anna Cradock, 20 Apr. 1791, Lawrence Butler Letters (photocopy), ViHi; Martineau, *Society in America*, 1:188.

3. Manuscript collections of southern families abound with letters to and from the Virginia Springs. Voluminous descriptions of life at the springs appeared in newspapers and published travel accounts. In spite of the wealth of manuscript sources, the Virginia Springs have been the subject of few published scholarly works. Most have focused upon the development of a single resort or discussed the folklore of the Virginia Springs or presented the history of the springs in an informal manner. The early twentieth-century works of William A. MacCorkle, *White Sulphur Springs,* and Dr. Quintard Taylor, *White Sulphur Springs: A Brief History,* are devoted entirely to one resort and are useful mainly for scientific and medical information. Other early works, such as J. T. McAllister, *Historical Sketches of Virginia Hot Springs, Warm Sulphur Springs and Bath County,* give brief histories of the development of certain resorts. Robert S. Conte, the current historian of the Greenbriar at White Sulphur Springs, has written an entertaining and informative history of that resort; see his *History of the Greenbriar.* Marshall W. Fishwick presents a fascinating collection of folklore in his *Springlore in Virginia.* Perceval Reniers's *Springs of Virginia* is the most widely used book on the subject, yet much of his evidence is presented as rumor and story without citations or sources. Similarly, Fay Ingalls's *Valley Road* is a memoir with stories about the

springs. Stan Cohen's *Historic Springs of the Virginias* is a helpful account of the Virginia Springs with pictures of the resorts and brief histories. See also his *Homestead and Warm Springs Valley, Virginia.* Many works on the antebellum South have mentioned the springs, such as Clinton, *Plantation Mistress,* 148−50, and Fox-Genovese, *Within the Plantation Household,* 69, 196. But Lawrence Brewster's *Summer Migrations and Resorts of South Carolina Low-Country Planters* is the only work that looks at the larger cultural significance of planters' summer travels. In his recent dissertation, "Fashionable Dis-Ease," Thomas A. Chambers compares the Virginia Springs and Saratoga Springs from 1790 to 1860.

4. For a discussion of the rituals and rules of plantation society from 1790 to 1860, see Smith, *Inside the Great House;* Isaac, *Transformation of Virginia;* Wyatt-Brown, *Southern Honor;* Harris, *Plain Folk and Gentry;* Stowe, *Intimacy and Power in the Old South;* Greenberg, *Honor and Slavery;* Stevenson, *Life in Black and White;* and Kierner, *Beyond the Household.* For discussions of the importance of social display, sociability, and gentility in colonial British America, see Bushman, *Refinement of America;* and Shields, *Civil Tongues and Polite Letters.*

5. For some of the major works that present the plantation as essentially deeply gender divided and patriarchal, see Clinton, *Plantation Mistress;* Wyatt-Brown, *Southern Honor;* Friedman, *Enclosed Garden;* Stowe, *Intimacy and Power in the Old South;* Fox-Genovese, *Within the Plantation Household;* Cashin, *Family Venture;* and Bardaglio, *Reconstructing the Household.* Other historians have found a more gender compatible and less patriarchal plantation. See Smith, *Inside the Great House;* Lewis, *Pursuit of Happiness;* Censer, *North Carolina Planters and Their Children;* and Buza, "'Pledges of Our Love.'" For the roles of hierarchies in the Slave South, see, in addition, Genovese, *Roll, Jordan, Roll;* Isaac, *Transformation of Virginia;* Oakes, *Ruling Race;* Burton, *In My Father's House;* Harris, *Plain Folk and Gentry;* McCurry, *Masters of Small Worlds;* and Stevenson, *Life in Black and White.*

6. See Lewis, *Pursuit of Happiness;* Censer, *North Carolina Planters and Their Children;* Fox-Genovese, *Within the Plantation Household;* Buza, "'Pledges of Our Love'"; and Jabour, *Marriage in the Early Republic.* Elizabeth Fox-Genovese and Suzanne Lebsock, in her *Free Women of Petersburg,* have found companionate marriage to be important to southerners but only in a form modified by the southern hierarchy of male dominance that made marriage unequal. Catherine Clinton, in *Plantation Mistress,* and Bertram Wyatt-Brown, in *Southern Honor,* claim that the oppressive patriarchy of men and the resultant subordination of women made companionate marriage impossible in the plantation South.

7. For some of the best works by historians of the nineteenth-century South who examine areas away from the usual plantation and farm districts, see Lebsock, *Free Women of Petersburg;* Pease, *Web of Progress;* Ayers and Willis, *Edge of the South;* Click, *Spirit of the Times;* Inscoe, *Mountain Masters;* and Morris, *Becoming Southern.*

8. For example, from around 1790 until around 1820, Virginian Charles Copland made a trip to the Virginia Springs every summer, except when traveling to the North or West ("Extracts from the Diary of Charles Copland," 217−30). Many historians have mentioned these lengthy absences from plantations, but few have examined them in any depth. See Brewster, *Summer Migrations;* Clinton, *Plantation Mistress,* 147; Pease, *Web of Progress;* Stowe,

Intimacy and Power in the Old South, 71; Fox-Genovese, *Within the Plantation Household,* 106–7; Cashin, "Structure of Antebellum Plantation Families"; and idem, *Family Venture,* 13–14. In his *Southern Odyssey,* John Hope Franklin has acknowledged the importance of looking at planters on trips off their plantations, but his emphasis is on their trips outside the South.

9. Joseph B. Skinner to Tristam L. Skinner, 1 Aug. 1844, Skinner Family Papers, NcU; Caroline Matilda Richardson to Sarah French, 8 Aug. 1835 (typescript), Sarah French Papers, ViHi; G. M. Yancey to John J. Ambler, 8 Aug. 1838, Ambler Family Papers, ViU.

10. See Isaac, *Transformation of Virginia,* and Bushman, *Refinement of America.*

11. For a good survey of the state of cultural history, see Bonnell and Hunt, *Beyond the Cultural Turn.* Even though she examines a later period, Grace Hale, in *Making Whiteness,* is concerned with similar issues of regional identity, place, gender, power, and the creation of communities among white southerners. Hale's late nineteenth- and twentieth-century white southerners, like those at the antebellum springs, used cultural forms to create "connections between categories of people and imagined spaces that moved far beyond local boundaries" and that served to set them apart (p. 6).

12. For two works that have moved beyond this eddy in the historiography and persuasively argued that capitalism and paternalism together shaped the plantation South, see Morris, *Becoming Southern,* and Young, *Domesticating Slavery.* Young concludes that "market capitalism and ideals of organic reciprocity evolved in tandem in the slave-owning South" (p. 5).

PART 1
The Scene

1. "Fauquier White Sulphur Springs" (advertisement), *Daily National Intelligencer,* 21 May 1835.

2. "Fauquier White Sulphur Springs" (advertisement), *Virginia Times,* 15 June 1839. The new bathhouse, which had the "appearance of extravagance," cost $750 (Fauquier White Sulphur Springs Co., *Extracts From Proceedings,* 4).

3. Burke, *Mineral Springs of Virginia,* 323.

4. Bushman, *Refinement of America,* 353.

"Solidity, Strength, and Grandeur"

1. See Amory, *Last Resorts;* Dulles, *History of Recreation;* Carson, "Early American Tourists"; Brown, *Inventing New England;* Martin, *Killing Time;* and Aron, *Working at Play.*

2. See Bridenbaugh, "Baths and Watering Places of Colonial America," 163; and Bowen, *Rambles in the Path of the Steam-Horse,* 240–43.

3. George Washington quoted in Bridenbaugh, "Baths and Watering Places of Colonial America," 160–61.

4. Robert Boyd to Henry Bouquet, 28 Oct. 1762, in Waddell, *Papers of Henry Bouquet,* 6:125–26.

5. For a detailed history of the development of these two spa towns, see Hendricks, "Health and Good Society."

6. Bayard, *Travels in the Interior of the United States,* 1; Waller Lewis to Lewis Holladay, 1 July 1784, Holladay Family Papers, ViHi. For George Washington, see Bridenbaugh, "Baths and Watering Places of Colonial America," 160–61.

7. John Gibson Worsham Jr., in "European Bathing Tradition and Its American Successors," has shown that the octagonal bathhouse could not have been built until after 1792.

8. Louisianna Cocke Faulcon to Louisa Cocke, 29 July 1828, Cocke Family Papers, ViU. By the late 1820s, many stage companies had established lines that ran from places such as Charleston, Charlottesville, Staunton, and Warrenton to the Virginia Springs (see Rice, *History of Greenbrier County;* "Stages Made by I. A. Coles in Journey to Missouri," 1 Sept.–7 Nov. 1825, Carter-Smith Family Papers, ViU). A host of letters attest to the benefits of improved river transportation on the trip to the Virginia Springs, especially Henry Clay's letters from the 1820s through the 1840s (see Hopkins, *Papers of Henry Clay*). For the variety of routes and modes of conveyance to the Virginia Springs from the 1830s to the 1850s, see *North American Tourist,* 413; and three works by Wellington Williams, *Appleton's Railroad and Steamboat Companion,* 286–87; *Appleton's Southern and Western Travellers' Guide;* and *Traveller's and Tourist's Guide.* For an account of one visitor's trip to the Virginia Springs via steamboat, railroad, and stagecoach, see William Stabler to Sally Stabler Jordan, 30 July–24 Aug. 1838, Jordan and Stabler Family Papers, ViHi. For canal improvements, see John Brockenbrough to William Wallace, 13 Dec. 1851, John Brockenbrough Papers, ViHi.

9. John H. Cocke to Ann Barraud Cocke, 12–15 Aug. 1811, Cocke Family Papers, ViU.

10. For examples of such reports, see Rouelle, *Complete Treatise on the Mineral Waters of Virginia;* and Baltzell, *Essay on the Mineral Properties of the Sweet Springs.*

11. Callahan, *History of West Virginia,* 1:180.

12. "Virginia Springs. Richmond & Danville, South-Side and Virginia and Tennessee Railroads!" (broadside), 7 May 1855, Blow Family Papers, ViHi; Noe, *Southwest Virginia's Railroad,* 66; Agnes S. B. Cabell to Louisa Carrington, 8 July 1858, Cabell-Carrington Papers, ViU. From the station, Montgomery White's rail cars used gravity to glide the passengers down to the resort; mules pulled the cars back up the mountain (Bodell, *Montgomery White Sulphur Springs,* 1).

13. Pencil, *White Sulphur Papers,* 25. Dorothy Bodell has stated that Exall was "one of the first builders to design and draw his own house plans" (*Montgomery White Sulphur Springs,* 2). Thomas Jefferson reputedly designed the main hotel at Sweet Springs, but there is no record amongst his voluminous writings to substantiate this claim. Alexander Jackson Davis's designs for a chapel, circular bathhouse, and circular hotel at White Sulphur Springs, from 1859 and 1860, still exist. But the Civil War prevented their construction (Lane, *Architecture of the Old South,* 248–49).

14. Mills Lane considers these two works the most influential Greek Revival pattern books in the South (Lane, *Architecture of the Old South,* 195). For Blue Ridge region architecture, including Roanoke Red Sulphur Springs, see Whitwell and Winborne, *Architectural Heritage of the Roanoke Valley,* especially 57–63.

15. Arese, *Trip to the Prairies,* 29–30.

16. For the importance of the Greek Revival in the United States, see Kennedy, *Greek Revival America;* and Sutton, *Americans Interpret the Parthenon.* For the impact of romanticism, see Early, *Romanticism and American Architecture.*

17. Windle, *Life at the White Sulphur Springs,* 74. Broad porches, or "galleries," also derived, in part, from French colonial building practices in the tropics, including French Louisiana.

18. All of the travel guides for the Virginia Springs included architectural descriptions. Newspapers, too, often gave extensive descriptions of resort buildings. For an excellent example, see the series of letters in the *Charleston Daily Courier,* 20 Aug.–18 Sept. 1855. Hundreds of guests' letters and journals included architectural details.

19. Buckingham, *Slave States of America,* 344; Martin, *New and Comprehensive Gazetteer,* 353.

20. Gaddis, *Foot-Prints of an Itinerant,* 315.

21. Richard Singleton built what was probably the first individually owned cottage at White Sulphur in 1825, but it was not on the grand and elegant scale of the later cottages, including the second one he built there in 1838. In 1855 the *Charleston Daily Courier* reported that "conspicuous among the buildings" at White Sulphur were "the residences of Colonels HAMPTON and SINGLETON of our State" (27 Aug. 1855).

22. A letter in a Washington, D.C., newspaper credited Fauquier White Sulphur's proprietor with that spring's landscape design ("Fauquier White Sulphur Springs," *Daily National Intelligencer,* 29 July 1858). But "the yard and pleasure grounds" of Amelia Springs had been "laid out by a celebrated English gardener" ("Public Sale of The Amelia Springs, &c.," *Richmond Enquirer,* 5 Sept. 1845). Two useful discussions of landscape architecture trends and styles in the early nineteenth century are O'Malley, "Landscape Gardening in the Early National Period," 133–59; and Leighton, *American Gardens of the Nineteenth Century.*

23. Jane Caroline North Diary, 29 Aug. 1851, in O'Brien, *Evening When Alone,* 169. Drawing from Loudon's "gardenesque" style, some of the resorts showcased rare and beautiful plants, and many integrated geometric patterns with irregular shapes. At Fauquier, "the walks on each side bloom[ed] with roses" (William F. Ritchie as quoted in Franck, "Virginia Legislature at the Fauquier Springs," 69). Seemingly uniquely, Fauquier White Sulphur's grounds were "in the French style of the Tuilleries and the Luxembourg" (Buckingham, *Slave States of America,* 2:559). The grounds took on a strong axiality, vastly unlike the tree-dotted and sweeping grounds of the English-type resorts. For examples of published guides or accounts with detailed descriptions of resort landscapes, see Paulding, *Letters from the South;* Prolix, *Letters Descriptive of the Virginia Springs;* Pencil, *White Sulphur Papers;* Buckingham, *Slave States of America;* Burke, *Mineral Springs of Western Virginia;* Windle, *Life at the White Sulphur Springs.*

24. Prolix, *Letters Descriptive of the Virginia Springs,* 34; Samuel Hoffman to Louisa Hoffman, 6 July 1832, Samuel Hoffman Papers, ViW; Pencil, *White Sulphur Papers,* 63. For a good discussion of the English landscape gardening tradition, see Batey, "High Phase of English Landscape Gardening," 44–50.

25. "Fauquier White Sulphur Springs," *Daily National Intelligencer,* 29 July 1858. Rhys

Isaac has found a similar architecture of "dominance and submission" on colonial plantations (*Transformation of Virginia*, 30–42 [quote from 38]). For more on plantation architecture in this period, see Hilliard, "Plantations and the Moulding of the Southern Landscape";
Wyckoff, "Landscapes of Private Power and Wealth"; Joseph, "White Columns and Black
Hands"; Vlach, *Back of the Big House;* Grootkerk, "Artistic Images of Mythological Reality."

26. Lucy W. Cocke Diary, 11 Sept. 1850, Cocke Family Papers, ViU.

27. William Cox to Rosanna Owens Cox, 29 Aug. 1804, Grigsby Papers, ViHi. For similar
sentiments, see John Baylor to John Baylor Jr., 26 Aug. 1805, Baylor Family Papers, ViU. Two
good works on the landscapes of Virginia plantations are Wells, "Planter's Prospect"; and
Cashin, "Landscape and Memory in Antebellum Virginia." Also helpful is Upton, "New
Views of the Virginia Landscape."

28. Jane Caroline North Diary, 29 Aug. 1851, in O'Brien, *Evening When Alone,* 169. For
comparisons to a rural village, see [Paulding], "Letters from Virginia," 424; and Pencil, *White
Sulphur Papers.* For comparisons to a park, see Buckingham, *Slave States,* 2:333; Edmund
Randolph to Marianne Old Meade, 4 Aug. 1840, Edmund Randolph Papers, ViHi; James
Alexander Seddon to Charles Bruce, 12 Aug. 1858, Bruce Family Papers, ViHi.

29. Grover, "Luxury and Leisure," 4.

30. Pencil, *White Sulphur Papers,* 23; Lucy Walton Diary, 1845, Lucy Muse (Walton)
Fletcher Papers, NcD. In his published work, John Disturnell declared White Sulphur a "truly
enchanting" site, "full of fascination" (*Springs, Water-falls, Sea-Bathing Resorts, and Mountain Scenery,* 125, 126). Another travel writer called one resort "a fairy spot" and another
"magical" ("Journal of a Trip to the Mountains, Caves and Springs of Virginia," 261, 385).
For remarks in a similar vein, see John S. Skinner, "Remarks . . . No. III, continued," 28 July
1847, in Bishko, "John S. Skinner Visits the Virginia Springs," 178; and anonymous woman to
"Pa," 1 Aug. 1847, Susan Bradford Eppes Papers, NcU. The architecture and landscape of the
popular northern resorts failed to achieve this same effect. Located in the midst of homes,
shops, churches, and even manufactories, Saratoga Springs' and Ballston Spa's resort buildings could not create for visitors, especially southern ones, an illusion of romance, intimacy,
and fantasy. See John Henry Strobia Diary, 27 and 28 Aug. 1817, ViHi; Prokopoff and Siegfried, *Nineteenth-Century Architecture of Saratoga Springs;* Broderick, "History in Towns,"
96–110.

31. Bushman, *Refinement of America,* 242.

32. Elizabeth M. Maben to Charles Campbell, 19 Aug. [1847], Charles Campbell Papers,
ViW; Edmund Randolph to Marianne Old Meade, 4 Aug. 1840, Edmund Randolph Papers,
ViHi; Samuel Hoffman to Louisa Hoffman, 6 Aug. 1840, Samuel Hoffman Papers, ViW.

"A Country More Wildly Picturesque"

1. Samuel Hoffman to Louisa Hoffman, 6 July 1832, Samuel Hoffman Papers, ViW;
Martineau, *Society in America,* 1:184–85.

2. The key works were Edmund Burke's *Philosophical Enquiry* (1757), William Gilpin's
Three Essays: on Picturesque Beauty; on Picturesque Travel; and on Sketching Landscape (1794),

and Sir Uvedale Price's *Essay on the Picturesque* (1794). Other influential works were Joseph Addison's *Spectator* (1712), William Hogarth's *Analysis of Beauty* (1753), and Thomas Whately's *Observations on Modern Gardening* (1770). See Myers, "On the Cultural Construction of Landscape Experience." Useful works on American attitudes toward nature include Huth, *Nature and the American;* Albanese, *Nature Religion in America;* Clarke, *American Landscape;* Crandell, *Nature Pictorialized,* chaps. 9 and 10.

3. Windle, *Life at the White Sulphur Springs,* 21–22; Edmund Burke, *Philosophical Enquiry,* 237–38; Downing, *Treatise on the Theory and Practice of Landscape Gardening,* 29. For a discussion of Americans and the changing concept of the sublime, see Novak, *Nature and Culture,* 34–38.

4. See Paulding, *Letters from the South;* Samuel Mordecai to Solomon Mordecai, 8 Aug. 1817, Mordecai Family Papers, NcU; Samuel Mordecai to Rachel Mordecai, 14 Aug. 1817, ibid. For the same phenomenon at Niagara Falls, see Sears, *Sacred Places,* 14. For the American romantic period, see Boas, *Romanticism in America;* Nye, *Society and Culture in America;* Foster, *Civilized Wilderness;* Jasen, "Romanticism, Modernity, and the Evolution of Tourism on the Niagara Frontier." For southern romanticism specifically, see Osterweis, *Romanticism and Nationalism in the Old South;* and Taylor, *Cavalier and Yankee.*

5. *Six Weeks in Fauquier,* 60; [Samuel or Moses] Mordecai to Ellen Mordecai, 19 July 1821, Mordecai Family Papers, NcU; Martha Terrell to Virginia Terrell, 30 Oct. [ca. 1820], Terrell-Carr Papers, ViU. Claude glasses were tinted pieces of glass that, when used to view a natural scene, presented an image with the same gold and brown tints of a Claude Lorrain painting. They were popular in the eighteenth century for tourists in search of picturesque views.

6. Martin, *New and Comprehensive Gazetteer,* 352; Pencil, *White Sulphur Papers,* 62. Dona Brown has found similar stock descriptions of the White Mountains from the 1840s to 1860 as has Patricia Jasen for Niagara Falls; see Brown, *Inventing New England,* 53–54; and Jasen, "Romanticism, Modernity, and the Evolution of Tourism on the Niagara Frontier," 287. Hans Huth found that "no [travel] author it seems ever tired of describing the sublimity and the grandeur of the scenery and the enchantment produced by it" (*Nature and the American,* 84). On the rise of tourism and travel writing in the United States, see Grover, "Luxury and Leisure"; Norris, "Reaching the Sublime," 53–59; Robertson, "Picturesque Traveler in America"; Sears, *Sacred Places;* Jasen, "Romanticism, Modernity, and the Evolution of Tourism on the Niagara Frontier"; Brown, *Inventing New England;* Martin, *Killing Time;* Aron, *Working at Play.*

7. Catherine Eliza Hall to Christian Elizabeth Price, 23 Aug. [1840], Price Family Papers, ViHi; Mary Jane Boggs Diary, June 1851, in Buni, "'Rambles among the Virginia Mountains,'" 83; *Trip to the Virginia Springs,* 12; C. O. Lyde Diary, 30 June 1841, NcD.

8. Mary Jane Boggs Diary, June 1851, in Buni, "'Rambles among the Virginia Mountains,'" 83. For two examples of visitors' copied descriptions, see Jerome Napoleon Bonaparte Jr.'s travel diary in Hoyt, "Journey to the Springs, 1846," 127; and Jane Caroline North Diary, 31 July–12 Oct. 1851, in O'Brien, *Evening When Alone,* 153–85. Peregrine Prolix's *Letters Descriptive of the Virginia Springs* seems to have been the most popular source from which

private writers as well as travel writers copied descriptions. See, for a published example, Tanner, *Geographical, Historical and Statistical View,* 469–70.

9. For a brief discussion of planter men's attitudes toward their plantation landscapes, see Cashin, "Landscape and Memory in Antebellum Virginia," 481 n. 7. In a previous work, Cashin noted that planter men and women shared "an enduring love for the land they lived on year after year" (*Family Venture,* 28). A thorough study of planter women's attitudes toward their home landscapes is needed, however. John F. Sears has similarly found no gender differences in the literature about tourist attractions in the nineteenth century and has concluded that these attractions were "free of being identified as either male or female space" (*Sacred Places,* 8). The writings of male and female visitors to the Virginia Springs stand in stark contrast to the findings of a number of scholars who have stated that men and women possessed opposing, or at least different, attitudes toward nature. These scholars have claimed that women were tender toward the environment and appreciated nature and that they sought harmony with the land in an organic relationship. Men, on the other hand, desired— in physical and sexual terms—to master, dominate, acquire, ravish, or lay waste to a fertile and feminine landscape. For interpretations that find distinct and separate masculine and feminine relationships with nature, see Anderson, *Sisters of the Earth;* Kolodny, *Lay of the Land* and *Land before Her;* Norwood, *Made from This Earth.*

"At Great Trouble and Expense"

1. For information on proprietors' backgrounds, see Morton, *History of Monroe County,* chap. 21, and his *Annals of Bath County,* 48; Callahan, *History of West Virginia;* Ingalls, *Valley Road,* 7–39; Semes, "Two Hundred Years at Rockbridge Alum Springs," 46–54; Cohen, *Historic Springs of the Virginias;* Rice, *History of Greenbrier County,* 147–50; Berdan, "The Spa Life," 110–19.

2. Brockenbrough might have inherited his spring property through his wife, Mary C. Bowyer of Lexington, Virginia. Additionally, the wealthy planter and author John D. Legare of South Carolina opened Gray Sulphur Springs in the early 1830s.

3. One exception seems to have been Red Sweet Springs proprietor C. Bias who, by 1855, owned nearly 1,800 acres of "highly cultivated land" (*Charleston Daily Courier,* 29 Aug. 1855). For the best account of antebellum southern yeomanry, see McCurry, *Masters of Small Worlds.* See also Ford, *Origins of Southern Radicalism.*

4. Salt Sulphur Springs Daybook, 6 Nov. 1821 and 8 Feb. 1822, Wv-Ar. Peregrine Echols of Bedford Alum Springs, Bedford County, purchased two sickly slave boys from William Massie for $500.00 in 1857, although he claimed "I have never went in to that sort of speculation" (P[eregrine] Echols to William Massie, 17 July 1857, William Massie Collection, TxU). Incorporated resorts did not own many slaves either. For example, the 1860 census listed only 5 slaves (all men, between 21 and 40 years old) owned by the Montgomery White Sulphur Springs Company (Bodell, *Montgomery White Sulphur Springs,* 3). In the records, it is difficult to distinguish between the numbers of slaves that proprietors owned and those that they hired because they paid taxes on both. See, for example, Fauquier White Sulphur Springs Co.

Culpeper Taxes, 1856, Keith Family Papers, ViHi. For hotelkeepers and slavery in the Blue Ridge Mountain region, see Inscoe, *Mountain Masters.* For slaveholding statistics for Appalachia in general between 1800 and 1860, see Murphy, "Slaveholding in Appalachia."

5. Financial Accounts for White Sulphur Springs Hotel, 1860, Cocke Family Papers, ViU. A close scrutiny of White Sulphur's accounts for 1860 reveals that all white workers, even "several Irish Women Employed at Scrubbing," were listed under "Salary." No individual lists existed for "Servant hire" or "Negro hire." Obviously, proprietors lumped slave workers into the two categories instead of listing them individually under salary. For an interesting analysis of slave hiring on another edge of the South, see Barton, "Good Cooks and Washers."

6. Salt Sulphur Springs Daybook, 1821–25, Wv-Ar. Henry Massie, who owned a plantation in Bath County, regularly sold meat and produce to Warm and Hot Springs as well as purchasing items from their stores and taverns year round (Account Book, Massie Family Papers, ViHi). In an advertisement for property he wanted to sell, Robert E. Lee made it clear that Warrenton Springs "affords a market at the door for meats, poultry, &c." ("Great Bargain!" *Virginia Times,* 8 Aug. 1840). For a discussion of the similar impact of summer tourism in the mountains of North Carolina, see Inscoe, *Mountain Masters.*

7. "Rockbridge Alum Springs, Va., August 2, 1855," *Charleston Daily Courier,* 7 Aug. 1855; Joseph C. Cabell to John H. Cocke, 9 Sept. 1849, Cocke Family Papers, ViU; Henry Clay to James Madison, 7 July 1828, in Hopkins, *Papers of Henry Clay,* 7:376 (Clay's letters to Caldwell are conveniently collected in Mayo, "Henry Clay," 301–17; the letters from Caldwell to Clay have not been found); William Bolling Diary, 30 Aug. 1841, ViHi; Richard D. Burroughs to Caroline Burroughs, [1857], Richard D. Burroughs Papers, NcD.

8. Salt Sulphur Springs Daybook, 1821–22, Wv-Ar.

9. Bailey, *Life and Adventures,* 219, 220, and 223. Some of the bathkeepers were European; see Larkin Newby Diary, 19 Aug. 1823, Larkin Newby Papers, NcU; and C. O. Lyde Diary, 15 Aug. 1841, NcD.

10. Willis Williams to his wife, 17 Sept. 1860, Willis Williams Papers, NcU; "Salary Acct.," 1860, Financial Accounts for White Sulphur Springs Hotel, Cocke Family Papers, ViU; J. Humphreys to Jeremiah Morton, 18 Dec. 1860, Morton-Halsey Papers, ViU. These figures do not include the hired slave servants and workers who were listed in the hiring and repair accounts.

11. Bailey, *Life and Adventures,* 66; Larkin Newby Diary, 16 Aug. 1823, Larkin Newby Papers, NcU. Another slave, owned by a guest from Baltimore, performed informally at White Sulphur in 1821 ([Samuel or Moses] Mordecai to Ellen Mordecai, 19 July 1821, Mordecai Family Papers, NcU).

12. Blair Bolling Diary, vol. 3, 14 Aug. 1838, ViHi. Bolling did not indicate whether the musicians were slave or free.

13. The band at White Sulphur in 1837 received $900.00 (Philippa Barbour to Mrs. Elizabeth [Barbour] Ambler, 1 Aug. 1837, Ambler Family Papers, ViU). Fifteen hundred dollars went to ten German musicians in 1841 at White Sulphur (William Bolling Diary, 19 Aug. 1841, ViHi). The ten-member band at White Sulphur in 1842 received $1,000.00 for the season

(Hugh Blair Grigsby Diary, 30 June 1842, ViHi). C. Volkindt, presumably a white musician, received over fourteen hundred dollars for the services of his band at White Sulphur Springs in 1860 ("Miscellaneous Expenses," Financial Accounts for the White Sulphur Springs Hotel, 1860, Cocke Family Papers, ViU). For one interesting exchange, see the series of letters from Christian Weber to Jones Green of Fauquier White Sulphur, 1842–43, Keith Family Papers, ViHi. See also the letters from a member of Weber's band, F. H. Knop, to Jones Green, 14 Mar. 1843, and from the man who "called the figures," [F. or P.] Arth, to Jones Green, 25 Apr. 1843, ibid.

14. "Bath Berkley Springs, Virginia," *Daily National Intelligencer*, 24 July 1819; George Mason Hooe to Daniel Ward, 18 Apr. 1842, Keith Family Papers, ViHi; John Turpin to Daniel Ward, 10 May 1843, ibid.; Helen Grinnan to John Gray, [ca. 1840], ibid.; Hezekiah Daggs Daybook, 1 Aug. 1834, ViRoH. In 1852, a former slave who had recently purchased his freedom from the proprietor remained at Warm Springs to tend bar ([Hoffman], "Trip to the Virginia Springs," 126). One hotel in the area employed only free servants (Sarah J. Burch Garland to James Garland, 20 Oct. [pre-1850], Sarah Garland Letter, ViHi). For other arrangements concerning hired slaves, see J. Stanard to John Green, 11 May 1846, ibid.; and P[eregrine] Echols to William Massie, 11 and 30 Aug., 6, 13, 20, 21 Sept., 11 Oct. 1855, 17 July 1857, William Massie Collection, TxU.

15. Henry Bright Diary, 20 June 1832, in Ehrenpreis, *Happy Country This America*, 177; Jeremiah Morton to George Morton, 13 June 1860, Morton Family Papers, ViU. Philip St. George Cocke's slave Henry wished to stop in Lexington on his way to his hired position at the springs to see his wife (Philip St. George Cocke to John H. Cocke, 10 July 1860, Cocke Family Papers, ViU).

16. Charles White to Hamilton Brown, 20 Dec. 1832, Hamilton Brown Papers, NcU. Even though no answer from Brown can be found, White's request was not totally successful. The following year, White remained in the county, but Brown had hired him out to another blacksmith (George Mayse to Hamilton Brown, 24 Oct. 1833, ibid.).

17. Federal Manuscript Census for Warrenton County, Fauquier White Sulphur Springs District, Virginia, 1860. In particular, four out of the five households contained a husband and wife. One family was headed by a woman. Four out of the five families had at least five children; the other contained no children. Four women apparently lived alone and were single. The adult women's ages ranged from the early 20s to 90. Most of the men were in their 40s. Slightly more than half were listed as "black," the rest as "mulatto." Almost all of the thirty-seven shared the surnames of Lancaster, Pinn, and Malvin.

18. Ibid. In addition to stonefencers and farmhands, the fathers and older sons listed their occupations as hotel waiter, "Ditcher," and "Quarrier." The women's occupations included not only laundresses and maids, but also a weaver and a couple of farmhands.

19. George Johnson to Marguerite Johnson, 14 Aug. 1853, George Nicolson Johnson Papers, ViHi; Lucy W. Cocke Diary, 15 Aug. 1850, Cocke Family Papers, ViU; James J. White to Mary Louisa White, 17 Aug. 1860, Cabell-Reid Papers, ViU; George E. Harrison to Anne H. Byrd, 11 Sept. 1828, Francis Otway Byrd Papers, ViHi. See also Sophie S. Wilson Diary, 10 Aug. 1831, DLC; and Jane Caroline North Pettigrew to Jane Petigru North, 10 Sept. 1855, Pettigrew Papers, NcU.

20. Robert Taylor Scott to William Aylett, 8 Sept. 1852, Aylett Family Papers, ViHi; Thomas Walker Gilmer to Samuel Minor, 27 July 1835, Randolph Family Papers, ViU. See also Dandridge Spotswood Sr. Diary, 6 Aug. 1848, ViHi; and Horace L. Hunley to Robert R. Barrow, 9 Aug. 1860 (typescript), Robert Ruffin Barrow Papers, LNHT. Historian John C. Inscoe has similarly argued that mountain slaves "generally enjoyed less restricted lives" than plantation slaves (*Mountain Masters*, 88). I have found no evidence concerning slave punishment at the springs.

21. Bath Alum Springs Account Book, 11–13 Aug. 1852, ViW; Maria C. Broadus to Eliza Tucker Harrison, 21 July 1857, Tucker-Harrison-Smith Papers, ViU; [Horner], *Observations on the Mineral Waters*, 19–20. For slaves who enjoyed their visits, see Louisianna Cocke to Louisa Cocke, 19 Aug. 1828, Charles Cary Cocke to John H. Cocke, 29 Aug. 1846, and Sally Cocke to John H. Cocke, 19 Aug. 1848, Cocke Family Papers, ViU; Nancy Evans to "Young Mistress," 6 Aug. 1856, Preston-Radford Papers, ViU.

22. Larkin Newby to Cecilia Newby, 25 June 1823, Larkin Newby Papers, NcD.

23. See "Bath Berkley Springs, Virginia," *Daily National Intelligencer*, 24 July 1819; "Botetourt Springs," ibid., 26 Apr. 1825; "Amelia Sulphur Springs" and "Augusta Springs," *Richmond Enquirer*, 21 June 1833; "Hugenot Springs" and "Fauquier White Sulphur Springs," ibid., 18 June 1847.

24. See, for example, Mütter, *Salt Sulphur Springs;* "Rockbridge Alum Springs and Bath Alum Springs, in Virginia," printed advertisement on verso of John H. Cocke to Cary Charles Cocke, 11 July 1853, Cocke Family Papers, ViU; and *Analysis of the Rockbridge Alum Springs.*

25. Miscellaneous Expenses, Financial Accounts for White Sulphur Springs Hotel, 1860, Cocke Family Papers, ViU. For more on resort advertising, see Charles Taylor to John Preston, 4 Feb. 1811, Preston Family Papers, ViHi.

26. Dr. William Burke of Red Sulphur and Dr. Thomas Goode of Hot Springs were two of the proprietors who wrote and published travel accounts of the Virginia Springs. Burke first published his book in 1842. Both works went through several editions. See Burke, *Mineral Springs of Western Virginia;* and Goode, *Invalid's Guide to the Virginia Hot Springs.*

27. Elizabeth H. Noel to "Julia," 1 Sept. 1860, Lewis Family Papers, ViU; "A List of Supplies for the Warrenton Springs," 22 Apr. 1839, Keith Family Papers, ViHi (Warrenton Springs was briefly the name of Fauquier White Sulphur); John Kettlered & Co. to Thomas Green, 11 June 1839, ibid.; J. Taylor to George Morton, [ca. 1860], Morton Family Papers, ViU. Another visitor to White Sulphur in 1860, Willis Williams, drew up a list to give his wife "something of an idea of what it takes to furnish the table." On 18 Aug., when the resort had 1,672 guests, "they cooked, 1238 lbs. of beef[,] 1020 of mutton, 420 of ham, 58 of [*illegible*], 101 of cornbeef, 132 gals. of milk, 300 doz. eggs for breakfast (none for dinner) three hundred chickens more for dinner. They use 195 lbs of coffee per day, about the same of tea, use three bar[rels] of sugar pr day & 36 gals. of molasses, 6 bar. of flour pr. day & one of [*illegible*], and 1 bushel corn meal" (Willis Williams to his wife, 17 Sept. 1860, Willis Williams Papers, NcU).

28. "Botetourt Springs," *Daily National Intelligencer*, 26 Apr. 1825; "Red Sulphur Springs," *Richmond Enquirer*, 10 May 1833.

29. "Rockbridge Alum Springs and Bath Alum Springs, in Virginia," printed advertise-

ment on verso of John H. Cocke to Cary Charles Cocke, 11 July 1853, Cocke Family Papers, ViU; Financial Accounts for White Sulphur Springs Hotel, 1860, ibid. See also "Fauquier White Sulphur Springs," *Daily National Intelligencer,* 21 May 1835. For the excitement over gas lighting and indoor water, see Calvin S. Campbell to Dr. Thomas E. Massie, 12 Mar. and 9 May 1857, Massie Family Papers, ViHi.

30. James C. Bruce to Eliza Bruce, 24 Aug. 1842, Bruce Family Papers, ViU; "Statement of Receipts & Expenditures of the White Sul. Springs Hotel for season of 1860," Financial Accounts for White Sulphur Springs Hotel, Cocke Family Papers, ViU. Many of the owners incorporated to acquire the necessary capital for the enormous expenditures to modernize their resorts. Both Sweet and Red Sweet Springs incorporated in 1836, and Fauquier White Sulphur did so in 1837. The White Sulphur Springs Company formed later, in 1854; Montgomery White Sulphur Springs Company followed in 1855. For the history of the rises and declines of Berkeley Springs (formerly Warm Springs), see Newbraugh, *Warm Springs Echoes;* and Morgan County Historical Society, *Morgan County.*

31. Robert E. Lee to Charles Carter Lee, 24 July 1843, Robert E. Lee Papers, ViU.

"Bribe High and You Live High"

1. John H. Cocke Diary, 13 Sept. 1818, Cocke Family Papers, ViU; Louisianna Cocke to John H. Cocke, 19 Aug. 1822, ibid.

2. Philip St. George Cocke to John H. Cocke, 30 Aug. 1856, ibid. (this letter is mistakenly filed under 1854).

3. "Rockbridge Alum Springs and Bath Alum Springs, in Virginia," printed advertisement on verso of John H. Cocke to Cary Charles Cocke, 11 July 1853, ibid.; Louisa Maxwell Holmes Cocke Diary, 31 Aug. 1816, ibid.; Sophie S. Wilson Diary, 26 July 1831, DLC (The diary is mistakenly attributed to Sophie; the author was actually her father, whose name is unknown); "Red Sulphur Springs," *Richmond Enquirer,* 10 May 1833; Terrill D. George to J. Halsey, 2 July 1858, Morton-Halsey Papers, ViU; Samuel Clayton to Henry Brown, 5 Aug. [1818], Brown-Coalter-Tucker Papers, ViW; Susanna I. Harrison to Mary Harrison, 24 Aug. 1831, Harrison Family Papers, ViHi. George Featherstonhaugh reported that one visitor found the heads and necks of chickens and a duck in his pillows (*Excursion through the Slave States,* 1:61–62).

4. James Cathcart Johnston to Mr. Hollwell, 8 Sept. 1857, Hayes Collection, Johnston Series, NcU. Similarly, a Mr. Wilson declared of White Sulphur: "In point of filth, dirt, and every other bad quality, we found it decidedly the meanest, most nasty place we ever visited" (Sophie S. Wilson Diary, 26 July 1831, DLC). For those who loved White Sulphur, see Jane Cary Fitzhugh (Harrison) Randolph to Randolph Harrison, 29 Aug. 1829, Harrison Family Papers, ViHi; anonymous woman to "Pa," 1 Aug. 1847, Susan Bradford Eppes Papers, NcU; Levin Joynes to Ann Joynes, 21 Aug. 1856, Joynes Family Papers, ViHi.

5. James Johnston Pettigrew to James Cathcart Johnston, 14 Aug. 1855, Pettigrew Papers, NcU.

6. James L. Petigru to Susan Petigru King, 21 Sept. 1845, in Carson, *Life, Letters and Speeches,* 250–51. Petigru also had a high opinion of Caldwell.

7. Wade Hampton III to Mary Fisher Hampton, 3 Aug. 1858, in Cauthen, *Family Letters of the Three Wade Hamptons,* 64.

8. James L. Petigru to Susan Petigru King, 13 Aug. 1845, in Carson, *Life, Letters and Speeches,* 244; William Bolling Diary, 28 Aug. 1841, ViHi. Similarly, one travel writer declared that the stage passenger "must submit his own claims . . . to the wealthy fashionable, who comes after him with a greater retinue" ("Journal of a Trip to the Mountains, Caves and Springs of Virginia," 262). At Capon Springs, one visitor declared that he "had been put in a room with forty *persons* to sleep" (Peter Daniel to Elizabeth Daniel, 3 Aug. 1851, Daniel Family Papers, ViHi). Foreigners could not understand or abide Americans' "subservient acquiescence" to hotelkeepers and managers (Buckingham, *Slave States,* 2:339). See also Featherstonhaugh, *Excursion through the Slave States,* 1:35 and 50.

9. "Memoir of Dr. John J. Moorman," 22; *Trip to the Virginia Springs,* 15; "Memoir of Dr. John J. Moorman," 22; *Trip to the Virginia Springs,* 16; Isaac Gorham Peck Diary, 9 Aug. 1833, ViHi. A foreign traveler adjudged Anderson one who "presume[d] not a little upon his power" and labeled him "despotic" (Marryat, *Diary in America,* 271). See also, "Journal of a Trip to the Mountains, Caves and Springs of Virginia," 262; Pencil, *White Sulphur Papers,* 36; Featherstonhaugh, *Excursion through the Slave States,* 1:51, 56, 72.

10. William Stabler to Sally (Stabler) Jordan, 30 July–24 Aug. 1848, Jordan and Stabler Family Papers, ViHi.

11. Samuel Hoffman to Louisa Hoffman, 21 July 1832, Samuel Hoffman Papers, ViW; John H. B. Latrobe, "Trip to the Virginia Springs," in Semmes, *John H. B. Latrobe,* 253 (see also 255–58). Numerous expense accounts kept by springs visitors included money given to servants. See, for example, David Watson Diary, June–July 1809, Watson Family Papers, ViU; John H. Cocke Diary, Aug.–Sept. 1818, Cocke Family Papers, ViU; and John Jarvis Diary, June–July 1849, ViU. Peregrine Prolix commented upon the bribing at the springs in print in his *Letters Descriptive of the Virginia Springs,* 36. William Burke also wrote about it in his *Mineral Springs of Virginia,* 131.

12. William Bolling Diary, 19 Aug. 1841, ViHi. William Stabler told of guests who made "obtrusive" scenes in their determination "not to be neglected" by waiters (William Stabler to Sally [Stabler] Jordan, 30 July–24 Aug. 1848, Jordan and Stabler Family Papers, ViHi). George Featherstonhaugh believed that the slaves kept the best cuts of meat for themselves (*Excursion through the Slave States,* 1:73 [see also 30, 32, 72, 77]).

13. John H. B. Latrobe, "Trip to the Virginia Springs," in Semmes, *John H. B. Latrobe,* 256.

PART 2

Healing Waters

1. John H. Cocke Diary, 21 Aug. 1851 and 3 Sept. 1844, Cocke Family Papers, ViU.

2. Philip St. George Cocke to John H. Cocke, 21 Aug. 1850, ibid.; Lucy W. Cocke Diary, 27 Nov. 1857, ibid.; Lucy Cocke to Cary Charles Cocke, 6 Sept. 1856, ibid.; Louisa Cocke to John H. Cocke, 6 Sept. 1840, ibid. In 1827, John Hartwell Cocke Jr. also tried the Virginia Springs for epilepsy, from which he suffered until his death at forty-two. His sister, Loui-

sianna Cocke Faulcon, visited the springs only months before her death in 1829 at the age of twenty-three.

3. John H. Cocke Diary, 13 Sept. 1851, ibid.

4. For the history of the use of mineral waters in the United States, see Crook, *Mineral Waters of the United States;* Sigerist, "American Spas in Historical Perspective"; Bridenbaugh, "Baths and Watering Places of Colonial America"; Kamenetz, "History of American Spas"; De Vierville, "American Healing Waters."

5. Mary Lee to Robert E. Lee, 3 Aug. 1857, Lee Family Papers, ViHi.

"King Cure All"

1. George Harrison to Anne H. Byrd, 12 Sept. 1829, Francis Otway Byrd Papers, ViHi; Robert Hubard to Edmund Hubard, 6 Aug. 1847, Hubard Family Papers, NcU; Thomas Gordon Pollock to Elizabeth Pollock, 3 Aug. 1860, Abram David Pollock Papers, NcU. For early accounts that noted the preponderance of pleasure-seekers, see Bayard, *Travels in the Interior of the United States,* 1; and Caldwell, *Tour Through Part of Virginia,* 26. Similarly, Janice Zita Grover has found that at Saratoga Springs in the nineteenth century it was difficult to discern the true invalids from the rest of the guests ("Luxury and Leisure," 164). This seems to have held true at other American spas; see Kamenetz, "History of American Spas," 172.

2. For the history of southern epidemic and endemic diseases in the nineteenth century, see Blanton, *Medicine in Virginia in the Nineteenth Century;* Rosenberg, *Cholera Years;* Savitt and Young, eds., *Disease and Distinctiveness in the American South;* K. David Patterson, "Disease Environments of the Antebellum South," in *Science and Medicine in the Old South,* ed. Numbers and Savitt, 152–65; Berdan, "Pestilence that Walketh in Darkness."

3. George Harrison to Anne H. Byrd, 17 Aug. [1833], Francis Otway Byrd Papers, ViHi; John Pendleton Kennedy to Peter H. Cruse, 4, 12, 23, 26 Aug. 1832, Peter Hoffman Cruse Papers, ViHi; Peyton H. Skipwith to John H. Cocke, 28 May 1849, Cocke Family Papers, ViU; Dr. Cary Charles Cocke to John H. Cocke, 12 Sept. 1846, ibid.

4. The link between yellow fever, cholera, and other diseases and the rise and decline of the Virginia Springs resorts lasted until the early twentieth century; see Baker, "Influence of Epidemic Diseases on the Virginia Springs." Occasionally, the Virginia Springs resorts became hotbeds for disease themselves with so many contagious persons visiting them for cures. A plague virtually closed down Berkeley Springs around 1800. In August 1823, Bedford, Berkeley, and Shannondale Springs were all, according to William Wirt, "said to be sickly. . . . So that every place in this valley between the Alleghany & Blue Ridge which people are in the habit of visiting for health has become dangerous even as a temporary residence" (William Wirt to Elizabeth Wirt, 31 Aug. 1823, William Wirt Papers, DLC). Many mothers feared their children might be exposed to whooping cough at the springs (see Agnes S. B. Cabell to Louisa Carrington, 11 Aug. [ca. 1836], Cabell-Carrington Papers, ViU; Lucy Ann Tucker to Elizabeth Tucker Bryan, [ca. 14 Sept. 1847], Bryan Family Papers, ViU; Lucy Cocke Diary, 20 Sept. 1850, Cocke Family Papers, ViU).

5. Diary entry of 7 Aug. 1820, in Adams, *Life and Writings of Jared Sparks,* 1:172.

6. Featherstonhaugh, *Excursion through the Slave States,* 69. See John Duffy, "Impact of Malaria on the South," and Jo Ann Carrigan, "Yellow Fever: Scourge of the South," in *Disease and Distinctiveness,* ed. Savitt and Young, 38, 58, respectively. For a thorough examination of the summer travels of South Carolina lowcountry planters to the Virginia Springs and elsewhere to escape the "sickly season," see Brewster, *Summer Migrations.*

7. William Gray to Lucy Gray, 14 Aug. 1798, Beverley Family Papers, ViHi.

8. Louisianna Cocke Diary, 13 Aug. 1822, typescript in author's possession.

9. For example, a published chemical analysis of Grey Sulphur Springs listed its mineral ingredients as follows: under "soluble ingredients," "Nitrogen, Hydro-Sulphuric Acid, Bi-Carbonate of Soda, a Superb Carbonate of Lime, Chloride of Calcium, Chloride of Sodium, Sulphate of Soda, and Alkaline or earthly Crenate, or both, Silicic Acid" and, under "insoluble ingredients," "Sulphuret of Iron, Crenate of Per Oxide of Iron, Silicic Acid, Alumina, Selicate of Iron" ([Miller], *Account of the Medical Properties of the Grey Sulphur Springs,* 2).

10. J. Taylor to George Morton, [ca. 1855], Morton Family Papers, ViU.

11. Burke, *Mineral Springs of Virginia,* 52.

12. Moorman, *Virginia Springs* (1859), 162; Edwin Bedford Jeffress Diary, 1 Sept. 1852, ViHi; "Red Sulphur Springs," *Richmond Enquirer,* 10 May 1833; Samuel Hoffman to Louisa Hoffman, 27–28 July 1833, Samuel Hoffman Papers, ViW. Some northern medical journals also published accounts of the healing powers of the Virginia Springs; see, for example, Hayward, "Remarks on Some of the Medicinal Springs of Virginia."

13. Charles Minor to John B. Minor, 25 Aug. 1836, Minor and Wilson Family Papers, ViU; Stringfellow, *Two Letters on Cases of Cure at Fauquier White Sulphur Springs.* Most of the testimonials followed the format of this one in support of Grey Sulphur Springs: "Dear Sir,—I take pleasure in stating that the waters of the Grey Sulphur have proved quite beneficial, during a visit of ten days, both to Mrs. S. and myself. . . . [We] experienced more benefit here than from any of the waters we have as yet visited" ([Miller], *Account of the Medical Properties of the Grey Sulphur Springs,* 5).

14. Zackary Taliaferro to Nicholas Cabell, 1 Sept. 1790, Cabell Family Papers, ViU; Randolph Harrison Sr. to John H. Cocke, 26 Aug. 1831, Cocke Family Papers, ViU; Helen Grinnan to John Gray, [ca. 1840], Keith Family Papers, ViHi; Peter Saunders to Elizabeth Saunders, 20 and 21 Aug. 1860, Saunders Family Papers, ViHi; R. T. W. Duke Jr., "Recollections," Duke Family Papers, ViU.

15. Zackary Taliaferro to Nicholas Cabell, 1 Sept. 1790, Cabell Family Papers, ViU; Sarah Isham Harrison to Randolph Harrison, 16 Sept. 1831, Harrison Family Papers, ViHi; Lizzy to William Massie, 6 Aug. [*sic:* Sept.] 1855, William Massie Collection, TxU; R. T. W. Duke Jr., "Recollections," Duke Family Papers, ViU; Jerome Napoleon Bonaparte Jr. Diary, in Hoyt, "Journey to the Springs," 129–30. For another slave left behind, see Jane Cary Randolph to Randolph Harrison, 29 Aug. 1829, Harrison Family Papers, ViHi. I have found no evidence of a separate bath for slaves, but slaves probably did not bathe with whites.

16. Dr. Charles Everette to Wilson C. Nicholas, 25 Aug. 1808, Edgehill-Randolph/Wilson Cary Nicholas Papers, ViU; William Wirt to Dabney Carr, 1–2 July 1820, William Wirt Papers, NcU; D. C. T. Davis to John B. Minor, 26 July 1854, Minor and Wilson Family Papers,

ViU; Thomas E. Massie to Thomas Massie, 23 July 1849, Massie Family Papers, ViHi; Richard
Burroughs to Caroline Burroughs, 25 Aug. 1857, Richard D. Burroughs Papers, NcD; R. G. H.
Kean to John B. Minor, 12 Aug. 1854, Minor and Wilson Family Papers, ViU.

17. Charlotte Stockdell (Meade) Ruffin to Edmund Ruffin Sr., 11 Sept. 1860, Edmund
Ruffin Papers, ViHi. See also John Francis Speight Jr. to Emma L. Speight, 29 July 1860, John
Francis Speight Papers, NcU.

18. William Gray to Lucy Gray, 14 Aug. 1798, Beverley Family Papers, ViHi.

19. [Paulding], "Letters from Virginia," 430.

20. See Betts, "Mind and Being in Early American Thought"; and Grover, "Luxury and
Leisure," 157.

21. Robert E. Lee to Charles Carter Lee, 2 Aug. 1836, Robert E. Lee Papers, ViU. See also
Emily and John Rutherfoord to John C. Rutherfoord, 22 Aug. 1850, John Rutherfoord Papers, NcD.

22. For the appeal of northern resorts' rural settings for urban visitors, see Grover,
"Luxury and Leisure," 4; Cayleff, *Wash and Be Healed,* 107; Brown, *Inventing New England.*

23. Morgan, *Description of the Peaks of Otter,* 85. Similarly, the *Richmond Enquirer* recommended Fauquier White Sulphur as "the most sovereign remedy for *ennui* and low-
spirits" ("Virginia Watering Place," 2 Sept. 1845).

24. *White Sulphur Springs, Greenbrier County,* 21; Tindall, *Observations on the Mineral
Waters,* 21; Jacob Hall to Christian Eliza (Hall) Price, 1 Sept. 1840, Price Family Papers,
ViHi. Kenneth Hawkins has explored the idea of a "therapeutic landscape" with respect to
nineteenth-century insane asylums in "Therapeutic Landscape."

25. Joseph C. Cabell to William B. Hare, 12 Nov. 1801, Cabell-Reid Papers, ViU; Alexander H. H. Stuart to Frances Stuart, 23 July [1837], Stuart Family Papers, ViHi; Rosalie Stier
Calvert to Henri J. and Marie Louise Peeters Stier, 28 June [1803], in Callcott, *Mistress of
Riversdale,* 52; Rosalie Stier Calvert to Isabelle Stier van Havre, 11 May and 24 Sept. 1820, ibid.,
359, 362.

26. John McLaughlin to Mary O. McLaughlin, 29 July 1814, McLaughlin-Redd Letters,
ViU; J[ames] Barbour to Frances T. Barbour, 4 Aug. 1847, Ambler Family Papers, ViU; Mary
Jane Boggs Diary, June 1851, in Buni, "'Rambles Among the Virginia Mountains,'" 89; Burke,
Mineral Springs of Western Virginia, 15.

27. Volumina Barrow to Horace Hunley, 12 July 1859, Robert Ruffin Barrow Papers,
LNHT; Caldwell, *Tour Through Part of Virginia,* 5; James White to Mary White, 17 Aug. 1860,
Cabell-Reid Papers, ViU.

28. Windle, *Life at the White Sulphur,* 24; James White to Mary White, 18 Aug. 1860,
Cabell-Reid Papers, ViU; William B. Hare to Joseph C. Cabell, 8 Sept. 1810, ibid.; Samuel
Hoffman to Louisa Hoffman, 17–18 and 13 July 1833, Samuel Hoffman Papers, ViW; Burke,
Mineral Springs of Western Virginia, 15. Upon a return trip in 1840, Hoffman again felt the
youthful powers of the springs, writing to his wife: "I feel as strong as a young Lion" (Samuel
Hoffman to Louisa Hoffman, 10 Aug. 1840, Samuel Hoffman Papers, ViW). See also Henry
Clay to Francis T. Brooke, 17 Apr. 1834, in Hopkins, *Papers of Henry Clay,* 8:715.

29. Thomas Jefferson Peyton to James Barbour Jr., 17 Aug. 1854, Barbour Family Papers, ViU.

"They All Drink the Waters without the Advice of Any Medical Man"

1. Most histories of medicine look at this subject from the point of view of published medical theories and the leading practitioners of orthodox medicine or health reforms. A few works examine the "average" town or rural doctor, but almost none look at therapeutics or ideas about health from the lay public's point of view. For examples of works that concentrate on leading practitioners and theory, see works cited in n. 2 below. For the "family and home contexts" of the small-town or rural doctor, see Leavitt, "'Worrying Profession.'" For a discussion of the average southern rural doctor, see Stowe, "Religion, Science, and the Culture of Medical Practice in the American South."

2. Benjamin Rush took the lead in the dissemination of heroic therapeutics in America. His influence on medical theory and therapy lasted throughout the nineteenth century and was especially strong in the South. The field of American medical history is extensive. Some works that examine the late eighteenth and nineteenth centuries are Shryock, *Medicine and Society in America* and *Medicine in America;* Rothstein, *American Physicians in the Nineteenth Century;* Bordley and Harvey, *Two Centuries of American Medicine;* Rosenberg, "Therapeutic Revolution"; Warner, *Therapeutic Perspective;* Armstrong and Metzger Armstrong, *Great American Medicine Show;* Murphy, *Enter the Physician;* Rosenberg, *Explaining Epidemics.* For medicine in the Antebellum South specifically, see Shryock, *Medicine in America,* 49–70; Blanton, *Medicine in Virginia in the Nineteenth Century;* Numbers and Savitt, *Science and Medicine in the Old South;* Stowe, "Religion, Science, and the Culture of Medical Practice in the American South."

3. Dr. Charles Everette to Wilson C. Nicholas, 25 Aug. 1808, Edgehill-Randolph/Wilson Cary Nicholas Papers, ViU; Newbraugh, *Warm Springs Echoes,* 27. See also Lawrence Butler to Anna Cradock, 17 Apr. 1790, Lawrence Butler Letters (photocopy), ViHi; Dow, *Vicissitudes Exemplified,* 93; Judith Randolph to John Randolph, 1 June 1813, Bryan Family Papers, ViU; Moncure Robinson to John Robinson, 17 Apr. 1828, in "Letters of Moncure Robinson," 13.

4. Larkin Newby Diary, 14 June–9 Sept. 1823, Larkin Newby Papers, NcU (even after undergoing all of these treatments during his lengthy stay at the springs, Newby died the following year); Nicholas Cabell to Peggy Cabell, 13 Aug. 1808, Cabell Family Papers, ViU; John Coalter to Frances Davenport, 14 July and 31 Aug. 1813, Grinnan Family Papers, ViHi.

5. Thomas and Mary Louisa Bolling to William Bolling, 13 Sept. 1832, William Bolling Papers, NcD; Larkin Newby Diary, 13 July 1823, Larkin Newby Papers, NcU.

6. Harvey Green has considered fresh air, sunshine, good diet, and exercise as therapeutics "closely allied" only with hydropathy and electrotherapy, and, after 1830, as the most recommended cures for consumption by regular physicians (*Fit for America,* 77). Nancy L. Struna has claimed that it was not until Catharine Beecher that "physical performance and sport" were linked to women's health ("'Good Wives' and 'Gardeners,' Spinners, and 'Fearless Riders,'" 249). Similarly, Nancy Cole Dosch has argued that before 1870 only health reformers, and not orthodox doctors, regarded exercise as an important element in the prevention of disease; see Dosch, "Exploring Alternatives." Charles E. Rosenberg, however, has shown that medical theory in the late eighteenth and early nineteenth centuries emphasized the relationship between "an individual's constitutional endowment and the environment"

and thus recommended a good regimen and diet "in the cause and cure of sickness" (*Explaining Epidemics*, 264).

7. Ferdinando Fairfax Diary, 14 July–31 Aug. 1792, ViU; Virginia Terrell to Nellie B. Carr, 22 Aug. 1813, Terrell-Carr Papers, ViU; Nicholas Faulcon to John H. Cocke, 30 Aug. 1822, Cocke Family Papers, ViU. See also William C. Latane to Warner Lewis, 7 Sept. 1826, Lewis and Latane Family Papers, ViU.

8. Some historians claim the change was revolutionary, while others believe the process was more gradual. See Coulter, *Divided Legacy;* Rosenberg, "Therapeutic Revolution"; Warner, *Therapeutic Perspective;* Murphy, *Enter the Physician.* For the post-1830 notice of the poor state of health of Americans, see Sklar, *Catharine Beecher;* Green, *Fit for America,* 14, 21; Albanese, *Nature Religion in America,* 120. Correspondingly, according to one historian, health captivated Victorians in England more than "religion, or politics, or Improvement, or Darwinism" (Haley, *Healthy Body and Victorian Culture,* 3).

9. Merit M. Robinson to John H. Cocke, 25 Sept. 1823, Cocke Family Papers, ViU. See Grover, "Luxury and Leisure," 149; Armstrong and Metzger Armstrong, *Great American Medicine Show,* 72; Dosch, "Exploring Alternatives," 316. Even those in "sophisticated medical circles" criticized traditional therapeutics by the 1830s (Rosenberg, "Therapeutic Revolution," 15).

10. For health reformers in the first half of the nineteenth century, see Morantz, "Making Women Modern"; Walters, *American Reformers,* especially chap. 7; Whorton, *Crusaders for Fitness;* Donegan, *"Hydropathic Highway to Health";* Green, *Fit for America;* Cayleff, *Wash and Be Healed;* Armstrong and Metzger Armstrong, *Great American Medicine Show;* Dosch, "Exploring Alternatives"; Haller, *Kindly Medicine.* For nineteenth-century Americans' beliefs in the healing power of nature, see Warner, "The Nature-Trusting Heresy"; Rosenberg, "Therapeutic Revolution," 15; Donegan, *"Hydropathic Highway to Health,"* xiv, 188–89; Cayleff, *Wash and Be Healed,* 11; Albanese, *Nature Religion in America,* 122, 136; Hawkins, "Therapeutic Landscape."

11. Haley, *Healthy Body,* 5.

12. Robert E. Lee to Mary Lee Custis, 26 July 1839, Lee Family Papers, ViHi; William Mackay to Catherine Mackay, 23 Aug. 1857, Mackay and Stiles Family Papers, NcU. See also John W. Wickham to John Carter, [ca. 1830], Carter-Smith Family Papers, ViU. For increasing distrust in orthodox physicians and theory, see also Merit M. Robinson to John H. Cocke, 25 Sept. 1823, Cocke Family Papers, ViU; Charles Campbell to [father?], 2 Sept. [ca. 1827], Charles Campbell Papers, ViW; Mary Louisa and Thomas Bolling to William and Mary Bolling, 12 Sept. 1832, William Bolling Papers, NcD; Louisa Cocke to John H. Cocke, 18 Aug. 1837, Cocke Family Papers, ViU.

13. Buckingham, *Slave States,* 2:346; Robert Hubard to Edmund Hubard, 3 Sept. 1852, Hubard Family Papers, NcU; John Francis Speight Jr. to Emma L. Speight, 29 July 1860, John Francis Speight Papers, NcU.

14. Dr. Edward H. Carmichael to St. George Tucker Coalter, 28 Apr. 1839, Brown-Coalter-Tucker Papers, ViW; Dr. Philip S. Physick to Henry Clay, 19 Apr. 1834, in Hopkins, *Papers of Henry Clay,* 8:716; Coulling, *Lee Girls,* 61, 65. Nelly Custis Lewis went to White

Sulphur for "Dropsey" and "liver disease" in 1834 (Nelly Custis Lewis to Elizabeth Bordley Gibson, 4 July 1834, in Brady, *George Washington's Beautiful Nelly*, 216). For southern doctors, see Duffy, "Medical Practice in the Ante-Bellum South"; and Stowe, "Seeing Themselves at Work."

15. Stowe, "Religion, Science, and the Culture of Medical Practice," 4. Charles Rosenberg has found that Americans in the first third of the nineteenth century felt little "conflict" between their beliefs in rational medicine and spiritual healing ("Therapeutic Revolution," 10).

16. Benjamin Grigsby to Rosanna Cox, 12 Aug. 1804, Hugh Blair Grigsby Papers, ViHi; Stringfellow, *Two Letters on Cases of Cure at Fauquier White Sulphur Springs*, 4, 12.

17. Levin Smith Joynes to Anne Joynes, 9 Aug. 1856, Joynes Family Papers, ViHi.

18. For the history of hydropathy in the United States, see Kamenetz, "History of American Spas and Hydropathy"; Donegan, *"Hydropathic Highway to Health"*; Cayleff, *Wash and Be Healed*.

19. "Rockbridge Alum Springs and Bath Alum Springs, in Virginia," printed advertisement on verso of John H. Cocke to Cary Charles Cocke, 11 July 1853, Cocke Family Papers, ViU; Nancy Evans to "My dear Young Mistress," 6 Aug. 1856, Preston-Radford Papers, ViU; J. Taylor to George Morton, [ca. 1855], Morton Family Papers, ViU; James Gray to William Gray, 12 Aug. 1853, William Gray Papers, ViHi. Agnes Cabell's relative also spent a season at the springs in 1817 recuperating from a miscarriage (Agnes S. B. Cabell to Louisa Cabell, 14 Aug. 1817, Cabell-Carrington Papers, ViU).

20. Almost all of the historical studies of women's health in the nineteenth century focus on northern attitudes and middle-class women. Very little has been written on southern medical attitudes and practice regarding white women. Sally McMillen's outstanding study on southern white women and childbirth stands virtually alone; see her *Motherhood in the Old South*. Elite southern women's pregnancy has also received attention in Lewis and Lockridge, "'Sally Has Been Sick.'" Little else has been written about southern white women and medical care. For the best discussions of medical attitudes concerning northern women and health in the first half of the nineteenth century, see Wood, "'Fashionable Diseases'"; Smith-Rosenberg and Rosenberg, "Female Animal"; Morantz, "Making Women Modern." Works that discuss the link between women's health and hydropathy include Donegan, *"Hydropathic Highway to Health"*; and Cayleff, *Wash and Be Healed*. See also Duffin, "Conspicuous Consumptive," and Apple, *Women, Health, and Medicine in America*, which focus primarily on the Gilded Age and the twentieth century, respectively. The fabled Victorian female "disease," neurasthenia, was not identified until after 1860.

21. Wood, "'Fashionable Diseases,'" 27.

22. Smith-Rosenberg and Rosenberg, "Female Animal." See also Wood, "'Fashionable Diseases.'" Hydropaths, however, did not adhere to this notion of reproductive organs as the major "physiological force" in women's health (Cayleff, *Wash and Be Healed*, 8–10).

23. See McMillen, *Motherhood in the Old South*, and letters cited throughout this section.

24. Bell, *On Baths and Mineral Waters*, 444; Moorman, *Water From the White Sulphur*

Springs, 6. Other resorts, such as Blue Sulphur and Red Sulphur, claimed similar cures for their mineral waters; see Martin, *New and Comprehensive Gazetteer of Virginia,* 353, 394; and William Burke, *Mineral Springs of Virginia,* 307.

25. John and Frances Coalter to Frances Davenport, [ca. 1813], Grinnan Family Papers, ViU; Agnes S. B. Cabell to Louisa Carrington, 18 July 1836, Cabell-Carrington Papers, ViU; Susanna I. Harrison to Mary Harrison, 24 Aug. 1831, Harrison Family Papers, ViHi; Ellen Tazewell Wirt to Henry Coalter Cabell, 23 Sept. 1833, Cabell Family Papers, ViHi; Sarah I. Harrison to Mary Harrison, 30 Aug. 1831, Harrison Family Papers, ViHi.

26. Moorman, *Virginia Springs* (1847), 80; George T. Sinclair to John H. Cocke, 25 Sept. 1860, Cocke Family Papers, ViU (mistakenly filed under 29 Oct.); Samuel Hoffman to Louisa Hoffman, 1 Aug. 1832, Samuel Hoffman Papers, ViW; Jane Caroline North Pettigrew to Jane Petigru North, 20 Aug. 1855, Pettigrew Papers, NcU.

27. W. H. Collins to James Barbour, 27 Mar. 1856, Barbour Family Papers, ViU; Bigelow, *Brief Exposition of Rational Medicine,* 46; Tindall, *Observations on the Mineral Waters of Western Virginia,* 24.

"Every Day Var[ies] a Little"

1. Similarly, homeopaths prescribed the same dosages and hydropaths administered the same water-cure treatment for men and women.

2. Levin Smith Joynes to Anne Joynes, 9 Aug. 1856, Joynes Family Papers, ViHi; Sarah J. Garland to James Garland, 20 Oct. [pre-1850], Sarah Garland Letter, ViHi; Susan Baldwin Stuart to Frances Baldwin Stuart, 31 July [ca. 1860], Stuart Family Papers, ViHi.

3. Pencil, *White Sulphur Papers,* 27–28; Burke, *Mineral Springs of Western Virginia,* 41; Larkin Newby Diary, 28 June 1823, Larkin Newby Papers, NcU. The water-drinking regimen at Saratoga Springs was quite similar; see Grover, "Luxury and Leisure," 100.

4. Anne Walke Smith and Mary E. Smith to Nannie Smith, 31 Aug. 1858, Smith Family Papers, ViHi.

5. Worsham, "European Bathing Tradition and Its American Successors." The bathhouses at Hot and White Sulphur and the Ladies' Bath built in 1836 at Warm Springs all had an octagonal shape. However, the bathhouses at Sweet Springs were square and built of brick, with Gothic towers later added to the corners. A castellated Gothic bathhouse held a prominent place at Fauquier White Sulphur.

6. C. O. Lyde Diary, 2 July 1841, NcD.

7. Thomas Gordon Pollock to Elizabeth Pollock, 12 Aug. 1860, Abram David Pollock Papers, NcU; [Horner], *Observations on the Mineral Waters,* 26; Thomas and Mary Louisa Bolling to William Bolling, 2 Sept. 1832, William Bolling Papers, NcD.

8. Some of the resorts charged extra for the use of their baths. In 1851, for example, Hot Springs charged fifty cents per day for the "Boiler" and twenty-five cents for the temperate bath (John H. Cocke Diary, 29 Aug. 1851, Cocke Family Papers, ViU). In 1848 Cocke paid a total of $10.00 for baths at Sweet and Hot Springs (John H. Cocke Diary, Aug.–Sept. 1848, ibid.). Benjamin Ogle Tayloe paid twenty-five cents per bath at Fauquier White Sulphur in 1839 (Fauquier White Sulphur Springs Bill, 18 July 1839, Benjamin Ogle Tayloe Scrapbook, ViHi).

9. Prolix, *Letters Descriptive of the Virginia Springs,* 26; Mary R. Harrison to Mary Harrison, 9 Aug. 1827, Harrison Family Papers, ViHi; [Horner], *Observations on the Mineral Waters,* 14.

10. Prolix, *Letters Descriptive of the Virginia Springs,* 82; Caldwell, *Tour Through Part of Virginia,* 31; Richard D. Burroughs to Caroline Burroughs, 25 Sept. 1857, Richard Burroughs Papers, NcD; Sarah Rutherfoord to John Rutherfoord, 12 July 1811, John Rutherfoord Papers, NcD. As early as 1792, blanket sweats were a part of the bathing regimen (see Ferdinando Fairfax Diary, 25 July 1792, ViU). In the 1840s, hydropaths adopted the blanket wraps and the spout baths as part of their regimen.

11. Few bathkeepers were referred to by name in visitors' or proprietors' records. An old Frenchman by the name of Jean Delorme was the bathkeeper at Sweet Springs in the 1830s (Prolix, *Letters Descriptive of the Virginia Springs,* 75–77). A "mulatto named Joseph Mackintosh" worked as a bathkeeper at White Sulphur in 1859 (entry of 22 Aug. 1859, in Scarborough, *Diary of Edmund Ruffin,* 1:332). For evidence that most of the servants were slaves, see Henry Bright Diary, 30 June 1852, in Ehrenpreis, *Happy Country This America,* 198. Like other servants at the resorts, bathkeepers and assistants expected tips.

12. Anne Smith to Nannie Smith, 31 Aug. 1858, Smith Family Papers, ViHi.

13. See Blair Bolling Diary, vol. 3, 24 Aug. 1838, ViHi; and John H. Cocke Diary, 6 Sept. 1844, Cocke Family Papers, ViU.

14. As quoted in Donegan, *"Hydropathic Highway to Health,"* 189.

15. James L. Petigru to Susan Petigru King, 21 Sept. 1845, in Carson, *Life, Letters and Speeches,* 250; J. Taylor to Dr. George Morton, [ca. 1860], Morton Family Papers, ViU; Otwayanna Carter to Betty Lewis Carter, 19 Aug. [ca. 1825], Tucker-Harrison-Smith Papers, ViU; Larkin Newby Diary, 22 July 1823, Larkin Newby Papers, NcU. For others who indulged in spa life, see Virginia Heth to Mary E. Carter, 3 Sept. 1822, Carter-Smith Family Papers, ViU; and Prolix, *Letters Descriptive of the Virginia Springs,* 65.

16. Bell, *On Baths and Mineral Waters,* 400–401. Dr. John J. Moorman of White Sulphur Springs copied these phrases, and others, verbatim into his *Virginia Springs* (1847), 79–80.

17. Moorman, *Virginia Springs* (1847), 76. See also Huntt, *Visit to the Red Sulphur Spring,* 7; and Burke, *Mineral Springs of Western Virginia,* 42.

18. John Howell Briggs Diary, 30 July 1804, ViHi; Jane Caroline North to Mary C. North, 17 Aug. 1851, Pettigrew Papers, NcU; Samuel Hoffman to Louisa Hoffman, 2 and 4 Aug. 1833, Samuel Hoffman Papers, ViW; Charles William Ashby to Sarah Elizabeth Ashby, 6 Aug. 1860, Charles William Ashby Papers, ViHi.

"The Most Delicious Sensations"

1. Ferdinando Fairfax Diary, 7 Aug. 1792, ViU; Robert Hubard to Edmund Hubard, 3 Sept. 1852, Hubard Family Papers, NcU; Larkin Newby Diary, 15 June 1823, Larkin Newby Papers, NcU.

2. Richard Burroughs to Caroline Burroughs, 20 Aug. 1857, Richard D. Burroughs Papers, NcD; Larkin Newby to Cecilia Newby, 25 June 1823, Larkin Newby Papers, NcD;

Thomas Gordon Pollock to Elizabeth Pollock, 12 Aug. 1860, Abram David Pollock Papers, NcU; William C. Latane to Warner Lewis, 7 Sept. 1826, Lewis and Latane Family Papers, ViU; Alexander H. H. Stuart to Frances Stuart, [1851], Stuart Family Papers, ViHi; Nicholas Faulcon to John H. Cocke, 21 Aug. 1821, Cocke Family Papers, ViU.

3. Samuel Hoffman to Louisa Hoffman, 25 and 29 July 1832, Samuel Hoffman Papers, ViW.

4. Hugh Blair Grigsby Diary, 2 July 1842, ViHi (Grigsby was reading a translation of Junius every day and falling asleep each time—hence the reference to Morpheus); Larkin Newby Diary, 14 June–9 Sept. 1823, Larkin Newby Papers, NcU; Memorandum of George Carr, 21 and 26 Aug. 1841, George Carr Papers, ViU.

5. John Guerrant to Robert P. Guerrant, 1 Aug. 1806, Goochland Court House Deposit, ViU; Ann Frances Bland Tucker to St. George Tucker, 17 Aug. 1801, St. George Tucker Papers, ViHi; Cary Charles Cocke to John H. Cocke, 5 Sept. 1850, Cocke Family Papers, ViU.

6. John Rutherfoord to Emily Rutherfoord, 16 Aug. 1849, John Rutherfoord Papers, NcD; Alexander H. H. Stuart to Frances Stuart, 30 July 1831, Stuart Family Papers, ViHi.

7. Thomas Jefferson to Martha Jefferson Randolph, 21 Aug. 1818, in Betts and Bear, *Family Letters of Thomas Jefferson,* 426. The trip home, troubled by his "imposthume and eruptions," reduced him "to the last stage of weakness and exhaustion" (ibid., 427).

8. Larkin Newby to Cecilia Newby, 25 June 1823, Larkin Newby Papers, NcD.

9. Benjamin Grigsby to Elizabeth Grigsby, 12 Aug. 1808, Hugh Blair Grigsby Papers, ViHi; Sophie S. Wilson Diary, 9 July 1831, DLC (the diary is mistakenly attributed to Sophie; the author was actually her father, whose name is unknown).

10. Sarah I. Harrison to Mary Harrison, 30 Aug. 1831, Harrison Family Papers, ViHi. Mary Harrison informed her mother that her husband was "well & fat & enjoys himself" (Mary R. Harrison to Mary Harrison, 27 Aug. 1827, ibid.).

11. Nicholas Faulcon to John H. Cocke, 6 Sept. 1822, Cocke Family Papers, ViU.

12. George T. Sinclair to John H. Cocke, 25 Sept. 1860, ibid. (mistakenly filed under 29 Oct.).

13. Willis Williams to "Neppie" [his wife], 28 Aug. and 10 Sept. 1858, Willis Williams Papers, NcU. Two years later, during his next trip to the Virginia Springs, Williams again kept close track of his weight (Willis Williams to "Neppie," 14 Sept. 1860, ibid.). Samuel Hoffman focused upon his weight during trips to the springs; see his letters to his wife Louisa during his 1832, 1833, and 1840 trips in Samuel Hoffman Papers, ViW.

14. Anonymous woman to "Pa," 1 Aug. 1847, Susan Bradford Eppes Papers, NcU. Samuel Hoffman considered his sister "wonderfully improved" after she gained thirteen pounds at the springs (Samuel Hoffman to Louisa Hoffman, 30–31 Aug. 1840, Samuel Hoffman Papers, ViW).

15. See Kasson, *Rudeness and Civility,* especially 124; and Bushman, *Refinement of America,* especially chap. 3.

16. Martineau, *Society in America,* 1:184; Edwin Bedford Jeffress Diary, 3 Sept. 1852, ViHi; Littleton Wickham to Elizabeth Wickham, 13 Aug. [ca. 1830], Wickham Family Papers, ViHi.

17. William C. Latane to Warner Lewis, 7 Sept. 1826, Lewis and Latane Family Papers, ViU; Sally Faulcon to Louisa Cocke, 2 Sept. 1822, Cocke Family Papers, ViU; Richard Burroughs to Caroline Burroughs, [1857] and 11 Sept. 1857, Richard D. Burroughs Papers, NcD. This sort of exchange occurred frequently at the springs. See also Larkin Newby Diary, 30 June 1823, Larkin Newby Papers, NcU; and Anne Walke Smith to Nannie Smith, 31 Aug. 1858, Smith Family Papers, ViHi.

18. Louisianna Cocke Faulcon to Louisa Cocke, 19 Aug. 1828, Cocke Family Papers, ViU; Samuel Hoffman to Louisa Hoffman, 9 July [*sic:* Aug.] 1832, Samuel Hoffman Papers, ViW.

19. Pencil, *White Sulphur Papers*, 18; Mackie, *From Cape Cod to Dixie,* 23−24; Martineau, *Society in America,* 1:187. For other stories about the spectacles at the scales, see Larkin Newby Diary, 11 Aug. 1823, Larkin Newby Papers, NcU; Pencil, *White Sulphur Papers,* 84; *Trip to the Virginia Springs,* 47.

20. Mildred Halsey to J. J. Halsey, 30 Aug. 1858, Morton-Halsey Papers, ViU.

21. Thomas Jefferson to Martha Jefferson Randolph, 7 Aug. 1818, in Betts and Bear, *Family Letters of Thomas Jefferson,* 424; Emily Rutherfoord to John C. Rutherfoord, 28 Sept. 1850, John Rutherfoord Papers, NcD; E. E. R. to Jane Randolph, 12 Sept. 1833, Randolph Family Papers, ViU; Susan Elizabeth Gordon Webb Diary, 15 Sept. 1858, ViHi.

22. Levin Joynes to Anne Joynes, 21 Aug. 1856, Joynes Family Papers, ViHi.

23. C. O. Lyde Diary, 14 Aug. 1841, NcD; Jane Caroline North Diary, 7 Aug. 1851, in O'Brien, *Evening When Alone,* 160; Featherstonhaugh, *Excursion through the Slave States,* 1:36.

24. Thomas Gordon Pollock to Elizabeth Pollock, 12 Aug. 1860, Abram David Pollock Papers, NcU; Mary Lee to Robert E. Lee, 7 July 1857, Lee Family Papers, ViHi; Mackie, *From Cape Cod to Dixie,* 47; Sally Faulcon to Louisa Cocke, 2 Sept. 1822, Cocke Family Papers, ViU; Lucy Baytop to James Baytop, [ca. 12 Aug. 1838], Baytop Family Papers, ViW.

25. *Trip to the Virginia Springs,* 46; Louisa Cocke Diary, 27 Aug. 1837, Cocke Family Papers, ViU; Jane Caroline North to Mary C. North, 11 Sept. 1851, Pettigrew Papers, NcU; Mary Pollard Diary, 6 Aug. 1836, Pollard Family Papers, ViHi. Later, Louisa Cocke's aunt, somewhat jokingly, warned her that if the waters were "so very exhilerating, perhaps it would be better for *Christians* not to frequent them to much"; she also hoped that Louisa "did not suffer" her "spirits" to be "too buoyant" (Helen Read to Louisa Cocke, 23 Sept. 1837, Cocke Family Papers, ViU).

26. Maria C. Broadus to Eliza Broadus, 13 July 1857, Tucker-Harrison-Smith Papers, ViU; Mary Lee to Robert E. Lee, 3 Aug. 1857, Lee Family Papers, ViHi; Windle, *Life at the White Sulphur Springs,* 75; Pencil, *White Sulphur Papers,* 19. For other accounts of women who enjoyed the sensuality of the baths, see Catherine Eliza (Moore) Hall to Christian Eliza (Hall) Price, 23 Aug. [1840], Price Family Papers, ViHi; Emily Rutherfoord to John C. Rutherfoord, 28 Sept. 1850, John Rutherfoord Papers, NcD; Jane Caroline North Diary, 13 Sept. 1851, in O'Brien, *Evening When Alone,* 174; C. S. to Frances Lea, 18 July 1854, Frances Lea Papers, NcD; Mary Lee to Robert E. Lee, 25 July 1857, Lee Family Papers, ViHi. Similarly, both Kathryn Kish Sklar and Susan Cayleff have found middle-class women at hydropathy establishments freely enjoying the sensual experiences of the water cure; see Sklar, *Catharine Beecher,* 207; and Cayleff, *Wash and Be Healed,* 145.

27. Biddle, *Autobiography of Charles Biddle*, 294; Blair Bolling Diary, vol. 3, 24 Aug. 1838, ViHi. See also Jerome Napoleon Bonaparte's travel diary in Hoyt, "Journey to the Springs," 129; and Thomas Pollard to Mary Pollard, 11 Sept. [1852], Pollard Family Papers, ViHi.

28. William Wirt to Dabney Carr, 1 July 1820, William Wirt Papers, NcU; *Charleston Daily Courier*, 20 Aug. 1855; Thomas Pollard to Mary Pollard, 11 Sept. [1852], Pollard Family Papers, ViHi (emphasis added); Mackie, *From Cape Cod to Dixie*, 48; Burke, *Mineral Springs of Virginia*, 191–92; John H. Cocke Diary, 6 Sept. 1844 and 27 Aug. 1851, Cocke Family Papers, ViU; James L. Petigru to Susan Petigru King, 12 Sept. 1845, in Carson, *Life, Letters and Speeches*, 248–49; Mackie, *From Cape Cod to Dixie*, 48. For George Featherstonhaugh, the "streams of gas" that "gently [crept] over his body as if little fishes were nibbling at him" turned Warm Springs' bath into a "perfect delight" (*Excursion through the Slave States*, 1:36–37). For other men who commented on the sensuality of the baths and towel rubs, see Thomas S. Massie to William Massie, 2 Sept. 1851, William Massie Papers, NcD.

29. Featherstonhaugh, *Excursion through the Slave States*, 1:37–38; *Trip to the Virginia Springs*, 46; Prolix, *Letters Descriptive of the Virginia Springs*, 82; Sarah Isham Harrison to Mary Harrison, 1 Sept. 1825, Harrison Family Papers, ViHi. For women bathing together, see also S. N. L. to Amilie Rives, 1 Sept. 1849, Rives Family Papers, ViU.

30. Larkin Newby Diary, 13 July 1823, Larkin Newby Papers, NcU; Peter Saunders to Elizabeth Saunders, 2 Sept. 1860, Saunders Family Papers, ViHi; Moore, "Old Dominion through Student Eyes," 316.

31. Sklar, *Catharine Beecher*, 206–7. For another discussion of the culture of women at water-cure establishments, see Cayleff, *Wash and Be Healed*.

32. "Journal of a Trip to the Mountains, Caves and Springs of Virginia," 305; Conway Whittle to Mary W. Neale, 16 Aug. 1858, Conway Whittle Family Papers, ViW. In 1850 Lucy Cocke and her party admired the tombstones in one resort graveyard, especially those of the infants (Lucy W. Cocke Diary, 10 Sept. 1850, Cocke Family Papers, ViU). See also Dandridge Spotswood Sr. Diary, 21 July 1848, ViHi.

33. For historians who argue that nineteenth-century Americans regarded sickness as a result of sin, see Daniel W. Foster, "Religion and Medicine: The Physician's Perspective" and Martin E. Marty, "The Intertwining of Religion & Health/Medicine in Culture: A View through the Disciplines," in *Health/Medicine and the Faith Traditions*, ed. Marty and Vaux, 245–70 and 27–50, respectively; and Dosch, "Exploring Alternatives," 337. Charles E. Rosenberg has found that Americans considered cholera "a scourge not of mankind but of the sinner" (*Cholera Years*, 40). Harvey Green has claimed that it was health reformers who equated physical debility with a moral or spiritual problem (*Fit for America*, 10). Out of the thousands of manuscripts examined for this work, I found only one letter that regarded sickness as a sin which "we have foolishly & wickedly brought upon ourselves" (Jonathan Minor to Alexander Garrett, 25 June 1848, Alexander Garrett Papers, ViU).

34. Sallie B. Cocke to John H. Cocke, 3 Sept. 1856, Cocke Family Papers, ViU; John H. Cocke to Cary Charles Cocke, 30 Aug. 1851, ibid.; Jane Caroline North Diary, 18 Sept. 1851, in O'Brien, *Evening When Alone*, 175–76; Samuel Clayton to Henry Brown, 25 Aug. 1818, Brown-Coalter-Tucker Papers, ViW.

35. Lucy Cocke to Louisa Cocke, 18 Sept. 1840, Cocke Family Papers, ViU.

PART 3
Community and Competition

1. Jane Caroline North Diary, 6 Aug. and 1 Sept. 1851, in O'Brien, *Evening When Alone,* 160, 170. In addition to her journal, see her letters to her family during her stay at the springs, Aug. through Sept. 1851, Pettigrew Papers, NcU.

2. Jane Caroline North Diary, 10 Sept., 9 Aug. and 29 Aug. 1851, in O'Brien, *Evening When Alone,* 173, 162, 167. See her entire travel journal 31 July–12 Oct. 1851, ibid., 153–85.

3. Ibid., 1 Sept. 1851, 170.

4. Jane Caroline North to Jane Petigru North, 5 Sept. 1851, Pettigrew Papers, NcU; Jane Carolina North Diary, 9, 11, 29, and 14 Aug. 1851, in O'Brien, *Evening When Alone,* 163, 163– 64, 167, 165; Jane Caroline North to Jane Petigru North, 5 Sept. 1851, Pettigrew Papers, NcU; Jane Caroline North Diary, 29 Aug. 1851, in O'Brien, *Evening When Alone,* 168, 167.

5. Burke, *Mineral Springs of Western Virginia,* 21–22; Elizabeth Ruffin Diary, 10 Aug. and 3 Sept. 1827, in O'Brien, *Evening When Alone,* 82, 95. Similarly, sportsman William Elliott of South Carolina found "not much sociability" at Saratoga in 1816 and barely "civil" matrons over twenty years later (William Elliott to Ann Smith, 24 July 1816, and William Elliott to Ann Elliott, 26 July 1839, in Scafidel, "Letters of William Elliott," 35–37, 385–89). See also "White Sulphur Springs," 226.

6. See Richard Bushman's *Refinement of America* for a similar analysis of gentility, but among eighteenth-century Americans not nineteenth-century southerners.

"A Never Ceasing Scene of Stir, Animation, Display, & Enjoyment"

1. Judith Walker Page Rives Autobiography (typescript), 1861, p. 53, Rives Family Papers, ViU; Account of John Wickham, 2–16 Sept. 1816, White Sulphur Springs Account Book, 1816–17, ViU (microfilm); Account receipt for "Chief Justice Taney and party" (typescript), 12 July–14 Oct. 1856, Fauquier White Sulphur Springs File, Fauquier County Library, Warrenton, Va. A lengthy stay at the resorts was quite expensive. In 1831 a Mr. Edmondston paid $114.50 for his family, servants, and horses for just twenty days at White Sulphur (Account of Mr. Edmondston, 11–31 Aug. 1831, White Sulphur Springs Account Book, 1831, ViU [microfilm]). By 1859 the bill of James Cathcart Johnston of South Carolina, his two servants, and two horses ran close to three hundred dollars for one month at the Healing Springs (Bill of James C. Johnston, [15 July 1859], Hayes Collection, Johnston Series, NcU). Customarily, the resorts charged full price for white adults and about half for children, servants, and horses. The charges for lodging, meals, liquor, laundry, and amusements varied from spa to spa. Some spas charged separately for the use of their mineral baths.

2. See DeBow, *Statistical View of the United States,* 164.

3. John H. B. Latrobe, "Trip to the Virginia Springs," in Semmes, *John H. B. Latrobe,* 256; Marryat, *Diary in America,* 271–72; Thomas Gordon Pollock to Elizabeth Pollock, 3 Aug. 1860, Abram David Pollock Papers, NcU. Joseph Packard also believed that the springs belonged to "the leaders of society" (*Recollections of a Long Life,* 103).

4. Reed and Matheson, *Narrative of the Visit to the American Churches,* 199; *Six Weeks in*

Fauquier, v–vi; *Baltimore Sun,* 17 Aug. 1843; Buckingham, *Slave States of America,* 2:317–18.

5. *Six Weeks in Fauquier,* vi; Jane Caroline North Diary, 9 Aug. 1851, in O'Brien, *Evening When Alone,* 163; *Trip to the Virginia Springs,* 29. Englishman George Featherstonhaugh comfortably left his wife at the Virginia Springs amid "the families of many opulent planters" (*Excursion through the Slave States,* 1:5). See also [Hoffman], "Trip to the Virginia Springs," 322. Thomas A. Chambers has found that within the "fluid society" at Ballston and Saratoga Springs detecting and protecting oneself from the pretender or seducer occupied the time of many genteel visitors, especially young women; see his "Fashionable Dis-Ease," chaps. 4 and 5. Similarly, Dona Brown has claimed that soon after Saratoga's rise as a resort in the 1820s, "it became notoriously difficult to distinguish between the genteel and the pretenders" (*Inventing New England,* 37).

6. Samuel Mordecai to Solomon Mordecai, 8 Aug. 1817, Mordecai Family Papers, NcU; Burke, *Mineral Springs of Virginia,* 42. Similarly, in 1835, L. H. Bolling happily informed his cousin, "The society I have met has been delightful, and I have never seen a collection of more polished and sensible people" (L. H. Bolling to Edmund Hubard, 15 Aug. 1835, Hubard Family Papers, NcU).

7. Dandridge Spotswood Sr. Diary, 23 July 1848, ViHi; J. Taylor to Dr. George Morton, [ca. 1860], Morton Family Papers, ViU.

8. Patrick Henry Aylett to Judith Page Aylett, 24 Aug. 1845, Aylett Family Papers, ViHi; Mackie, *From Cape Cod to Dixie,* 52. Mackie found that "the Irish immigrant" in "Northern hotels" "carries in his face no sign of summer-day satisfaction," unlike the Virginia Springs servant. See also his stereotypical description of one of the "black boys" who served him at the springs (ibid., 52, 20–23 and 28). Many guests similarly depicted the Virginia Springs slave servants as happy and eager to serve.

9. William Stabler to Sally Stabler Jordan, 30 July 1838, Jordan and Stabler Family Papers, ViHi.

10. [Paulding], "Letters from Virginia," 425; Mary B. Blackford to William Blackford, 12 Aug. 1844, Blackford Family Papers, ViU; Royall, *Black Book,* 1:18–19. Foreign travelers often preferred the exclusive and orderly Virginia Springs over Saratoga, too. Englishman James S. Buckingham detested the "humblest mechanics," "small shopkeepers, clerks, and even white servants" who enjoyed Saratoga Springs and disrupted its order (*Slave States of America,* 2:318). Similarly, Michael Chevalier of France believed the spas of Europe could "lose their charm" once "democracy" spread into their confines as it had at Saratoga (*Society, Manners and Politics in the United States,* 315–16). Only on very rare occasions did a country outsider interrupt the pleasant routine and pleasurable diversions of life at the springs. In 1838 at White Sulphur, Blair Bolling felt that the "tranquility" of the day had been disrupted when a man, who had shot and killed another man at a house half a mile away, came to the resort looking for a lawyer. "This rash and cruel act was the cause of a numerous collection of spectaters on the lawn where Gwatkins [the killer] was apprehended." Later, the incident "became the subject of general conversation and animadversion during the ballance of the evening" (Blair Bolling Diary, vol. 3, 20 Aug. 1838, ViHi).

11. J. Taylor to George Morton, [ca. 1860], Morton Family Papers, ViU; Thomas Smith

to William P. Smith, 1 Sept. 1826, William Patterson Smith Papers, NcD; *Six Weeks in Fauquier*, 58. See also James, "Life in Virginia," 280.

12. Prolix, *Letters Descriptive of the Virginia Springs*, 36; Elizabeth Moore Taylor to Judith P. Aylett, 11 Sept. [ca. 1845], Aylett Family Papers, ViHi. See also Lucy Ann Tucker to Elizabeth Tucker Bryan, [ca. 14 Sept. 1847], Bryan Family Papers, ViU.

13. Mary Thompson to Mary Neale, [ca. 31 Aug. 1848], Conway Whittle Family Papers, ViW; Jane Caroline North Diary, 8 Aug. 1851, in O'Brien, *Evening When Alone*, 161. In 1857 William Pettigrew detailed the intricacies of seeking an introduction to a young lady at the springs (William Pettigrew Diary, 21 Aug. 1857, Pettigrew Papers, NcU).

14. Mary Thompson to Mary W. Neale, [ca. 31 Aug. 1848], Conway Whittle Family Papers, ViW; Sarah I. Harrison to Mary Harrison, 30 Aug. 1831, Harrison Family Papers, ViHi; Judith Walker Page Rives Autobiography (typescript), 1861, p. 53, Rives Family Papers, ViU. Many women worried about returning visits and not snubbing their callers. See, for example, Maria C. Broadus to Eliza Tucker Harrison, 21 July 1857, Tucker-Harrison-Smith Papers, ViU. Men, too, never forgot to whom they owed visits and whom they wanted to meet. See, for example, Conway Whittle to Frances M. Lewis, 13 Aug. 1832, Conway Whittle Family Papers, ViW.

15. Mary Thompson to Frances Lewis, 27 Aug. 1856, Conway Whittle Family Papers, ViW; *Trip to the Virginia Springs*, 26; John H. B. Latrobe, "Trip to the Virginia Springs," in Semmes, *John H. B. Latrobe*, 257.

16. Bayard, *Travels in the Interior of the United States*, 45; Playfair, *Recollections of a Visit to the United States*, 171–85; L. L. D. to John B. Minor, 22 Aug. 1855, Minor and Wilson Family Papers, ViU.

17. James Alexander Seddon to Charles Bruce, 12 Aug. 1858, Bruce Family Papers, ViHi. Visitors at White Sulphur found it very difficult to visit with friends and meet acquaintances because of its lack of a parlor or drawing room before the late 1850s; see [Hoffman], "Trip to the Virginia Springs," 220.

18. John Howell Briggs Diary, 15 and 1 Aug. 1804, ViHi; Packard, *Recollections of a Long Life*, 103. Similarly, at Dibrell's Springs in 1852, Edwin Jeffress complained not about the gambling going on in the room next to him but about the noise: "I did not rest well last night, having the same noisy neighbors. Money rattled, oaths, cards, with now and then the phrase 'I will stand,' another, 'I will go 2-1/2 better' & so on until I became interested in the game & could not get to sleep until 12 o'clock. They played nearly or quite all night" (Edwin Bedford Jeffress Diary, 8 Aug. 1852, ViHi). Some guests, especially evangelicals, did find the informal gambling among visitors offensive. At Sweet Springs in 1818, John Cocke noted "that the odious & destructive vice of Gaming is secretly carried on here & at the Sulphur Spring to great extent" (John H. Cocke Diary, 12 Sept. 1818, Cocke Family Papers, ViU).

19. Joseph C. Cabell to Ira Garrett, 20 Aug. 1851, Cabell Family Papers, ViU.

20. Bayard, *Travels in the Interior of the United States*, 50–51; Jerome Napoleon Bonaparte Jr. Diary, in Hoyt, "Journey to the Springs," 127; Pencil, *White Sulphur Papers*, 100; John Wickham to Littleton Waller Tazewell Wickham, [ca. 24 Aug. 1844], Wickham Family Papers, ViHi; Peter Saunders to Elizabeth Saunders, 29 Aug. 1860, Saunders Family Papers,

ViHi. Dr. Bayliss reappeared in 1849 at Fauquier White Sulphur during the Virginia legislature's temporary session there to examine "the crania of the Legislature" (William Ritchie, 22 June 1849, for *Richmond Enquirer,* quoted in Franck, "Virginia Legislature at the Fauquier Springs," 73).

21. Jane Caroline North Pettigrew to Jane Petigru North, 10 Sept. 1855, Pettigrew Papers, NcU.

22. John Brodnax to Mary Brodnax, 23 Aug. 1860, John Grammar Brodnax Papers, NcU; Emily Rutherfoord to John C. Rutherfoord, 28 Aug. 1849, John Rutherfoord Papers, NcD; St. George Tucker Coalter to Judith H. Coalter, 16 July 1833, Brown-Coalter-Tucker Papers, ViW. From the 1820s through the 1850s, the Rutherfoords regularly traveled to the Virginia Springs to reunite with kin.

23. J. Taylor to Dr. George Morton, [ca. 1860], Morton Family Papers, ViU; Walter E. Preston to John Preston, 23 July 1839, Preston Family Papers, ViHi; Philippa Barbour to Elizabeth Ambler, 3 Sept. 1837, Ambler Family Papers, ViU; Bell, *Mineral and Thermal Springs of the United States,* 188−89; Sophie S. Wilson Diary, 15 July 1831, DLC. Bell continued by stating that the company at the Virginia Springs "always exhibit[ed] a large share of intelligence, good taste and sociability."

24. Anna Cora Ritchie to Mary Roane, July 1854, in *Fauquier County, Virginia,* 139; Louisa Emmerson Memoirs (typescript), [pre-1861], ViU; *Six Weeks in Fauquier,* 27; James Alexander Seddon to Charles Bruce, 12 Aug. 1858, Bruce Family Papers, ViHi; James L. Petigru to Susan Petigru King, 29 Aug. 1845, in Carson, *Life, Letters and Speeches,* 245.

25. James White to Mary White, 18 Aug. 1860, Cabell-Reid Papers, ViU; Lucy W. Cocke Diary, 23 Aug. 1850, Cocke Family Papers, ViU.

26. Blair Bolling Diary, vol. 3, 11 Aug. 1838, ViHi; C. S. to Frances Lea, 18 July 1854, Frances Lea Papers, NcD.

27. *Six Weeks at Fauquier,* 15; Bell, *Mineral and Thermal Springs of the United States,* 189; Royall, *Sketches of History,* 32. Similarly, travel writer Mark Pencil admitted that "the general interchange of civilities exist to a greater degree among the company at these springs than at those of the North" (*White Sulphur Papers,* 41). For the "southernness" of the manners at the springs, see also [Horner], *Observations on the Mineral Waters,* 19; Edwin Hall to Cyrus Woodman, 30 Aug. 1837, quoted in Jones, *Plantation South,* 42−44; James, "Life in Virginia," 282; Mackie, *From Cape Cod to Dixie,* 50.

28. Featherstonhaugh, *Excursion through the Slave States,* 1:93; Blair Bolling Diary, vol. 3, 11 Aug. 1838, ViHi; Hoffman, *Winter in the West,* 2:294; Burke, *Mineral Springs of Virginia,* 293. For more on these points, see also Buckingham, *Slave States,* 2:307; [Hoffman], "Trip to the Virginia Springs," 322; "Journal of a Trip to the Mountains, Caves and Springs of Virginia," 516; Prolix, *Letters Descriptive of the Virginia Springs,* 43.

29. Burke, *Mineral Springs of Western Virginia,* 12−13.

"Forming Violent Friendships in Three Days Time"

1. For some of the major works that essentially present the plantation as gender divided and patriarchal, see Clinton, *Plantation Mistress;* Wyatt-Brown, *Southern Honor;* Friedman,

Enclosed Garden; Stowe, *Intimacy and Power in the Old South;* Fox-Genovese, *Within the Plantation Household;* Cashin, *Family Venture;* Bardaglio, *Reconstructing the Household.* Other historians have found a more gender-compatible and less patriarchal plantation. See Smith, *Inside the Great House;* Lewis, *Pursuit of Happiness;* Censer, *North Carolina Planters and Their Children;* Buza, "'Pledges of Our Love.'"

2. D. Blanding DeSaussure to Charles Stroman, 27 July 1854, Charles J. Stroman Papers, NcD.

3. Larkin Newby Diary, 19 Aug. 1823, Larkin Newby Papers, NcU; Charlotte Ruffin to Edmund Ruffin Sr., 11 Sept. 1860, Edmund Ruffin Papers, ViHi; Anna Cora Ritchie to Mary Roane, July 1854, in *Fauquier County, Virginia,* 138. Similarly, Mary Blackford regarded ten-pins as entirely suitable for genteel ladies, but only at the springs. In town the game was "the resort of low company" (Mary B. Blackford to William Blackford, 19 Sept. 1844, Blackford Family Papers, ViU).

4. Sarah I. Harrison to Mary Harrison, 5 Sept. and 30 Aug. 1831, Harrison Family Papers, ViHi; Prolix, *Letters Descriptive of the Virginia Springs,* 44.

5. Pencil, *White Sulphur Papers,* 42; Paulding, *Letters from the South by a Northern Man,* 2:164; Pencil, *White Sulphur Papers,* 77. Pencil also described at length a grand picnic at White Sulphur in the late 1830s (ibid., 102–7).

6. See Smith, *Inside the Great House,* esp. chap. 4; Lewis, *Pursuit of Happiness,* esp. chap. 5; Censer, *North Carolina Planters and Their Children;* Lebsock, *Free Women of Petersburg;* Fox-Genovese, *Within the Plantation Household;* Buza, "'Pledges of Our Love'"; Jabour, *Marriage in the Early Republic.* In a classic article Carroll Smith-Rosenberg defined a "female world of love and ritual" in which women found true, loving, emotional, and equal relationships only with other women (Smith-Rosenberg, "Female World of Love and Ritual").

7. Eliza Harwood to Tristam L. Skinner, 20 Aug. 1846, Skinner Family Papers, NcU; Eliza Branch Cave Friendship Book, 1831–34, Eliza Branch Cave Papers, ViU; J. K. [Lee] to "Charlie," 5 Sept. 1854, Carrington Family Papers, ViHi. See also James White to Mary White, 17 Aug. 1860, Cabell-Reid Papers, ViU.

8. William Elliott to Ann Elliott, 8 Sept. [1851], in Scafidel, "Letters of William Elliott," 650–54; Louisa Maxwell Holmes Cocke Diary, 1 and 3 Sept. 1816, Cocke Family Papers, ViU; Jane Caroline North to Mary C. North, 17 Aug. 1851, Pettigrew Papers, NcU; Louisa Maxwell Holmes Cocke Diary, 2 Sept. 1816, Cocke Family Papers, ViU.

9. H. B. Tomlin to Cary Charles Cocke, 29 June 1849, Cocke Family Papers, ViU (first emphasis added); Edwin Bedford Jeffress Diary, 1 Sept. 1852, ViHi; Samuel Hoffman to Louisa Hoffman, 21 July 1833, Samuel Hoffman Papers, ViW; Charles Bruce to Sarah Alexander Bruce, 15 July 1859, Bruce Family Papers, ViHi. For more examples of the easy mixing of married people at the springs, see Otwayanna Carter to Betty Lewis Carter, 19 Aug. [ca. 1825], Tucker-Harrison-Smith Papers, ViU; Samuel Hoffman to Louisa Hoffman, 10 Aug. 1833, Samuel Hoffman Papers, ViW; Robert E. Lee to Mary Lee, 4 Aug. 1840, Lee Family Papers, ViHi; Richard D. Burroughs to Caroline Burroughs, [1857], Richard D. Burroughs Papers, NcD.

10. D. Blanding DeSaussure to Charles Stroman, 27 July 1854, Charles J. Stroman Papers, NcD; Louisa M. Collins to Mercer Harrison, 31 [*sic*] Sept. 1837, Byrd Family Papers, ViHi;

Mildred Halsey to J. Halsey, 15 Aug. 1858, Morton-Halsey Papers, ViU; Alexander H. H. Stuart to Frances Stuart, 26 July 1838, Stuart Family Papers, ViHi. Bachelor Thomas Gordon Pollock also participated in similar flirtations with married women (Thomas Gordon Pollock to Elizabeth Pollock, 3 Aug. 1860, Abram David Pollock Papers, NcU).

11. Louisa Maxwell Holmes Cocke Diary, 4 Sept. 1816, Cocke Family Papers, ViU.

12. Samuel Hoffman to Louisa Hoffman, 17 July 1832, Samuel Hoffman Papers, ViW. Eleanor Parke Custis Lewis, George Washington's granddaughter, visited with the entire party at Berkeley Springs later in the season. She gave no indication of an affair between Rogers and Poinsett in a letter to her longtime confidant Elizabeth Bordley Gibson. She called Mrs. Rogers "lovely & interesting as ever" and Poinsett "a charming companion" "as he always is," though she also considered him "a Wolf in Sheep's clothing." Lewis apparently saw nothing unseemly between Poinsett and Rogers nor, presumably, heard any of the gossip spreading around the resorts or the young ladies' confidences (Eleanor Parke Custis Lewis to Elizabeth Bordley Gibson, 24 Aug. 1832, in Brady, *George Washington's Beautiful Nelly*, 201). For another possible affair that was prevented by the return of the woman's husband, see [Hoffman], "Trip to the Virginia Springs," 143.

13. Louisa Maxwell Holmes Cocke Diary, 3 Sept. 1816, Cocke Family Papers, ViU.

"You Might Have Supposed Them All Quite Intimate"

1. John H. Cocke to Joseph C. Cabell, 14 Sept. 1822, Cabell Family Papers, ViU; Robert Waller Blow to Eliza Blow, 21 Oct. 1826, Blow Family Papers, ViHi. For other women who sought the excitement of a springs trip, see Sally Faulcon Cocke to John H. Cocke, [June 1833], Cocke Family Papers, ViU; John Herritage Bryan to Ebenezer Pettigrew, 23 May 1836, in Lemmon, *Pettigrew Papers*, 2:301–2; James Gray to William Gray, 12 Aug. 1853, William Gray Papers, ViHi. For plantation women's work and responsibilities, see Scott, *Southern Lady;* Clinton, *Plantation Mistress;* Fox-Genovese, *Within the Plantation Household;* Weiner, *Mistresses and Slaves.*

2. See Sklar, *Catharine Beecher*, 215; Wood, "'Fashionable Diseases,'" 35; Cayleff, *Wash and Be Healed,* 141; D'Emilio and Freedman, *Intimate Matters,* 81.

3. Lucy W. Cocke Diary, 2 Aug. 1850, Cocke Family Papers, ViU; Elizabeth H. Noel to "Julia" [her daughter], 1 Sept. 1860, Lewis Family Papers, ViU.

4. Mary Thompson to Mary W. Neale, 16 Oct. 1848, Conway Whittle Family Papers, ViW. Similarly, probably not until her stay at the springs did Mary Steger characterize herself as "a lady of leisure" (Mary Pendleton Steger to Martha F. Hunter, 5 Aug. 1847, Hunter Family Papers, ViHi). For corresponding sentiments by women about the abundance of leisure and freedom from daily labors at the springs, see Sarah Rutherfoord to John Rutherfoord, 12 July 1811, John Rutherfoord Papers, NcD; Sarah C. Carter to Mary E. Carter, 22 Aug. 1832, Carter-Smith Family Papers, ViU; Agnes S. B. Cabell to Louisa Carrington, 4 Aug. 1858, Cabell-Carrington Papers, ViU; F. B. E. Brown to Georgia Grinnan, 11 Sept. 1859, Grinnan Family Papers, ViU.

5. Buckingham, *Slave States of America,* 2:563; C. O. Lyde Diary, 9 Aug. 1841, NcD; "Life

at the Rockbridge Alum Springs," *Charleston Daily Courier*, 15 July 1858. See also "CS" to Frances Lea, 18 July 1854, Frances Lea Papers, NcD. Women's pleasure and participation in these outdoor activities, often ungloved and unbonneted, undermines the suggestion, according to one scholar, that elite southern women had an "obsession with keeping a delicate, pale skin tone" (Norwood, *Made from This Earth*, 3).

6. Bayard, *Travels in the Interior of the United States*, 40; Willis Williams to his wife, 22 Aug. 1858, Willis Williams Papers, NcU; Buckingham, *Slave States of America*, 2:359.

7. Wade Hampton III to Mary Fisher Hampton, 14 Aug. 1858, in Cauthen, *Family Letters of the Three Wade Hamptons*, 65; Anne Walke Smith, Mary E. Smith, and Robert Manson Smith to Nannie Smith, 31 Aug. 1858, Smith Family Papers, ViHi; Eliza Harwood to Tristam L. Skinner, 20 Aug. 1846, Skinner Family Papers, NcU; Sarah Brunet to Louisa Maxwell, 25 Aug. 1807, Cocke Family Papers, ViU; Mildred Halsey to J. J. Halsey, 30 Aug. 1858, Morton-Halsey Papers, ViU. Similarly, Mary Thompson claimed that at Sweet Springs "the girls go in troops" about the place and into the woods (Mary Thompson to Frances Lewis, 27 Aug. 1856, Conway Whittle Papers, ViW). For the social prohibitions on elite white women's movements around their home environments and farther afield, see Fox-Genovese, *Within the Plantation Household*, 69; and Cashin, *Family Venture*, 15.

8. John C. Rutherfoord to Sarah G. Stevenson, 30 Sept. 1837, John Rutherfoord Papers, NcD; Mary B. Blackford to William Blackford, 12 Aug. 1844, Blackford Family Papers, ViU; Agnes S. B. Cabell to Louisa Carrington, 14 July 1842, Cabell-Carrington Papers, ViU; D. Blanding DeSaussure to Charles Stroman, 27 July 1854, Charles J. Stroman Papers, NcD. In 1816 Louisa Maxwell Holmes met several women at various springs awaiting the arrival of their husbands to take them home (Louisa Maxwell Holmes Cocke Diary, 17 Aug.–3 Oct. 1816, Cocke Family Papers, ViU).

9. Henry Clay to James Caldwell, 7 May 1834, in Hopkins, *Papers of Henry Clay*, 8:724; Henry Clay to Lucretia Hart Clay, 9 Aug. 1847, ibid., 10:344.

10. Randolph Ross to John Preston, 31 July 1817, Preston-Radford Papers, ViU; Mildred Halsey to J. J. Halsey, 2 Sept. 1858, Morton-Halsey Papers, ViU. See also E. Cabell to Edmund Hubard, 8 Oct. 1832, Hubard Family Papers, NcU.

11. Philip St. George Ambler to John Jaquelin Ambler, 7 Aug. 1829, Ambler Family Papers, ViU; Philip St. George Ambler to Catharine Ambler, 15 Aug. 1829, ibid.; James Bruce to James C. Bruce, 17 July 1834, Bruce Family Papers, ViU; George Hancock to James Breckenridge, 17 Oct. 1805, James Breckinridge Papers, ViU; Thomas Walker Gilmer to Samuel Minor, 27 July 1835, Randolph Family Papers, ViU; Horace L. Hunley to Robert Ruffin Barrow, 9 Aug. 1860 (typescript), Robert Ruffin Barrow Papers, LNHT. See also Dandridge Spotswood Sr. Diary, 6 Aug. 1848, ViHi.

12. William Mackay to "Kate," 8 Sept. 1858, Mackay and Stiles Family Papers, NcU; Nicholas Cabell to Peggy Cabell, 13 Aug. 1808, Cabell Family Papers, ViU; Richard Burroughs to Caroline Burroughs, 20 Aug. and 11 Sept. 1857, Richard D. Burroughs Papers, NcD. John Cocke relied as heavily upon his first wife; see John H. Cocke to Ann Barraud Cocke, 8 and 12 Aug. 1811, Cocke Family Papers, ViU. See also Peter Saunders to Elizabeth Saunders, 26 Aug. 1860, Saunders Family Papers, ViHi.

13. Moses and Henry to William Pettigrew, 2 Aug. 1856, Pettigrew Papers, NcU. Earlier, Pettigrew had warned the two that if things at home took "an unfavorable turn," not only would he be "distressed," but "you & all your people" would be "disgraced in my estimation" (William Pettigrew to Moses and Henry, 12 July 1856, ibid.).

14. Larkin Newby to Cecilia Newby, 6 July 1823, Larkin Newby Papers, NcD; Benjamin Temple to Lucy Temple, 13 Sept. 1828, Harrison Family Papers, ViHi; Willis Williams to his wife, 11 Sept. 1860, Willis Williams Papers, NcU.

15. James C. Bruce to Eliza Bruce, 16 Aug. 1842, Bruce Family Papers, ViU. Nothing "but the pressure of public duties at the University and at Richmond: & my perfect conviction that they [his wife and invalid niece] will be well taken care of" by several friends could induce Joseph C. Cabell to leave them (Joseph C. Cabell to John H. Cocke, 24 Sept. 1839, Cabell Family Papers, ViU).

16. Louisianna and John Faulcon to Louisa Cocke, 19 Aug. 1828, Cocke Family Papers, ViU; George E. Harrison to Anne H. Byrd, 11 Sept. 1828, Francis Otway Byrd Papers, ViHi. Doctors especially considered themselves authorities on their wives' health. Dr. Cary Charles Cocke determined his wife's regimen and progress, whether he accompanied her to the springs or not (see Cary Charles Cocke to Lucy Cocke, 29 Aug. and 22 Sept. 1846, and 6 Sept. 1856, Cocke Family Papers, ViU). Brenda Stevenson similarly has found that planter wives often received counsel about their health from their husbands (*Life in Black and White*, 77).

17. Similarly, Elizabeth Fox-Genovese has claimed that through schools, resorts, extended visits, and correspondence, slaveholding women "could transcend the material limitations of a particular locality" and form networks of friendship. But, curiously, Fox-Genovese states, in the following paragraph, that "the predominantly rural character of southern society" prevented southern women from "develop[ing] sustained female networks" (*Within the Plantation Household*, 69, 70). The question of whether a community or even a culture of slaveholding women existed in the antebellum South has attracted much attention from historians. Catherine Clinton and Jean E. Friedman have agreed with Fox-Genovese's last statement. Clinton has characterized life on the plantation as extremely isolating for women, arguing that planter women "had no comparable sense of community" to that of slave or northern women (*Plantation Mistress*, 165). Friedman has stated that southern women "formed few bonds" with each other as women, depending upon their families and church for support rather than a "women's network" (*Enclosed Garden*, 20). Another set of historians has persuasively argued that a strong sense of community characterized the lives of elite southern women. Suzanne Lebsock, in her path-breaking work *Free Women of Petersburg*, has found not just strong female ties in the town of Petersburg, but also a women's culture based upon a distinctly female set of values that she labeled "personalism." In *Southern Honor*, Bertram Wyatt-Brown has argued that planter women developed strong female relationships for companionship and to compensate for their tense and distant relationships with men (see especially 249–51). Similarly, Melinda Buza has discovered that "strong, loving relations" and "deep emotional ties flourished" among antebellum Virginia women who depended upon one another, though unlike Wyatt-Brown, she has suggested that they still maintained loving relationships with their husbands ("'Pledges of Our Love,'" 11, 29). Mary

S. Hoffschwelle has discovered that Tennessee slaveholding women "participated in vibrant female networks and rituals" ("Women's Sphere and the Creation of Female Community in the Antebellum South," 80). Christie Anne Farnham has explored the importance of schoolmates in young women's lives in *Education of the Southern Belle*. In *Family Venture*, Joan E. Cashin has found that women cherished their relationships with one another and dreaded moving west primarily because they feared losing them. More recently and more forcefully, Cashin has argued, in her editorial introduction to *Our Common Affairs*, that elite southern women formed a "culture of resignation" based upon their own "sense of commonality" and their "shared exclusions" from male culture (Introduction: "Culture of Resignation," Cashin, *Our Common Affairs*, 2, 10). See also her article, "'Decidely Opposed to *the Union.*'"

18. Formal organizations, however, need not be requisite for a community of women. See Stansell, *City of Women,* for a discussion of the informal yet strong community of working-class women in New York City, for example.

19. A few historians have explored the significance of visiting and traveling or emphasized the importance of correspondence in the lives of women during the late eighteenth and nineteenth centuries. Carroll Smith-Rosenberg has mentioned the importance for women of summer reunions at resorts or each others' houses and the role of visits and letters in "provid[ing] an important sense of continuity" ("Female World of Love and Ritual," 11). For southern women specifically, Joan E. Cashin's *Family Venture* stresses the value that planter women placed upon extensive visits and correspondence in women's relationships and emotional well-being. See also Cashin's "Structure of Antebellum Planter Families" for the crucial role that visits between relatives played in binding a family together. For the importance of women's networks for childbirth among slaveholding women, see McMillen, *Motherhood in the Old South,* 57–65.

20. Similarly, Steven M. Stowe has concluded that "letters often were the very substance of relationships. . . . Such letters existed as a bond and a commentary on the bond" (*Intimacy and Power in the Old South,* 4). For similar conclusions, see also Lewis, *Pursuit of Happiness,* 224; and Rothman, *Hands and Hearts,* 11.

21. Emily Rutherfoord to John C. Rutherfoord, 28 Aug. 1849, John Rutherfoord Papers, NcD; Mary Randolph Harrison to Mary Harrison, 27 Aug. 1827, Harrison Family Papers, ViHi. See also "Sister" to Ann Rutherfoord, 9 Aug. 1858, John Rutherfoord Papers, NcU.

22. Kathryn Sklar has discovered a similar female communality at water-cure establishments founded upon the intimate and sensual environment of a "female-oriented culture" (*Catharine Beecher,* 204–16, quote on 206).

23. Catherine Eliza Hall to Christian Hall Price, 23 Aug. [1840], Price Family Papers, ViHi. See also "Virginia" to Frances Aglionby, 20 Nov. 1848, Frances Walker Yates Aglionby Papers, NcD; and Jane Caroline North Pettigrew to Mary North, 9 Sept. 1855, Pettigrew Papers, NcU.

24. James L. Petigru to Susan Petigru King, 13 Aug. 1845, in Carson, *Life, Letters and Speeches,* 244.

25. Bayard, *Travels in the Interior of the United States,* 97; Jane Caroline North Diary, 11 Aug. 1851, in O'Brien, *Evening When Alone,* 163. North made many close friends among

women visitors on both of her trips to the springs. See Jane Caroline North to Mary C. North, 17 Aug. 1851, Pettigrew Papers, NcU; Jane Caroline North to Jane Petigru North, 5 Sept. 1851, ibid.; Jane Caroline North Pettigrew to Jane Petigru North, 20 Aug. 1855, ibid.

26. Horace L. Hunley to Robert R. Barrow, 9 Aug. 1860, Robert Ruffin Barrow Papers, LNHT; Volumina W. Barrow to Horace L. Hunley, 12 July 1859, ibid.; Hannah and George Cabell to Joseph Cabell, 2 Sept. 1812, Cabell Family Papers, ViU; Mary Louisa and Thomas Bolling to William and Mary Bolling, 12 Sept. 1832, William Bolling Papers, NcD.

27. Virginia Heth to Mary E. Carter, 3 Sept. 1822, Carter-Smith Family Papers, ViU. See also Otwayanna Carter to Betty Lewis Carter, 19 Aug. [ca. 1825], Tucker-Harrison-Smith Papers, ViU; Jane Caroline North Diary, 29 Aug. 1851, in O'Brien, *Evening When Alone,* 167; and Elizabeth H. Noel to her mother, 1 Sept. 1860, Lewis Family Papers, ViU. For such close relationships among young southern women, see especially Buza, "'Pledges of Our Love'"; and Farnham, *Education of the Southern Belle.*

28. Helen Fitzhugh to Fanny B. Coalter, 5 Aug. [1858], Brown-Coalter-Tucker Papers, ViW; Conway Whittle to Mary W. Neale, 16 Aug. 1858, Conway Whittle Family Papers, ViW. For similar friendships, see C. O. Lyde Diary, 2 Aug. 1841, NcD.

29. Louisa Maxwell Holmes Cocke Diary, 4 Sept. and 23 Aug. 1837, Cocke Family Papers, ViU; Bettie Fontaine to Mrs. John B. (Martha) Minor, 17 Oct. 1846, Minor and Wilson Family Papers, ViU; Jane Caroline North to Jane Petigru North, 5 Sept. 1851, Pettigrew Papers, NcU; Jane Caroline North Pettigrew to Jane Petigru North, 10 Sept. 1855, ibid. For Seaton's invitation, see Jane Caroline North to Mary C. North, 17 Aug. 1851, ibid.

30. Robert Hubard to Edmund Hubard, 3 Sept. 1852, Hubard Family Papers, NcU; William C. Rives Jr. to John C. Rutherfoord, 24 July 1846, John Rutherfoord Papers, NcD; Robert Taylor Scott to William Aylett, 28 July 1852, Aylett Family Papers, ViHi; Thomas Gordon Pollock to Elizabeth Pollock, 12 Aug. 1860, Abram David Pollock Papers, NcU; Samuel Hoffman to Louisa Hoffman, 21 July 1833, Samuel Hoffman Papers, ViW. See also Larkin Newby to Cecilia Newby, 7 Aug. 1823, Larkin Newby Papers, NcD; Larkin Newby Diary, 14 and 27 Aug. 1823, Larkin Newby Papers, NcU; William Collins to Benjamin Johnson Barbour, 14 Aug. 1854, Barbour Family Papers, ViU. Based upon the correspondence of early nineteenth-century Virginia men, Melinda Buza similarly has concluded that elite southern men had their own version of the "female world of love and ritual" ("'Pledges of Our Love,'" 29). For discussions of nineteenth-century male culture, but primarily in the North, see Carnes and Griffen, *Meanings for Manhood;* Rotundo, *American Manhood;* Kimmel, *Manhood in America.* Kenneth S. Greenberg examines elite southern male community and culture in depth in his *Honor and Slavery.* See also Wyatt-Brown, *Southern Honor;* and Ownby, *Subduing Satan.*

31. Thomas Rutherfoord to John Rutherfoord, 15 Aug. 1836, John Rutherfoord Papers, NcD.

32. Charles William Ashby to Sarah Elizabeth Ashby, 24 July 1860, Charles William Ashby Papers, ViHi.

33. Burke, *Mineral Springs of Virginia,* 43; Henry Clay to Phillip R. Fendall, 4 Aug. 1832, in Hopkins, *Papers of Henry Clay,* 8:558; Robert Hubard to Edmund Hubard, 3 Sept. 1852, Hubard Family Papers, NcU.

34. William Bolling Diary, 24 Aug. 1841, ViHi. For information on the meeting of the legislature at the springs, see John Jarvis Diary, 10 June–20 Aug. 1849, ViU; scattered reports in the *Richmond Enquirer*, June–Aug. 1849; Franck, "Virginia Legislature at the Fauquier Springs."

35. James L. Petigru to Alfred Huger, 5 Sept. 1860, in Carson, *Life, Letters and Speeches,* 356; Horace L. Hunley to Robert Ruffin Barrow, 9 Aug. 1860, Robert Ruffin Barrow Papers, LNHT; entries of 7, 12, 25, and 29 Aug. 1860, in Scarborough, *Diary of Edmund Ruffin,* 1: 447–53.

36. Agnes S. B. Cabell to Louisa Carrington, 29 Oct. 1821, Cabell-Carrington Papers, ViU; Caldwell, *Tour Through Part of Virginia,* 27–28. Samuel Hoffman was attended by "the most attentive, tender, affectionate, and companionable of Fathers" whose attentions were "like the most devoted husband to his wife" during his illness at the springs in 1832 (Samuel Hoffman to Louisa Hoffman, 1 and 21 July 1832, Samuel Hoffman Papers, ViW). Conversely, when his father was sick, Samuel "kept almost constantly by his side" (Samuel Hoffman to Louisa Hoffman, 12 July 1832, ibid.). Many histories of planter families have concentrated on the caregiving roles of mothers and female friends and have neglected to look at fathers and male friends in this capacity. One important exception is McMillen, "Antebellum Southern Fathers and the Health Care of Children," which argues that antebellum southern fathers, not just mothers, held a deep concern for the welfare of their children and often attended them in sickness.

37. Edwin Bedford Jeffress Diary, 28 Aug. 1852, ViHi; William Pettigrew to Mary B. Pettigrew, 23 June 1856, Pettigrew Papers, NcU. Many men tended their male friends with great care. Benjamin Grigsby accompanied his friend William Cox who suffered from alcoholism to the springs in 1804 and hoped that with his help and God's Cox could be cured. Grigsby regularly sent letters to Cox's wife, keeping her informed and hopeful. See Benjamin Grigsby to Rosanna Cox, 9, 11, 12, 14, 18, and 23 Aug. and 6 Sept. 1804, Hugh Blair Grigsby Papers, ViHi; and William Cox to Rosanna Cox, 29 Aug. 1804, ibid.

38. John H. Cocke Diary, 12 Sept. 1818, Cocke Family Papers, ViU.

39. Pencil, *White Sulphur Papers,* 107.

"You Are Now Just Entering upon That School of Life"

1. Alexander H. H. Stuart to Frances, Susan, and Mary Stuart, [20 Aug. 1840], Stuart Family Papers, ViHi.

2. John H. Cocke to Sally F. Cocke, 17 Aug. 1833, Cocke Family Papers, ViU. Similarly, in 1822 he required his eldest daughter, Louisianna, to keep a journal of her springs trip to record her reflections and learn from them later (Louisianna Cocke Diary, Aug. 1822, typescript in possession of author). For a similar experience, see P. W. Carr to Martha M. Davis, 6 Oct. 1830, Minor Family Papers, ViU.

3. Lucy W. Cocke Diary, 1 Sept. 1850, Cocke Family Papers, ViU.

4. John C. Rutherford to John Rutherfoord, 20 Aug. 1841, John Rutherfoord Papers, NcD; John Rutherford to John C. Rutherfoord, 30 Aug. 1841, ibid.

5. Henry D. Mandeville Sr. to his daughters, 23 Aug. 1854, Henry D. Mandeville Papers, LU; Henry D. Mandeville Jr. to his sisters, 24 Aug. 1854, ibid.

6. Henry D. Mandeville Jr. to his sisters, 24 Aug. 1854, Henry D. Mandeville Papers, ibid. For discussions of the coming of age of planter children in the late eighteenth and early nineteenth centuries, see Smith, *Inside the Great House;* Wyatt-Brown, *Southern Honor,* especially chaps. 6 and 7; Censer, *North Carolina Planters and Their Children,* especially chap. 3; Steven M. Stowe, "The Not-So-Cloistered Academy: Elite Women's Education and Family Feeling in the Old South," in *Web of Southern Social Relations,* ed. Fraser, 90–106; Stowe, *Intimacy and Power in the Old South,* especially chap. 3; Farnham, *Education of the Southern Belle;* Kilbride, "Philadelphia and the Southern Elite," chaps. 5 and 6. For an excellent history of adolescence in America, see Kett, *Rites of Passage.*

7. Henry D. Mandeville Jr. to his sisters, 24 Aug. 1854, Henry D. Mandeville Papers, LU; John Rutherfoord to Ann Roy, 13 Sept. 1856, John Rutherfoord Papers, NcU; C. O. Lyde Diary, 10 Aug. 1841, NcD; anonymous woman to "Pa," 1 Aug. 1847, Susan Bradford Eppes Papers, NcU. For a similar duty-bound occasion, see John C. Rutherfoord to John Rutherfoord, 20 Aug. 1841, John Rutherfoord Papers, NcD. Like Mandeville, Sally Warwick spied another couple "out walking alone until a very late hour" (Sally M. Warwick to Sarah Warwick, 24 Aug. 1841, John Warwick Daniel Papers, ViU).

8. Reed and Matheson, *Narrative of the Visit to the American Churches,* 208; Julia Watson to Nancy Watson, 23 and 27 Aug. [1838], Watson Family Papers, ViHi; Thomas White Jr. to Thomas White, 23 Aug. 1850, Thomas White Jr. Papers, NcD. The coming-of-age behavior of male planter youths has been discussed in Smith, *Inside the Great House,* chap. 3; Wyatt-Brown, *Southern Honor,* chaps. 6 and 7; Stowe, *Intimacy and Power in the Old South,* chap. 3.

9. Prolix, *Letters Descriptive of the Virginia Springs,* 38; Robert Taylor Scott to William Aylett, 8 Sept. 1852, Aylett Family Papers, ViHi; F. R. Bolling to William Bolling, 9 Sept. 1827, Cabell Family Papers, ViU; D. Blanding DeSaussure to Charles Stroman, 27 July 1854, Charles J. Stroman Papers, NcD. See also Robert Scott to William Aylett, 20 Aug. 1852, Aylett Family Papers, ViHi. White Sulphur's resident physician, Dr. John J. Moorman, included a lengthy discussion of the "extraordinary powers" of White Sulphur water in "eradicating the lurking poison" of venereal diseases in a published pamphlet. He also claimed that "scores of patients" came every season to cure venereal diseases, especially syphilis (*Water from the White Sulphur Springs, Greenbrier County, VA,* [ca. 1840], ViU, 7).

10. Ferdinando Fairfax Diary, 22 and 23 July 1792, ViU; Samuel Hoffman to Louisa Hoffman, 28 Aug. 1840, Samuel Hoffman Papers, ViW; Richard Burroughs to Caroline Burroughs, 20 Aug. 1857, Richard D. Burroughs Papers, NcD; Windle, *Life at the White Sulphur Springs,* 82–83. Kenneth Greenberg has discussed the unusual but not infrequent occurrence of honorable men, especially young ones, wearing women's clothing in *Honor and Slavery,* 24–33.

11. Isabella Ritchie to Annie Cross, 21 Aug. 1859, Ritchie-Harrison Papers, ViW; Louisa M. Collins to Mercer Harrison, 31 [*sic*] Sept. 1837, Byrd Family Papers, ViHi.

12. Emily Rutherfoord to John C. Rutherfoord, 28 Aug. 1849, John Rutherfoord Papers, NcD. Many young people apologized for not writing in a timely fashion because of all of

the activities and people that preoccupied them; see also, for example, George Harrison to Anne H. Byrd, 23 Aug. 1836, Francis Otway Byrd Papers, ViHi.

13. Pencil, *White Sulphur Papers*, 40−41.

14. Eliza Harwood to Tristam L. Skinner, 20 Aug. 1846, Skinner Family Papers, NcU; Philippa Barbour to Elizabeth Ambler, 3 Sept. 1837, Ambler Family Papers, ViU; Ann Frances Bland Tucker to St. George Tucker, 17 Aug. 1801, St. George Tucker Papers, ViHi; Louisa M. Collins to Mercer Harrison, 31 [*sic*] Sept. 1837, Byrd Family Papers, ViHi; S. N. L. to Amilie Rives, 1 Sept. 1849, Rives Family Papers, ViU. See also Louisianna Cocke to John H. Cocke, 19 Aug. 1822, Cocke Family Papers, ViU.

15. Levin Joynes to Anne Joynes, 28 Sept. 1856, Joynes Family Papers, ViHi. See also Nicholas Faulcon to John H. Cocke, 21 Aug. 1821 [*sic:* 1822], Cocke Family Papers, ViU; and Roberta Page Burwell to Lucy Tidball, [ca. Aug. 1840], Louise Patten Papers, ViHi.

16. Samuel Hoffman to Louisa Hoffman, 16 Aug. 1840, Samuel Hoffman Papers, ViW; James White to Mary White, 18 Aug. 1860, Cabell-Reid Papers, ViU.

17. Mary Jane Boggs Diary, June 1851, in Buni, "'Rambles Among the Virginia Mountains,'" 88; Robert Taylor Scott to William Aylett, 20 Aug. 1852, Aylett Family Papers, ViHi.

18. Jane Caroline North to Mary C. North, 17 Aug. 1851, Pettigrew Papers, NcU.

19. Jane Caroline North Pettigrew to Jane Petigru North, 1 Aug. 1855, ibid.

"A Great Deal Is Affected, but Nothing on the Heart in It"

1. Philippa Barbour to Elizabeth Ambler, 3 Sept. 1837, Ambler Family Papers, ViU. For the tradition of competition and display and communal status among southern gentry, see Isaac, *Transformation of Virginia,* especially chap. 5; Wyatt-Brown, *Southern Honor,* especially part 3; Greenberg, *Honor and Slavery;* Kierner, "Hospitality, Sociability, and Gender in the Southern Colonies"; Rozbicki, *Complete Colonial Gentleman.* For eighteenth- and nineteenth-century gentry in general, see Bushman, *Refinement of America.* David Shields has found that British spas were "hypercompetitive arenas of social display" (*Civil Tongues and Polite Letters,* 41).

2. Levin Joynes to Anne Joynes, 28 Sept. 1856, Joynes Family Papers, ViHi; Martha Terrell to Dabney Terrell, 29 Nov. [ca. 1820], Terrell-Carr Papers, ViU; Walter E. Preston to John Preston, 23 July 1839, Preston Family Papers, ViHi.

3. Thornton Harrington's Account, 23 July 1825, Hubard Family Papers, NcU.

4. Otwayanna Carter to Betty Lewis Carter, 19 Aug. [ca. 1825], Tucker-Harrison-Smith Papers, ViU; Philippa Barbour to Elizabeth Ambler, 1 Aug. 1837, Ambler Family Papers, ViU; Martineau, *Society in America,* 1:182; William Elliott to Ann Elliott, 9 July 1850, in Scafidel, "Letters of William Elliott," 611−13.

5. Henry Clay to James Caldwell, 30 July 1832, in Hopkins, *Papers of Henry Clay,* 8:556; Isaac Gorham Peck Diary, 9 Aug. 1833, ViHi; Packard, *Recollections of a Long Life,* 103; W. S. Harding to Fannie Harding, 17 Aug. 1856, Rosamonde E. and Emile Kuntz Collection, LNHT. Dr. John J. Moorman, the resident physician of White Sulphur, remembered an-

other guest bringing twenty-six horses and thirteen servants ("Memoir of Dr. John J. Moorman," 27). The Bath Alum Springs Account Book shows eighty sets of visitors during August 1852: seventeen brought servants and twenty-three brought horses, some came with two or three servants and two or three horses each (Bath Alum Springs Account Book, Aug. 1852, ViW).

6. George W. Randolph to Mary Randolph, 8 Aug. 1859, Randolph Family Papers, ViU; J. Taylor to George Morton, [ca. 1860], Morton Family Papers, ViU; Benjamin Temple to Lucy Temple, 13 Sept. 1828, Harrison Family Papers, ViHi; Prolix, *Letters Descriptive of the Virginia Springs*, 31.

7. *Trip to the Virginia Springs*, 15; W. S. Harding to Fannie Harding, 17 Aug. 1856, Rosamonde E. and Emile Kuntz Collection, LNHT; Levin Joynes to Anne Joynes, 21 Aug. and 28 Sept. 1856, Joynes Family Papers, ViHi; James Cathcart Johnston to Mr. Hollwell, 8 Sept. 1857, Hayes Collection, Johnston Series, NcU. On the other hand, William Burke proclaimed that "there is no place in the mountains, where the society is more select, more charming, more intellectual, than it is at the Salt Sulphur" (*Mineral Springs of Virginia*, 153).

8. "Memoir of Dr. John J. Moorman," 10. Mary Pendleton Steger believed that if Clay were not *the* Henry Clay he would have been "held up as a model of ugliness"; instead, he possessed a "commanding apperance" and a near perfect "human nature" (Mary Pendleton Steger to Martha F. Hunter, 5 Aug. 1847, Hunter Family Papers, ViHi).

9. Windle, *Life in Washington*, 180; James L. Petigru to Susan Petigru King, 29 Aug. 1845, in Carson, *Life, Letters and Speeches*, 245; Louisa Carrington to Sarah E. Reid, 22 July 1838, Cabell-Reid Papers, ViU; Thomas Gordon Pollock to Elizabeth Pollock, 3 Aug. 1860, Abram David Pollock Papers, NcU.

10. Women at northern resorts were often criticized for their slavish pursuit of fashion. For the shift of northerners from gentility to respectability, see the brilliant Bushman, *Refinement of America*. See also Halttunen, *Confidence Men and Painted Women;* and Kasson, *Rudeness and Civility*.

11. Bertram Wyatt-Brown has examined in depth this characteristic of southern white society in his *Southern Honor*. Similarly, Steven Stowe has found "a remarkable degree of continuity in elite [southerners'] habits and values" as compared to northerners' over the first half of the nineteenth century (*Intimacy and Power*, 253). See also Greenberg, *Honor and Slavery*.

12. Volumina Barrow to Horace L. Hunley, 12 July 1859, Robert Ruffin Barrow Papers, LNHT; Mary Thompson to Frances Lewis, 27 Aug. 1856, Conway Whittle Family Papers, ViW; Mildred Halsey to J. Halsey, 15 Aug. 1858, Morton-Halsey Papers, ViU.

13. Elizabeth M. Maben to Charles Campbell, 19 Aug. [1847], Charles Campbell Papers, ViW; Charles Bruce to Sarah Alexander Bruce, 15 July 1859, Bruce Family Papers, ViHi; Larkin Newby to Cecilia Newby, 7 Aug. 1823, Larkin Newby Papers, NcD.

14. Louisianna Cocke to John H. Cocke, 2 Sept. 1856, Cocke Family Papers, ViU; Samuel Hoffman to Louisa Hoffman, 14 July 1832, Samuel Hoffman Papers, ViW. For a travel account with a section on spa customs, see *Trip to the Virginia Springs*, 20−43.

15. *Trip to the Virginia Springs*, 20; William Stabler to Sally Stabler Jordan, 30 July 1838,

Jordan and Stabler Family Papers, ViHi; Mary Pendleton Steger to Martha F. Hunter, 5 Aug. 1847, Hunter Family Papers, ViHi. See also [Hoffman], "Trip to the Virginia Springs," 326.

16. For the importance of bodily movement and restraint to gentility, see Bushman, *Refinement of America,* especially 63−69.

17. Mary Jane Boggs Diary, June 1851, in Buni, "'Rambles Among the Virginia Mountains,'" 82.

18. Henry D. Mandeville Sr. to his daughters, 23 Aug. 1854, Henry D. Mandeville Papers, LU; Susanna I. Harrison to Mary Harrison, 24 Aug. 1831, Harrison Family Papers, ViHi.

19. Samuel Hoffman to Louisa Hoffman, 16 Aug. 1840, Samuel Hoffman Papers, ViW; Moore, "The Old Dominion through Student Eyes," 317.

20. John Rutherfoord to Emily Rutherfoord, 16 Aug. 1849, John Rutherfoord Papers, NcD; "Life at the Rockbridge Alum Springs," *Charleston Daily Courier,* 30 July 1858. Dance had a long history with the southern gentry as a convivial event, an opportunity for social competition, and an attempt for status recognition; see Isaac, *Transformation of Virginia,* 80−87. For a detailed discussion of the proper etiquette and fashionable dances in nineteenth-century ballrooms, see Aldrich, *From the Ballroom to Hell.*

21. Courtney Bowdoin to Louisa Cocke, 19 Aug. 1833, Cocke Family Papers, ViU; C. O. Lyde Diary, 26 July 1841, NcD; Eliza Harwood to Tristam L. Skinner, 20 Aug. 1846, Skinner Family Papers, NcU.

22. John Rutherfoord to Emily Rutherfoord, 16 Aug. 1849, John Rutherfoord Papers, NcD; William Elliott to Ann Elliott, 15 Sept. 1851, in Scafidel, "Letters of William Elliott," 654−57; Mary Cameron to Duncan Cameron, 22 Aug. 1834, Cameron Family Papers, NcU; Blair Bolling Diary, vol. 3, 10 Aug. 1838, ViHi; James C. Johnston to James J. Pettigrew, 30 Aug. 1855, Pettigrew Papers, NcU. For the importance of familiarity with the latest dance steps, see also James J. White to Mary Louisa White, 16 Aug. 1860, Cabell-Reid Papers, ViU. For another condemnation of an excessive display in the ballroom, see Courtney Bowdoin to Louisa Cocke, 19 Aug. 1833, Cocke Family Papers, ViU.

23. Levin Joynes to Anne Joynes, 21 Aug. 1856, Joynes Family Papers, ViHi; Pencil, *White Sulphur Papers,* 85; Windle, *Life in Washington,* 197; Roberta Page Burwell to Lucy Tidball, [ca. Aug. 1840], Louise Patten Papers, ViHi. In addition to paying constant attention to their clothes while at the resorts, visitors devoted great effort before the trip to selecting an appropriate wardrobe.

24. Maria Louisa Fontaine to Kate Meade, 10 Aug. 1860, Meade Family Papers, ViHi.

25. Jane Harrison Randolph to Mary Harrison, 25 Aug. 1829, Harrison Family Papers, ViHi; Paulding, *Letters from the South by a Northern Man,* 2:171; Volumina W. Barrow to Horace L. Hunley, 12 July 1859, Robert Ruffin Barrow Papers, LNHT. For similar sentiments, see also Jane Caroline North Diary, 6 Sept. 1851, in O'Brien, *Evening When Alone,* 172.

26. For drinking and gambling in the plantation environment, see Wyatt-Brown, *Southern Honor,* especially 278−80 and 339−50; and Greenberg, *Honor and Slavery.*

27. Before the 1839 season, the proprietor of Fauquier White Sulphur ordered from Robert Bulord and Company "50 baskets" of champagne, "12 boxes" of claret and six of "Sack," "1 quarter cask of your best Pale sherry," and one of brown sherry, "2 half Pipes of

your *best* old Cognac Brandy," "1 barrel of best Jamaican Rum & one of best Holland Gin," "6 crates of wine," "10 gallons best Irish whiskey and a barrell of best Peach brandy," and "4 barrells of best whiskey" (Robert E. Lee to [probably] Robert Bulord and Company, 22 Apr. 1839, Keith Family Papers, ViHi).

28. John H. Cocke Diary, 13 and 6 Sept. 1851, Cocke Family Papers, ViU; Bayard, *Travels in the Interior of the United States,* 51; William Gray to Lucy Gray, 14 Aug. 1798, Beverley Family Papers, ViHi; Lucy Ann Tucker to Elizabeth Tucker Bryan, [ca. 14 Sept. 1847], Bryan Family Papers, ViU.

29. For similar conclusions about the power gentility gave to southern women, see Fox-Genovese, *Within the Plantation Household,* especially 196–97 and 230; Kilbride, "Philadelphia and the Southern Elite," 31–36; Kierner, *Beyond the Household,* chap. 2.

30. Windle, *Life at the White Sulphur Springs,* 60; Bayard, *Travels in the Interior of the United States,* 47; Paulding, *Letters from the South by a Northern Man,* 2:166. See also Louisa Maxwell Holmes Cocke Diary, 14 Sept. 1840, Cocke Family Papers, ViU; Elizabeth H. Noel to Julia Noel, 1 Sept. 1860, Lewis Family Papers, ViU; Paulding, *Letters from the South by a Northern Man,* 2:171; Windle, *Life in Washington,* 176. Similarly, Fox-Genovese has stated that "slaveholding women, including those who usually demonstrated graciousness, generosity, and compassion, proved ruthless in their demarcation of class lines" (*Within the Plantation Household,* 225).

31. Thomas Gordon Pollock to Elizabeth Pollock, 3 Aug. 1860, Abram David Pollock Papers, NcU; Paulding, *Letters from the South by a Northern Man,* 2:171. See also William Daniel to Margaret Daniel, 22 Aug. 1822, John Warwick Daniel Papers, ViU.

32. Volumina W. Barrow to Horace L. Hunley, 12 July 1859, Robert Ruffin Barrow Papers, LNHT. Similarly, another woman looked in the eyes of a reported beauty and believed her to be "capable of flashing with anger" (anonymous woman to "Pa," 1 Aug. 1847, Susan Bradford Eppes Papers, NcU).

33. Elizabeth Fox-Genovese has drawn a similar conclusion for plantation circles; see *Within the Plantation Household,* 230.

34. Bayard, *Travels in the Interior of the United States,* 47.

35. See John Howell Briggs Diary, 1 Aug. 1804, ViHi; and James Alexander Seddon to Charles Bruce, 12 Aug. 1858, Bruce Family Papers, ViHi.

36. *Trip to the Virginia Springs,* 45, 20–21; Littleton Waller Tazewell Wickham to Elizabeth S. Wickham, 28 Aug. 1843, Wickham Family Papers, ViHi; C. O. Lyde Diary, 8 Aug. 1841, NcD; Levin Joynes to Anne Joynes, 21 Aug. 1856, Joynes Family Papers, ViHi; Otwayanna Carter to Betty Lewis Carter, 19 Aug. [ca. 1825], Tucker-Harrison-Smith Papers, ViU.

37. Hannah Cabell to Joseph Cabell, 2 Sept. 1812, Cabell Family Papers, ViU; Mary Thompson to Frances Lewis, 23 Aug. 1827, Conway Whittle Papers, ViW; George W. Randolph to Mary Randolph, 8 Aug. 1859, Randolph Family Papers, ViU.

38. Mary Jane Boggs Diary, 21 June 1851, in Buni, "'Rambles Among the Virginia Mountains,'" 104–5; Peter Daniel to Elizabeth Daniel, 29 July 1851, Daniel Family Papers, ViHi.

39. Samuel Hoffman to Louisa Hoffman, 6 Sept. and 10 Aug. 1840, Samuel Hoffman Papers, ViW; Robert E. Lee to Mary Lee, 4 Aug. 1840, Lee Family Papers, ViHi; Otwayanna Carter to Betty Lewis Carter, 19 Aug. [ca. 1825], Tucker-Harrison-Smith Papers, ViU; Jane

Caroline North to Jane Petigru North, 5 Sept. 1851, Pettigrew Papers, NcU; Samuel Hoffman to Louisa Hoffman, 1 Aug. 1832, Samuel Hoffman Papers, ViW; James C. Johnston to James J. Pettigrew, 30 Aug. 1855, Pettigrew Papers, NcU.

40. Roberta Page Burwell to Lucy Tidball, [ca. Aug. 1840], Louise Patten Papers, ViHi; Mary B. Pettigrew to William Pettigrew, 2 Aug. 1856, Pettigrew Papers, NcU; Henry D. Mandeville Jr. to his sisters, 24 Aug. 1854, Henry D. Mandeville Papers, LU.

41. Thomas Gordon Pollock to Elizabeth Pollock, 3 Aug. 1860, Abram David Pollock Papers, NcU.

42. Alexander H. H. Stuart to Frances Stuart, 26 July 1838, Stuart Family Papers, ViHi; George Johnson to Marguerite Johnson, 3 Aug. 1846, George Nicholson Johnson Papers, ViHi.

43. See Windle, *Life at the White Sulphur Springs,* especially 26–78, and *Life in Washington,* especially 170–73 and 197–98.

44. "Life at the Rockbridge Alum Springs," *Charleston Daily Courier,* 30 July 1858. See also *Alexandria Gazette,* Aug. 1849; *Charleston Daily Courier,* Aug.–Sept. 1855; *Knickerbocker Magazine,* July–Nov. 1852 and Feb. 1853; *National Intelligencer,* 26 Aug. 1848; *New England Magazine,* Sept. 1832; *Richmond Enquirer,* 2 Sept. 1845; *Richmond Whig,* July–Aug. 1849. John S. Skinner, the editor of *Farmers' Library and Monthly Journal of Agriculture,* sent a series of letters naming names and giving details of resort life to the *New York Tribune, Baltimore American,* and *Richmond Enquirer* as well as publishing letters in his own journal during his trip to the Virginia Springs in the summer of 1847. See *New York Tribune,* 16 June, 3, 23, 28, and 30 July, 5 and 7 Aug., and 7 Sept. 1847; *Baltimore American,* 5 and 7 Aug. and 3 Sept. 1847; *Richmond Enquirer,* 30 July and 17 and 20 Aug. 1847; and *Farmers' Library,* Aug., Sept., and Oct. 1847 issues.

45. James C. Johnston to James J. Pettigrew, 30 Aug. 1855, Pettigrew Papers, NcU; Julia M. Watson to Miss Watson, 22 and 23 Aug. [1838], Watson Family Papers, ViHi; Mary Thompson to Mary W. Neale, [ca. 31 Aug. 1848], Conway Whittle Family Papers, ViW; Henry D. Mandeville Sr. to his daughters, 23 Aug. 1854, Henry D. Mandeville Papers, LU; John C. Rutherfoord to Sarah G. Stevenson, 30 Sept. 1837, John Rutherfoord Papers, NcD.

"Love-Making May Fairly Be Set Down as One of the
Amusements of the Virginia Springs"

1. Mackie, *From Cape Cod to Dixie,* 76; Judith Walker Page Rives Autobiography (typescript), 1861, Rives Family Papers, ViU. Many historians have found companionate marriage and its ideas of supportiveness, affection, and mutual dependence important to southerners in the early nineteenth century. See, for example, Smith, *Inside the Great House,* especially chap. 4; Lewis, *Pursuit of Happiness,* especially chap. 5; Censer, *North Carolina Planters and Their Children;* Buza, "'Pledges of Our Love'"; Jabour, *Marriage in the Early Republic.* Suzanne Lebsock, *Free Women of Petersburg,* and Elizabeth Fox-Genovese, *Within the Plantation Household,* have found companionate marriage to be important to southerners, but only in a form modified by the southern hierarchy of male dominance that made marriage unequal. Other historians argue that patriarchy prohibited marital companionship in the ante-

bellum South. See Clinton, *Plantation Mistress;* Wyatt-Brown, *Southern Honor;* Cashin, *Family Venture.*

2. Levin Joynes to Anne Joynes, 21 Aug. 1856, Joynes Family Papers, ViHi; Paulding, *Letters from the South by a Northern Man,* 2:166; Kitty Heth Harrison to Isaetta Carter, [pre-1824], Carter-Smith Family Papers, ViU; Richard D. Burroughs to Caroline Burroughs, 25 Aug. 1857, Richard D. Burroughs Papers, NcD. Nathan Ryno Smith similarly described antebellum belles as "merchandise" "effectually displayed" at the springs in his post–Civil War *Legends of the South,* 17.

3. *Six Weeks in Fauquier,* 58–59; Mackie, *From Cape Cod to Dixie,* 61; Levin Joynes to Anne Joynes, 21 Aug. 1856, Joynes Family Papers, ViHi; Alexander H. H. Stuart to Frances Stuart, [23 July 1837], Stuart Family Papers, ViHi. Wyth Munford was the same man who, two months later, participated in the late-night race of two women at White Sulphur. Apparently, he was not engaged to E. Cabell because, after losing the race, he "had concluded to console himself with the *winning nag* Miss Erskine, and has accordingly followed her to the Salt S. to obtain her acceptance of his hand & heart" (Louisa M. Collins to Mercer Harrison, 31 [*sic*] Sept. 1837, Byrd Family Papers, ViHi). Two other travel accounts give lengthy, detailed descriptions of belles—and beaux—at the Virginia Springs; see the aptly titled *Trip to the Virginia Springs, or the Belles and Beaux of 1835;* and Windle, *Life at the White Sulphur Springs.*

4. Alexander H. H. Stuart to Frances Stuart, [23 July 1837], Stuart Family Papers, ViHi; Louisa Maxwell Holmes Cocke Diary, 16 Aug. 1837, Cocke Family Papers, ViU; Jacob Hall to Christian Elizabeth Price, 1 Sept. 1840, Price Family Papers, ViHi; [J. K. Lee] to "Charlie," 5 Sept. 1854, Carrington Family Papers, ViHi. See also John C. Rutherfoord to Sarah G. Stevenson, 30 Sept. 1837, John Rutherfoord Papers, NcD; and Samuel Hoffman to Louisa Hoffman, 16 Aug. 1840, Samuel Hoffman Papers, ViW.

5. Samuel Hoffman to Louisa Hoffman, 10 Aug. 1840, Samuel Hoffman Papers, ViW; Jane Caroline North Diary, 29 Aug. 1851, in O'Brien, *Evening When Alone,* 168; Virginia Heth to Mary E. Carter, 3 Sept. 1822, Carter-Smith Family Papers, ViU. See also Robert E. Lee to Mrs. B. C. Mason, 9 Aug. 1840, Lee Family Papers, ViHi; and William Pettigrew Diary, 31 Aug. 1857, Pettigrew Papers, NcU.

6. Virginia Heth to Mary E. Carter, 3 Sept. 1822, Carter-Smith Family Papers, ViU; S. N. L. to Amilie Rives, 1 Sept. 1849, Rives Family Papers, ViU; Courtney Bowdoin to Louisa Cocke, 19 Aug. 1833, Cocke Family Papers, ViU. Emily Rutherfoord was thrilled that her cousin Isaetta Coles "has been much admired & attended to" (Emily Rutherfoord to John C. Rutherfoord, 28 Aug. 1849, John Rutherfoord Papers, NcD). Another woman reported that both Isaetta and Emily were successes at the springs that season (S. N. L. to Amilie Rives, 1 Sept. 1849, Rives Family Papers, ViU). Brenda Stevenson has found that public courting in plantation communities, however, could lead to "fierce matches between women for male attention" (*Life in Black and White,* 54).

7. Bayard, *Travels in the Interior of the United States,* 140; L. H. Bolling to Edmund Hubard, 15 Aug. 1835, Hubard Family Papers, NcU; Alfred Jones to Duncan Cameron, 16 Aug. 1835, Cameron Family Papers, NcU.

8. Windle, *Life in Washington,* 168; John Coalter to St. George Tucker, [ca. 24 Aug. 1811],

Bryan Family Papers, ViU; Paulding, *Letters from the South by a Northern Man,* 2:165; Little-ton Waller Tazewell Wickham to Elizabeth S. W. Wickham, 21 Aug. 1848, Wickham Family Papers, ViHi; Thomas Gordon Pollock to Elizabeth Pollock, 3 Aug. 1840, Abram David Pollock Papers, NcU.

9. Paulding, *Letters from the South by a Northern Man,* 2:166; George William Bagby to Ellen A. Turner, 17 Aug. 1856, George William Bagby Papers, ViHi; "Lou" to Ann Oliver, 18 Aug. 1846, Oliver Family Papers, ViU. Jane Turner Censer has found similar descriptions among planter families of courtship as a "battle" (*North Carolina Planters and Their Children,* 77).

10. See Clinton, *Plantation Mistress,* 62; Censer, *North Carolina Planters and Their Children,* 78; Farnham, *Education of the Southern Belle,* 127.

11. Helen Fitzhugh to Fanny B. Coalter, 5 Aug. [1858], Brown-Coalter-Tucker Papers, ViW; anonymous friend to Louisiana Hubard, 4 Sept. 1832, Hubard Family Papers, NcU; Lucia C. Harrison to Mary Harrison, 13 Aug. 1827, Harrison Family Papers, ViHi. For the writings of other belles, see Martha B. Daniel to Sarah Warwick, 28 July 1841, John Warwick Daniel Papers, ViU; Peter Carr to Lucy Minor, 21 Aug. 1843, Terrell-Carr Papers, ViU; Betty Fontaine to Martha Minor, 17 Oct. 1846, Minor and Wilson Family Papers, ViU; Kate Fontaine to Lucy L. Braxton, 19 Aug. 1853, Meade Family Papers, ViHi.

12. Jane Caroline North to Mary C. North, 17 Aug. 1851, Pettigrew Papers, NcU; Jane Caroline North Diary, 29 Aug. 1851, in O'Brien, *Evening When Alone,* 169; Jane Caroline North to Mary C. North, 17 Aug. 1851, Pettigrew Papers, NcU; Jane Caroline North Diary, 29 Aug., 2, 3, 11, and 15 Sept. 1851, in O'Brien, *Evening When Alone,* 169, 170, 171, 173, 174. See also Jane Caroline North to Jane Petigru North, 5 Sept. 1851, Pettigrew Papers, NcU. For a similar discussion of Jane Caroline North as a quintessential southern belle, see Michael O'Brien's editorial introduction to *Evening When Alone,* 22–30; and Pease and Pease, *Family of Women,* especially chap. 6.

13. James White to Mary White, 21 Aug. 1860, Cabell-Reid Papers, ViU; *Trip to the Virginia Springs,* 26; George Harrison to Anne H. Byrd, 12 Sept. 1829, Francis Otway Byrd Papers, ViHi. Jane Turner Censer has stated that planters considered courtship something of a game, with the players and "spectators" keeping "'score'" of the number of beaux attracted and rejected (*North Carolina Planters and Their Children,* 77). Springs visitors apparently did, too. See Alexander H. H. Stuart to Frances Stuart, 26 July 1838, Stuart Family Papers, ViHi; James C. Bruce to Eliza Bruce, 24 Aug. 1842, Bruce Family Papers, ViU; John Rutherfoord to Emily Rutherfoord, 16 Aug. 1849, John Rutherfoord Papers, NcD; William Elliott to Ann Elliott, 8 Sept. [1851], in Scafidel, "Letters of William Elliott," 650–54; Jane Caroline North Pettigrew to Jane Petigru North, 20 Aug. 1855, Pettigrew Papers, NcU; James Jones White to his wife, 19 Aug. 1860, James Jones White Papers, NcU.

14. Emily Rutherfoord to John C. Rutherfoord, 28 Aug. 1849, John Rutherfoord Papers, NcD; Windle, *Life at the White Sulphur Springs,* 69–70; Windle, *Life in Washington,* 166. For courtship in plantation society, see Smith, *Inside the Great House,* chap. 4; Clinton, *Plantation Mistress,* chap. 4; Wyatt-Brown, *Southern Honor,* chap. 8; Lewis, *Pursuit of Happiness,* chap. 5; Stowe, "'The *Thing* Not Its Vision'"; Censer, *North Carolina Planters and Their Children,*

chap. 4; Stowe, *Intimacy and Power*, chap. 2; Stevenson, *Life in Black and White*, chap. 2. For the general history of courtship in the United States, see Rothman, *Hands and Hearts;* and Lystra, *Searching the Heart*. Rothman excluded the South from her study and Lystra failed to address the South seriously.

15. Burr Powell to Elizabeth Powell, 7 June 1827, Holmes Conrad Papers, ViHi; Robert Conrad to Elizabeth Powell, [July 1827], ibid.; Robert Conrad to Catherine Conrad, 14 July 1851, ibid.; John Rutherfoord to Emily Rutherfoord, 16 Aug. 1849, John Rutherfoord Papers, NcD; Emily and John Rutherfoord to John C. Rutherfoord, 22 Aug. 1850, ibid.; W. S. Harding to Fannie Harding, 17 Aug. 1856, Rosamonde E. and Emile Kuntz Collection, LNHT. Similarly, Jane Turner Censer has found courting couples making or breaking promises of marriage, unknown to their parents (*North Carolina Planters and Their Children*, 78).

16. Pencil, *White Sulphur Papers*, 133. For other published odes from the Virginia Springs, see Cornelia Rives Harrison, "Bubbles from Bedford Springs" (broadside), (Providence: E. L. Freeman & Company, undated, ViU); *Banco: or, the Tenant of the Spring;* Gilman, *Poetry of Travelling in the United States*, 348–49; Carlisle, *Travels in America*, 65. A melodramatic romance set at the Virginia Springs, written by William Alexander Caruthers, was published in *The Magnolia; or, Southern Apalachian* in 1842.

17. H. B. Tomlin to Cary Charles Cocke, 29 June 1849, Cocke Family Papers, ViU. Like other visitors, Agatha Towles and Robert Carter each composed a "farewell" poem to the springs about the sadness of parting with friends and good times (Agatha Towles, "A sorrowful farwel to the Sweet Springs," [ca. Aug. 1798], Agatha Towles Papers, ViHi; Robert W. Carter, "Lines on revisiting Jordan's Springs," 1849, Carter Family Papers, ViU).

18. Entry of 2 Sept. 1775, in Albion, *Philip Vickers Fithian*, 2:126.

19. "Journal of a Trip to the Mountains, Caves and Springs of Virginia," 304. See also Pencil, *White Sulphur Papers*, 79–81.

20. Pencil, *White Sulphur Papers*, 95 (emphasis added); *Trip to the Virginia Springs*, 16, 25. For other belles and beaux playing their parts, see George W. Munford to Lucy L. Taylor, 9 Sept. 1828, Munford-Ellis Papers, NcD; and John D. Munford to George W. Munford, 14 Sept. 1838, ibid.

21. Pencil, *White Sulphur Papers*, 89, 105; Robert Young Conrad to Elizabeth Powell, [July 1827], Holmes Conrad Papers, ViHi.

22. William Pettigrew Diary, 21 and 8 Sept. 1857, Pettigrew Family Papers, NcU; anonymous friend to Louisiana Hubard, 4 Sept. 1832, Hubard Family Papers, NcU; John H. B. Latrobe to Charles Carroll Harper, 25 and 30 Aug. 1832, in Semmes, *John H. B. Latrobe*, 262–63.

23. William Daniels Cabell to his grandmother, 1 Mar. 1857, William D. Cabell Papers, ViU; Ann Barraud Cocke to Ann B. Barraud, 6 Oct. 1811, Cocke Family Papers, ViU; "Coles Homes on the Green Mountain and Their Mistresses," 17, Robert Coles Papers, ViU; Virginia Terrell to Lucy Terrell, 18 July 1810, Terrell Family Papers, ViU; entry of 1 Aug. 1859, in Turner, *Diary of Henry Boswell Jones*, 78.

24. Sally L. Taylor to Ella Rives, 18 July 1857, Rives Family Papers, ViU; Pencil, *White Sulphur Papers*, 113–14.

"They Seemed to Sink into the Deepest Insignificance"

1. William Elliott to Ann Elliott, 9 July 1850, in Scafidel, "Letters of William Elliott," 611–13.

2. Charles Bruce to Sarah Seddon Bruce, 15 July 1859, Bruce Family Papers, ViHi; Louisa Venable to her mother, 27 Aug. 1860, William Patterson Smith Papers, NcD; L. H. Bolling to Edmund Hubard, 15 Aug. 1835, Hubard Family Papers, NcU. In 1833 Virginian St. George Tucker Coalter informed his wife that "Virginians & Southerners are now beginning to drop in" (St. George Tucker Coalter to Judith H. Coalter, 24 July 1833, Brown-Coalter-Tucker Papers, ViW). See also "Letter from Mrs Elizabeth Taylor to Mrs Judith Page Aylett," 150–51.

3. Edward T. Tayloe to Benjamin Ogle Tayloe, 17 Aug. 1832, Tayloe Family Papers, ViU. See also John Pendleton Kennedy to Peter H. Cruse, 4 Aug. 1832, Peter Hoffman Cruse Papers, ViHi; and St. George Tucker Coalter to Judith H. Coalter, 2 Aug. 1833, Brown-Coalter-Tucker Papers, ViW.

4. James L. Petigru to Alfred Huger, 8 Sept. 1852, in Carson, *Life, Letters and Speeches,* 292–93. The "fuss" may have come about, as William Elliott noted, because "Virginia has no toleration for disunion principles," adding, "it is mortifying to feel that our state is looked upon, as being at the command of [Robert Barnwell] Rhett and his faction" (William Elliott to Ann Elliott, 1 Sept. 1851, in Scafidel, "Letters of William Elliott," 643–47).

5. Agnes S. B. Cabell to Louisa Cabell Carrington, 17 Aug. [ca. 1836], Cabell-Carrington Papers, ViU; Alexander H. H. Stuart to Frances Stuart, 26 July 1838, Stuart Family Papers, ViHi. See also Royall, *Sketches of History,* 32; and Hoffman, *Winter in the West,* 2:294.

6. William Short to John H. Cocke, 28 May 1833, Cocke Family Papers, ViU. Cocke responded that he would be "sorry" if Short could not "get over the difficulty which seemed to stand in your way of visiting our springs this season" (John H. Cocke to William Short, 1 July 1833, William Short Papers, DLC). There is no evidence that Short made the trip.

7. Emily Rutherfoord to John C. Rutherfoord, 28 Sept. 1850, John Rutherfoord Papers, NcD.

8. Jane Caroline North Diary, 29 Aug. 1852, in O'Brien, *Evening When Alone,* 167; Richard D. Burroughs to Caroline Burroughs, 13 Aug. 1857, Richard D. Burroughs Papers, NcD.

9. Edmund Randolph to Marianne Old Meade, 4 Aug. 1840, Edmund Randolph Papers, ViHi.

10. Larkin Newby Diary, 19 Aug. 1823, Larkin Newby Papers, NcU; Nelly Custis Lewis to Elizabeth Bordley Gibson, 4 July 1834, in Brady, *George Washington's Beautiful Nelly,* 216–19; Larkin Newby Diary, 19 Aug. 1823, Larkin Newby Papers, NcU; Martineau, *Society in America,* 1:188. From an early date, the Virginia Springs' remote, less-policed location and wealthy clientele attracted professional gamblers. From 1790 through 1860, gamblers increasingly prowled the springs, keeping along the fringes and away from the local authorities. At Sweet Springs and, later, White Sulphur, groups of gamblers owned cabins that all of the visitors, including women, knew housed gaming activities (see David Watson Diary, 2 Aug. 1822, Watson Family Papers, ViU; Mary Thompson to Frances Lewis, 23 Aug. 1827, Conway Whittle Papers, ViW; Knepper, *Travels in the Southland,* 64; Semmes, *John H. B. Latrobe and His*

Times, 254). In his 1844 travel account, English traveler George Featherstonhaugh informed his readers that White Sulphur Springs rented a house "to a set of sharpers, who keep a public gaming-table, that is open day and night. . . . Thus every direct encouragement is given to vice" (*Excursion through the Slave States,* 1:79). For the important role of gambling in gentry culture, especially before the nineteenth century, see Breen, "Horses and Gentlemen"; Isaac, *Transformation of Virginia;* Fabian, *Card Sharps, Dream Books, and Bucket Shops.*

11. Henry Watson Jr. to Sophia Watson, 28 Aug. 1856, Henry Watson Jr. Papers, NcD.

12. Horace Hunley to Robert R. Barrow, 9 Aug. 1860 (typescript), Robert Ruffin Barrow Papers, LNHT. Physician John Bell concurred, claiming "it must, after all, appear ridiculous, in the midst of woods and rocks, to make those sacrifices to fashion, which are barely supportable in a crowded and wealthy capital" (*On Baths and Mineral Waters,* 400). See also Benjamin Temple to Lucy Temple, 4 Sept. 1837, Harrison Family Papers, ViHi.

13. Mary M. Brison to Mary Stewart Harrison, 16 July [pre-1850], Tucker-Harrison-Smith Papers, ViU; Robert Hubard to Edmund Hubard, 5 Aug. 1838, Hubard Family Papers, NcU.

14. Elizabeth Tucker Bryan to Georgia Sereven, 30 Nov. 1838, Grinnan Family Papers, ViU; Robert Eden Peyton to Editor, *Virginia Times,* July 1840, Peyton Family Papers, ViHi. In spite of Peyton's fears, there is no evidence of cockfighting at the Virginia Springs. That sport would have been highly unusual in such a genteel environment. "Warrenton Springs" was an earlier name for Fauquier White Sulphur.

15. Entries of 8 Aug. 1789 and 7 June 1793, in Clark, *Journal and Letters of Francis Asbury,* 1:607, 760; Lucy Baytop to daughter Ann, postscript added to Thomas Baytop to Jeff W. Stubbs, 28 Aug. 1838, Baytop Family Papers, ViW; Paulina Storrs to Cornelia Storrs, 27 Aug. 1838, Cornelia Storrs Papers, NcD; Joseph Burwell Ficklen to Anne Eliza Fitzhugh Ficklen, 6 Sept. 1857, Joseph Burwell Ficklen Letters, ViU. For similar sentiments, see Nicholas Faulcon to John H. Cocke, 30 Aug. 1822, Cocke Family Papers, ViU; Richard Burroughs to Caroline Burroughs, 25 Aug. 1857, Richard D. Burroughs Papers, NcD; Buckingham, *Slave States of America,* 2:348.

16. Lucy Cocke to Cary Charles Cocke, 6 Sept. 1856, Cocke Family Papers, ViU; newspaper clipping, Buffalo Springs File, Amherst County Historical Museum, Amherst, Virginia; Mary B. Blackford to John B. Minor, 22 Sept. 1844, Minor and Wilson Family Papers, ViU; John H. Cocke Diary, 13 Sept. 1851, Cocke Family Papers, ViU.

17. Louisa Cocke to John H. Cocke, 14 Aug. 1837, Cocke Family Papers, ViU.

18. James Pleasants to Ann Eliza Pleasants, 15 Aug. 1854, Massie Family Papers, ViHi; Caroline Matilda Richardson to Sarah French, 8 Aug. 1835, Sarah French Papers, ViHi; C. Matilda (Richardson) Henry to Sarah French, 23 Aug. 1837, ibid.; Alexander H. H. Stuart to Frances Stuart, [ca. 1837], Stuart Family Papers, ViHi. Robert E. Lee's daughter Agnes also feared her "weakness" against the "temptations" at the springs (Mary and Agnes Lee to Robert E. Lee, 4 Aug. 1857, Lee Family Papers, ViHi).

19. Louisa Maxwell Holmes Cocke Diary, 17 Sept. 1840, Cocke Family Papers, ViU; John H. Cocke Diary, 12 Sept. 1818, 6 Sept. 1851, 10 and 3 Sept. 1844, 27 Aug. 1851, ibid.

20. James McHenry to Peggy McHenry, 8 and 18 Aug. 1794, James McHenry Papers, ViU; Robert Hubard to Louisiana Hubard, 19 Aug. 1825, Hubard Family Papers, NcU.

21. See Samuel Hoffman to Louisa Hoffman, 17 July 1832, Samuel Hoffman Papers, ViW.

22. Featherstonhaugh, *Excursion through the Slave States,* 1:55; "Journal of a Trip to the Mountains, Caves and Springs of Virginia," 302. For a similar comment, see Larkin Newby Diary, 22 June 1823, Larkin Newby Papers, NcU. See also [Hoffman], "Trip to the Virginia Springs," 441.

23. Elizabeth Ann Valentine Gray to William F. Gray, 26 Sept. 1856, Edward Pleasants Valentine Papers, ViV. I am indebted to Gregg Kimball for bringing this group of letters to my attention.

24. "To the Proprietors of the White Sulphur Springs, Greenbrier County, Va.," *Charleston Daily Courier,* 30 July 1858. The author doubted that even "the fanatics of Boston [would] have countenanced such a proceeding."

25. Ibid.

26. Elizabeth Ann Valentine Gray to William F. Gray, 29 and 26 Sept. 1856, Edward Pleasants Valentine Papers, ViV.

27. Marryat, *Diary in America,* 273. The English novelist Frederick Marryat spoke with Mayr about and saw the painting. After noticing that "one man was missing" from the band of musicians, Marryat asked, "'Why did you not put him in?'" Mayr replied, "'Why, Sir, I could not put him in; it was impossible; he never *plays in tune.* Why, if I put him in, Sir, he would spoil the *harmony* of my whole picture!'" (ibid.). For discussions of Mayr's work by art historians, see Williams, *Mirror to the American Past,* 77–78; Hills, *Painter's America,* 58; McElroy, *Facing History,* xvii, 33; Johns, *American Genre Painting,* 114 and 231, n. 18. For a discussion of the depiction of servants, including slaves, in art, see O'Leary, *At Beck and Call.* Mayr painted other scenes of black men and women at the Virginia Springs, but they are unfortunately lost.

"Honor to Those Days of Chivalry"

1. Alexander H. H. Stuart to Frances Peyton Stuart, Susan Baldwin Stuart, and Mary Stuart, 20 Aug. [ca. 1840], Stuart Family Papers, ViHi; Pencil, *White Sulphur Papers,* 56. For the definitive work on southern romanticism, see Osterweis, *Romanticism and Nationalism.* For chivalry and southern honor, see Taylor, *Cavalier and Yankee;* Wyatt-Brown, *Southern Honor;* Ayers, *Vengeance and Justice;* Greenberg, *Honor and Slavery.* For medievalism and nineteenth-century Americans, see Kenney and Workman, "Ruins, Romance, and Reality." The influence of Sir Walter Scott's novels, especially the *Waverley Novels* and *Ivanhoe,* should not be underestimated. Between 1813 and 1823, five millon cheap copies of the Waverley series alone were published in the United States. Southerners constantly referred to Scott or passages from his novels and took the author seriously as a "cultural arbiter" (Kenney and Workman, "Ruins, Romance, and Reality," 152). Osterweis has concluded that, while many Americans read the *Waverley Novels* "with enthusiasm," "the South sought to live them" (*Romanticism and Nationalism,* 215).

2. Henry D. Mandeville Sr. to his daughters, 23 Aug. 1854, Henry D. Mandeville Papers, LU; Windle, *Life at the White Sulphur Springs*, 78, 79; entry of 24 Aug. 1859, in Scarborough, *Diary of Edmund Ruffin*, 1:334. The *Charleston Daily Courier* described a costume ball at Red Sweet Springs complete with a Hamlet, Rob Roy, Spanish maidens, and a group of men dressed as exotic animals (18 Sept. 1855).

3. [J. K. Lee] to "Charlie," 5 Sept. 1854, Carrington Family Papers, ViHi.

4. *National Intelligencer* (Washington, D.C.), 26 Aug. 1848; Pencil, *White Sulphur Papers*, 143. In his *Springs of Virginia*, Perceval Reniers claimed, with no supporting evidence, that tournaments originated at Fauquier White Sulphur Springs. In 1854 Anna Cora Ritchie claimed to have heard that the annual Fauquier White Sulphur tournament began before Lord Eglinton held his famous and trend-setting medieval tournament for aristocrats in Scotland in 1839 (Anna Cora Ritchie to Mary Roane, July 1854, in *Fauquier County, Virginia*, 139). For Lord Eglinton's tournament and the cult of chivalry in Great Britain, see Girouard, *Return to Camelot*. An excellent description of a tournament at Fauquier White Sulphur appeared in the *Richmond Enquirer*, 2 Sept. 1845. For another at Shannondale, see *Baltimore Herald*, 2 Aug. 1848. For other tournament descriptions, see Samuel Hoffman to Louisa Hoffman, 20 and 28 Aug. 1840, Samuel Hoffman Papers, ViW; Eliza Harwood to Tristam L. Skinner, 20 Aug. 1846, Skinner Family Papers, NcU; William C. Carrington to Maria Dabney Carrington, 17 Sept. 1848, Cabell-Carrington Papers, ViU; *Virginia Free Press*, 28 Aug. and 11 Sept. 1851; James, "Life in Virginia," 282.

5. Robert Taylor Scott to William Aylett, 8 Sept. 1852, Aylett Family Papers, ViHi; Samuel Hoffman to Louisa Hoffman, 28 and 20 Aug. 1840, Samuel Hoffman Papers, ViW; *Baltimore Herald*, 2 Aug. 1848, as quoted in Theriault, "Shannondale Springs," 9; [Hoffman], "Trip to the Virginia Springs," 143. For another tournament crowd description, see E. H. Taylor to Isabella H. Harrison, 27 Aug. 1842, Ritchie-Harrison Papers, ViW.

6. *Baltimore Herald*, 2 Aug. 1848, as quoted in Theriault, "Shannondale Springs," 9; Samuel Hoffman to Louisa Hoffman, 20 Aug. 1840, Samuel Hoffman Papers, ViW; James, "Life in Virginia," 282; Samuel Hoffman to Louisa Hoffman, 28 Aug. 1840, Samuel Hoffman Papers, ViW. For similar feudal sentiments, see "Virginia Watering Place," *Richmond Enquirer*, 2 Sept. 1845. For detailed descriptions of post-tournament costume balls, see *Richmond Enquirer*, 2 Sept. 1845; and *Baltimore Herald*, 2 Aug. 1848.

7. *Baltimore Herald*, 2 Aug. 1848, as quoted in Theriault, "Shannondale Springs," 9; Burke, *Mineral Springs of Virginia*, 177.

8. On the myths and images of southern women, see Clinton, "Women and Southern History." Like the fair maidens at the springs, May Day queens in school pageants "provided a glorious symbolic representation of the chivalric ideal" (Farnham, *Education of the Southern Belle*, 168). See also Cook, "Growing Up White, Genteel, and Female." For an excellent exploration of the meaning and variety of ways women functioned in public during the nineteenth century, see Ryan, *Women in Public*.

9. "Virginia Watering Place," *Richmond Enquirer*, 2 Sept. 1845; James, "Life in Virginia," 282.

10. C. O. Lyde Diary, 29 July 1841, NcD.

CONCLUSION

1. Entries of 6, 7, and 11 July 1861, in Woodward, *Mary Chesnut's Civil War,* 92, 93, 95.

2. Cohen, *Historic Springs of the Virginias,* 45.

3. George Tucker to Eliza Tucker Harrison, 25 July 1860, Tucker-Harrison-Smith Papers, ViU.

4. Burwell, *Girl's Life in Virginia,* 117–18. For the postwar Virginia Springs, see McAllister, *Historical Sketches of Virginia;* Taylor, *White Sulphur Springs;* Cohen, *Historic Springs of the Virginias;* Conte, *History of the Greenbriar.*

5. For the rise of new forms of leisure, resorts, and vacations over the nineteenth century, see Aron, *Working at Play.* See also Dulles, *History of Recreation;* and Braden, *Leisure and Entertainment in America.*

6. Louisa Maxwell Holmes Cocke Diary, 3 Sept. 1816, Cocke Family Papers, ViU.

7. William P. Taylor to Pattie Waller Aylett, 21 Sept. 1857, Aylett Family Papers, ViHi.

8. William Maxwell to Louisa Maxwell Holmes, 2 Sept. [ca. 1811–15], Cocke Family Papers, ViU; A. Braxton to Cary Charles Cocke, 8 Oct. 1849, ibid.

Works Cited

Manuscript Collections

Amherst County Historical Museum, Amherst County, Virginia.
    Buffalo Springs File
Barker Texas History Center, University of Texas–Austin. TxU.
    William Massie Collection
Special Collections Library, Duke University, Durham, North Carolina. NcD.
    Frances Walker Yates Aglionby Papers
    William Bolling Papers
    Richard D. Burroughs Papers
    Frances Lea Papers
    C. O. Lyde Diary
    William Massie Papers
    Larkin Newby Papers
    John Rutherfoord Papers
    Charles J. Stroman Papers
    Henry Watson Jr. Papers
Fauquier County Library, Warrenton, Virginia.
    Fauquier White Sulphur Springs File
Hollins College Archives, Hollins College, Roanoke, Virginia. ViRoH.
    Hezekiah Daggs Daybook
Manuscripts Division, Library of Congress, Washington, D.C. DLC.
    William Short Papers (microfilm edition)
    Sophie S. Wilson Diary
    William Wirt Papers

Special Collections, Hill Memorial Library, Louisiana State University, Baton Rouge. LU.
    Henry D. Mandeville Papers
Southern Historical Collection of the Manuscripts Department, University of North Carolina, Chapel Hill. NcU.
    John Grammar Brodnax Papers
    Hamilton Brown Papers
    Calder Family Papers
    Cameron Family Papers
    Susan Bradford Eppes Papers
    Hayes Collection, Johnston Series
    Hubard Family Papers
    Mackay and Stiles Family Papers
    Mordecai Family Papers
    Larkin Newby Papers
    Pettigrew Papers
    Abram David Pollock Papers
    Skinner Family Papers
    John Frances Speight Papers
    James Jones White Papers
    Willis Williams Papers
    William Wirt Papers
Special Collections Division, Howard-Tilton Library, Tulane University, New Orleans, Loui-
siana. LNHT.
    Robert Ruffin Barrow Papers
    Rosamonde E. and Emile Kuntz Collection
Valentine Museum, Richmond, Virginia. ViV.
    Edward Pleasants Valentine Papers
Special Collections Department, University of Virginia, Charlottesville. ViU.
    Ambler Family Papers
    Barbour Family Papers
    Baylor Family Papers
    Blackford Family Papers
    James Breckenridge Papers
    Bruce Family Papers
    Bryan Family Papers
    Cabell Family Papers
    Cabell-Carrington Papers
    Cabell-Reid Papers
    William D. Cabell Papers
    George Carr Papers
    Carter-Smith Family Papers
    Eliza Branch Cave Papers
    Cocke Family Papers

Robert Coles Papers
Duke Family Papers
Edgehill-Randolph / Wilson Cary Nicholas Papers
Louisa Emmerson Memoirs
Ferdinando Fairfax Diary
Joseph Burwell Ficklen Letters
Alexander Garrett Papers
Goochland Court House Deposit
John W. Jarvis Diary
Robert E. Lee Papers
Lewis Family Papers
Lewis and Latane Family Papers
James McHenry Papers
McLaughlin-Redd Letters
Dolley Madison Papers
Minor Family Papers
Minor and Wilson Family Papers
Morton Family Papers
Morton-Halsey Papers
Oliver Family Papers
Preston-Radford Papers
Randolph Family Papers
Rives Family Papers
Tayloe Family Papers
Terrell Family Papers
Terrell-Carr Papers
Tucker-Harrison-Smith Papers
Warm Springs Daybook
Watson Family Papers
White Sulphur Springs Account Books
Virginia Historical Society, Richmond. ViHi.
Charles William Ashby Papers
Aylett Family Papers
George William Bagby Papers
Beverley Family Papers
Blow Family Papers
Blair Bolling Diary
William Bolling Diary
John Howell Briggs Diary
John Brockenbrough Papers
Bruce Family Papers
Buffalo Lithia Springs Hotel Guest Register
Lawrence Butler Letters

Byrd Family Papers
Francis Otway Byrd Papers
Cabell Family Papers
Henry Coalter Cabell Accounts
Carrington Family Papers
Holmes Conrad Papers
Peter Hoffman Cruse Papers
Daniel Family Papers
Fauquier White Sulphur Springs Accounts
Sarah French Papers
Sarah Garland Letter
William Gray Papers
Grigsby Papers
Hugh Blair Grigsby Diary
Hugh Blair Grigsby Papers
Grinnan Family Papers
Harrison Family Papers
Holladay Family Papers
Hunter Family Papers
Edwin Bedford Jeffress Diary
George Nicolson Johnson Papers
Jordan and Stabler Family Papers
Joynes Family Papers
Keith Family Papers
Lee Family Papers
Massie Family Papers
Meade Family Papers
Louise Patten Papers
Isaac Gorham Peck Diary
Thornton Perry Papers
Peyton Family Papers
Pollard Family Papers
Preston Family Papers
Price Family Papers
Edmund Randolph Papers
Edmund Ruffin Papers
Saunders Family Papers
John Armistead Selden Diary
Smith Family Papers
Dandridge Spotswood Sr. Diary
John Henry Strobia Diary
Stuart Family Papers

Benjamin Ogle Tayloe Scrapbook
Agatha Towles Papers
St. George Tucker Papers
Susan Elizabeth Gordon Webb Diary
Wickham Family Papers
Yellow Sulphur Springs Guest Register
West Virginia Division of Culture and History, Charleston. Wv-Ar.
Red Sulphur Springs Account Book
Salt Sulphur Springs Daybook
University Manuscripts and Rare Books Department, Swem Library, College of William and
Mary, Williamsburg, Virginia. ViW.
Bath Alum Springs Account Book
Baytop Family Papers
Brown-Coalter-Tucker Papers
Charles Campbell Papers
Samuel Hoffman Papers
Ritchie-Harrison Papers
Conway Whittle Family Papers

Newspapers

Alexandria Gazette (Alexandria, Va.)
Baltimore American
Baltimore Sun
Charleston Daily Courier (Charleston, S.C.)
Daily National Intelligencer (Washington, D.C.)
New York Tribune
Richmond Enquirer (Richmond, Va.)
Richmond Whig (Richmond, Va.)
Virginia Times (Warrenton, Va.)

Primary Sources

Adams, Herbert Baxter. *The Life and Writings of Jared Sparks, Comprising Selections from His Journals and Correspondence.* 2 vols. Boston and New York: Houghton, Mifflin & Co., 1893.
Addison, Joseph. *The Spectator.* Vol. 6. Edinburgh: A. Donaldson, 1766.
Albion, Robert Greenhalgh, and Leonidas Dodson, eds. *Philip Vickers Fithian: Journal, 1775 – 1776.* 2 vols. Princeton, N.J.: Princeton University Press, 1934.
Analysis of the Rockbridge Alum Springs in Virginia; With Some Account of their History, and the Properties of the Water, in Letters of Eminent Physicians and Other Gentlemen. Richmond, Va.: N.p., 1857.

Arese, Count Francesco. *A Trip to the Prairies and in the Interior of North America (1837–1838)*. Translated by Andrew Evans. New York: Harbor Press, 1934.

Bailey, Robert. *The Life and Adventures of Robert Bailey*. Richmond, Va.: N.p., 1822; reprint, Marceline, Mo.: Walsworth Publishing Company for Warm Spring Echoes Book Company, Berkeley Springs, W.Va., 1978.

Baltzell, John. *An Essay on the Mineral Properties of the Sweet Springs of Virginia*. Baltimore: Warner and Hanna, 1802.

Banco; or, the Tenant of the Spring. A Legend of the White Sulphur. Philadelphia: C. Sherman and Company, 1839.

Bayard, Ferdinand M. *Travels in the Interior of the United States, to Bath, Winchester, in the Valley of the Shenandoah, etc., etc., during the Summer of 1791*. N.p.: N.p., 1797; reprint, translated and edited by Ben C. McCary, N.p.: N.p., 1950.

Bell, John, M.D. *The Mineral and Thermal Springs of the United States and Canada*. Philadelphia: Parry and McMillan, 1855.

———. *On Baths and Minerals Waters*. Philadelphia: Henry H. Porter, 1831.

Betts, Edwin Morris, and James Adam Bear Jr., eds. *The Family Letters of Thomas Jefferson*. Columbia: University of Missouri Press, 1966.

Beyer, Edward. *Album of Virginia; or, Illustration of the Old Dominion*. Richmond, Va.: N.p., 1858.

Biddle, Charles. *Autobiography of Charles Biddle, Vice-President of the Supreme Executive Council of Pennsylvania. 1745–1821*. Philadelphia: E. Claxton and Company, 1883.

Bigelow, Jacob, M.D. *Brief Exposition of Rational Medicine: To Which Is Prefixed the Paradise of Doctors, a Fable*. Boston: Phillips, Sampson and Company, 1858.

Bishko, Lucretia Ramsey, ed. "John S. Skinner Visits the Virginia Springs, 1847." *Virginia Magazine of History and Biography* 80 (April 1972): 158–92.

Bowen, Ele. *Rambles in the Path of the Steam-Horse*. Philadelphia: Wm. Bromwell and Wm. White Smith, 1855.

Brady, Patricia, ed. *George Washington's Beautiful Nelly: The Letters of Eleanor Parke Custis Lewis to Elizabeth Bordley Gibson, 1794–1851*. Columbia: University of South Carolina Press, 1991.

Buckingham, James Silk. *The Slave States of America*. 2 vols. London: Fisher, Son, and Company, 1842.

Buni, Andrew, ed. "'Rambles Among the Virginia Mountains': The Journal of Mary Jane Boggs, June 1851." *Virginia Magazine of History and Biography* 77 (January 1969): 78–111.

Burke, Edmund. *A Philosophical Enquiry Into the Origin of Our Ideas of the Sublime and Beautiful: With an Introductory Discourse Concerning Taste, and Several Other Additions*. Reprint, London: N.p., 1812.

Burke, William, M.D. *The Mineral Springs of Virginia: With Remarks on Their Use, and the Diseases to Which They Are Applicable, and in Which They Are Contra-Indicated*. Richmond, Va.: Morris and Brother, 1851.

———. *The Mineral Springs of Western Virginia; With Remarks on Their Use, and the Diseases to Which They Are Applicable*. 2d ed. New York: Wiley and Putnam, 1846.

Burwell, Letitia M. *A Girl's Life in Virginia Before the War.* 2d ed. New York: Frederick A. Stokes Company, 1895.

Callcott, Margaret Law, ed. *Mistress of Riversdale: The Plantation Letters of Rosalie Stier Calvert, 1795–1821.* Baltimore: Johns Hopkins University Press, 1991.

Caldwell, John Edwards. *A Tour Through Part of Virginia, in the Summer of 1808.* Belfast: Smyth and Lyons, 1810; reprint, edited by William M. E. Rachal, Richmond, Va.: The Dietz Press, 1951.

Carlisle, George William. *Travels in America.* New York: G. P. Putnam, 1851.

Carson, James Petigru. *Life, Letters and Speeches of James Louis Petigru.* Washington, D.C.: N.p., 1920.

Caruthers, William Alexander. "Excerpts from the Port Folio of a Physician: Love and Consumption." *The Magnolia; or, Southern Apalachian* 1 (July 1842): 35–38, (August 1842): 103–8, (September 1842): 177–82.

Cauthen, Charles E., ed. *Family Letters of the Three Wade Hamptons, 1782–1901.* Columbia: University of South Carolina Press, 1953.

Chevalier, Michael. *Society, Manners and Politics in the United States: Being a Series of Letters on North America.* Boston: Weeks and Jordan, 1839.

Clark, Elmer T., et al., eds. *The Journal and Letters of Francis Asbury.* 3 vols. London: Epworth Press and Nashville: Abingdon Press, 1958.

DeBow, J. D. B. *Statistical View of the United States.* Washington, D.C.: N.p., 1854.

Disturnell, John. *Springs, Water-falls, Sea-Bathing Resorts, and Mountain Scenery of the United States and Canada.* New York: J. Disturnell, 1855.

Dow, Peggy. *Vicissitudes Exemplified; or the Journey of Life.* New York: John C. Totten, 1814.

Downing, A. J. *A Treatise on the Theory and Practice of Landscape Gardening Adapted to North America.* New York: Wiley and Putnam, 1841.

Ehrenpreis, Anne Henry, ed. *Happy Country This America: The Travel Diary of Henry Arthur Bright.* Columbus: Ohio State University Press, 1978.

"Extracts From the Diary of Charles Copland." *William and Mary Quarterly,* 1st ser., 14 (April 1906): 217–30.

Fauquier White Sulphur Springs Company. *Extracts From Proceedings of the Fauquier White Sulphur Company, in their Meeting, on the 28th Day of September, 1839.* Richmond, Va.: Shepherd and Colin, 1839.

Featherstonhaugh, George W. *Excursion through the Slave States, From Washington on the Potomac to the Frontier of Mexico; with Sketches of Popular Manners and Geological Notices.* 2 vols. London: John Murray, 1844.

Gaddis, Maxwell Pierson. *Foot-Prints of an Itinerant.* Cincinnati: N.p., 1855.

Gilman, Caroline. *The Poetry of Travelling in the United States.* New York: S. Colman, 1838.

Gilpin, William. *Three Essays: On Picturesque Beauty; On Picturesque Travel; and on Sketching Landscape: To Which is Added a Poem, on Landscape Painting.* London: N.p., 1794.

Goode, Thomas, M.D. *The Invalid's Guide to the Virginia Hot Springs: Containing an Account of the Medical Properties of these Waters, with Cases Illustrative of their Effects.* Richmond, Va.: P. D. Bernard, 1846.

Hayward, George, M.D. "Remarks on Some of the Medicinal Springs of Virginia." *Boston Medical and Surgical Journal* 21 (October 23, 1839): 169–75.

Hoffman, Charles F. *A Winter in the West.* Vol. 2. New York: Harper and Brothers, 1835.

[Hoffman, David]. "A Trip to the Virginia Springs. By Viator." *Knickerbocker Monthly Magazine* 40 (July 1852): 20–27, (August 1852): 124–29, (September 1852): 214–21, (October 1852): 316–27, (November 1852): 440–45, 41 (February 1853): 140–45.

Hopkins, James F., et al., eds. *The Papers of Henry Clay.* 10 vols. and supplement. Lexington: University Press of Kentucky, 1959–92.

[Horner, Edmondson, M.D.]. *Observations on the Mineral Waters in the South Western Part of Virginia.* Philadelphia: N.p., 1834.

Hoyt, William D., Jr., ed. "Journey to the Springs, 1846." *Virginia Magazine of History and Biography* 54 (April 1946): 119–36.

Huntt, Henry. *A Visit to the Red Sulphur Spring of Virginia, During the Summer of 1837: with Observations on the Waters.* Washington, D.C.: N.p., 1838.

James, G. P. R. "Life in Virginia." *Knickerbocker Magazine* 52 (September 1858): 269–82.

"Journal of a Trip to the Mountains, Caves and Springs of Virginia. By a New-Englander." *Southern Literary Messenger* 4 (February 1838): 89–93, (March 1838): 196–201, (April 1838): 261–64, (May 1838): 302–6, (June 1838): 384–87, (August 1838): 513–18.

Knepper, George W., ed. *Travels in the Southland, 1822–1823: The Journal of Lucius Verus Bierce.* Columbus: Ohio State University Press, 1966.

Lemmon, Sarah McCulloh, ed. *The Pettigrew Papers.* Vol. 2. Raleigh: North Carolina Department of Cultural Resources, 1988.

"Letter From Mrs Elizabeth Taylor to Mrs Judith Page Aylett." *Virginia Magazine of History and Biography* 45 (April 1937): 150–51.

"Letters of Moncure Robinson to his Father John Robinson, Clerk of Henrico Court." *William and Mary Quarterly,* 2d ser., 9 (January 1929): 13–33.

Lewis, Helen Beall, ed. "Journal of Alexander Dick in America, 1806–1809." M.A. thesis, University of Virginia, 1984.

Mackie, J. Milton. *From Cape Cod to Dixie and the Tropics.* New York: G. P. Putnam, 1864.

Marryat, Frederick. *Diary in America, with Remarks on its Institutions.* Philadelphia, 1839; reprint, edited by Jules Zanger, Bloomington: Indiana University Press, 1960.

Martin, Joseph. *A New and Comprehensive Gazetteer of Virginia.* Charlottesville, Va.: Joseph Martin, 1835.

Martineau, Harriet. *Society in America.* 2 vols. 3d ed. New York: Saunders and Otley, 1837.

Maury, Ann Fontaine, ed. *Intimate Virginiana: A Century of Maury Travels by Land and Sea.* Richmond, Va.: The Dietz Press, 1941.

Mayo, Bernard, ed. "Henry Clay, Patron and Idol of White Sulphur Springs: His Letters to James Calwell." *Virginia Magazine of History and Biography* 55 (October 1947): 301–17.

"The Memoir of Dr. John J. Moorman, Resident Physician at White Sulphur Springs." *Journal of the Greenbrier Historical Society* 3 (1980): 5–29.

[Miller, A. E.]. *Account of the Medical Properties of the Grey Sulphur Springs.* 2d ed. Charleston, Va.: N.p., 1837.

Moore, John H. "The Old Dominion through Student Eyes, 1852–1855: The Reminiscences of Thomas Hill Malone." *Virginia Magazine of History and Biography* 71 (July 1963): 294–326.

Moorman, John J., M.D. *A Guide to the Virginia Springs*. Staunton, Va.: Robert Cowan, 1851.

———. *The Virginia Springs: How to Reach Them and How to Use Them*. Philadelphia: J. B. Lippincott and Company, 1859.

———. *The Virginia Springs, with Their Analysis; and Some Remarks on Their Character, Together with a Directory for the Use of the White Sulphur Water, and an Account of the Diseases to Which It Is Applicable*. Philadelphia: Lindsay and Blakiston, 1847.

———. *Water From the White Sulphur Springs, Greenbrier County, VA*. N.p., 1840.

Morgan, Henry. *A Description of the Peaks of Otter, with Sketches and Anecdotes of Patrick Henry, John Randolph and Thomas Jefferson, and Other Distinguished Men, Who Have Visited the Peaks of Otter, or Resided in That Part of the State; Also a Description on the Natural Bridge and Other Scenery in Western Virginia*. Lynchburg, Va.: N.p., 1853.

Mütter, Thomas D., M.D. *The Salt Sulphur Springs, Monroe County, Va*. Philadelphia: T. K. and P. G. Collins, 1840.

The North American Tourist. New York: A. T. Goodrich, 1839.

O'Brien, Michael, ed. *An Evening When Alone: Four Journals of Single Women in the South, 1827–67*. Charlottesville: University Press of Virginia, 1993.

Packard, Joseph. *Recollections of a Long Life*. Washington, D.C.: Byron S. Adams, 1902.

Paulding, James Kirke. *Letters from the South by a Northern Man*. 2 vols. 2d ed. New York: Harper and Brothers, 1835.

———. *Letters from the South Written During an Excursion in the Summer of 1816*. 2 vols. New York: James Eastburn and Co., 1817.

[Paulding, James Kirke]. "Letters from Virginia. By a Northern Man." *The Analectic Magazine* 9 (May 1817): 418–30.

Pencil, Mark [Mary M. Hagner]. *The White Sulphur Papers, or Life at the Springs of Western Virginia*. New York: Samuel Colman, 1839.

Playfair, Robert. *Recollections of a Visit to the United States and the British Provinces of North America, in the Years, 1847, 1848, and 1849*. Edinburgh: Thomas Constable and Company, 1856.

Prolix, Peregrine [Philip Holbrook Nicklin]. *Letters Descriptive of the Virginia Springs: the Roads Leading Thereto, and the Doings Thereat*. Philadelphia: H. S. Tanner, 1837.

Reed, Andrew, and James Matheson. *A Narrative of the Visit to the American Churches, by the Deputation from the Congregational Union of England & Wales*. London: Jackson and Walford, 1835.

Rouelle, John, M.D. *A Complete Treatise on the Mineral Waters of Virginia: Containing a Description of Their Situation, Their Natural History, Their Analysis, Contents, and Their Use in Medicine*. Philadelphia: John Rouelle, 1792.

Royall, Anne. *The Black Book; Or, a Continuation of Travels in the United States*. Vol. 1. Washington, D.C.: N.p., 1828.

———. *Sketches of History, Life, and Manners in the United States*. New Haven: N.p., 1826.

Scafidel, Beverly Robinson. "The Letters of William Elliott." Ph.D. diss., University of South Carolina, 1978.

Scarborough, William Kaufmann, ed. *The Diary of Edmund Ruffin.* 2 vols. Baton Rouge: Louisiana State University Press, 1972.

Semmes, John E. *John H. B. Latrobe and His Times, 1803–1891.* Baltimore: The Norman Remington Co., 1917.

Six Weeks in Fauquier. Being the Substance of a Series of Familiar Letters, Illustrating the Scenery, Localities, Medicinal Virtues, and General Characteristics of the White Sulphur Springs, at Warrenton, Fauquier County, Virginia. New York: Samuel Colman, 1839.

Stringfellow, Rev. Thomas. *Two Letters on Cases of Cure at Fauquier White Sulphur Springs; Embracing Also, Mineral Waters in General.* Washington, D.C.: N.p., 1851.

Tanner, H. S. *A Geographical, Historical and Statistical View of the Central or Middle United States.* Philadelphia: H. Tanner Jr., 1841.

Tindall, P. B., M.D. *Observations on the Mineral Waters of Western Virginia.* Richmond, Va.: Chas. H. Wynne, 1858.

A Trip to the Virginia Springs, or the Belles and Beaux of 1835, by a Lady. Lexington, Va.: N.p., 1843.

Turner, Charles W., ed. *The Diary of Henry Boswell Jones of Brownsburg (1842–1871).* Verona, Va.: McClure Press, 1979.

Waddell, Louis M., ed. *The Papers of Henry Bouquet.* Vol. 6. Harrisburg: Pennsylvania Historical and Museum Commission, 1994.

Whately, Thomas. *Observations on Modern Gardening, Illustrated by Descriptions.* 2d ed. London, 1770.

"The White Sulphur Springs." *New England Magazine* (September 1832): 222–27.

The White Sulphur Springs, Greenbrier County, Virginia. Philadelphia: J. B. Lippincott & Co., 1860.

Williams, Wellington. *Appleton's Railroad and Steamboat Companion.* New York: D. Appleton and Company, 1849.

———. *Appleton's Southern and Western Travellers' Guide.* New York: D. Appleton and Company, 1851.

———. *The Traveller's and Tourist's Guide through the United States of America, Canada, Etc.* Philadelphia: Lippincott, Grambo and Company, 1855.

Windle, Mary J. *Life at the White Sulphur Springs; or, Pictures of a Pleasant Summer.* Philadelphia: J. B. Lippincott and Company, 1857.

———. *Life in Washington, and Life Here and There.* Philadelphia: J. B. Lippincott and Company, 1859.

Woodward, C. Vann, ed. *Mary Chesnut's Civil War.* New Haven: Yale University Press, 1981.

Secondary Sources

Books

Albanese, Catherine L. *Nature Religion in America: From the Algonkian Indians to the New Age.* Chicago: University of Chicago Press, 1990.

Aldrich, Elizabeth. *From the Ballroom to Hell: Grace and Folly in Nineteenth-Century Dance.* Evanston, Ill.: Northwestern University Press, 1991.

Amory, Cleveland. *The Last Resorts.* New York: Harper and Brothers, 1952.

Anderson, Lorraine, ed. *Sisters of the Earth: Women's Prose and Poetry about Nature.* New York: Vintage Books, 1991.

Apple, Rima D., ed. *Women, Health, and Medicine in America.* New York: Garland Publishing, 1990.

Armstrong, David, and Elizabeth Metzger Armstrong. *The Great American Medicine Show, Being an Illustrated History of Hucksters, Healers, Health Evangelists, and Heroes From Plymouth Rock to the Present.* New York: Prentice-Hall, 1991.

Aron, Cindy S. *Working at Play: A History of Vacations in the United States.* New York: Oxford University Press, 1999.

Ayers, Edward L. *Vengeance and Justice: Crime and Punishment in the Nineteenth-Century American South.* New York: Oxford University Press, 1984.

Ayers, Edward L., and John C. Willis, eds. *The Edge of the South: Life in Nineteenth-Century Virginia.* Charlottesville: University Press of Virginia, 1991.

Bardaglio, Peter W. *Reconstructing the Household: Families, Sex, and the Law in the Nineteenth-Century South.* Chapel Hill: University of North Carolina Press, 1995.

Blanton, Wyndham B. *Medicine in Virginia in the Nineteenth Century.* Richmond, Va.: Garrett and Massie, 1933.

Boas, George, ed. *Romanticism in America.* Baltimore: Johns Hopkins Press, 1940.

Bodell, Dorothy H. *Montgomery White Sulphur Springs: A History of the Resort, Hospital, Cemeteries, Markers, and Monument.* Blacksburg, Va.: Pocahontas Press, 1993.

Bonnell, Victoria E., and Lynn Hunt, eds. *Beyond the Cultural Turn: New Directions in the Study of Society and Culture.* Berkeley: University of California Press, 1999.

Bordley, James, and A. McGehee Harvey. *Two Centuries of American Medicine, 1776–1976.* Philadelphia: W. B. Saunders Company, 1976.

Braden, Donna R. *Leisure and Entertainment in America.* Dearborn, Mich.: Henry Ford Museum and Greenfield Village, 1988.

Brewster, Lawrence Fay. *Summer Migrations and Resorts of South Carolina Low-Country Planters.* Durham, N.C.: Duke University Press, 1947.

Brown, Dona. *Inventing New England: Regional Tourism in the Nineteenth Century.* Washington, D.C.: Smithsonian Institution Press, 1995.

Burton, Orville Vernon. *In My Father's House Are Many Mansions: Family and Community in Edgefield, South Carolina.* Chapel Hill: University of North Carolina Press, 1985.

Bushman, Richard L. *The Refinement of America: Persons, Houses, Cities.* New York: Alfred A. Knopf, 1992.

Callahan, James Morton. *History of West Virginia, Old and New.* Vol. 1. Chicago and New York: American Historical Society, 1923.

Carnes, Mark C., and Clyde Griffen, eds. *Meanings for Manhood: Constructions of Masculinity in Victorian America.* Chicago: University of Chicago Press, 1990.

Cashin, Joan E. *A Family Venture: Men and Women on the Southern Frontier.* New York: Oxford University Press, 1991.

————, ed. *Our Common Affairs: Texts from Women in the Old South*. Baltimore: Johns Hopkins University Press, 1996.

Cayleff, Susan E. *Wash and Be Healed: The Water-Cure Movement and Women's Health*. Philadelphia: Temple University Press, 1987.

Censer, Jane Turner. *North Carolina Planters and Their Children, 1800–1860*. Baton Rouge: Louisiana State University Press, 1984.

Clarke, Graham. *The American Landscape*. Vol. 2, *The American Image: Landscape as Symbol and Myth in the Nineteenth Century*. New York: Routledge Press, 1993.

Click, Patricia C. *The Spirit of the Times: Amusements in Nineteenth-Century Baltimore, Norfolk, and Richmond*. Charlottesville: University Press of Virginia, 1989.

Clinton, Catherine. *The Plantation Mistress: Woman's World in the Old South*. New York: Pantheon Books, 1982.

Cohen, Stan. *Historic Springs of the Virginias: A Pictorial History*. Charleston, W.Va.: Pictorial Histories Publishing Co., 1981.

————. *The Homestead and Warm Springs Valley, Virginia: A Pictorial Heritage*. Charleston, W.Va.: Pictorial Histories Publishing Co., 1984.

Conte, Robert S. *The History of the Greenbriar: America's Resort*. Charleston, W.Va.: Pictorial Histories Publishing Company, 1989.

Coulling, Mary P. *The Lee Girls*. Winston-Salem, N.C.: John F. Blair, 1987.

Coulter, Harold L. *Divided Legacy: A History of the Schism in Medical Thought*. Vol. 3, *Science and Ethics in American Medicine: 1800–1914*. Washington, D.C.: Wehawken Book Company, 1973.

Crandell, Gina. *Nature Pictorialized: "The View" in Landscape History*. Baltimore: Johns Hopkins University Press, 1993.

Crook, James K. *The Mineral Waters of the United States and Their Therapeutic Uses*. New York: Lea Brothers and Co., 1899.

D'Emilio, John, and Estelle B. Freedman. *Intimate Matters: A History of Sexuality in America*. New York: Harper and Row, 1988.

Donegan, Jane B. *"Hydropathic Highway to Health": Women and Water-Cure in Antebellum America*. Westport, Conn.: Greenwood Press, 1986.

Dulles, Foster Rhea. *A History of Recreation: America Learns to Play*. 2d ed. Englewood Cliffs, N.J.: Prentice-Hall, 1965.

Early, James. *Romanticism and American Architecture*. New York: A. S. Barnes and Co., 1965.

Fabian, Ann. *Card Sharps, Dream Books, and Bucket Shops: Gambling in Nineteenth-Century America*. Ithaca, N.Y.: Cornell University Press, 1990.

Farnham, Christie Anne. *The Education of the Southern Belle: Higher Education and Student Socialization in the Antebellum South*. New York: New York University Press, 1994.

Fauquier County, Virginia, 1759–1959. Fauquier Bicentennial Commission, 1979.

Fishwick, Marshall W. *Springlore in Virginia*. Bowling Green, Ohio: Bowling Green State University Press, 1978.

Ford, Lacy K., Jr. *Origins of Southern Radicalism: The South Carolina Upcountry, 1800–1860*. New York: Oxford University Press, 1988.

Foster, Edward Halsey. *The Civilized Wilderness: Backgrounds to American Romantic Literature, 1817–1860*. New York: The Free Press, 1975.

Fox-Genovese, Elizabeth. *Within the Plantation Household: Black and White Women of the Old South*. Chapel Hill: University of North Carolina Press, 1988.

Franklin, John Hope. *A Southern Odyssey: Travelers in the Antebellum North*. Baton Rouge: Louisiana State University Press, 1976.

Fraser, William J., Jr., et al., eds. *The Web of Southern Social Relations: Women, Family, and Education*. Athens: University of Georgia Press, 1985.

Friedman, Jean E. *The Enclosed Garden: Women and Community in the Evangelical South, 1830–1900*. Chapel Hill: University of North Carolina Press, 1985.

Genovese, Eugene. *Roll, Jordan, Roll: The World the Slaves Made*. New York: Pantheon Books, 1974.

Girouard, Mark. *The Return to Camelot: Chivalry and the English Gentleman*. New Haven: Yale University Press, 1981.

Green, Harvey. *Fit for America: Health, Fitness, Sport and American Society*. New York: Pantheon Books, 1986.

Greenberg, Kenneth S. *Honor and Slavery: Lies, Duels, Noses, Masks, Dressing as a Woman, Gifts, Strangers, Humanitarianism, Death, Slave Rebellions, the Proslavery Argument, Baseball, Hunting, and Gambling in the Old South*. Princeton, N.J.: Princeton University Press, 1996.

Hale, Grace Elizabeth. *Making Whiteness: The Culture of Segregation in the South, 1890–1940*. New York: Pantheon Books, 1998.

Haley, Bruce. *The Healthy Body and Victorian Culture*. Cambridge, Mass.: Harvard University Press, 1978.

Haller, John S., Jr. *Kindly Medicine: Physio-Medicalism in America, 1836–1911*. Kent, Ohio: Kent State University Press, 1997.

Halttunen, Karen. *Confidence Men and Painted Women: A Study of Middle-Class Culture in America, 1830–1870*. New Haven: Yale University Press, 1982.

Harris, J. William. *Plain Folk and Gentry in a Slave Society: White Liberty and Black Slavery in Augusta's Hinterlands*. Middletown, Conn.: Wesleyan University Press, 1985.

Hills, Patricia. *The Painter's America: Rural and Urban Life, 1810–1910*. New York: Praeger, 1974.

Huth, Hans. *Nature and the American: Three Centuries of Changing Attitudes*. Berkeley: University of California Press, 1957; reprint, Lincoln: University of Nebraska Press, 1972.

Ingalls, Fay. *The Valley Road*. Cleveland: World Publishing Co., 1949.

Inscoe, John C. *Mountain Masters, Slavery, and the Sectional Crisis in Western North Carolina*. Knoxville: University of Tennessee Press, 1989.

Isaac, Rhys. *The Transformation of Virginia, 1740–1790*. Chapel Hill: University of North Carolina Press, 1982.

Jabour, Anya. *Marriage in the Early Republic: Elizabeth and William Wirt and the Companionate Ideal*. Baltimore: Johns Hopkins University Press, 1998.

Johns, Elizabeth. *American Genre Painting: The Politics of Everyday Life*. New Haven: Yale University Press, 1991.

Jones, Katharine M. *The Plantation South.* Indianapolis: Bobbs-Merrill Company, 1957.

Kasson, John F. *Rudeness and Civility: Manners in Nineteenth-Century Urban America.* New York: Hill and Wang, 1990.

Kennedy, Roger G. *Greek Revival America.* New York: Stewart, Tabori, and Chang, 1989.

Kett, Joseph F. *Rites of Passage: Adolescence in America, 1790 to the Present.* New York: Basic Books, 1977.

Kierner, Cynthia A. *Beyond the Household: Women's Place in the Early South, 1700–1835.* Ithaca, N.Y.: Cornell University Press, 1998.

Kimmel, Michael. *Manhood in America: A Cultural History.* New York: The Free Press, 1996.

Kolodny, Annette. *The Land before Her: Fantasy and Experience of the American Frontiers, 1630–1860.* Chapel Hill: University of North Carolina Press, 1984.

———. *The Lay of the Land: Metaphor as Experience and History in American Life and Letters.* Chapel Hill: University of North Carolina Press, 1975.

Lane, Mills. *Architecture of the Old South: Virginia.* Savannah: The Beehive Press, 1987.

Lebsock, Suzanne. *The Free Women of Petersburg: Status and Culture in a Southern Town, 1784–1860.* New York: W. W. Norton and Company, 1984.

Leighton, Ann. *American Gardens of the Nineteenth Century: "For Comfort and Affluence."* Amherst: University of Massachusetts Press, 1987.

Lewis, Jan. *The Pursuit of Happiness: Family and Values in Jefferson's Virginia.* New York: Cambridge University Press, 1983.

Lystra, Karen. *Searching the Heart: Women, Men, and Romantic Love in Nineteenth-Century America.* New York: Oxford University Press, 1989.

McAllister, J. T. *Historical Sketches of Virginia Hot Springs, Warm Sulphur Springs and Bath County, Virginia.* Salem, Va.: N.p., 1908.

MacCorkle, William A. *White Sulphur Springs.* New York: Neale Publishing Company, 1916.

McCurry, Stephanie. *Masters of Small Worlds: Yeoman Households, Gender Relations, and the Political Culture of the Antebellum South Carolina Low Country.* New York: Oxford University Press, 1995.

McElroy, Guy C. *Facing History: The Black Image in American Art, 1710–1940.* San Francisco: Bedford Arts in association with the Corcoran Gallery of Art, 1990.

McMillen, Sally G. *Motherhood in the Old South: Pregnancy, Childbirth, and Infant Rearing.* Baton Rouge: Louisiana State University Press, 1990.

Martin, Scott C. *Killing Time: Leisure and Culture in Southwestern Pennsylvania, 1800–1850.* Pittsburgh: University of Pittsburgh Press, 1995.

Marty, Martin E., and Kenneth L. Vaux. *Health/Medicine and the Faith Traditions: An Inquiry into Religion and Medicine.* Philadelphia: Fortress Press, 1982.

Mitchell, Robert D. *Commercialism and Frontier: Perspectives on the Early Shenandoah Valley.* Charlottesville: University Press of Virginia, 1977.

Morgan County Historical and Geological Society. *Morgan County, West Virginia and Its People.* Berkeley Springs, W.Va.: Morgan County Historical and Geological Society, 1981.

Morris, Christopher. *Becoming Southern: The Evolution of a Way of Life, Warren County and Vicksburg, Mississippi, 1770–1860.* New York: Oxford University Press, 1995.

Morton, Oren F. *Annals of Bath County Virginia.* Staunton, Va.: McClure Co., 1917.

———. *A History of Monroe County, West Virginia.* Dayton, Va.: Ruebush-Elkins Co., 1916.

Murphy, Lamar Riley. *Enter the Physician: The Transformation of Domestic Medicine, 1760–1860.* Tuscaloosa: University of Alabama Press, 1991.

Newbraugh, Frederick T. *Warm Springs Echoes: About Berkeley Springs and Morgan County.* 2d ed. Vol. 1. N.p., 1967.

Noe, Kenneth W. *Southwest Virginia's Railroad: Modernization and the Sectional Crisis.* Urbana: University of Illinois Press, 1994.

Norwood, Vera. *Made from This Earth: American Women and Nature.* Chapel Hill: University of North Carolina Press, 1993.

Novak, Barbara. *Nature and Culture: American Landscape and Painting, 1825–1875.* New York: Oxford University Press, 1980.

Numbers, Ronald L., and Todd L. Savitt, eds. *Science and Medicine in the Old South.* Baton Rouge: Louisiana State University Press, 1989.

Nye, Russel Blaine. *Society and Culture in America, 1830–1860.* New York: Harper and Row, 1974.

Oakes, James. *The Ruling Race: A History of American Slaveholders.* New York: Alfred A. Knopf, 1982.

O'Leary, Elizabeth L. *At Beck and Call: The Representation of Domestic Servants in Nineteenth-Century American Painting.* Washington, D.C.: Smithsonian Institution Press, 1996.

Osterweis, Rollin G. *Romanticism and Nationalism in the Old South.* New Haven: Yale University Press, 1949.

Ownby, Ted. *Subduing Satan: Religion, Recreation, and Manhood in the Rural South, 1865–1920.* Chapel Hill: University of North Carolina Press, 1990.

Pease, Jane H., and William H. Pease. *A Family of Women: The Carolina Petigrus in Peace and War.* Chapel Hill: University of North Carolina Press, 1999.

———. *The Web of Progress: Private Values and Public Styles in Boston and Charleston, 1828–1843.* New York: Oxford University Press, 1985.

Prokopoff, Stephen S., and Joan C. Siegfried. *The Nineteenth-Century Architecture of Saratoga Springs: Architecture Worth Saving in New York State.* N.p.: New York State Council on the Arts, 1970.

Reniers, Perceval. *The Springs of Virginia: Life, Love, and Death at the Waters, 1775–1900.* Chapel Hill: University of North Carolina Press, 1941.

Rice, Otis K. *A History of Greenbrier County.* Lewisburg, W.Va.: Greenbrier Historical Society, 1986.

Rosenberg, Charles E. *The Cholera Years: The United States in 1832, 1849, and 1866.* Chicago: University of Chicago Press, 1962.

———. *Explaining Epidemics and Other Studies in the History of Medicine.* Cambridge: Cambridge University Press, 1992.

Rothman, Ellen K. *Hands and Hearts: A History of Courtship in America.* Cambridge, Mass.: Harvard University Press, 1987.

Rothstein, William G. *American Physicians in the Nineteenth Century.* Baltimore: Johns Hopkins Press, 1972.

Rotundo, E. Anthony. *American Manhood: Transformations in Masculinity from the Revolution to the Modern Era.* New York: Basic Books, 1993.

Rozbicki, Michal J. *The Complete Colonial Gentleman: Cultural Legitimacy in Plantation America.* Charlottesville: University Press of Virginia, 1998.

Ryan, Mary P. *Women in Public: Between Banners and Ballots, 1825–1880.* Baltimore: Johns Hopkins University Press, 1990.

Savitt, Todd L., and James Harvey Young, eds. *Disease and Distinctiveness in the American South.* Knoxville: University of Tennessee Press, 1988.

Scott, Anne Firor. *The Southern Lady: From Pedestal to Politics, 1830–1930.* Chicago: University of Chicago Press, 1970.

Sears, John F. *Sacred Places: American Tourist Attractions in the Nineteenth Century.* New York: Oxford University Press, 1989.

Shields, David S. *Civil Tongues and Polite Letters in British America.* Chapel Hill: University of North Carolina Press, 1997.

Shryock, Richard Harrison. *Medicine and Society in America, 1660–1860.* New York: New York University Press, 1960.

———. *Medicine in America: Historical Essays.* Baltimore: Johns Hopkins Press, 1966.

Sklar, Kathryn Kish. *Catharine Beecher: A Study in American Domesticity.* New Haven: Yale University Press, 1973.

Smith, Daniel Blake. *Inside the Great House: Planter Family Life in Eighteenth-Century Chesapeake Society.* Ithaca, N.Y.: Cornell University Press, 1980.

Smith, Nathan Ryno. *Legends of the South.* Baltimore: N.p., 1869.

Stansell, Christine. *City of Women: Sex and Class in New York, 1789–1860.* New York: Alfred A. Knopf, 1986.

Stevenson, Brenda E. *Life in Black and White: Family and Community in the Slave South.* New York: Oxford University Press, 1996.

Stowe, Steven M. *Intimacy and Power in the Old South: Ritual in the Lives of the Planters.* Baltimore: Johns Hopkins University Press, 1987.

Sutton, Robert Kent. *Americans Interpret the Parthenon: The Progression of Greek Revival Architecture from the East Coast to Oregon, 1800–1860.* Niwot: University Press of Colorado, 1992.

Taylor, Quintard, M.D. *White Sulphur Springs: A Brief History.* N.p., 1923.

Taylor, William R. *Cavalier and Yankee: The Old South and American National Character.* Cambridge, Mass.: Harvard University Press, 1979.

Vlach, John Michael. *Back of the Big House: The Architecture of Plantation Slavery.* Chapel Hill: University of North Carolina Press, 1993.

Walters, Ronald G. *American Reformers, 1815–1860.* New York: Hill and Wang, 1978.

Warner, John Harley. *The Therapeutic Perspective: Medical Practice, Knowledge, and Identity in America, 1820–1885.* Cambridge, Mass.: Harvard University Press, 1986.

Weiner, Marli F. *Mistresses and Slaves: Plantation Women in South Carolina, 1830–80.* Urbana: University of Illinois Press, 1998.

Whitwell, W. L., and Lee W. Winborne. *The Architectural Heritage of the Roanoke Valley.* Charlottesville: University Press of Virginia, 1982.

Whorton, James C. *Crusaders for Fitness: The History of American Health Reformers.* Princeton, N.J.: Princeton University Press, 1982.

Williams, Herman Warner, Jr. *Mirror to the American Past: A Survey of American Genre Painting, 1750–1900.* Greenwich, Conn.: New York Graphic Society, 1973.

Wyatt-Brown, Bertram. *Southern Honor: Ethics and Behavior in the Old South.* New York: Oxford University Press, 1982.

Young, Jeffrey Robert. *Domesticating Slavery: The Master Class in Georgia and South Carolina, 1670–1837.* Chapel Hill: University of North Carolina Press, 1999.

Articles and Chapters in Books

Baker, James P. "The Influence of Epidemic Diseases on the Virginia Springs." *Journal of the Greenbrier Historical Society* 1 (September 1965): 5–10.

Barton, Keith C. "'Good Cooks and Washers': Slave Hiring, Domestic Labor, and the Market in Bourbon County, Kentucky." *Journal of American History* 84 (September 1997): 436–60.

Batey, Mavis. "The High Phase of English Landscape Gardening." *Eighteenth-Century Life* 8 (1983): 44–50.

Berdan, Marshall S. "The Pestilence that Walketh in Darkness: The Cholera Epidemic of 1832." *Virginia Cavalcade* 43 (Summer 1993): 14–23.

———. "The Spa Life: Taking the Cure in Antebellum Bath County." *Virginia Cavalcade* 40 (Winter 1991): 110–19.

Betts, John Rickards. "Mind and Being in Early American Thought." *Journal of American History* 54 (December 1968): 787–805.

Breen, T. H. "Horses and Gentlemen: The Cultural Significance of Gambling among the Gentry of Virginia." *William and Mary Quarterly,* 3d ser., 34 (April 1977): 239–57.

Bridenbaugh, Carl. "Baths and Watering Places of Colonial America." *William and Mary Quarterly,* 3d ser., 3 (April 1946): 151–81.

Broderick, Mosette Glaser. "History in Towns: Saratoga Springs, New York, the Queen of American Resorts." *Antiques* 128 (July 1985): 96–110.

Buza, Melinda S. "'Pledges of Our Love': Friendship, Love, and Marriage among the Virginia Gentry, 1800–1825." In *The Edge of the South: Life in Nineteenth-Century Virginia,* ed. Edward L. Ayers and John C. Willis, 9–36. Charlottesville: University Press of Virginia, 1991.

Cashin, Joan E. "'Decidely Opposed to *the Union*': Women's Culture, Marriage, and Politics in Antebellum South Carolina." *Georgia Historical Quarterly* 78 (Winter 1994): 735–59.

———. "Landscape and Memory in Antebellum Virginia." *Virginia Magazine of History and Biography* 102 (October 1994): 477–500.

———. "The Structure of Antebellum Plantation Families: 'The Ties that Bound Us Was Strong.'" *Journal of Southern History* 56 (February 1990): 55–70.

Clinton, Catherine. "Women and Southern History: Images and Reflections." In *Perspectives on the American South: An Annual Review of Society, Politics, and Culture*, Vol. 3, ed. James C. Cobb and Charles R. Wilson, 45–62. New York: Gordon and Breach Science Publishers, 1985.

Duffin, Lorna. "The Conspicuous Consumptive: Woman as an Invalid." In *The Nineteenth-Century Woman: Her Cultural and Physical World*, ed. Sara Delamont and Lorna Duffin, 26–56. New York: Barnes and Noble, 1978.

Duffy, John. "Medical Practice in the Ante-Bellum South." *Journal of Southern History* 25 (February 1959): 53–72.

Franck, Frederick William. "The Virginia Legislature at the Fauquier Springs in 1849." *Virginia Magazine of History and Biography* 58 (January 1950): 66–83.

Grootkerk, Paul. "Artistic Images of Mythological Reality: The Antebellum Plantation." *Southern Quarterly* 32 (Summer 1994): 33–44.

Hilliard, Sam B. "Plantations and the Moulding of the Southern Landscape." In *The Making of the American Landscape*, ed. Michael P. Conzen, 104–26. Boston: Unwin Hyman, 1990.

Hoffschwelle, Mary S. "Women's Sphere and the Creation of Female Community in the Antebellum South: Three Tennessee Slaveholding Women." *Tennessee Historical Quarterly* 50 (Summer 1991): 80–89.

Jasen, Patricia. "Romanticism, Modernity, and the Evolution of Tourism on the Niagara Frontier, 1790–1850." *Canadian Historical Review* 72 (September 1991): 283–318.

Joseph, J. W. "White Columns and Black Hands: Class and Classification in the Plantation Ideology of the Georgia and South Carolina Lowcountry." *Historical Archaeology* 27, no. 3 (1993): 57–73.

Kamenetz, Herman. "History of American Spas and Hydropathy." In *Medical Hydrology*, ed. Sidney Licht, 160–88. New Haven: Elizabeth Licht, 1963.

Kenney, Alice P., and Leslie J. Workman. "Ruins, Romance, and Reality: Medievalism in Anglo-American Imagination and Taste, 1750–1840." *Winterthur Portfolio* 10 (1975): 131–63.

Kierner, Cynthia A. "Hospitality, Sociability, and Gender in the Southern Colonies." *Journal of Southern History* 62 (August 1996): 449–80.

Leavitt, Judith Walzer. "'A Worrying Profession': The Domestic Environment of Medical Practice in Mid-Nineteenth-Century America." *Bulletin of the History of Medicine* 69 (Spring 1995): 1–29.

Lewis, Jan, and Kenneth A. Lockridge. "'Sally Has Been Sick': Pregnancy and Family Limitation among Virginia Gentry Women, 1780–1830." *Journal of Social History* 22 (Fall 1988): 5–19.

McMillen, Sally G. "Antebellum Southern Fathers and the Health Care of Children." *Journal of Southern History* 60 (August 1994): 513–32.

Morantz, Regina M. "Making Women Modern: Middle-Class Women and Health Reform in Nineteenth-Century America." *Journal of Social History* 10 (Summer 1977): 490–507.

Murphy, James B. "Slaveholding in Appalachia: A Challenge to the Egalitarian Tradition." *Southern Studies* 3 (Spring 1992): 15–33.

Myers, Kenneth John. "On the Cultural Construction of Landscape Experience: Contact to 1830." In *American Iconology: New Approaches to Nineteenth-Century Art and Literature*, ed. David C. Miller, 58–79. New Haven: Yale University Press, 1993.

Norris, Darrell A. "Reaching the Sublime: Niagara Falls Visitor Origins, 1831–1854." *Journal of American Culture* 9 (Spring 1986): 53–59.

O'Malley, Therese. "Landscape Gardening in the Early National Period." In *Views and Visions: American Landscape before 1830*, ed. Edward J. Nygren, 133–59. Washington, D.C.: Corcoran Gallery of Art, 1986.

Robertson, Bruce. "The Picturesque Traveler in America." In *Views and Visions: American Landscape before 1830*, ed. Edward J. Nygren, 189–211. Washington, D.C.: Corcoran Gallery of Art, 1986.

Rosenberg, Charles E. "The Therapeutic Revolution: Medicine, Meaning, and Social Change in Nineteenth-Century America." In *The Therapeutic Revolution: Essays in the Social History of American Medicine*, ed. Morris J. Vogel and Charles E. Rosenberg, 3–25. Philadelphia: University of Pennsylvania Press, 1979.

Semes, Robert Louis. "Two Hundred Years at Rockbridge Alum Springs." In *Proceedings of the Rockbridge Historical Society, 1966–1969*, ed. Anne Brandon Heiner, 46–54. Lexington, Va.: Rockbridge Historical Society, 1970.

Sigerist, Henry E. "American Spas in Historical Perspective." *Bulletin of the History of Medicine* 11 (1942): 133–47.

Smith-Rosenberg, Carroll. "The Female World of Love and Ritual: Relations between Women in Nineteenth-Century America." *Signs: A Journal of Women in Culture and Society* 1 (August 1975): 1–29.

Smith-Rosenberg, Carroll, and Charles Rosenberg. "The Female Animal: Medical and Biological Views of Woman and Her Role in Nineteenth-Century America." *Journal of American History* 60 (September 1973): 332–56.

Stowe, Steven M. "Religion, Science, and the Culture of Medical Practice in the American South, 1800–1870." In *The Mythmaking Frame of Mind: Social Imagination and American Culture*, ed. James Gilbert et al., 1–24. Belmont, Calif.: Wadsworth Publishing Company, 1993.

———. "Seeing Themselves at Work: Physicians and the Case Narrative in the Mid-Nineteenth-Century American South." *American Historical Review* 101 (February 1996): 41–79.

———. "'The *Thing* Not Its Vision': A Woman's Courtship and Her Sphere in the Southern Planter Class." *Feminist Studies* 9 (Spring 1983): 113–30.

Struna, Nancy L. "'Good Wives' and 'Gardeners,' Spinners, and 'Fearless Riders': Middle- and Upper-rank Women in the Early American Sporting Culture." In *From "Fair Sex" to Feminism: Sport and the Socialization of Women in the Industrial and Post-Industrial Eras*, ed. J. A. Mangan and Roberta J. Park, 235–55. London: Frank Cass and Company, 1987.

Theriault, William D. "Shannondale Springs." *West Virginia History* 57 (1998): 1–26.

Upton, Dell. "New Views of the Virginia Landscape." *Virginia Magazine of History and Biography* 96 (October 1988): 403–70.

Warner, John Harley. "'The Nature-Trusting Heresy': American Physicians and the Concept of the Healing Power of Nature in the 1850's and 1860's." *Perspectives in American History* 11 (1977–78): 289–324.

Wells, Camille. "The Planter's Prospect: Houses, Outbuildings, and Rural Landscapes in Eighteenth Century Virginia." *Winterthur Portfolio* 28 (Spring 1993): 1–31.

Wood, Ann Douglas. "'The Fashionable Diseases': Women's Complaints and Their Treatment in Nineteenth Century America." *Journal of Interdisciplinary History* 4 (Summer 1973): 25–52.

Wyckoff, William K. "Landscapes of Private Power and Wealth." In *The Making of the American Landscape*, ed. Michael P. Conzen, 335–54. Boston: Unwin Hyman, 1990.

Dissertations and Other Unpublished Works

Chambers, Thomas A. "Fashionable Dis-Ease: Promoting Health and Leisure at the Virginia Springs and Saratoga Springs, New York, 1790–1860." Ph.D. diss., College of William and Mary, 1999.

Cook, Florence Elliott. "Growing Up White, Genteel, and Female in a Changing South, 1865 to 1915." Ph.D. diss., University of California-Berkeley, 1992.

De Vierville, Jonathan Paul. "American Healing Waters: A Chronology (1513–1946) and Historical Survey of America's Major Springs, Spas, and Health Resorts Including a Review of Their Medicinal Virtues, Therapeutic Methods, and Health Care Practices." Ph.D. diss., University of Texas-Austin, 1992.

Dosch, Nancy Cole. "Exploring Alternatives: The Use of Exercise as a Medical Therapeutic in Mid-Nineteenth Century America, 1830–1870." Ph.D. diss., University of Maryland, 1993.

Grover, Janice Zita. "Luxury and Leisure in Early Nineteenth-Century America: Saratoga Springs and the Rise of the Resort." Ph.D. diss., University of California-Davis, 1973.

Hawkins, Kenneth. "The Therapeutic Landscape: Nature, Architecture, and Mind in Nineteenth Century America." Ph.D. diss., University of Rochester, 1991.

Hendricks, Christopher. "Health and Good Society: The Development of the Spa Town in Colonial Virginia." Paper presented at the Museum of American Frontier Culture, Staunton, Va., January 1992.

Kilbride, Daniel. "Philadelphia and the Southern Elite: Class, Kinship, and Culture in Antebellum America." Ph.D. diss., University of Florida, 1997.

Worsham, John Gibson, Jr. "The European Bathing Tradition and Its American Successors in the Eighteenth and Early Nineteenth Century." Unpublished paper, 1992.

Index

The American South Series